Bill Markham

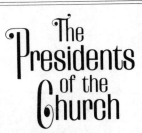

The Presidents of the Church

PRESTON NIBLEY

The Presidents of the Church

PRESTON NIBLEY

"One comfort is, that Great Men taken up in any way, are profitable company. We cannot look, however imperfectly, upon a great man, without gaining something from him. He is the living light-fountain, which it is good and pleasant to be near."

—*Thomas Carlyle.*

Deseret Book

Salt Lake City, Utah

1971

Library of Congress Catalog Card No. 73-157300

SBN NO. 87747-414-1

COPYRIGHT 1971
THE DESERET BOOK COMPANY
SALT LAKE CITY, UTAH

FIRST PRINTING SEPTEMBER, 1941
SECOND PRINTING JANUARY, 1942
THIRD PRINTING MAY, 1943
FOURTH PRINTING NOVEMBER, 1944
FIFTH PRINTING SEPTEMBER, 1947
SIXTH PRINTING AUGUST, 1950
SEVENTH PRINTING AUGUST, 1956
EIGHTH PRINTING SEPTEMBER, 1959
NINTH PRINTING JUNE, 1960
TENTH PRINTING FEBRUARY, 1965
ELEVENTH PRINTING FEBRUARY, 1968
Revised and Enlarged Edition, April, 1971

Printed and bound by the Deseret News Press
Salt Lake City, Utah

FOREWORD

This book contains brief biographies of the ten great men who have presided over The Church of Jesus Christ of Latter-day Saints from its organization in April, 1830, until the present time. Those biographies are designed for those readers who are making their first acquaintance with the lives and activites of the Presidents and who do not have time or opportunity for extensive reading and investigation.

Every effort has been made to present exact historical information, and wherever possible the words of the leaders themselves have been quoted.

While writing these biographies I have been deeply impressed with the faith and devotion, the heroism and greatness of the men who have presided over the Church. Such men have seldom lived in the world; men devoted to the purpose of having God's word become an actuality in their lives and in the lives of their followers; men who labored with the sublime object of building God's kingdom on earth, where only righteousness would prevail. These are the select men of the earth; the true benefactors of mankind. Time will award them an honored place among the shining lights of history.

Preston Nibley,
Salt Lake City, Utah

CONTENTS

JOSEPH SMITH

JOSEPH SMITH—THE PROPHET

(1805-1844)

I

I N HIS life and work and in the nature of his great accomplishments, Joseph Smith, the Prophet, stands apart
from all other men. He came into the world at a time
when it was generally taught and believed that prophets
were men of the "old ages" and that God's written word
was complete as recorded in the Holy Book. These beliefs
he was to deny and successfully disprove, and, before his
early death, he was to lay the foundation of a "church and
kingdom" which, he declared on numerous occasions,
would grow and flourish "until it filled the whole earth."
Time is gradually establishing his claims; his followers regard him as one of the greatest prophets in the annals of
mankind.

For the beginning of the activities of this remarkable man, one must look to New England, in the early part
of the nineteenth century. The parents, Joseph Smith
and Lucy Mack Smith, were farming people who had
settled in Orange County, Vermont. Three children
were born to them there. For a time they prospered in
their agricultural activities. When reverses came they
moved to Windsor County and rented a farm from Mrs.
Smith's father. There, on the 23rd of December, 1805,
the third son and fourth child was born, whom the parents
named Joseph Jr.

During his early youth ill fortune pursued the family of Joseph Jr. The good father tried farming in several

localities but could not quite succeed in any of them. When the boy was six years old, he and his brothers and sisters (two more children having arrived) were stricken with typhus fever. Joseph Jr. soon recovered but was left with a painful sore on his leg that infected the bones between the knee and the foot. Physicians were called in, and after some consultation they decided to operate on the leg and remove the infected bones. Chloroform or anesthetics of any kind were unknown in those days. The boy was urged to drink brandy or wine to dull the pain, but refused to do so, saying, "If my father will sit on the bed and hold me in his arms, I will do whatever is necessary in order to have the bone taken out." And so, the primitive operation was performed. Strangely enough there were no disastrous results. With the tender care of the mother, the wound soon healed, although the boy was lame for a number of years.

In 1816, when Joseph Jr. was ten years old, the father, thinking to better his fortunes, left Vermont and moved with his family to western New York, locating in the village of Palmyra. Here he and his sons did whatever work came to hand in order to support themselves. They were poor, but they were honest and honorable Christian people.

About 1818 the father purchased one hundred acres of timber land two miles south of Palmyra. Here the family soon located, and the father and sons constructed a log cabin home. Their desire now was to remain on this farm permanently and make themselves independent. In a short time they cleared a considerable acreage, planted wheat and corn, and set out sugar trees.

In 1820 the Smith family became actively interested in the subject of religion. Revival meetings were being held in Palmyra and efforts were being made by the various churches to gain converts. Mrs. Smith, her son Hyrum, and her daughter Sophronia united with the Presbyterian Church. The boy, Joseph Jr., became acquainted with the Methodist minister and was inclined toward that sect, although he did not formally join. Then came an event in the boy's life that, after more than one hundred years, is still a thrilling and inspiring narrative—one that will continue to thrill and inspire the hearts of believers throughout the ages to come. Joseph Jr. relates that he decided to go into a grove on his father's farm and kneel down and ask God to make known to him which of all the churches was true and which he should join.

He did so, and in broad daylight there appeared before him, "standing above me in the air," "two Personages, whose brightness and glory defy all description. . . .One of them spake unto me, calling me by name, and said, pointing to the other—This is My Beloved Son. Hear Him!"

Joseph inquired of the two heavenly beings which of all the churches was right and which he should join. He was informed that the true church was not upon the earth. "He forbade me to join any of them; and many other things did he say unto me, which I cannot write at this time."

The followers of Joseph Smith, known as Latter-day Saints, and now numbering in the millions, located in all parts of the world, accept this vision as the greatest event in modern history. This vision restored God to the world! At a time when the very existence of God was denied, this vision revealed the personages of the Father and the Son and made known to mankind that they rule and reign in the heavens and that they are mindful of those who seek them.

After this great vision, there were no special events in the life of the boy Joseph Jr. for more than three years. He continued to work with his parents and brothers and sisters on the farm. The family was endeavoring to build a new home for themselves, and they were having a severe struggle. However, they managed to complete it, and it stands to this day.

On the night of September 21, 1823, Joseph Jr. had retired to his bed and was engaged in prayer when the second of his remarkable visions took place. The room was filled with light, and a heavenly messenger stood before

him and announced that his name was Moroni; that he was
sent from the presence of God; that God had an important
work for the youth to do, "and that my name should be
had for good and evil among all nations." Continuing
further, "He said there was a record deposited [in a nearby
hill], written upon gold plates, giving an account of the
former inhabitants of this continent, and the source from
whence they sprang. He also said that the fulness of the
everlasting Gospel was contained in it, as delivered by
the Savior to the ancient inhabitants; Also, that there
were two stones in silver bows—and these stones, fastened
to a breastplate, constituted what is called the Urim and
Thummim—deposited with the plates; and the possession and use of these stones were what constituted 'seers'
in ancient or former times; and that God had prepared
them for the purpose of translating the book."

This is the correct story of the origin of the Book of
Mormon, as given to us by the Prophet himself. After he
waited four years, in which time he endeavored to prepare
himself for his great work, the plates were finally delivered
into Joseph's hands on September 22, 1827, by the same
messenger who had informed him about them.

Meantime, on January 18, 1827, Joseph had married Miss Emma Hale of Harmony, Pennsylvania. After
receiving the plates, Joseph went to his father-in-law's
home in Harmony, and in April, 1828, the translation of
the sacred record began, with Martin Harris, a resident
of Palmyra, acting as scribe. One hundred sixteen pages
of manuscript were completed when Martin asked permission of Joseph to return to Palmyra and show the same
to relatives and friends. This precious document was
never returned to the youthful Prophet, but through
the treachery of those who did not believe in his divine
calling it was lost or destroyed. Joseph was greatly discouraged with this loss and did not begin the work of translation again until April, 1829, when a young schoolteacher,
Oliver Cowdery, came from Palmyra and offered to assist

him. The work now proceeded rapidly, and was completed sometime in June, 1829, at the home of Peter Whitmer, in Fayette, New York.

To add to the marvelous wonders that had taken place in his life, Joseph informed his relatives and friends that during the work of translation, he and Oliver Cowdery had been visited by John the Baptist, who had ordained them to the Aaronic Priesthood and commanded them to baptize each other by immersion in a nearby river. They had also been visited by the ancient apostles Peter, James, and John, who had ordained them to the apostleship in the Melchizedek Priesthood.

Futhermore, the vision of the Three Witnesses, as recorded in the Book of Mormon, took place sometime in June, 1829, when Oliver Cowdery, David Whitmer, and Martin Harris were shown the sacred plates by the angel Moroni and heard the voice of God declare that a correct translation had been made.

Joseph experienced considerable difficulty in finding a publisher for his sacred manuscript. He was alone, without funds, and was ridiculed everywhere he went for his pretentious claims. But the loyalty of Martin Harris, his Palmyra neighbor, again asserted itself. Martin offered to mortgage his farm to pay for the printing of the book. With this security, arrangements were soon made with E. B. Grandin, of Palmyra, to print an edition of five thousand copies for the sum of $3,000. In March, 1830, the work was completed.

The Book of Mormon might be called the American volume of scripture, equal in importance to the Bible. At first it was not well received by the citizens of Palmyra, who refused to buy it, believing that it was a fraud and deception. But gradually, and on its own merits, the book has made its way. In the years that have passed since the first edition in 1830, many other editions have been published, in the United States and in other countries. Latter-day Saints believe that the Book of Mormon has now established the claims that Joseph Smith made for it in 1830; that it is a true record of ancient peoples who once inhabited this continent; that Christ visited them here after his ministry in Palestine, and established his church among them.

A few weeks after the publication of the Book of Mormon on April 6, 1830, Joseph met with five young men at the home of Peter Whitmer, in Fayette, New York, and formally organized the Church of Jesus Christ. These first members were Oliver Cowdery, David Whitmer, Peter Whitmer, Jr., and two of Joseph's brothers, Hyrum and Samuel Smith. Hyrum Smith was the oldest of the group, having just passed his thirtieth birthday, and the youngest was Samuel Smith, who, three weeks previously, had turned twenty-two. The Church was therefore distinctly a church of young men.

After the organization of the Church, Joseph's course before him was clear, and the work he sought to do was definite in his mind. First, the newly revealed gospel, as set forth in the Book of Mormon and in the revelations that came to him from time to time, was to be preached to all the world. Then those who truly believed and yielded obedience to the principles and teachings were to gather together, in a place yet to be designated in the land of America, and a holy city was to be built, a place where they could worship the Lord in righteousness and in peace. It was a glorious objective, and yet the young men who were called upon to undertake the work were unlearned and poor in worldly possessions. But Joseph set his face as flint to carry out the mandates God had given him. He was not to be discouraged.

II

All the miraculous events pertaining to the rise of the Church had taken place in western New York, yet Joseph had met with little response from the inhabitants there and little encouragement or success, except from his own family and a few friends. By the people generally he was misunderstood, ridiculed, and persecuted, even to the extent of doing him bodily harm. Missionaries who had gone to Ohio, Oliver Cowdery, Parley P. Pratt, and others, had met with more success in obtaining converts than Joseph had had in New York. During the latter part of 1830 and the first few months of 1831, nearly 1,000 converts had been baptized in the neighborhood of Mentor, Ohio. Then the word of the Lord came to the young Prophet, under date of January 2, 1831: ". . . I gave unto you the commandment that ye should go to Ohio; and there I will give unto you my law; and there you shall be endowed with power from on high; And from thence, whosoever I will shall go forth among all nations, and it shall be told them what they shall do; for I have a great work laid up in store, for Israel shall be saved, and I will lead them whithersoever I will, and no power shall stay my hand." (D&C 38:32-33.)

Thus Ohio became the first designated gathering place *Feb 1831* for the Saints, and in a few weeks the Prophet transferred his place of residence there, making the journey in a sleigh and arriving in Kirtland early in February. Practically all the members in New York followed him during the spring and summer of 1831. New proselytes were constantly being gained in Ohio, and by the first of June, 1831, the membership of the Church numbered nearly two thousand souls.

On the 6th of June, 1831, a conference of the entire Church was held at Kirtland. While it was still in session the Prophet received a revelation that the next conference was to be held in Missouri, "upon the land which I will consecrate unto my people; the land of your inheritance." Thus the permanent gathering place of the Saints was designated; it was to be in the western part of Missouri, "on the border by the Lamanites."

On the 19th of June, Joseph, Sidney Rigdon, Martin

19 Jun 1831

Harris, and others of the brethren left Kirtland for Missouri to view for the first time "the land of our inheritance, even the place for the city of the New Jerusalem." The journey was made by wagon, stage, and boat as far as St. Louis. From this place Joseph, Martin Harris, William W. Phelps, and others walked overland to Independence, a distance of nearly three hundred miles. The day after their arrival a revelation was given to Joseph designating Independence and the lands surrounding as the gathering place, "and the Lord designated the exact spot on which a temple was to be erected to his glory."

Almost immediately after this revelation the Saints began to gather to Jackson County, and by fall several hundred of them were located there. The publication of a newspaper was begun at Independence, called the *Evening and Morning Star*.

Meantime Joseph had returned to Kirtland and resumed his work of revising and clarifying the Bible. This and other duties pertaining to his office as President of the Church occupied his time during the winter of 1831 and 1832. In March, 1832, while residing at the home of John Johnson in Hiram, Ohio, Joseph was dragged from his bed at night by a mob, taken into a nearby field, given a coat of tar and feathers, and left beaten and bruised. This was the work of certain apostates from the Church and sectarian priests who had sworn to destroy him.

Soon recovering from the effects of the treatment of the mob, Joseph spent the spring and part of the summer of 1832 in again visiting the Saints who had settled in Missouri. It was a great joy for them to have the Prophet among them. He was always an inspiration to his people.

Returning to Kirtland in late summer, Joseph resumed his work of "translating" the scriptures. Meantime the Church at Kirtland was continually being strengthened by the arrival of new converts. In November, Brigham Young and Heber C. Kimball made the journey from western New York and met the Prophet for the first time. At the time of this meeting Brigham Young was thirty-one years of age and the Prophet lacked a few months of being twenty-seven. Joseph is said to have remarked on this occasion that the time would come when Brigham Young would preside over the Church.

Early in 1833, at Kirtland, a revelation known as the Word of Wisdom was given out by the Prophet. This revelation, which advises against the use of tobacco, intoxicating liquors, and hot drinks of all kinds, has played a great part in molding the lives of the Latter-day Saints and in making them a sober, industrious people.

Early in the summer of 1833, a group of Missourians, said to have numbered three hundred, came together at Independence for the purpose of making plans to keep the Mormons from settling in western Missouri and to expel those who were already there. Their main fear was that the Latter-day Saints would come into the country in such large numbers that they would control the election vote and take over the various county offices. There was perhaps some ground for this fear, as the Saints were continually gathering in and around Independence, and by July it was estimated that about twelve hundred of them had settled in Jackson County.

During the latter part of July, a mob of five hundred men, led by politicians and sectarian priests, gathered at Independence and issued an edict that the Saints were to immediately leave Jackson County. The Saints asked for ten days' time in which to consider the edict but were told that "fifteen minutes" was sufficient. The mob then began burning the homes of the Saints, whipping the men, driving away their stock, and destroying their crops. All the Saints were ordered to leave the county and not return again. If they did return, they were informed, their lives would be taken.

The Prophet Joseph was in Kirtland at the time of the Missouri mob violence. It was indeed painful news for him to hear that the Saints had been expelled from Jackson

County. He wrote to them and urged them to bear their afflictions patiently. He told them that those who were called upon to lay down their lives in the cause of Christ would be rewarded with life eternal. "After much tribulation cometh the blessing." He also promised them that in some future time, "Zion would be redeemed in power."

Early in 1834 the Prophet organized a group of men in Kirtland, known as Zion's Camp (205 in number) who expressed their willingness to go with him to Missouri and do all that could be done to relieve the persecuted and harassed Saints. The long journey of one thousand miles was made, and the members of Zion's Camp arrived in western Missouri during the latter part of June. While in Missouri the Prophet did everything possible to alleviate the sufferings of the Saints and to have them restored to their rightful possessions. He found, however, that the officials of Missouri were working with the mob and that the Saints were too weak in numbers to withstand their persecutors. In July, Joseph and a number of his brethren, after perfecting the organization of the Saints, made their way back to the headquarters of the Church in Kirtland.

During the remaining months of 1834 Joseph devoted his time principally to the work of assisting in the construction of the Kirtland Temple. He labored in the stone quarry and helped in hauling the stone to the temple ground. This temple, the first to be erected by the Latter-day Saints, was to be the scene of many wonderful events and glorious visions that unfolded and made manifest the greatness of the latter-day work.

About the middle of February, 1835, Joseph called an assemblage of all the brethren who had composed Zion's Camp. From this group he requested the Three Witnesses of the Book of Mormon, Oliver Cowdery, David Whitmer, and Martin Harris, to choose twelve men who would be known as the Quorum of Twelve Apostles. These men were selected and ordained, Brigham Young, Heber C. Kimball, Parley P. Pratt, and Orson Pratt being among the

number. It was the duty of the twelve to be "special witnesses of the name of Christ in all the world." The labors
and sacrifices of these men form a great part of the history
of the Church during the following thirty or forty years.

During all of the year 1835 work on the Kirtland
Temple was continued, and by the early spring of 1836
the building was ready for dedication. These solemn ceremonies took place on Sunday, March 27, 1836. The Prophet
himself offered the dedicatory prayer, which closed with
the following words:

". . . hear us, O Lord. And answer these petitions, and
accept the dedication of this house unto thee, the work of
our hands, which we have built unto thy name;

"And also this church, to put upon it thy name; and
help us by the power of thy Spirit, that we may mingle
our voices with those bright, shining seraphs around thy
throne, with acclamations of praise, singing Hosanna to
God and the Lamb;

"And let these, thine anointed ones, be clothed with
salvation, and thy saints shout aloud for joy. Amen and
amen." (D&C 109:78-80.)

By a vote of the entire congregation, Joseph was sustained as the Prophet and Seer of the Church. In closing,
"the Prophet made a short exhortation in tongues, and then
blessed the congregation and dismissed them in the name
of the Lord."

One week after this meeting, while Joseph and Oliver
Cowdery were alone in the temple, they knelt in prayer
and afterwards beheld a glorious vision. They testified
that they saw the Lord, "standing upon the breastwork of
the pulpit." Then, "Moses appeared before us and committed unto us the keys of the gathering of Israel. . . . After
this, Elias appeared, and committed the dispensation of
the gospel of Abraham." When this vision had closed, "Elijah the prophet, who was taken to heaven without tasting
death," appeared before them, testifying that the time had
fully come which was spoken of by the mouth of Malachi,

when the hearts of the fathers would be turned to the children and the children to the fathers lest the earth should be smitten with a curse.

The glorious manifestations that came to Joseph and Oliver that day will be an inspiration to the people of God throughout all time to come.

In July, 1836, Joseph, with his brother Hyrum, Sidney Rigdon, and Oliver Cowdery, left Kirtland on a mission to the eastern states. During this journey they traveled as far as Salem, Massachusetts, and did much effective work in stimulating the membership of the branches that were visited.

III

The year 1837 was a difficult one for the Prophet. Due to misunderstandings and causes that were beyond his control, such as the failure of the Kirtland Safety Society Bank, some of the Saints became embittered and drew away from the Church. Even members of the Twelve were so far disaffected that they became Joseph's avowed enemies. On one occasion, during this year, a meeting was held "in the upper room of the Kirtland Temple" attended by "several of the Twelve, the Witnesses of the Book of Mormon, and others of the authorities of the Church." The object of this meeting was to ascertain how the Prophet Joseph could be deposed and David Whitmer appointed president of the Church. Brigham Young, who was present, reports the proceedings as follows: "Father John Smith, brother Heber C. Kimball and others were present, who were opposed to such measures. I rose up and in a plain and forcible manner told them that Joseph was a prophet, and I knew it, and that they might rail and slander him as much as they pleased, they could but destroy their own authority, cut the thread that bound them to the Prophet of God and sink themselves to hell."

Twenty-seven years after this event, President Brigham Young again took occasion to refer to the trying year of 1837 at Kirtland. "Some of the leading men at Kirtland were much opposed to Joseph the Prophet meddling with temporal affairs. They did not believe that he was capable of dictating to the people upon temporal matters, thinking that his duty embraced spiritual things alone, and that the people should be left to attend to their temporal affairs without any interference whatever from Prophets or Apostles. Men in authority there would contend with Joseph on this point, not openly, but in their councils. After awhile, the matter culminated into a public question; it became so public that it was in the mouth of almost everyone. In a public meeting of the Saints I said: 'Ye elders of Israel: Now, will some of you draw the line of demarcation between the spiritual and temporal in the Kingdom of God, so that I may understand it!' Not one of them could do it. When I saw a man standing in the path before the Prophet, I felt like hurling him out of the way, and branding him as a fool."

A few stalwarts like Brigham Young stood firm for the Prophet, but they were too few in numbers to withstand the opposition. In the month of December, both Joseph *Dec /1837* and Brigham fled from Kirtland, as the mob had threatened "publicly and privately" to take their lives. Thus the Prophet of God was forced to leave his own home, the beautiful temple that he had assisted in building, his friends, his relatives, and many of the Saints who were still loyal to him and, in the dead of winter, take up his journey toward the scattered settlements of the Saints of Missouri. He no doubt felt discouraged and depressed, and yet his determination to carry on was invincible.

Arriving at Far West, Missouri, the headquarters of *Mar /1838* the Saints, on March 14, 1838, after a difficult and trying journey, Joseph was astonished to find that "the same evil spirit which had gained such sway in Kirtland had begun to assert itself in Missouri." The spirit of disaffection was

there also, and some of the chief men in the Church were
guilty of wrong doing and evil speaking, which made them
undesirable members. About one month after Joseph's arrival in Missouri, a trial was held, at which time Oliver
Cowdery, David Whitmer, Luke Johnson, Lyman E. Johnson, John F. Boynton, and others were excommunicated
from the Church. The two former were witnesses of the
Book of Mormon, and the three latter were members of
the Quorum of Twelve Apostles. It was a sad day for Joseph
when he lost the companionship of these men, some of
whom had been with him and assisted him from the beginning of the work. But he could not allow them to take a
wrong course or do anything that would impede the great
work that had been committed into his hands. And, let
the reader think of this: Had there been any fraud connected with the coming forth of the Book of Mormon,
would not now David Whitmer and Oliver Cowdery have
exposed it? History shows that both of them remained firm
and true to the testimonies they had given of the divine
origin of the sacred record. Ten years after his excom-
munication Oliver Cowdery came back to the Church and
asked for admittance by baptism. David Whitmer did not
join the Church again, but he did not deny his testimony
as it is published in the Book of Mormon. He reaffirmed
it throughout his lifetime, and on his death bed, nearly
forty years after the events about which we are writing,
he gave his solemn word that his testimony was true.

On July 4, 1838, Joseph assisted in laying the cornerstone of "a house of the Lord" to be built at Far West, and
on July 8 he received a revelation in which John Taylor,
John E. Page, Wilford Woodruff, and Willard Richards
were to be appointed members of the Twelve, "in place
of those who have fallen."

For a number of months, during the spring and summer of 1838, events moved peacefully and quietly with
the Saints in Missouri, but now, dark clouds of persecution loomed on the horizon. The chief difficulty again was

that sectarian priests and politicians raised the cry that the Saints were becoming so numerous they would control the elective offices of the counties and state and persecute and drive out the Missourians. At an election held in Daviess County on the 6th of August, a determined effort was made to keep the Saints away from the polls. This led to an open clash, in which some of the brethren were injured. An attempt was also made to arrest the Prophet, charging him with being the instigator of the "insurrection." This agitation, and "the perjuries of foiled mobbers," caused Lilburn W. Boggs, the governor of the state, to call out part of the state militia in the number of four hundred mounted men "armed and equipped" to preserve the public order. Events subsequently proved that this was the beginning of a deliberate movement to drive the Saints out of Missouri.

It is not necessary, in this short sketch, to go into all the details connected with the Missouri outrage. It might be sufficient here to say that on October 27, 1838, Governor Boggs issued his infamous "extermination order" against the Saints, in the following words: "The Mormons must be treated as enemies, and must be exterminated or driven from the State, if necessary for the public good. Their outrages are beyond all description." The Saints were represented by the governor as being a most wicked and diabolical people whose very presence endangered the morals and lives of the Missourians. Boggs himself published the most infamous falsehoods against the Saints and did all he could to incite the mob to rob, plunder and "exterminate" them.

On October 20, a mob militia of 2,000 men appeared at Far West. They demanded that the Prophet, Sidney Rigdon, Parley P. Pratt, Lyman Wight, and George W. Robinson be surrendered to them. Joseph and his brethren, realizing the helpless condition of the Saints, gave themselves up to the militia, although they knew that their lives were in extreme danger.

The following day, November 1, a court martial convened at the headquarters of General Lucas. The verdict, which was given after a few minute's deliberation, was that Joseph and his companions were "to be shot at nine o'clock the next morning, November 2nd, 1838, on the public square at Far West." This verdict would have been carried out had it not been for General Doniphan, one of the commanders of the militia. "I wash my hands of this thing," he said; "it is murder." The order was reconsidered, and it was decided to take the brethren (Hyrum Smith and Amasa M. Lyman having been added to their number) to Independence as prisoners. Here they were kept four days while the officials were endeavoring to determine what charges should be made against them. They were then carried to Richmond, Missouri, and placed in chains to prevent their escape. From Richmond they were transferred to Liberty Jail, in Clay County, and held on the charge of "murder and treason."

Joseph and Hyrum and their companions were held in Liberty Jail through the winter of 1838 and 1839. They were confined in one room with two small windows. No provision had been made to heat the room; there was no chimney to draw out the smoke. The brethren slept on piles of straw on the floor. Their food was of the coarsest kind. And yet, from that prison came some of the most beautiful thoughts and writings that Joseph Smith has left to the world. Sections 121, 122, and 123 of the Doctrine and Covenants will endure among the sacred writings of the Church for all time.

On April 16, 1839, while the brethren were being transferred to Boone County for trial, their guards became intoxicated and Joseph informed his companions that this was a favorable opportunity for them to escape. After traveling by night and suffering all manner of privations, they arrived in a few days at Quincy, Illinois, and joined their families and friends. "It was one of the most joyful scenes of my life," relates Brigham Young, "to once more shake

hands with the Prophets and behold them free from the
hands of their enemies. Joseph conversed with us like a
man who had just escaped from a thousand oppressions
and was now free in the midst of his children."

IV

The immediate prospect now before the Prophet was
to find another place of gathering for his scattered and
persecuted people. A few days after his arrival in Quincy,
he and a number of leading brethren of the Church traveled northward about forty miles to a village called Commerce, where a large tract of land had been offered for
sale. Here Joseph purchased property and located, and here
he was to spend the few remaining years of his life.

The name of the village was soon changed from Commerce to Nauvoo (meaning the fair or beautiful) and word
was sent out to the scattered Saints throughout the world
that this place was to be the headquarters of the Church.
In a short time hundreds of families who had been driven
from Missouri were wending their way toward the new
gathering place. Most of them were in a pitiable plight,
as they had lost everything they possessed, but their faith
in the Church and in the divine calling of their leader had
not been lessened. When a siege of illness overtook those
who had gathered at Nauvoo, Joseph went among them and
blessed them as did the Savior with his following during
his ministry in Palestine. He was always a source of strength
to the Saints; he inspired them and encouraged them to go
forward and build up the kingdom in power.

In the fall of 1839, while the Saints were endeavoring
to make a new beginning at Nauvoo, Joseph requested the
Twelve to depart for England and proclaim the principles _fall 1839_
of the gospel in that land. How could they do this task?
Most of them were ill and all of them were desperately
poor. None of them had money or proper clothing with
which to begin the journey. But all of them were filled

with mighty faith; and without hesitation, at the command of their Prophet and with his blessing, they departed on this difficult mission. I shall pass over their struggles in reaching England, but I cannot refrain from giving a brief account of their success, which was the greatest that ever came to a similar number of missionaries in the history of the Church. I select the following from Brigham Young's journal under date of April 20, 1841, as he was leaving Liverpool, on his return journey to the United States:

"It was with a heart full of gratitude to God, my Heavenly Father, that I reflected upon His dealings with me and my brethren of the Twelve during the past year of my life, which was spent in England. It truly seemed a miracle to look upon the contrast between our landing and departing from Liverpool. We landed in the Spring of 1840, as strangers in a strange land and penniless, but through the mercy of God we have gained many friends, established churches in almost every noted town and city in the Kingdom of Great Britain, baptized between seven and eight thousand, printed 5,000 Books of Mormon, 3,000 Hymn Books, 2,500 volumes of the Millennial Star, and 60,000 tracts, and emigrated to Zion 1,000 souls, established a permanent shipping agency, which will be a great blessing to the Saints, and have left sown in the hearts of many thousands the seeds of eternal truth, which will bring forth fruit to the honor and glory of God, and yet we have lacked nothing to eat, drink or wear: in all these things I acknowledge the hand of God."

The Prophet's wisdom and inspiration in sending these brethren of the Twelve to England were abundantly justified.

On October 29, 1839, Joseph, accompanied by Sidney Rigdon and Elias Higbee, left Nauvoo on a journey to Washington, D. C. It was his intention to lay before the President of the United States and Congress the wrongs that the Saints had endured at the hands of the Missouri mobs and to see if redress could be obtained. The brethren traveled by stage and boat and in one month they reached Washington. A few days later they were admitted to the White House and given an interview with the President, Martin Van Buren. Mr. Van Buren listened attentively to Joseph's recital of the Missouri troubles and outrages, and then calmly replied, "Gentlemen, your cause is just, but I can do nothing for you." And then further on in the conversation, he added, "If I take this up for you, I shall lose the votes of Missouri."

Joseph was disappointed and disgusted with the reception he received both from the President and from members of Congress whom he interviewed. After remaining in Washington a few weeks, he left Judge Higbee to continue to press the claims of the Saints, and departed for his home. Arriving in Nauvoo, he recorded the following in his history: "I arrived safely at Nauvoo, after a wearisome journey, through alternate snow and mud, having witnessed many vexatious movements in government officers, whose sole object should be the peace and prosperity and happiness of the whole people; but . . . I discovered that popular clamor and personal aggrandizement were the ruling principles of those in authority; and my heart faints within me when I see, by the visions of the Almighty, the end of this nation, if she continues to disregard the cries and petitions of her virtuous citizens. . . ."

During the balance of the year 1840, Joseph remained in Nauvoo and vicinity and directed the affairs of the Church, which now, with approximately twenty thousand members, were becoming very extensive. Settlements of the Saints were being formed in all directions from Nauvoo. The city was growing more rapidly than any other city in Illinois. The missionaries throughout the United States and in England were reaping an unprecedented harvest; thousands of honest souls were preparing to emigrate to the land of Zion. It was during this year and the few succeeding years of the Prophet's life that he had the opportunity to demonstrate what a marvelous work he could accomplish, if left to pursue his tasks unmolested. But the growing kingdom and its inspired leader were not to find peace in this world.

On September 14, 1840, the Prophet's father, Joseph Smith, Sr., died at his home in Nauvoo. He was sixty-nine years of age; he had been well and strong until he had suffered from the persecutions of the mob in Missouri. Regarding his father the Prophet wrote:

"He was the first person who received my testimony after I had seen the angel, and exhorted me to be faithful and diligent to the message I had received. He was baptized April 6th, 1830.

"In August, 1830, in company with my brother Don Carlos, he took a mission to St. Lawrence county, New York, touching on his route at several of the Canadian ports, where he distributed a few copies of the Book of Mormon. He also visited his father, brothers and sister residing in St. Lawrence county, bore testimony to the truth which resulted eventually in all the family coming into the Church, excepting his brother Jesse and sister Susan. . . .

"He was one of the most benevolent of men; opening his house to all who were destitute."

At the October conference at Nauvoo in 1840, the Prophet put forth the proposition of constructing a temple "in this city." It was to be built, as far as possible, by donation labor, each individual giving "every tenth day of labor." The work was soon begun and went forward rapidly, though Joseph did not live to see the completion of this beautiful structure.

At this conference Joseph expressed his gratitude for the favorable condition of the Saints: "Two years ago mobs were threatening, plundering, driving and murdering the Saints. Our burning houses enlightened the canopy of heaven. Our women and children, houseless and destitute, had to wander from place to place to seek shelter from the rage of persecuting foes. Now we enjoy peace, and can worship the God of heaven and earth without molestation, and expect to be able to go forward and accomplish the great and glorious work to which we have been called."

But not long was the Prophet to enjoy peace. On the 5th of June, 1841, while returning from Quincy, where he had visited with the governor of Illinois, Thomas Carlin, Joseph was overtaken by the sheriff of Adams County and served with a writ of arrest, on the ground that he was a fugitive from justice from the state of Missouri. He returned with the officers to Quincy and there obtained a hearing on the writ before Judge Stephen A. Douglas. Joseph secured the services of attorney O. H. Browning, who later became Secretary of the Interior in President Andrew Johnson's Cabinet. Mr. Browning plead for the protection of Joseph from his Missouri enemies and gave a clear exposition of the persecutions of the Saints at the hands of the Missouri mobs. Judge Douglas then rendered his decision, which freed the Prophet from arrest. On his return to Nauvoo, Joseph was met by a large group of Saints who extended to him a joyful welcome.

At the October conference in 1841, Joseph gave instructions to the Saints on the subject of "baptism for the dead." His remarks were a comfort to those who had sorrowed that their ancestors had been deprived from hearing the gospel truths.

On the 17th of March, 1842, the Prophet organized at Nauvoo "The Female Relief Society," an organization of the sisters that was to devote itself to the work of charity. This society has done untold good during the years of its existence.

In 1842, when only thirty-six years of age, Joseph began to give warning of his early death. On the 9th of April, in a public meeting, he said: "Some of the Saints have supposed that Brother Joseph could not die, but this is a mistake. It is true that there have been times when I have had the promise of my life to accomplish certain things, but, having now done these things, I have no longer any lease of my life. I am as liable to die as other men."

On the 6th of August, 1842, while Joseph was visiting
with several of his brethren at Montrose, Iowa, he made the
significant statement "that the Saints would continue to
suffer much affliction and would be driven to the Rocky
Mountains, many would apostatize, others would be put
to death by our persecutors or lose their lives in consequence of exposure or disease; and some of you will live to
go and assist in making settlements and build cities and
see the Saints become a mighty people in the midst of the
Rocky Mountains."

Throughout his lifetime Joseph was harassed by enemies both without and within the Church. The summer and
fall of 1842 were darkened for the Saints at Nauvoo by
the apostasy of John C. Bennett, the mayor of the city
and one who stood high in the councils of the presiding
brethren. Never did a more bitter and vindictive enemy
turn loose calumny and vituperation upon an innocent
people. This man seemed to be the very incarnation of
Satan. He went about writing for newspapers, lecturing, and
effectively poisoning the public mind against the Prophet
and the Saints. His book *Mormonism Exposed* I regard as
the bitterest attack ever made against the Church, even
to this day.

Joseph felt this attack keenly, but it did not deter him
in the least from continuing on with his great work of
founding the kingdom. In a public meeting at Nauvoo on
August 26, he addressed the people "with all his wonted
fire, and advised them concerning all the exigencies of their
situation. He reminded the people that the falsehoods of
John C. Bennett were being scattered over the land and
called for Elders to go abroad to declare the truth and re-
fute the slanders which the enemies of the Prophet and
the Church were circulating." "While he talked," relates
George Q. Cannon, "an indescribable transport of joy was
manifested by the assembly; and when he concluded, three
hundred and eighty Elders volunteered to go immediately
into the east, upon the proposed mission of enlightenment."

During the summer of 1842 a further attempt was made by the officials of Missouri to arrest Joseph, and for a time he was forced to go into retirement. From the home of Edward Hunter he wrote the following, which is an excerpt from An Epistle to the Saints. It reveals his ever optimistic and courageous spirit.

"Now what do we hear in the gospel which we have received? 'A voice of gladness! A voice of mercy from heaven, and a voice of truth out of the earth; glad tidings for the dead; a voice of gladness for the living and the dead; glad tidings of great joy. . . .'

"Brethren, shall we not go on in so great a cause? Go forward and not backward? Courage, brethren, and on, on to the victory! Let your hearts rejoice, and be exceeding glad. Let the earth break forth into singing. . . . Let the sun, moon, and the morning stars sing together, and let the sons of God shout for joy. And let the eternal creation declare His name for ever and ever. And again I say, how glorious is the voice we hear from heaven, proclaiming in our ears, glory, and salvation, and honor, and immortality and eternal life, kingdoms, principalities and powers. Behold the great day of the Lord is at hand; and who can abide the day of His coming, and who can stand when He appeareth?"

On December 26, 1842, Joseph submitted to voluntary *Dec 1842* arrest on the Missouri writ and was taken to Springfield for trial. The case was called before Judge Pope, who, after listening to the evidence and calmly weighing the same, gave the Prophet his freedom. This was again the cause of much rejoicing among the Saints at Nauvoo.

On Wednesday, January 18, 1843, Joseph and his wife entertained a large company of brethren and sisters at their home in Nauvoo in honor of the fifteenth anniversary of their wedding and in celebration of Joseph's release from "the Missouri writ." It was one of the happiest occasions of his life, a life that had been filled with so much trouble and care.

Four days after the above event Joseph addressed a
public meeting in Nauvoo and again gave an ominous fore-
cast of his death:

"God Almighty is my shield; and what can man do if
God is my friend? I shall not be sacrificed until my time
comes; then I shall be offered freely."

According to President Brigham Young, it was in this
year, 1843, that the Prophet realized that the great work of
his life was finished. In a letter from President Young to
Orson Spencer, under date of January 23, 1848, I find the
following:

"Joseph told the Twelve, the year before he died,
'There is not one key or power to be bestowed upon this
Church, to lead the people into the celestial gate, but I
have given you, showed you and talked it over to you; the
Kingdom is set up, and you have the perfect pattern, and
you can go and build up the Kingdom, and go in at the
celestial gate, taking your train with you.' "

50,000 Saints   Joseph no doubt had great satisfaction in his accomplishments. He had built up a large following during the
years of his ministry, estimated to have numbered fifty
thousand people, located in various parts of the civilized
world. In five years Nauvoo had become the largest city in
Illinois, with some 20,000 inhabitants. The kingdom was
prospering both at home and abroad. Joseph had lived to
see that his life's efforts had been successful. And in his
high position he was loved and sustained by his people.
At the April conference in 1843, Brigham Young made the
motion to sustain Joseph Smith as President of the whole
Church, and "one vast sea of hands was presented," carrying the motion unanimously.

One other act of this conference was to send out one
hundred fifteen missionaries "to go forth into the vineyards,
and build up churches." Until his death Joseph did not
cease his efforts to have the missionaries proclaim the gospel
"in all the world."

In the summer and fall of 1843 the Saints at Nauvoo were subjected to the same treatment that had caused them so much trouble in Missouri. In August, a number of brethren who had been elected to county offices went to Carthage to give bonds and take the official oath. "While these men were before the court, a rabble, consisting of Constable Harmon T. Wilson and about fifteen others came in armed with hickory clubs, knives and pistols, and swore that the bonds should not be approved nor the men from Nauvoo inducted into office." On August 19, a mob from Hancock County numbering several hundred met in the courthouse at Carthage and passed resolutions stating that the Mormons should be expelled from Illinois as they had been from Missouri. This was the beginning of a lawless tirade of abuse and a campaign of vicious persecution, which exceeded anything that the Saints had previously experienced and resulted in the great exodus to the West.

Joseph was less fearful of the acts of the mobs than he was of those who might prove to be traitors among his own people. Before the city council of Nauvoo he made this significant statement in December, 1843. "I am exposed to far greater danger from traitors among ourselves than from enemies without. . . . All the enemies upon the face of the earth may roar and exert all their power to bring about my death, but they can accomplish nothing unless some who are among us, who have enjoyed our society, have been with us in our councils, participated in our confidence, taken us by the hand, called us brother, saluted us with a kiss, join with our enemies, turn our virtues into faults, and, by falsehood and deceit, stir up their wrath and indignation against us, and bring their united vengeance upon our heads."

The history of the following few months clearly shows that Joseph was right in his fear that traitors within his own ranks would do him harm. One of his own counselors, William Law, assisted in betraying him into the hands of his enemies.

Politics played an important part in Joseph's life during the first few months of 1844. It was a presidential year, and the issues of the campaign were being discussed on every side. At a meeting of the leading brethren, held at Nauvoo on January 29, it was decided that the Saints could support neither Martin Van Buren nor Henry Clay, the presidential candidates. Both had refused to help them obtain redress for the wrongs done them in Missouri, Clay's reply being, "You had better go to Oregon for redress." Consequently it was natural that Willard Richards should put a motion before the brethren—

"That we will have an independent electoral ticket and Joseph Smith will be a candidate for the next Presidency; and that we will use all honorable means in our power to secure his election."

At the April conference, 244 elders volunteered to go throughout the states and present the Prophet's name and his "views on the powers and policy of the government of the United States" to the people. Brigham Young had under his direct supervision the activities of these elders and their assignments to their fields of labor. In his instructions to them he said that they were to seek diligently to get electors who would vote for Joseph for the presidency; they were to be faithful "in preaching the Gospel in its simplicity and beauty, in all meekness, humility, long-suffering and prayerfulness; and the Twelve will devote the season to traveling, and will attend as many conferences as possible."

The April conference at Nauvoo in 1844 was the largest ever held in the history of the Church. It was estimated that some twenty thousand people were in attendance. Joseph spoke to the great congregation on the subject of "the death of Elder King Follett," who had been accidentally killed a few days previously. "In this address," relates George Q. Cannon, who was present, "he uplifted the souls of the congregation to a higher comprehension of the glory which comes after death to the faithful. His address ceased to be a mere eulogy of an individual, and became a revelation of eternal truths concerning the glories of immortality. The address occupied three hours and a half in delivery, and the multitude was held spellbound by its power. The Prophet seemed to rise above the world. It was as if the light of heaven encircled his physical being." The "King Follett Address," after nearly one hundred years, is today regarded as a classic in the literature of the Church.

During the early part of May, 1844, a small group of men in Nauvoo who were or had been members of the Church and who had been privately and publicly reprimanded by the Prophet for their evil ways began preparations to set up a newspaper in which they hoped to expose the Prophet and the Saints and do them every possible harm. One of these men was William Law, Joseph's former counselor in the Presidency. On June 7, the first and only issue of *The Nauvoo Expositor* appeared. It was filled with vicious falsehoods and its whole intent was to arouse the citizens of Illinois against the Prophet and his people. Three days later, at a meeting of the city council, at which Joseph presided as mayor, the *Expositor* was declared to be a public nuisance and was ordered to be abated. Marshal John P. Greene, with his assistants, proceeded to the office of the *Expositor* and destroyed the press and type. Immediately after this was done the owners of the paper fled to Carthage, where they demanded the arrest of Joseph and the members of the city council of Nauvoo. On June 12, Constable David Bettisworth of Carthage arrived in Nauvoo with warrants for the arrest of these men. The warrants had been issued upon a complaint, "sworn to by Francis M. Higbee [a former member of the Church] charging the parties named with having committed a riot."

Events now moved swiftly. Inflamed by the appeals of the agitators, a mob of several hundred men gathered at Carthage. Arms were brought from Warsaw and Quincy, and the newspapers in those cities were filled with flaming headlines calling upon the people of Illinois to drive out the Mormons or exterminate them.

Joseph felt that his final hour was approaching. He said to his brother Hyrum, "Hyrum, take your family on the next boat to Cincinnati. I want you to live to avenge me." Hyrum replied, "Joseph, I will not leave you."

On June 21, Thomas Ford, governor of Illinois, arrived in Carthage, having been summoned there by the leaders of the mob. This man Ford was to lure the Prophet Joseph Smith to his death. He sent word to Joseph, informing him that he would guarantee him the full protection of the state of Illinois if he would come to Carthage and surrender for trial. Joseph agreed to this proposition and informed Ford that he would arrive in Carthage on Monday, June 24. In sending this word, Joseph remarked to his brother Hyrum, "We are going back to be butchered." On his way to Carthage, he remarked to his brethren, "I am going like a lamb to the slaughter, but I am as calm as a summer's morning. I have a conscience void of offense toward God and toward all men."

The day after Joseph's arrival in Carthage he presented himself, together with his brethren who were under arrest, to Constable Bettisworth, who held the original writ against them. At four o'clock in the afternoon the brethren were taken before Justice Robert F. Smith, where they were admitted to bail in the sum of $7,500. Immediately after this procedure Joseph and Hyrum were arrested again, upon warrants issued by Justice Smith, charging them with treason. The mob had determined that Joseph and Hyrum should not escape from its cruel and deadly clutches, no matter what method had to be pursued to retain them. One of the mob was heard to remark at this time, "There is nothing against these men; the law cannot reach them, but powder and ball shall. They will never get out of Carthage alive."

Immediately after the second arrest Joseph and Hyrum were taken to the county jail, a few blocks from the courthouse. Several of the brethren accompanied them, among whom were Elders John Taylor and Willard Richards of

the Quorum of the Twelve. These men were not under
arrest, but gladly acted as guards, to protect, if possible,
the lives of their beloved leaders.

The following day, June 26, was spent by the brethren
in the "upper room" of Carthage jail. About nine o'clock
in the morning, in response to an urgent request from
Joseph, Governor Ford came to the jail and the brethren
had a lengthy interview with him. Not much satisfaction
was obtained from this interview, but on leaving, the governor promised Joseph and Hyrum— "pledging his faith, the
honor of his officers, and the good name of the state of
Illinois"—that they would be protected. Subsequent events
proved that this and all other promises of the Illinois governor were shallow, unfaithful, and treacherous.

During the evening, "Hyrum read from the Book of
Mormon concerning the sufferings and deliverance of the
servants of God from the hands of their enemies. Joseph arose
and bore a powerful testimony to the guards, of the divinity
of the book; he declared that the Gospel had been restored
and that the Kingdom of God was again established on the
earth, for the sake of which he was then incarcerated in
prison, and not because he had violated any law of God
or man." The brethren retired to rest late at night, several
of them sleeping on the floor.

June 27 dawned fair and clear at Carthage, but the
atmosphere was tense among the mob soldiery lounging
about the public square, and in the little county jail, where
the greatest and most gifted man of modern ages awaited
the uncertainty of events.

Sometime during the forenoon, Governor Ford, accompanied by a body of troops, left for Nauvoo. Arriving
there in the afternoon, he addressed a congregation of
assembled Saints, at which time he is reported to have said,
"A crime has been done by destroying the Expositor press,
and placing the city under martial law. A severe atone-
ment must be made, so prepare your minds for the
emergency."

During the afternoon at the jail, John Taylor sang a plaintive song that had recently been introduced into Nauvoo, entitled "A Poor Wayfaring Man of Grief." It had many verses. When he concluded the Prophet asked him to sing it again, but Brother Taylor excused himself, saying that he did not feel much like singing.

Shortly after five o'clock John Taylor, who was looking out a front window, saw a group of armed men, with blackened and painted faces, march around the corner of the jail. At their appearance the guard fled, and as many of the ruffians as could do so climbed the stairs to the room where the brethren were confined. "The four prisoners sprang against the door," relates George Q. Cannon, who was in Nauvoo at the time of the murder and was intimately acquainted with all the details, "but the murderers burst it partly open and pushed their guns into the room. John Taylor and Willard Richards, each with a cane, tried to knock aside the weapons. A shower of bullets came up the stairway and through the door. Hyrum was in front of the door when a ball struck him in the face, and he fell back saying:

"'I am a dead man.'

"As he was falling, another bullet from the outside passed through his swaying form, and two others from the doorway entered his body a moment later. When Hyrum fell, Joseph exclaimed, 'Oh, my dear brother Hyrum!' and opening the door a few inches he discharged his pistol into the stairway—but two or three barrels missed fire.

"When the door could no longer be held, and when he could no longer parry the guns, Elder Taylor sprang toward the window. A bullet from the doorway struck his left thigh. Paralyzed and unable to help himself he fell on the window sill, and felt himself falling out, when, by some means which he did not understand at the time, he was thrown back into the room. A bullet fired from the outside struck his watch and the watch saved his life in two ways, it stopped the bullet, which probably would have killed him,

and the force of the ball in striking it, threw him back into
the room. The watch stopped at 16 minutes and 26 seconds
past 5 o'clock. After he fell into the room, three other
bullets struck him spattering his blood upon the walls and
floor.

"Joseph saw that there was no longer safety in the
room; and thinking he would save the life of Willard
Richards, if he himself should spring from the room, he
turned immediately from the door, dropped his pistol and
leaped into the window. Instantly two bullets pierced him
from the door, and one entered his right breast from without, and he fell outward into the hands of his murderers,
exclaiming:

"'Oh Lord, My God.'

"When his body struck the ground he rolled instantly
upon his face—Dead."

V

The day following the murder the bodies of Joseph and
Hyrum were conveyed across the prairie eighteen miles to
Nauvoo, where they were received by sorrowing relatives
and friends, prepared for burial, and viewed by thousands
of Saints. The martyrs were then laid to rest in the soil of
the city they had founded and made famous.

VI

The following description of the Prophet and tribute
to his accomplishments was written by George Q. Cannon,
who came to Nauvoo as an emigrant boy from England in
1842.

"Joseph Smith had been a retiring youth—the Spirit
made him bold to declare to rulers and potentates and all
mankind, the Gospel again revealed. He had been a humble
farmer lad—divine authority sat so becomingly upon him

that men looked at him with reverent awe. He had been
unlearned in the great things of art and science—he walked
with God until human knowledge was to his eye an open
book; the celestial light beamed through his mind. His lofty
soul comprehended the grandeur of his mission upon earth;
and with divine fortitude he fulfilled the destiny which
God had ordained for him.

"When he had achieved the prime of his manhood, he
seemed to combine all attractions and excellence. His
physical person was the fit habitation of his exalted spirit.
He was more than six feet in height, with expansive chest
and clean cut limbs—a staunch and graceful figure. His
head, crowned with a mass of soft, wavy hair, was grandly
poised. His face possessed a complexion of such clearness
and transparency that the soul appeared to shine through.
He wore no beard, and the full strength and beauty of his
countenance impressed all beholders at a glance. He had
eyes which seemed to read the hearts of men. His mouth
was one of mingled power and sweetness. His majesty of
air was natural, not studied. Though full of personal and
prophetic dignity, whenever occasion demanded, he could
at other times unbend, and be as happy and unconventional
as a boy. This was one of his most striking characteristics. . . .

"But whether engaged in manly sport, during hours of
relaxation, or proclaiming words of wisdom in pulpit or
grove, he was ever the leader. His magnetism was masterful, and his heroic qualities won universal admiration.
Where he moved, all classes were forced to recognize in
him the man of power. Strangers, journeying to see him
from a distance, knew him the moment their eyes beheld
his person. Men have crossed ocean and continent to meet
him and have selected him instantly from a multitude. . . .

"The Prophet's life was exalted and unselfish. His
death was a sealing martyrdom."

VII

I shall close this sketch with the following tribute taken from section 135 of Doctrine and Covenants, one of the standard works of the Church. It was written shortly after the Prophet's death:

"Joseph Smith, the Prophet and Seer of the Lord, has done more, save Jesus only, for the salvation of men in this world, than any other man that ever lived in it. In the short space of twenty years, he has brought forth the Book of Mormon, which he translated by the gift and power of God, and has been the means of publishing it on two continents; has sent the fulness of the everlasting gospel, which it contained, to the four quarters of the earth; has brought forth the revelations and commandments which compose this book of Doctrine and Covenants and many other wise documents and instructions for the benefit of the children of men; gathered many thousands of the Latter-day Saints, founded a great city, and left a fame and name that cannot be slain. He lived great, and he died great in the eyes of God and his people; and like most of the Lord's anointed in ancient times, has sealed his mission and his works with his own blood. . . ." (D&C 135:3.)

BRIGHAM YOUNG

BRIGHAM YOUNG

(1801-1877)

O N THE day of the tragedy at Carthage, June 27, 1844, Brigham Young was in Boston, Massachusetts, engaged in missionary work for the Church. He had left Nauvoo five weeks previously, at the request of the Prophet Joseph Smith, to supervise the work of a large group of missionaries who had been sent out for the summer to present to the people the Prophet's "views on the powers and policy of the government of the United States," and to do missionary work whenever and wherever the opportunity was afforded.

On the first of June, while on his journey to the East, Brigham passed his forty-third birthday. He was a strong, vigorous man, sound in body and sound in mind. He was a man whose judgment was good; a clear-thinking, forward-looking, determined man; a man who knew where he wanted to go and what he wanted to accomplish. The lessons he had learned in life he had gained wholly from life, from nature herself; a natural man, taught in the rugged school of experience; a successful man, one who understood the principles that would prosper in this world and applied those principles with all his strength. Of book learning, school education, he had little; or it might be said, none at all, only "eleven days" in some backwoods school during his boyhood.

His present work, which he thoroughly enjoyed and

understood and to which he gave himself wholeheartedly, was that of a missionary, an apostle in The Church of Jesus Christ of Latter-day Saints. He was an official of the Church, the President of the Quorum of Twelve Apostles. Next to the Prophet Joseph Smith, Brigham no doubt carried more responsibility than any other man in the organization. For this work he received no material compensation, but he felt in his soul that it was God's behest that he should labor in it with all his might.

The tragedy at Carthage jail changed the course of Brigham Young's life. Had the Prophet lived, Brigham would no doubt have continued to serve his friend and leader well, for he was a true and devoted servant. But now, suddenly, the responsibility of leadership of a great religious people was to be placed upon him. How he carried this responsibility and with what degree of success he led the Latter-day Saints during the following thirty-three years is history that is fairly well known.

For the beginning of the life of this remarkable man, as was the case with Joseph Smith, we must look to New England in the early years of the nineteenth century. John Young, the father, was a soldier in the Revolutionary War, under General Washington. Returning from the war, he married Abigail Howe at Hopkinton, Massachusetts, in 1785 and settled down to the life of a farmer. Several children were born to this wedded pair at Hopkinton. About the beginning of the century, John Young, looking for better opportunities, moved with his family to Vermont and located on a farm at Whittingham. There, on June, 1801, was born the ninth child, whom the parents named Brigham.

When Brigham was two years old, the parents moved westward again and located in Chenango County, New York, where a settlement called Smyrna was forming. Here the family remained until Brigham was fourteen years of age. The boy had very few advantages in his youth. He relates that he had "no opportunity for letters," but "I had the privilege of picking up brush, chopping down trees, rolling

logs and working among the roots, getting my shins, feet
and toes bruised." And yet, his education was practical: "I
learned how to make bread, wash the dishes, milk the cows
and make butter. . . . Those are about all the advantages I
gained in my youth. I learned how to economize, for my
father had to do it."

At the age of fourteen, a tragedy came into the boy's
life. He lost his noble and splendid mother in death. She
had been his mainstay and support, and throughout his
future years he always spoke of her with the greatest reverence. "Of my mother—she that bore me—I can say, no
better woman ever lived in the world than she was," he
said in a sermon at Salt Lake City on August 15, 1852.
"While she lived, she taught her children all the time to
honor the name of the Father and Son, and to reverence
the Holy Book." Brigham's strong religious nature was no
doubt inherited, in a great measure, from his God-fearing
mother.

After the death of his mother, Brigham was "farmed
out" among the neighbors, and from that time on he made
his way alone. But he had already learned to work, and to
work at useful and necessary things. He soon found that he
could take care of himself. Somewhere, somehow, he learned
the carpenter trade, and at the age of twenty-two we find
him at Port Byron, New York, on the Erie Canal, able to
call himself a "carpenter, joiner, painter, and glazier." As
a boy he seems to have been as solid and substantial as he
was later on when grown to manhood.

At Port Byron Brigham joined the Methodist Reformed
Church. Three of his older brothers and a brother-in-law,
John P. Greene, were itinerant preachers in this organization,
but Brigham never became very enthusiastic about it; there
was not sufficient power in it to stir his soul.

On October 8, 1824, in the town of Aurelius, Cayuga
County, New York, Brigham married Miriam Works. He had
turned twenty-three years of age the previous June and was
now fairly prosperous in his occupation as a carpenter. Two

of his youthful friends at this time were Henry Wells, founder of the Wells-Fargo Express Company, and Isaac Singer, inventor of the Singer Sewing Machine. D. B. Smith, of Cayuga County, who knew Brigham well at this time, said later, "Brigham Young was as fine a specimen of young manhood as I have ever known, and would have made his mark in whatever community his lot might have been cast."

In the spring of 1829, Brigham moved to Mendon, Monroe County, New York, where most of his brothers and sisters resided. It was there, the following year, that he heard strange rumors of a "golden Bible" that a young man had found in a hill at Palmyra in Wayne County, and that the record had been translated and published in a book called the Book of Mormon. A few weeks after these rumors began to circulate, one of the books came into Brigham's hands. It was a small event and yet it was to change his life and perhaps the history of this nation. Destiny hangs upon small events. Brigham read the book and was profoundly impressed by it. His brother Phinehas relates in his history that "about this time, my brother Brigham came to see me, and very soon told me he was convinced that there was something in 'Mormonism.'"

Up to this time Brigham had not seen or heard any missionaries of the Church, but the following year he relates, "Elders Alpheus Gifford, Elial Strong and others came to Mendon to preach the everlasting Gospel, as revealed to Joseph Smith the Prophet, which I heard and believed."

It was fortunate for Brigham Young that he had a believing mind. "A man lives by believing something," writes Thomas Carlyle, "not by debating and arguing about many things. . . . We have our mind given us, not that it may cavil and argue, but that it may see into something, give us clear belief and understanding about something, whereon we are then to proceed to act."

Brigham was baptized at Mendon and made a member of the Church on April 14, 1832, by Elder Eleazer Miller. "We returned home," he relates, "about two miles, the weather being cold and snowy, and before my clothes were dry on my back he laid his hands on me and ordained me an Elder, at which I marveled." From this day on, until the day of his death, Brigham Young's activities were devoted almost wholly to the advancement of his chosen religion. Few men have ever worked with greater singleness of purpose.

In September, 1832, Brigham, accompanied by his brother Joseph and Heber C. Kimball, set out for Kirtland, Ohio, to visit the Prophet Joseph Smith, who had moved there the previous year and whom they had never seen. Brigham relates that on arriving, "we went to his father's house and learned that he was in the woods, chopping. We immediately went to the woods, where we found the Prophet and two or three of his brothers, chopping and hauling wood. Here my joy was full at the privilege of shaking the hand of the Prophet of God, and I received the sure testimony, by the spirit of prophecy, that he was all that any man could believe him to be, as a true Prophet. He was happy to see us and made us welcome. We soon returned to his house, he accompanying us."

This was a historic meeting. It is my opinion that, at that time, Joseph Smith and Brigham Young were the two most important men living in the world. Yet, see their humble circumstances! Truly the Almighty does use the humble things of the world to confound the wise and the powerful.

The same evening after their arrival, Brigham relates, Joseph called a few of the brethren together, and "we conversed on the things of the kingdom. He [Joseph] called upon me to pray; in my prayer I spoke in tongues. As soon as we arose from our knees the brethren flocked around him and asked his opinion concerning the gift of tongues that was upon me. He told them it was the pure Adamic language. Some said to him they expected he would condemn the gift Brother Brigham had, but he said, 'No, it is of God, and the time will come when Brother Brigham Young will preside over the Church.' "

The Prophet Joseph Smith had never heard the gift of tongues until he heard it from Brigham that day, and by the gift of prophecy he knew that a great man and a great leader had joined his standard.

II

In September, 1833, Brigham moved from Mendon, where he had lived four years, to Kirtland, Ohio, the home of the Prophet and headquarters of the Church. The previous year Brigham's wife Miriam had died, leaving him with two little girls, Elizabeth, age seven, and Vilate, two. A few months after his arrival in Kirtland, in February, 1834, Brigham married Mary Ann Angell, a faithful and devout woman, who proved truly to be an angel in his household. In Kirtland he soon established himself and became known for his diligence, his loyalty to the brethren and the Church, and his devotion to the kingdom, as the following instance from his journal will show:

"In the fall of 1833, many of the brethren had gathered to Kirtland, and not finding suitable employment, and having some difficulty in getting their pay after they had labored, several went off to Willoughby, Painesville and Cleveland. I told them I had gathered to Kirtland because I was so directed by the Prophet of God, and I was not going away to Willoughby, Painesville, Cleveland, nor anywhere else to build up the Gentiles, but I was going to stay here and seek the things that pertained to the Kingdom of God, by listening to the teachings of His servants, and I should work for my brethren, and trust in God and them that I would be paid. I labored for brother Cahoon and finished his house, and although he did not know he could pay me when I commenced, before I finished he had paid me in full. I then went to work for Father John Smith and others, who paid me, and I sustained myself in Kirtland, and when the brethren who had gone out to work for the Gentiles returned, I had means, though some of them were scant."

In February, 1835, the first Quorum of Twelve Apostles was organized, and Brigham Young was made a member. This was a high honor to a young man who had been in the Church less than three years. But his devotion and ability had been recognized. His new position made him one of the officials of the Church, and from this time on he was able to contribute splendidly to its advancement.

During the summers of 1835 and 1836 Brigham labored as a missionary for the Church in the eastern states. In the winter months he returned home and supported himself and his family by working at his trade as carpenter.

The year 1837 was a difficult one for the Prophet Joseph and all those at Kirtland who were loyal to him. Through the failure of the Kirtland Safety Society Bank and through the persecution of priests and apostates, many members had become embittered and sought to destroy the Prophet. Brigham stood firm and loyal to his leader, but the persecution finally became so intense that both he and the Prophet were forced to flee for their lives. Late in December they left Kirtland, riding horseback, and began their journey toward the scattered settlements of the Saints in Missouri. After a difficult trip of nearly three months, they arrived at Far West, the principal gathering place. Here they were welcomed by the Missouri Saints, and for a time all went well. But in the fall of 1838, persecutions began to break out in Missouri, and a determined effort was made by disgruntled ministers, politicians, and state officials to drive the Mormons from the state. In their scattered condition the Saints were unable to defend themselves, and by midwinter between twelve and fifteen thousand people were fleeing for their lives before a wicked and murderous mob. The Prophet Joseph Smith and several officials of the Church had been arrested and placed in Liberty jail. Brigham made his way out of Missouri early in March, 1839, and arrived in Quincy, Illinois. Here he labored with all his might to assist in rescuing "the poor Saints" from the ravages of the Missouri mob. His labors did not cease until all of them had removed to nearby states.

In April, 1839, the Prophet escaped from his persecutors and made his way to Illinois, where he was welcomed by the Saints. A few weeks later he located at Commerce, Illinois, and began another gathering place or headquarters for the Church. Brigham Young and many others joined him there and a prosperous settlement, which was named Nauvoo, was begun.

In the fall of 1839, before Brigham had had time to construct a home or establish himself, he began preparations to depart for a mission to England, as he and the other members of the Twelve had been commanded in the revelation of July, 1838. His faith taught him that, even though he were ill and penniless, he should be obedient to the revelations of his Heavenly Father as made known to the Prophet. Heber C. Kimball records the following regarding Brigham's condition. "September 14th, 1839, President Brigham Young left his home at Montrose to start on the mission to England. He was so sick that he was unable to go to the Mississippi, a distance of thirty rods, without assistance. After he had crossed the river he rode behind Israel Barlow on his horse to my house, where he continued sick until the 18th. He left his wife sick with a babe only ten days old, and all his children were sick and unable to wait upon each other. Not one soul of them was able to go to the well for a pail of water, and they were without a second suit to their backs, for the mob in Missouri had taken nearly all they had."

While his family did not have "a second suit for their backs," Brigham scarcely had one for his own. The cap he wore had been made "out of a pair of old pantaloons," and further, "I had not even an overcoat; I took a small quilt from the trundle bed while I was traveling to the state of New York where I had a coarse satinette overcoat given to me." Thus did Brigham Young go forth on his mission to England, sick, penniless, in threadbare clothing; but within his breast there was the heart of a lion, a determination to do or to die.

I do not have space here to go into the details of this

mission to England. The brethren of the Twelve were in England "one year and sixteen days" and it is safe to say that in that time they accomplished more than was ever accomplished since by a similar group of missionaries. The Church was established on a firm foundation in England; branches were organized in almost every noted town and city; and between seven and eight thousand converts were baptized. This great success was due in part to Brigham's fine leadership, his faith, his devotion, his unceasing energy and labor. Never did a man give himself more wholeheartedly to a righteous cause.

With a number of his brethren, Brigham sailed from Liverpool on his return journey on April 20, 1841. Thirty days later the ship *Rochester* arrived in New York City; and after an uneventful trip overland, by stage and boat, he reached Nauvoo July 1 and was warmly welcomed by his family and friends. Among the first to give him his hand as the boat docked at Nauvoo was the Prophet Joseph Smith.

The first thing that confronted Brigham on his return home was to provide comfortable living quarters for himself and his family. He relates, "On my return from England I found my family living in a small unfinished log cabin, situated on a low wet lot, so swampy that when the first attempt was made to plow it the oxen mired." He went to work and largely with his own hands built a comfortable brick home, which stands to this day. Brigham was constantly at the call of the Church, and what means he did acquire for himself he had to acquire in his spare time. From the Church he received no material compensation at all. In a sermon delivered years later at Salt Lake City I find the following:

"I came into this Church in the Spring of 1832. Previous to my being baptized I took a mission to Canada at my own expense; and from the time that I was baptized until the day of our sorrow and affliction at the martyrdom of Joseph and Hyrum, no summer passed over my head but what I was traveling and preaching, and the only thing I ever received from the Church, during over twelve years, and the only means that were ever given me by the Prophet, that I now recollect, was in 1842, when Brother Joseph gave me the half of a small pig that the brethren had brought to him."

During 1842 and 1843 Brigham labored principally in and around Nauvoo. The Prophet announced in August, 1841, that the time had come "when the Twelve should be called upon to stand in their place next to the First Presidency, and attend to the settling of the emigrants and the business of the Church at the Stakes, and assist to bear off the Kingdom victorious to the nations; and as they had been faithful and had borne the burden in the heat of the day, that it was right that they should have an opportunity of providing something for themselves and families."

Nauvoo was growing rapidly during these years. It was estimated in 1842 that the population had reached approximately 10,000. The city had already outdistanced Chicago in its number of inhabitants, and it soon became the largest city in Illinois.

During the year 1843 Brigham took one missionary trip to the East. He traveled as far as New York City and visited the various branches of the Church on the way. His principal object on this journey was to raise money to assist in the construction of the temple in Nauvoo.

At the April conference in 1844, the Prophet requested a number of the brethren to go throughout the eastern states and present his "views on the power and policy of the government of the United States" to the people. Two hundred and forty-four elders volunteered for this mission, and Brigham Young was placed in charge of their activities. He was in the East engaged in this labor when he learned of the death of the Prophet.

President Young's first reaction to the news of the death of the Prophet was this: "Has Joseph taken with him the keys of the kingdom?" He answered the question himself as he spoke to those about him in the home of "Brother

Bement" at Petersboro, New Hampshire, where the first definite word of the tragedy came to him. "Bringing my hand down on my knee I said, 'The keys of the kingdom are right here with the Church.' " To many others, the situation of the Church after the death of the Prophet Joseph was not clear, but Brigham knew that the Prophet had conferred upon the Twelve "the keys of the kingdom," and it must have flashed across his mind at that instant the burden of leadership was upon him. He was aware that in the absence of the First Presidency, the Quorum of Twelve was the governing body of the Church.

Brigham summoned to Boston all of the Twelve who were in the East, and together they made their way to Nauvoo, where they arrived in the evening of August 6. Their arrival at that time was fortunate, as Sidney Rigdon, the counselor to the Prophet, had appointed a meeting of the Saints the following day to present his claim for the position of guardian of the Church. Brigham went to this meeting and spoke in such plain, unmistakable language that the Saints were soon convinced that Sidney Rigdon was not the man to lead the Church. "Joseph conferred upon our heads," he said, speaking for himself and the Twelve, "all the keys and powers belonging to the apostleship which he himself held before he was taken away, and no man or set of men can get between Joseph and the Twelve, in this world or in the world to come. How often has Joseph said to the Twelve, 'I have laid the foundation and you must build thereon, for upon your shoulders the kingdom rests.' "

The following day, a large congregation of Saints again assembled and a vote was taken. Sidney Rigdon's claim for the guardianship of the Church was rejected and the Quorum of the Twelve was sustained as the Presidency of the Church. From that day on, for over thirty-three years, Brigham Young stood at the head of The Church of Jesus Christ of Latter-day Saints.

After Brigham was sustained as leader of the Saints, his course before him was clear and the objects he sought to attain were definite in his mind. "We will carry out all the measures of Joseph," he said. He did not attempt to originate anything new. He maintained that the gospel in its purity and fullness had been revealed to the Prophet, and that the foundation of the kingdom had been laid. He and his followers would build upon that foundation.

The first proposition that came before Brigham was to complete the construction of the Nauvoo Temple, as the Saints had been requested to do by the Prophet Joseph. Brigham knew that a move to the West was imminent, and he did not want the Saints to go into the wilderness "without their blessings." Every sacrifice was therefore made to complete this great building, and on May 24, 1845, "amidst shouts of hosanna from the Saints" the capstone was laid. Never did a people more willingly perform a great labor than was done in the construction of the Nauvoo Temple.

The second proposition before President Young was to prepare the people for their great exodus to the West, for he and his brethren had determined that there would be no peace for the Saints among the people of Illinois. He was not long in beginning this work, and on November 30, 1845, he was able to report that "every hundred (referring to groups of Saints) have established one or more wagon shops: wheelwrights, carpenters and cabinet makers are nearly all former wagon makers, and many not mechanics are at work in every part of the town preparing timber for making wagons. . . . Teams are sent to all parts of the country to purchase iron; blacksmiths are at work night and day and all hands are busily engaged getting ready for our departure westward, as soon as possible."

On the last day of 1845, Brigham recorded the following in his history: "Elder Heber C. Kimball and I superintended the operations in the Temple, examined maps with reference to selecting a location for the Saints, west of the Rocky Mountains, and read various works written by travelers in those regions."

III

On February 15, 1846, Brigham, with his family in a wagon, his teams, his cattle, and what possessions he could carry away, left his comfortable brick home in Nauvoo, his farm, his stores and city lots, the beautiful temple, which had almost cost him his life's blood, the graves of his beloved friends the Prophet and Patriarch, and ferried across the river to the Iowa side. It was a cold, bitter day. Before him was the great West, stretching 2,000 miles to the Pacific Ocean, with its vast plains and mountains, its deserts and uninhabitable wastes, its roving tribes of Indians, its wild beasts and reptiles; a region little known and explored except by the daring spirits who went forth in search of furs and skins of wild animals. Somewhere in this vast region he hoped to find a place of security, a resting place, for his long harassed and persecuted people. From maps, charts, and reports he had read and studied, he had fastened somewhat vaguely on the Salt Lake Valley, just beyond the Rocky Mountains, in the center of the Great Basin. Other than this he knew not of his destiny. But Brigham faced the future unafraid; his faith taught him that all was well. No picture in America is more sublime to me than that of this rugged man of faith, this strong man of God, going forth into the wilderness at the head of his little band of Saints to found an empire.

In a few weeks it was reckoned that about three thousand people had left their homes in Nauvoo and joined the caravan. Then the journey across Iowa toward Council Bluffs was begun. There were no roads, only trails in the soft mud, made by those who had gone ahead. Frequent heavy rains held them back so that often only two to five miles could be made in a day. At times the nights were cold, and occasionally snow fell to the depth of several inches. Many went without sufficient food; some died and were buried by the wayside. It was not until June 14 that Brigham came in sight of Council Bluffs on the Missouri River. He had been four months making the journey across Iowa.

I shall not be able to go into detail regarding the vast camp that was formed by the Saints on both sides of the Missouri River during the summer and fall of 1846 except to say that it was computed that twelve thousand refugees had gathered there or were in the plains of Iowa. Of their hardships I would almost rather not write at all, as they were the cause of much grief and sorrow. But under the leadership of President Brigham Young and the members of the Twelve, the Saints had constant encouragement and inspiration. Never was a people more fortunate in its leadership.

I must not forget to mention here that while at Council Bluffs, the Saints were called upon by General Kearney of the United States Army to furnish five hundred men to join the army in the war against Mexico. He sent Captain James Allen from Fort Leavenworth to interview President Young. The President, after weighing the matter carefully, called the Saints together and agreed to the proposition. He stated: "I propose that five hundred volunteers be mustered, and I will do my best to see that all their families are brought forward, so far as my influence can be extended, and to feed them when I have anything to eat myself." The story of the soldiers of the Mormon Battalion and their unparalleled march to California is one of the most thrilling in our Church history.

Early in April, 1847, a small group of pioneers, consisting of 143 men, three women, and two children, left Winter Quarters to search out a permanent home for the Saints, somewhere west of the Rocky Mountains. At the head of this group was President Brigham Young. He held the company to military rules, and the entire journey was made with safety and precision. In what is now western Wyoming, the brethren met James Bridger, who perhaps was the most famous of the western scouts. He did all he could to discourage President Young from trying to form a settlement in the Great Basin, stating that he would give $1,000 for the first bushel of corn grown there. President Young replied, "Wait a year or two and we will show you what can be done."

After traveling nearly four months and experiencing many hardships, the company entered Salt Lake Valley. As Brigham viewed the valley for the first time, on July 24, he said: "This is the right place."

After remaining in the valley a few weeks and giving instructions as to the location of a city, and how the lands were to be divided, President Young and a part of the pioneer company began their return journey to Winter Quarters. Although they experienced considerable difficulties, such as the loss of twenty-eight horses stolen by the Indians, the brethren made the journey to Winter Quarters in safety, arriving on the 31st of October. President Young later wrote: "We drove into the town about an hour before sunset. The streets were crowded with people to shake hands as we passed through the lines. We were truly rejoiced to once more behold our wives, children and friends, after an absence of over six months, having traveled more than two thousand miles, sought out a location for the Saints to dwell in peace, and accomplished the most interesting mission in this last dispensation. Not a soul of our camp died, and no serious accident happened to any, for which we praise the Lord."

The principal event of the winter of 1847 was a meeting of the Twelve that was held at the home of Orson Hyde, on the Iowa side of the river, on December 5. At this meeting a reorganization of the First Presidency of the Church was effected. Brigham Young was named President, and he selected as his counselors Heber C. Kimball and Willard Richards.

During February, March, and April of 1848, preparations for a general exodus of the Saints from Winter Quarters were being made. Three great caravans, presided over by Brigham Young, Heber C. Kimball, and Willard Richards, were to undertake the journey. By the latter part of May, President Young's company, which was to take the lead, was ready. It consisted of the following: "397 wagons, 1229 souls, 74 horses, 19 mules, 1275 oxen, 699 cows, 184 cattle,

411 sheep, 141 pigs, 605 chickens, 37 cats, 82 dogs, 3 goats, 10 geese, 2 beehives, 8 doves and 1 crow." Thus did the pioneers of Utah, like the Israelites of old, with wives and children, flocks and herds, journey forth into the wilderness. And at their head was a modern Moses, ready and able to lead them to a "promised land."

This second journey across the plains proved to be more wearisome and difficult than the first had been. The company was large and cumbersome and progress slow. When they reached the Sweetwater River in what is now western Wyoming, Brigham wrote back to Orson Hyde at Kanesville, "We have been sixty-three days in traveling from the Elkhorn to the last crossing of the Sweetwater, at an average of 12 miles a day, resting 22, including Sundays, to recruit and strengthen our cattle. The very dry season, the scarcity of grass, the heavy, dragging, dusty roads, and inhaling so much of the alkali by breathing, eating and drinking, has been the cause of our losing many of our cattle."

On August 28, Brigham's eyes and heart were gladdened by the timely arrival from the valley of his brother Lorenzo and Abraham O. Smoot, accompanied by forty-seven wagons and one hundred twenty-four yoke of oxen, "to give him help over the mountains." More rapid progress was now made, and on September 7 the company reached Green River. On September 12 the company arrived at Fort Bridger and camped there for the night. On the 19th, Brigham, riding in his carriage with his brother Lorenzo, crossed over the summit of Big Mountain; and the following day, from the mouth of Emigration Canyon, he was able to behold his little growing city in the wilderness. He had been one hundred sixteen days on the journey from Winter Quarters.

IV

During the first few years in the Salt Lake Valley, many of the Saints were not satisfied with their new location. The land was dry and barren and crops would not grow without irrigation. There was no timber in the valley; it had to be reached in the rocky and almost impassable canyons. Food supplies were short and some of the settlers were forced to subsist on roots or the flesh of wild animals. A feeling grew among the Saints that they would be better off if they moved to California or some more favorable location. "At this time of gloom," relates James Brown, one of the pioneers, "President Young stood before the whole people, and said in substance that some people had misgivings, and some were murmuring and had not faith to go to work and make their families comfortable; they had got the gold fever and were going to California. Said he, 'Some have asked me about going. I have told them that God has appointed this place for the gathering of His Saints, and you will do better right here than you will by going to the gold mines. Some have thought they would go there and get fitted out and come back, but I told them to stop here and get fitted out. Those who stop here and are faithful to God and His people will make more money and get richer than you that run after the God of this world; and I promise you in the name of the Lord that many of you that go, thinking that you will get rich and come back, will wish you had never gone away from here, and will long to come back, but will not be able to do so. Some of you will come back, but your friends who remain here will have to help you; and the rest of you who are spared to return will not make as much money as your brethren do who stay here and help build up the Church and Kingdom of God; they will prosper and be able to buy you twice over. Here is the place God has appointed for his people.' "

By the strength of his great personality and by the inspirational words that flowed from his lips on this occasion, Brigham was able to stem the tide of discontent and keep the Saints permanently in Salt Lake Valley.

Early in 1849 attention was paid to the matter of civil government. At a convention held in Salt Lake City, a memorial was drawn up asking the Congress of the United States for a territorial government, the territory "to be known by the name of Deseret." The memorial was carried to Washington by Dr. John M. Bernhisel. Congress did not act on this matter until September, 1850, at which time a bill passed both houses and was signed by President Millard Fillmore, creating the Territory of Utah. President Fillmore appointed Brigham Young to be the first governor of the new territory. News traveled so slowly in those days that Brigham did not learn of the action of Congress and his appointment as governor until January, 1851, on his return from a visit to the settlers at Ogden. Needless to say there was rejoicing among the Saints, and President Young was pleased with the honor that had been conferred on him.

During the summer of 1851, the selection of a site for the capitol of the new territory was made, one hundred fifty miles south of Salt Lake City. It was called Fillmore, in honor of the President. Dr. Bernhisel was named as the representative of the people of the territory to Washington.

The years of 1850 to 1854 in Utah were years of progress. Thousands of emigrants made their way across the plains to cast their lot with the Saints in the valleys, and many new settlements were formed. Abroad, the missionaries of the Church were preaching the gospel with great enthusiasm. President Young, in his dual capacity of President of the Church and governor of the territory, was a pronounced success in all he undertook to do. Seldom has the world seen a more capable executive. He had a profound understanding of human nature, and he knew what people should do to succeed and prosper.

On April 6, 1853, the cornerstones of the great Salt Lake Temple were laid, with President Young presiding at the ceremony. "Seven years ago," he said, "I crossed the Mississippi River with my brethren, not knowing at that time whither we were going, but firmly believing that the Lord had in reserve for us a good place in the mountains, and that He would lead us directly to it. It is but seven years since we left Nauvoo and we are now ready to build another temple." President Young did not live long enough to see the Salt Lake Temple completed, but under his guiding genius the work was planned and carried forward until it could be successfully finished by those who came after him.

In 1854, when President Young's first term as governor was about to expire, President Franklin Pierce offered the appointment to Edward J. Steptoe, a colonel in the United States Army. Colonel Steptoe came to Utah, visited with the people, and made an investigation of conditions. He thereupon recommended that Brigham Young be reappointed to the office, "as he possesses in an eminent degree every qualification necessary for the discharge of his official duties and is decidedly the most suitable person that can be selected for that office." Upon receipt of this word, the President reappointed Governor Young for a second four-year term.

Among the federal appointments made by President Pierce at this time was that of William W. Drummond of Illinois to the office of associate justice of the territorial supreme court. This man was to cause a great deal of trouble for President Young and the Saints. Drummond is described as having been "dishonest and licentious." "He left his wife and family in Illinois without means of support, and brought with him to the territory a common courtesan whom he introduced as his wife." When this situation became known, Drummond departed for Nevada to hold court and did not return. He continued on to Washington, where he made grave charges against President Young and the Saints. He declared that "the records of the supreme court of Utah had been destroyed; that Brigham Young had given his approval to this treasonable deed and with his knowledge it was done; that Brigham Young, as governor, had pardoned Mormon criminals and imprisoned innocent Gentiles; that he had insulted federal judges; that the American Government had been traduced and men insulted, harassed and murdered for doing their duty." These and other charges made by Judge Stiles, Indian agent Garland Hurt, and W. M. Magraw (the latter having lost a mail contract which had been given to a member of the Church) induced President James Buchanan to act without making further investigation. He determined to release Brigham Young from his position as governor of Utah and to appoint a new governor and new judges for the territorial supreme court. "He further directed that an army was to accompany the new appointees, to sustain these officers and suppress rebellion among the Mormon people." This hasty action was to cost the government millions of dollars and become known as "Buchanan's blunder."

President Brigham Young and a large group of Saints were at Silver Lake, at the head of Big Cottonwood Canyon, July 24, 1857, celebrating Pioneer Day, when they learned of the coming of the army and the appointment of a new governor. President Young was surprised, but it did not take him long to make up his mind as to what course he would pursue. As for the appointment of governor, he was not greatly concerned whether he or some other man held that office; but he would, with all his might, oppose the coming of the army to Utah. Addressing the Saints at Salt Lake City on Sunday, September 14, 1857, he said:

"I have been in this kingdom a good while—twenty-five years and upwards—and I have been driven from place to place, my brethren have been scattered and peeled, and every time without any provocation on our part, only that we were united, obedient to the laws of the land, and striving to worship God. Mobs repeatedly gathered against this people, but they never had any power to prevail until governors issued their orders and called out a force, under the letter of the law, to hold the Mormons while infernal scamps cut their throats. I have had all that before me through the night past, and it makes me too angry to preach. Also to see that we are in a government whose administrators are always trying to injure us, while we are

constantly at the defiance of all hell to prove any just
grounds for their hostility against us; and yet they are organizing their forces to come here and protect infernal
scamps, who are anxious to come and kill whom they
please, destroy whom they please, and finally exterminate
us.

"This people are free. They are not in bondage to any
government on God's footstool. We have transgressed no
law, and we have no occasion to do so, neither do we in-
tend to; but as for any nations' coming to destroy this people, God Almighty being my helper, they cannot come here."

On September 15, Governor Young issued a proclamation placing the territory of Utah under martial law, "for-
bidding all armed forces of every description from coming
into the territory, under any pretense whatever." General
Wells of the Nauvoo Legion established headquarters in
Echo Canyon and instructed his men to do everything possible to impede the progress of the troops: "Stampede their
cattle; set fire to their trains; burn the whole country before
them and on their flanks; keep them from sleeping by
night surprises; blockade the road; but avoid strictly the
taking of life."

In November, as cold weather came on, General Albert
Sidney Johnston decided wisely that the troops that had
reached western Wyoming would make winter camp at
Fort Bridger and would not attempt to pursue their march
further until spring. This fortunate delay provided time in
which the difficulties between the Saints and the government could be talked over and solved.

In February, 1858, Colonel Thomas L. Kane, President
Young's friend from Philadelphia, arrived in Salt Lake City
"by the southern route," bearing instructions from the
President of the United States and offering his services as
a mediator between the Saints and army and civil officers.
After spending several days in Salt Lake City and inter-
viewing President Young and the brethren, Colonel Kane
went to Fort Bridger and met Alfred Cumming, the new

governor, and General Johnston. By his arrangements, Governor Cumming was induced to come to Salt Lake City and take the oath of office for his new position. On his arrival he was shown the records of the court that Judge Drummond had reported as having been burned. Governor Cumming found that the Saints and President Young had been grossly misrepresented to President Buchanan, and both he and Colonel Kane sent word to President Buchanan that a peace commission should be ordered to Utah to investigate conditions and restore peace and order. President Buchanan acted favorably on this suggestion—the first sensible thing he had done in the matter, it seems to me—and in June Senator L. W. Powell of Kentucky and Major Ben McCulloch of Texas arrived in Salt Lake City to bring about, if possible, a settlement of the difficulties. President Young and a number of leading brethren met with them in the old Council House. President Young related the persecutions that the Saints had been subjected to in Ohio, Missouri, and Illinois, and warned the commissioners that before he or the Saints would submit to further persecution, they would burn their homes and destroy their possessions and go elsewhere. "No mob can live in the homes we have built in the mountains," he concluded. "If you want war, you can have it; but if you wish peace, peace it is; we shall be glad of it."

The commissioners declared for peace. It was decided that the army should be allowed to enter the valley, but that it should not form a permanent camp within forty miles from the city. These arrangements were carried out, but as President Young did not trust the officials of the government or the army, he ordered the Saints to evacuate Salt Lake City and all the settlements north and to move into Utah and Juab valleys until it could be proven that General Johnston meant to keep his word. It is to his honor that General Johnston did not allow his soldiers to molest the homes or possessions of the Saints and that he took them into camp in Cedar Valley, forty miles from Salt Lake City.

Thus ended the Utah War, which accomplished nothing except the expenditure of millions of dollars, and which, as I stated before, became known in the east for many years as "Buchanan's Blunder."

Freed from his responsibilities as governor of the territory, President Young was now at liberty to continue the peaceful and delightful labors of "building up the kingdom." This was the work he desired above all else to do; his heart was in the progress of the work of God. Yet he did not relax his efforts to oppose any who would injure the Saints or detract from their righteous accomplishments.

After peace was restored, travel was resumed across the plains, and several noted visitors called at Salt Lake City. On July 10, 1859, the Overland Stage brought Horace Greeley, famed editor of the *New York Tribune*. During his stay in the city he had a two-hour interview with President Young. He has left his impression of the President in the following description: "As President Young is the first minister of the Mormon Church, and bore the principal part in the conversation, I have reported his answers alone to my questions and observations. The others appeared uniformly to defer to his views, and to acquiesce fully in his responses and explanations. He spoke readily, not always with grammatical accuracy, but with no appearance of hesitation or reserve, and with no apparent desire to conceal anything; nor did he repel any of my questions as impertinent. He was very plainly dressed, in thin summer clothing, and with no air of sanctimony or fanaticism. In appearance he is a portly, frank, good-natured, rather thick-set man of fifty-five [this should have been fifty-eight] seeming to enjoy life and to be in no particular hurry to get to heaven."

In the spring of 1860 President Young, accompanied by a large party of his brethren, visited the settlements of the Saints north of Salt Lake City and for the first time viewed the growing colonies in Cache Valley. His instructions to the Saints were wise and timely; he knew what they should do to establish themselves and improve the country.

With the outbreak of the Civil War in 1861—after the troops had been called away from Cedar Valley—President Young instructed the Saints that "he did not wish Utah mixed up with the secession movement." When the first transcontinental telegraph line was completed in October, 1861, he sent a wire to the president of the company, J. H. Wade, in which he said, "Utah has not seceded, but is firm for the Constitution and laws of our once happy country."

It was in this year, 1861, that President Young began the construction of the Salt Lake Theatre, one of the most beautiful buildings of its kind in the United States. The President was fond of drama and seldom missed attending a "performance" when he was in the city. He encouraged the members of his family to take part in the plays, which, in the beginning, consisted entirely of home talent.

In 1863 a concerted effort was made by non-Mormons to develop mining in Utah. President Young took an active stand against opening the mines. "Can you not see," he said, "that silver and gold rank among the things that we are least in want of? . . . It is a fearful deception which all the world labors under, and many of this people too, who profess to be not of the world, that gold is wealth. On the bare report that gold was discovered in these west mountains, men left their threshing machines, and their horses at large, to eat up and trample down and destroy the precious bounties of the earth. They at once sacrificed all at the glittering shrine of the popular idol, declaring they were now going to be rich, and would raise wheat no more. Should this feeling become universal upon the discovery of gold mines in our immediate vicinity, nakedness, starvation, utter destitution and annihilation would be the inevitable lot of this people." The wisdom of Brother Brigham's words and advice cannot be doubted.

During the years of 1864 and 1865 President Young visited the settlements of the Saints both north and south of Salt Lake City. Everywhere he encouraged the people and taught them the doctrines of the Church. During these years he also sent many teams across the plains to Omaha "to assist the poor Saints to the valleys." The one central purpose of all his thoughts and labors was "to build up the kingdom of God" in all the world.

The Salt Lake Tabernacle, one of the most interesting and commodious structures ever built for public worship, was constructed during 1866 and 1867, under the supervision of President Young. The immense roof, like an inverted bowl, was built almost entirely of wood, as the Saints did not possess iron or steel in quantities at that time. This roof, set down upon stone columns, was unique in structure and design, and to this day it is the chief auditorium for the conferences of the Latter-day Saints.

Another improvement of immense importance during these years was the beginning of the construction of the Union Pacific Railroad from Omaha, Nebraska, to Ogden, Utah, a distance of one thousand miles. President Young took an active part in this great enterprise and entered into a contract with the railroad company to construct seventy miles of grade and tunnel work, from the head of Echo Canyon to the shore of Great Salt Lake. This work was faithfully completed, and on May 10, 1869, the last spike was driven at Promontory, Utah, and the Union Pacific and Central Pacific railroads were united. The nation was spanned by a band of steel from New York City to San Francisco. The days of the ox team, the pony express and the stage coach were over.

In 1871, when President Young was nearing the end of his great and useful life, he was subjected to severe persecution on the part of the federal government, which had determined, at all costs, to end the practice of polygamy. On October 2, at his home on South Temple Street, he was arrested by United States Marshal Patrick. One week later he appeared before Judge McKean and posted bail in the amount of $5,000. Shortly thereafter he departed for St. George, where, on November 9, he dedicated a site

Nov 9, 1871 *dedicated a site*

for the St. George Temple. While at St. George he learned that the non-Mormon grand jury had filed a charge of murder against him. This charge grew out of the confessions of the notorious Bill Hickman and dated back to the year 1857, when, Hickman related, a certain Richard Yates had been put to death in Echo Canyon at the instance of President Young.

Returning immediately from St. George, in the inclement winter season of the year, President Young appeared in Judge McKean's court on January 2, 1872. When the attorney for President Young asked for bail, it was refused by Judge McKean, who ordered that the President be held a prisoner in his own house, under guard for the United States marshal, until his case could be tried. Thus President Brigham Young became a prisoner in his own home, in the city he had founded. He was not freed until the Supreme Court of the United States rendered a decision on April 15, 1872, stating that the grand jury that had indicted him was illegal. However, the non-Mormon federal officers of Utah did not cease with this attempt to arrest and imprison him. Their persecution of him ended only with his death.

During the summers 1873 and 1874 President Young *1873-74* launched his last great enterprise among the Latter-day Saints—that of attempting to establish the "United Order." "I have been steadily watching and waiting," he said, "just as steadily and earnestly and faithfully as ever a mother watched over an infant child, to see when this people would be ready to receive the doctrine, or the first revelations given when the Center Stake of Zion was first located, to consecrate their property, and be indeed the servants and handmaidens of the Lord, and labor with all their hearts to do His will and build up His Kingdom on the earth, and I have never seen the time when we could organize one little society, or one little ward; but, thank God, the time has come; the spirit of the Lord is upon the people."

The object of the United Order, said the President,
was to unite the labors and resources of the Latter-day
Saints. "Let some of the brethren raise cattle and sheep,
some fruit, some grain and vegetables; and when they have
raised these products, every particle will be gathered into
a storehouse and storehouses, and everyone have what is
needed to sustain him. . . . We want the time of this people called Latter-day Saints, that we can organize this
time systematically and make this people the richest people
on the face of the earth."

Thus poverty would be done away with, the Saints
would be self-sustaining, and there would be a large sur-
plus to be used in the building of the kingdom. To President Young the plan was perfectly clear and feasible—all
parts of it fitted in so as to work harmoniously together.
It is to be regretted that he did not live long enough to
perfect this interesting plan, which many today believe
would solve all the economic problems of mankind.

In April, 1877, the St. George Temple was ready for
dedication, and President Young instructed the Saints to
gather there for the annual conference of the Church.
Meetings were held for three days, and he spoke at several
of the sessions. "As to my health," he said in one of his
sermons, "I feel many times that I could not live an hour
longer, but I mean to live just as long as I can. I know
not how soon the messenger will call for me, but I calcu-
late to die in the harness."

He continued on with his work and during the summer
attended several of the stake conferences of the Church.
His last public discourse was at Brigham City, on August
19, "where he addressed a congregation of at least two
thousand five hundred people." On Monday, August 20,
he returned by train to Salt Lake City.

Throughout the following Thursday, August 23, while
working in his office, the President complained of a feeling
of nausea, "with an inclination to vomit." At eleven o'clock
at night, on retiring, he was seized with a severe attack of

"cholera morbus." This continued until five o'clock in the morning, when, to relieve his suffering, a mild oiate was administered by Drs. F. D. Benedict and Seymour B. Young, who had been called to his bedside during the night.

All day Friday he was in considerable pain, "but endured it cheerfully, and occasionally made humorous remarks when he saw those about him inclined to be troubled." On Saturday afternoon "inflammation of the bowels" set in. He slept fitfully during the night and frequently moaned in his sleep. When asked if he suffered great pain, he replied, "No, I don't know that I do."

During Sunday and Monday, he seemed to revive somewhat, "being frequently administered to by some of his brethren," but on Monday evening he sank into a comatose condition, from which it was difficult to arouse him. At four o'clock Tuesday morning "he sank down in bed apparently lifeless." Artificial respiration was immediately resorted to, and "hot poultices were placed over the heart to stimulate action." "For nine consecutive hours artificial respiration was continued. At that time he seemed greatly revived and spoke to those around him, saying he felt better and wished to rest."

On Wednesday, August 29, it was apparent to anxious watchers at his bedside that the end was near. His last words, as he gazed fixedly upwards, were "Joseph, Joseph, Joseph," as though he communed with his beloved Prophet. At one minute past four o'clock in the afternoon his breathing ceased; his great heart was stilled. The mortal life of one of God's noblest sons had come to an end.

V

The funeral of President Young was held in the great Tabernacle on Sunday, September 2, 1877, at 12 o'clock noon. It was estimated that at least 12,000 persons were in attendance, "with as many more on the grounds of the Tabernacle, or on the streets outside." The speakers were

Daniel H. Wells, Wilford Woodruff, Erastus Snow, George
Q. Cannon and John Taylor. All praised President Young's
faith and devotion, his great work and accomplishments.
Following the services the body was conveyed to a private
burial ground on First Avenue in Salt Lake City. All that
was mortal of him was given back to mother earth.

VI

In a letter written four years before his death, to the
editor of the *New York Herald*, President Young made the
following statement:

"My whole life is devoted to the Almighty's service,
and while I regret that my mission is not better understood
by the world, the time will come when I will be understood, and I leave to futurity the judgment of my labors
and their result as they shall become manifest."

Nearly a century has passed since the above significant statement was made, and it is no doubt true that
those years have brought about a better understanding of
President Brigham Young's life and work. Louis Bromfield,
the author, in an interview given to the press in Salt Lake
City, said, when speaking of Brigham Young, "He was one
of the six or seven greatest Americans." In a letter to this
writer a few years ago, Harry Chandler, publisher of the
Los Angeles Times, paid President Young this high tribute:
"I regard him as an outstanding citizen of the world."

In conclusion, may I add my tribute, which was published in my *Life of Brigham Young*:

"If I were asked to point out the principal thing,
which, more than all others, made President Young the
great man he was, I think I should reply, without hesitation, that it was his ability to believe—his great faith.
First, faith in a living God, to whom he felt personally
responsible and to whom he felt obligated to render up an
accounting for all the deeds done in the flesh. Second,

faith in every principle and doctrine revealed and taught
by the Prophet Joseph Smith, and a firm and unyielding
determination to shape his life according to those principles.
Third, faith in himself, and in his ability to carry on the
great work of establishing the Kingdom of God, the leadership of which had come to him after the death of the
Prophet. Time and time again, in this history, I have been
astounded by the strength of this man's faith; such faith I
have never encountered in any other person. On his tomb-
stone one might well have written, HE BELIEVED. Yes,
he believed his religion, this great man, and he shaped his
life to its principles, to his dying day.

"Once possessing this great faith, this great belief, all
things followed naturally in their course. He became a loyal
man.

"How curious it is in the early history of our Church
that so many of the prominent men fell by the wayside—
six of the Apostles, the three witnesses of the Book of Mormon and several of Joseph's counselors. Something happened
that shook them from the tree of life, and they fell to the
ground like dead leaves. But where in all the Church history is one single instance to show that Brigham Young
ever faltered; ever proved disloyal or unfaithful to a trust?
There is not one. Always to the day of his death he was
faithful, loyal, true. The Prophet soon learned that here was
a man he could depend upon. He therefore elevated him to
a prominent place in the councils of the Saints, and made
him a close friend and companion. When trouble became
desperate around the Prophet, Brigham was there to defend
him. He could say in later years:

" 'Scores and scores of nights I have lain on the floor,
with a loaded revolver under my pillow, to protect the
life of the Prophet Joseph.'

"There was loyalty that brooked no questioning. Without that quality President Young could never have risen
to greatness. Possessing it, he could in a few years, assume
a high place in the estimation of the Saints and his brethren about him.

"Throughout this history I have been impressed, time and time again, with President Young's practical judgment, wisdom and good, sound common sense.

"At all times and on all occasions he seemed to know what was the practical, the best thing to do. Had he not possessed this quality he might have failed in his great undertakings. With his faith, with his loyalty, he was also blessed with the quality of being a wise man—a man whose judgment in temporal matters was sound. When he gave advice, it was good. The Saints built up in confidence in the history of this Church. To go against President Young's advice was to court failure. He seemed to weigh all sides of a question, and to invariably decide wisely.

"As to his practical judgment, I have noted with interest, that during the first trip across the plains, it was President Young who rode horseback ahead and selected the route. It was he who chose the camping grounds; he noted every man's wagon, and the load it carried; he noted the strength of the team, and its ability to pull the load. His precaution against Indian attacks was carried on with precision; he himself frequently standing guard under the stars, with rifle in hand. When he reached the valley, he could say that he had made the one thousand mile journey 'without the loss of a man or a horse.'

"Of his selection of these valleys as a permanent place of residence for the Saints, with the historic declaration, 'This is the right place,' what can we say of that? Did not that show the superlative good judgment of the man? A grateful generation which has followed him has erected a one hundred thousand dollar monument on the site where those historic words were uttered. The Empire of the West was born that day—July 24th, 1847.

"His founding of cities and towns in this intermountain region, and his selection of the men who were to preside over them, were carried out with a profound understanding of agricultural conditions and of human nature. In most instances he himself designated the ground where the settlement was to be built, he directed the location of the canals, the land that was to be irrigated, and he 'blessed and set apart' the men who were placed to preside. During his last years he could look about him and behold upwards of two hundred villages, settlements, towns and cities, peopled with more than one hundred thousand inhabitants, prosperous, independent—out of debt mostly—all constructed during his thirty years of residence here, and under his immediate supervision and direction.

"His building of Temples, the great Salt Lake Tabernacle, of telegraph lines and of railroads which extended north and south through the Territory, all betoken his genius as a master builder.

"However, I do not wish to misinform my readers as to the central purpose of President Young's activities here in the west. It was not to build up an empire. The central purpose of all his activities, throughout all his life, from the time he joined the Church in 1832, until his death in 1877, was to build up, here on earth 'the Church and Kingdom of God.' He himself, in his sermons, on hundreds of occasions, enunciated this purpose. At the time of the death of the Prophet he declared it to the Saints in Nauvoo. 'Brother Joseph has laid the foundation, and we can build upon it—we can build a Kingdom such as there never was in this world.' All the activities of his life centered around this one purpose.

"His knowledge of spiritual matters became as profound as his knowledge of practical affairs. On all points of doctrine, pertaining to the Kingdom, he became an authority. I have been amazed at the number and extent of purely doctrinal sermons, and with what ease and clearness he could discourse on such subjects as death, the resurrection, immortality and eternal life.

"It was as a leader of the Saints that President Young was supreme. He had been a faithful servant in the days of Joseph. When Joseph was taken away, he stepped forth in his place and took command. Immediately the Saints recognized that God had raised up a new leader in Israel, and they gathered loyally around him. Their confidence in him increased with the years—soon he was designated by them as 'The Lion of the Lord.' Confidence grew into love and affection. Frequently, as he went about among the settlements, thousands would stand on the roadside to greet him, and ofttimes, flowers were strewn in his path. I do not recall any leader of any people who was more honored and loved than was Brigham Young.

"Yet, at no time did he lose 'the common touch.' He was always one with the people, and thousands familiarly called him 'Brother Brigham.' He did not set himself up to be great; he set himself up to be a servant of God, and he was one, in word and in deed.

"President Young's life is a priceless heritage to the Latter-day Saints. All that we teach, and all that we stand for, are embodied in him. Generations yet unborn will turn to him for inspiration, counsel and advice. Even though dead, he lives in the hearts of all those who are engaged in the grand task of building on earth 'the Kingdom of God.' "

JOHN TAYLOR

JOHN TAYLOR

(1808-1887)

W HEN President Brigham Young died, "at one minute past four o'clock" on the afternoon of August 29, 1877, the burden of guiding the hosts of Israel fell upon the broad and capable shoulders of President John Taylor. President Taylor was then in his sixty-ninth year, rapidly approaching the allotted three-score and ten, but he was still in the vigor of manhood, sound in judgment, firm and invincible in the faith, an able executive, a capable leader, a true man of God.

For over forty years President Taylor had been a constant laborer in the kingdom. He had given his all to its upbuilding. And by reason of his splendid qualities, his intelligence, his ability, his loyalty, his spirit of cooperation, he had risen to the presidency of the Twelve; and therefore, upon the death of President Young, the right to preside was his.

By birth, President Taylor was an Englishman, and he possessed all the finest characteristics of that people: honest, industrious, loving liberty within truth and right living. One who knew him well has described him to me as "an English gentleman." Sweet-spirited, kind to friend and stranger alike, tolerant, he nevertheless set his face as flint against any form of evil or wrongdoing. I call him a true man of God, a great, exemplary Latter-day Saint. It is an honor to speak or write about such a man.

The parents of John Taylor resided in the town of Milnthorpe, Westmoreland County, England, when he was born there on the first day of November, 1808. The father's name was James Taylor and the mother's name, before her marriage, was Agnes Taylor, though they were not relatives, as far as I have been able to learn. Ten children were born to James and Agnes Taylor—eight sons and two daughters. Three of the children died in infancy. When Edward, the eldest son, died at the age of twenty-two, John, the second son and the subject of this sketch, stood next to his father, the head of the family.

When John was eleven years of age his parents settled on a small estate they had inherited, near the town of Hale, England. At fourteen there was some discussion in the family as to what trade the boy should learn now that he was approaching young manhood. It was finally decided that he should learn the trade of cooper, and accordingly he was apprenticed to a manufacturer in Liverpool, but in a few months his employer failed in business and John was forced to return home. Being determined to learn a trade, he went shortly afterward to Penrith in Cumberland, where he undertook to learn the trade of wood turner. Here he remained from his fifteenth to his twentieth years, laboring diligently with his hands until he had mastered his task.

In the year 1830, which is a significant year in our Church history, the parents of John Taylor, together with his brothers and sisters, took ship at Liverpool and sailed for Canada. John was left in England to settle affairs and dispose of some of his father's property, and it was two years before he was able to rejoin them. Arriving in New York City in the fall of 1832, John made his way by stage and boat to Toronto, Ontario, Canada, where he joined his family. It was not long until he had set himself up in his trade as a wood turner and with confidence looked forward to a life of happiness, peace, and prosperity.

Being of a strong religious nature, John allied himself with the Methodist Church in Toronto soon after his arrival there, and within a few months he became a class leader and itinerant preacher for the organization. His natural bent was to be an expounder of the gospel, to bring souls to a knowledge of God, and to make the world a better place in which to live; that task became the hope, the dream, and the ambition of his life. He was to live to fulfill that ambition.

It was while John was attending the meetings of the Methodist Church in Toronto that he met and married Leonora Cannon, daughter of Captain George Cannon of Peel, the Isle of Man. Leonora was a refined, educated woman, witty, gifted, with rare conversational powers, possessed of a deep religious nature and withal a fitting companion for John Taylor.

Everything looked favorable for this newly married couple as they set up homemaking in Toronto. John's weekdays were spent in his wood-turning shop and his Sundays with the congregation of the Methodist Church, where he took an active interest. However, as time moved on and he grew in knowledge and understanding, he began to question some of the dogmas taught by the Methodist leaders. A little group of the congregation joined him in these inquiries, and it was not long until they were known as "Dissenters." They were looking for a new gospel, where the power of God would be made manifest. The doctrines taught by the Methodists failed to satisfy them.

It was at this critical time in the life of John Taylor that Parley P. Pratt, an apostle of The Church of Jesus Christ of Latter-day Saints, arrived in Toronto. He came for the purpose of delivering an important message to the people, and he traveled, as did the ancient apostles, "without purse or scrip," depending upon God to direct him to the honest in heart. Elder Pratt began holding meetings at the home of a Mrs. Walton, and among those who attended were John Taylor and his wife. "John wrote down eight sermons which Apostle Pratt preached," relates B. H. Roberts, "and compared them with the scripture." He also investigated the evidences of the divine authenticity of the Book of Mormon and the Doctrine and Covenants. "I made a regular business of it for three weeks," John relates, "and followed Brother Parley from place to place." The result of this thorough investigation was that John Taylor and his wife were baptized on May 9, 1836, by Elder Parley P. Pratt.

John immediately became an active member of the Church and within a few weeks was ordained to the office of elder. Together with Elder Pratt he began preaching in the countryside around Toronto, and new converts were daily added to the fold. When Elder Pratt departed for his home in Kirtland in the fall of 1836, he left Elder Taylor "in charge of all the Saints and branches in Upper Canada."

In March, 1837, Elder Taylor set out for Kirtland, to visit the Saints there and meet the Prophet Joseph Smith for the first time. On his arrival the Prophet received him cordially and entertained him in his own home. This was the beginning of a friendship that was to continue throughout the lifetime of the Prophet. His last hours in mortality —indeed, his very last hour—were to be soothed and comforted by the tender and wholesome spirit and loving friendship of John Taylor.

In August, 1837, the Prophet Joseph, accompanied by Sidney Rigdon and Thomas B. Marsh, paid a return visit to Elder Taylor in Canada. "This was as great a treat to me as I ever enjoyed," records Elder Taylor. "I had daily opportunity of conversing with them, of listening to their instructions, and in participating in the rich store of intelligence that flowed continually from the Prophet Joseph."

Before the Prophet left Canada he ordained Elder Taylor to the office of high priest and reappointed him to preside over the Church there.

II

In the fall of 1837, Elder Taylor received word from the Prophet that he would like to have him wind up his affairs in Canada and join the main body of the Saints in Missouri. John Taylor now cast his lot with the Latter-day Saints. He gave up his comfortable home and business in Toronto, and together with an Elder Mills, departed for Kirtland. As the winter season was on, "they fitted up a covered sleigh for their families to ride in, while their goods were conveyed in wagons." After a long and difficult trip, during part of which time Brother Taylor remained in Indiana and worked for means to continue his journey, he arrived with his family at Far West, Missouri, about October 1, 1838.

It was while he was making his weary journey from Canada that he was called to the apostleship in a revelation received by the Prophet Joseph on July 8, 1838.

Unfortunately, the persecution of the Saints by the Missouri settlers was at its height at the time of John Taylor's arrival at Far West. One month later, the Prophet Joseph and several of the leaders of the Church were taken prisoner by the mob militia, and all of the Saints in Missouri were ordered to leave the state. In the midst of this confusion, at a meeting of the high council in Far West, on the evening of December 19, 1838, John Taylor was ordained an apostle, "under the hands of Brigham Young and Heber C. Kimball." Shortly afterwards, he too, with his wife and family, was fleeing eastward to the new gathering place of the Saints in Illinois.

For a time John Taylor remained at Quincy, where a number of the brethren of the Twelve had located. Shortly thereafter, under the leadership of the Prophet Joseph, the city of Nauvoo was founded and Elder Taylor and his family moved to that location. However, not finding suitable accommodations for living quarters, he crossed the river to the Iowa side and moved "into one room of an old military barracks." It was while living in these humble circumstances that he began preparations to depart for a mission to England, to which he and the brethren of the Twelve had been called.

I cannot give more at this time than a brief account of John Taylor's excellent missionary labors in England, but I do want to say that he exhibited all those sterling qualities which brought him a high place in the estimation of the Latter-day Saints. He made his way to England, ill and penniless, but by the strength of his great character and testimony he succeeded in bringing many families to a knowledge of the truth. Among his converts were his wife's brother, George Cannon, and family of Liverpool. What this remarkable family has added to the Church and what the hundreds of descendants are contributing today is beyond estimation. Elder Taylor continued his work in England until April, 1841, when, together with his brethren of the Twelve, he departed for his home in Nauvoo. Prior to leaving England he published a report of his labors in the *Millennial Star*, part of which follows:

"I feel to rejoice before God that He has blessed my humble endeavors to promote His cause and Kingdom and for all the blessings I have received from this island; for although I have traveled 5,000 miles without purse or scrip, besides traveling so far in this country on railroads, coaches, steamboats, wagons, on horseback, and almost every way, and been amongst strangers and in strange lands, I have never for once been at a loss for either money, clothes, friends or a home, from that day until now; neither have I ever asked a person for a farthing. Thus I have proved the Lord, and I know that He is according to His word. And now as I am going away, I bear testimony that this work is of God—that He has spoken from the heavens— that Joseph Smith is a Prophet of the Lord—that the Book of Mormon is true; and I know that this work will roll on until 'the kingdoms of this world become the Kingdoms of our God and His Christ.' "

Leaving England in April, 1841, the brethren of the Twelve, including John Taylor, arrived in New York City after a voyage of one month. They then proceeded to Nauvoo, where they arrived on the 1st of July. "We landed

Jul 1841

in Nauvoo," records Heber C. Kimball, "on the 1st of
July, and when we struck the dock, I think there were
about 300 Saints there to meet us, and a greater manifestation of love and gladness I never saw before. President
Smith was the first one that caught us by the hand. I never
saw him feel better in my life than he does at this time;
this is the case with the Saints in general. . . . We found
our families well, except Sister Taylor who was quite low."

Upon his arrival in Nauvoo, John found his family
living under rather distressing conditions. His wife was in
ill health, but through kind care and attention, she was
quickly restored. Elder Taylor at once became active in
all the affairs of the Church. In August he was elected
"a regent in the University of Nauvoo." Almost daily he
met with his brethren of the Twelve, for whom he wrote
many letters and epistles. At the October conference held
in Nauvoo, "the conference appointed Elias Higbee, John
Taylor and Elias Smith to petition for redress of wrongs
sustained in Missouri; and John Taylor to present the
petition."

Elder Taylor spent many hours with the Prophet,
and between the two there was formed a close friendship.
In January, 1842, the Prophet records in his history: "I
read the Book of Mormon, transacted a variety of business
in the store and city, and spent the evening in the office
with Elders Taylor and Richards."

In February, 1842, the Church purchased the printing
office of the *Times and Seasons* from Ebenezer Robinson,
and the Prophet requested John Taylor and Wilford Woodruff to assume the management of the publication. John
now found a work for which he was especially qualified.
He was an able writer and editor, and during his subsequent residence in Nauvoo he contributed many articles
to the various issues of this publication. In the fall of 1842
he began a weekly newspaper called *The Nauvoo Neighbor.*

On the 1st of November, 1842, Elder Taylor celebrated
his thirty-fourth birthday. With his wife and four small chil-

dren well and favorably located, with his standing in the
Church as an apostle, and with a growing and profitable
business, he looked forward to a life of happiness, peace
and prosperity.

Throughout the year of 1843 Elder Taylor worked
diligently at his tasks as a publisher. It may seem strange
that one of his difficulties was to secure a sufficient supply
of paper. When the Mississippi River was frozen over in
the winter, practically all transportation with the outside
world ceased. I find the following in the *Times and Seasons*
under date of April, 1843. It is part of an editorial by
Elder Taylor:

"We have to apologize to our readers for this number
issued so much later than the day of publication. We had
run short of paper, expecting that the river would have
opened long before it did; and as it was impossible with
the state of the roads to bring it by land, we had no other
alternative but to wait until the river opened. We are
sorry for the delay, but assure our friends that it was un-
avoidable on our part. Every arrangement, however, is
entered into that is necessary to make up for lost time,
as we have engaged two sets of hands to keep the work
progressing, night and day, until the time is made up,
which we expect will be about three weeks."

The year 1844 dawned favorably for John Taylor—and
yet it was to be such a fatal year. It is perhaps fortunate
that we cannot see or know what is before us from day to
day. Among the chief enjoyments that came to him was
that he had the confidence and companionship of the
Prophet. I find the following in the Prophet's history, under date of January 1, 1844:

"A large party took a New Year's supper at my house,
and had music and dancing till morning. I was in my private room with my family, Elder John Taylor and other
friends."

And again on Tuesday, February 6: "Very cold day.
I spent the evening with my brother, Hyrum, Sidney

Rigdon and the Twelve Apostles and their wives at Elder John Taylor's: took supper and had a very pleasant time."

The year 1844 was a presidential year, and political affairs were being discussed on all sides. It was the decision of the leaders of the Saints that they could not support the major political parties or their candidates. In order to pursue a middle course, the Prophet was requested to announce that he was a candidate for the presidency, and the Saints were to support him and labor for his election. To this end, in April 244 elders, including all of the Twelve Apostles except John Taylor and Willard Richards, left Nauvoo and journeyed to the various states in the East.

While they were away an anti-Mormon newspaper was set up in Nauvoo which viciously attacked the Prophet and the Saints. This paper was ordered, by the Nauvoo city council, "to be destroyed," and the order was carried out. Warrants were immediately issued for the arrest of the Prophet, his brother Hyrum, John Taylor, and others who were members of the city council. It was while awaiting trial that the tragedy at Carthage jail occurred, on the 27th of June, 1844. The Prophet and Patriarch were killed, and John Taylor was severely wounded. The details of this tragedy are given in full in the chapter on the Prophet Joseph Smith in this volume, and I shall not repeat them here.

Elder Taylor was conveyed to his home in Nauvoo a few days after the tragedy, and it was many weeks before he was able to resume his normal work. The council meetings of the Twelve were frequently held at his house while he was recovering from his wounds. Once on his feet again, he continued with his publications, besides his Church activities and a splendid farm that he operated near Nauvoo. However, it was known to the leading brethren during 1845 that the Saints would have to leave Nauvoo if peace were to be obtained, and preparations were begun during the fall and winter of 1846-47 for the great migration westward.

It was on February 16, 1846, that Elder Taylor took his departure from Nauvoo and crossed the river to the Iowa side. To get some idea as to the sacrifice he made at that time, it is related that he left at Nauvoo "a large two-story brick house, well-furnished, with a brick store on one side, and a new brick building that he had erected for a printing office on the other, with a large barn in the rear. The lot and buildings were worth $10,000. In addition to this property, a short distance east of Nauvoo, he had a farm of 106 acres, another of 80 acres, forty of which were under cultivation and forty in timber. He also owned a corner lot, 101x85 feet on Main and Water streets." All this property Elder Taylor abandoned in Nauvoo as he pursued the weary journey into the western wilderness. But the thought and belief that the Saints could find a place where they could worship God in peace and dwell in security without being molested by wicked mobs led him onward toward the setting sun.

III

The journey across Iowa in the rain and mud took four months' time. On July 14, Elder Taylor arrived at Council Bluffs on the Missouri River. Here a temporary halt was made. At this place word was received from the organizations of the Church in England that all was not going well there. The Council of the Twelve took the matter under consideration, and as a result John Taylor, Orson Hyde, and Orson Pratt were requested by President Young to depart for England and set the churches in order. Leaving their families in wagons to face the rigors of a winter on the banks of the Missouri, the brethren took their departure. After a difficult journey by land and by sea they arrived in Liverpool, England, on October 3, 1846.

Elder Taylor and his brethren spent four months in England and accomplished the work they were requested to do by the presiding brethren. On his return voyage, which took thirty-six days, he sailed to New Orleans. From New Orleans he took a river steamer to St. Joseph, Missouri. From there he made his way to the camp of the Saints and arrived just in time to have an interview with President Young, who was leaving for the West with the pioneer company. Elder Taylor brought with him several valuable scientific instruments, listed as two sextants, two barometers, two artificial horizons, one circular reflector, several thermometers, and a telescope, which proved to be of great value to the pioneers.

When President Young and his pioneer company left for the West in April, 1847, to find a suitable location for the Saints, Elder Taylor remained for a time at Winter Quarters to organize the Saints into groups to follow them. By the latter part of June a large party was ready to begin the long journey of 1,000 miles. In this party there were 1,533 people, 600 wagons, 2,213 oxen, 124 horses, and 887 cows. Thus, with flocks and herds the Latter-day Saints journeyed forth into the wilderness. Elders John Taylor and Parley P. Pratt presided over this large group.

The journey across the plains was slow and wearisome, from five to twenty miles a day being made, according to the condition of the country through which they were traveling. The camp usually rested on Sundays, when religious services were held, "and the stillness of the great wilderness of the west was broken by the Saints singing songs of Zion."

When the members of the caravan led by John Taylor approached the upper crossing of the Sweetwater, in what is now western Wyoming, they came upon the returning pioneers under President Young, who announced to them that a permanent gathering place for the Saints had been selected in the Salt Lake Valley. In order to do honor to these pioneers John Taylor requested the women of his company to prepare a dinner for them, and accordingly, what was later known as "the feast in the wilderness" was enjoyed by them in this lonely mountain retreat. "Several improvised tables covered with snow-white linen," writes B. H. Roberts, "gave evidence that a surprise was in store for the weary pioneers. The fatted calf was killed, game and fish were prepared in abundance; fruits, jellies and relishes for special occasions were brought out, until it truly was a royal feast." The dinner over, the brethren and sisters spent the evening in dancing. "And soon was added to the sweet confusion of laughter and cheerful conversation, the merry strains of a violin and the strong, clear voice of the prompter, directing the dancers through the mazes of quadrilles, scotch-reels, french-fours, and other harmless dances," suitable to the occasion.

The following morning the two companies separated and each pursued its way, President Young and his pioneers going back to Winter Quarters and John Taylor and his company continuing on to Salt Lake Valley, where they arrived on the afternoon of October 5, 1847.

Now located with the Saints, John Taylor's first efforts were to build a home for himself and family. "Our houses," he writes, "were built on the outside line of the fort in shanty form, the highest wall outside, the roof sloping towards the interior. The windows and doors were placed on the side facing the enclosure, the outside being left solid, excepting loopholes for protection. About Christmas [1847] I had put up, enclosed and covered, about ninety feet of building made of split logs. In addition to this I had built corrals and stables behind, and enclosed a garden spot in front. I assisted in all this labor of sawing, building and hauling."

John Taylor remained in Salt Lake Valley for two years (from October, 1847, to October, 1849), during which time he took an active part in all the affairs of the Saints. He attended the meetings of the Twelve; he spoke at the conferences of the Saints; he made every effort to provide the comforts of life for his family. He was a personal witness to that remarkable occurrence when thousands of gulls flew in from the lake and destroyed the myriads of crickets that were devastating the meager crops of the Saints. Under every condition John Taylor was a leader. "Many leaned on Elder Taylor's strength in those days," writes B. H. Roberts. "When despair settled over the colony, he infused it with hope; when the weak faltered, he strengthened them; those cast down with sorrow, he comforted and cheered. His faith and trust in God and in His power to preserve and deliver His people, were as unshaken in the midst of the difficulties they encountered in settling the desert valleys of Utah as they had been in the midst of mob-violence in Missouri and Illinois."

IV

At the October conference in 1849, John Taylor was was called by the First Presidency of the Church to introduce the gospel to the people of France. He readily accepted this important call and on the 19th of October departed for the East with a number of his fellow missionaries. The trip across the plains was a difficult one at that inclement season of the year, as the cold winds, with flurries of snow, swept across the prairies. But the brethren continued on from day to day and in two months arrived at Kanesville, Iowa, where a number of the Saints still resided, and by whom they were warmly welcomed. From Kanesville Elder Taylor made his way by wagon and boat to St. Louis, where he remained for several weeks, "visiting the Saints and studying the French language." The journey was then undertaken to New York City, and from that place he sailed for England. After an uneventful voyage he arrived at Liverpool on May 27, 1850.

Remaining in England for a few weeks only, to renew old acquaintances and meet with the Saints, Elder Taylor departed for France and made his headquarters at Boulogne-sur-Mer. His companions were Elders Curtis Bolton and William Howell.

Because of the limited Protestant population in Boulogne, the missionaries did not make much headway. Elder Taylor engaged in a public debate with two ministers from England, which attracted considerable attention, but it was not long until he left for a larger field of activity in Paris. Here he soon baptized a number of people and founded a small branch of the Church. He also made arrangements for the publication of the Book of Mormon in the French language and for the printing of a small monthly publication called the *Etoile du Deseret.* However, the political agitation in France at this time was such that the government soon prohibited the elders from promulgating the principles of the gospel. In August, 1851, Elder Taylor went to Hamburg, Germany, where he was successful in getting the Book of Mormon translated into the German language and establishing a small monthly paper called *Zions Panier.*

Elder Taylor arrived back in Paris in December, 1851, only to find that the country was in a state of revolution and that the city was in the hands of soldiers. With this uncertain condition he thought it best to leave France. He therefore called a conference with the Saints and bade them farewell, leaving for England the following day and considering that his mission for the time being was at an end.

It was while on this mission that Elder Taylor wrote his admirable pamphlet, *The Government of God.* Of this work Historian Bancroft writes, "As a dissertation on a general and abstract subject it probably has not its equal in point of ability within the range of Mormon literature."

Elder Taylor sailed from England on March 6, 1852, on his return to America. After visiting friends in Philadelphia and Washington, he made his way by train and boat to Kanesville, Iowa, and from that settlement joined an emigrant caravan to Utah. After the usual weary trip across the plains, he was welcomed by his loved ones and friends on his arrival in Salt Lake City, on the 20th of August. after an absence of nearly three years.

No doubt Elder Taylor was now anxious to look after his personal affairs and improve his financial condition, after his long absence in Europe, but the presidency of the Church evidently thought too highly of his ability as a missionary to let him remain long at home. In the summer of 1854 he was again sent east to "preside over the churches in the eastern states, supervise the emigration and publish a paper in the interests of the Church." These tasks did not prove to be easy, as there was a feeling of ill will against the Latter-day Saints in the East at the time, due to the reports of the "run-away judges" and other territorial officials who had returned to their homes there. Yet Elder Taylor went fearlessly forward and accomplished the work that had been assigned to him. A paper called the *Mormon* was begun at New York City on February 17, 1855.

As an editor, Elder Taylor was one of the most able and fearless the Church has produced. The great daily papers of New York City took particular delight in attacking the *Mormon* and the doctrines of the Church, but Elder Taylor was equal to any occasion and replied in a manner that often silenced his critics.

V

Elder Taylor remained in the East throughout the stormy period of 1856 and the early months of 1857, when it was announced that President Buchanan had ordered an army sent to Utah and a new governor to replace Brigham Young. Feeling that the time had come when he should report personally to President Young, he left New York City and after another weary trip across the plains arrived in Utah in August, 1857.

In the old Tabernacle, the Sunday after his arrival, President Young praised Elder Taylor for his editorial work in the East.

"With regard to the labors of Brother Taylor in editing the paper called the *Mormon*, published in the city of New York, I have heard many remarks concerning the editorials in that paper, not only from the Saints, but from those who do not profess to believe the religion we have embraced; and it is probably one of the strongest edited papers that is now published. I can say, as to its editorials, that it is one of the strongest papers ever published, so far as my information extends; and I have never read one sentence in them, but what my heart could bid success to it, and beat a happy response to every sentence I have read or heard read. Brother Taylor, that is for you; and I believe that these are the feelings and sentiments of all this community who have perused that paper."

Meantime the United States Army was marching to the west and rapidly approaching the borders of Utah Territory. About a month after Elder Taylor's return Captain Van Vliet, assistant quartermaster on General Harney's staff, arrived in Salt Lake City to purchase supplies for the oncoming forces. While in the city Captain Van Vliet attended a service in the Tabernacle, at which Elder Taylor made a stirring speech. "What would be your feelings if the United States wanted to drive us from our own homes," he asked the Saints. "Would you, if necessary, brethren, put the torch to your buildings and lay them in ashes and wander houseless into the mountains? I know what you would say and what you would do."

At this point President Young called out, "Try the vote."

Elder Taylor then continued, "All you that are willing to set fire to your property and lay it in ashes rather than submit to their military rule and oppression, manifest it by raising your hands."

It is reported that four thousand of the Saints raised their hands in unanimous approval.

Such were the stirring scenes in which Elder Taylor actively participated on his arrival in Utah.

That the Saints were in real earnest with regard to "laying waste to their fields and homes" is evidenced by the fact that early in the spring of 1858, President Young ordered the evacuation of all the northern settlements, including Salt Lake City, and again a great migration of the Latter-day Saints was begun. Elder Taylor participated in this migration and moved his family to Utah County until the fear of a clash with the army was over. He took part in the conference with the peace commissioners and made an effective speech that assisted in adjusting the differences between the Saints and the government. Writing of John Taylor's activities at this time, B. H. Roberts pays him the following tribute:

"Confident as he ever was, that God held the destiny of this people and that of their enemies in His own hands, he was ready for peace or war; or for the abandonment and destruction of his home, if such were the will of God. This spirit of confidence and trust in the Lord, he not only possessed himself, but he had also the faculty of imbuing others with it. He encouraged the disheartened, cheered the sorrowful, strengthened the weak, reproved the fearful, convinced the unbelieving, counseled even the wise; and throughout those dark and turbulent times, bore himself with dignity, courage and true manliness, which intensified the love of the Saints for him, and called for the admiration of his brethren."

The twenty years intervening between 1857, when Elder Taylor arrived home from his eastern mission, and 1877, when President Brigham Young died, were filled with various activities, both civil and religious, confined mostly to the valleys of the mountains. During these entire twenty years Elder Taylor served as a member of the Utah territorial legislature, and during five successive sessions he was elected Speaker of the House. In 1868 he was elected probate judge of Utah County and continued in the office until the December term of that court in 1870.

Both summer and winter, during all this time, Elder

Taylor was constantly active in his Church duties and in his calling as an apostle. He accompanied President Brigham Young on almost all of his annual preaching tours, both north and south of Salt Lake City. His printed sermons during these years, which were invariably of excellent quality, would fill several volumes. His presentation of the doctrines and policies of the Church was always masterful.

VI

On August 29, 1877, as stated in the beginning of the chapter, President Brigham Young died in Salt Lake City. The passing of this notable man dissolved the First Presidency and left the Church without a president. The responsibility of governing the Saints therefore devolved upon the Quorum of Twelve Apostles, with John Taylor at its head.

"Great energy characterized President Taylor's administration of affairs in the Church, both in Zion and abroad," writes his biographer, B. H. Roberts. "He pushed forward with increased zeal the work on the temples, of which three were in course of erection at the time of his taking control of affairs. He required bishops to hold weekly priesthood meetings in their wards; presidents of stakes to hold general priesthood meetings monthly in their respective stakes; and appointed quarterly conferences in all the stakes of Zion, publishing the dates for holding them for half a year in advance, a custom which has continued until the present. He personally attended as many of these quarterly conferences as he could, without neglecting the executive branch of his calling. But where he could not go himself he sent members of his quorum, so that the Saints received much teaching and instructions from the Apostles, more perhaps than at any previous time in the history of the Church. The result was a great spiritual awakening among the Saints."

President Taylor also stimulated the missionary work of the Church by calling out a larger number of elders than had previously been sent into the world. The missionary work was featured on Pioneer Day, July 24, 1880. In the parade on this occasion "a man and a woman, dressed in native costume, represented each country; the colors and the name of the nation represented where the missionaries of the Church had labored." Afterwards these nationalities, twenty-five in number, were arranged on a platform in front of the pulpit in the Tabernacle. Elder Orson Pratt read a brief account of the introduction of the gospel to each of the various countries. President Taylor followed with this statement: "The Lord commanded his servants to go forth to all the world to preach the Gospel to every creature. We have not yet been to all the world, but here are twenty-five nations represented today, and thus far we have fulfilled our mission; and it is for us to continue our labors until all the world shall hear us, that all who are desirous may obey, and we may complete the mission given us."

The annual General Conference of the Church, held in April, 1880, was known as the "Jubilee Conference," it having been fifty years since the Church was organized. "It occurred to me," said President Taylor on this occasion, "that we ought to do something, as they did in former times, to relieve those that are oppressed with debt, to assist those that are needy, to break off the yoke of those that may feel themselves crowded upon, and to make it a time of general rejoicing."

He then explained that many of the Saints were indebted to the Perpetual Emigration Fund for money that had been advanced to them by the Church to emigrate to Zion. This large sum, which had accumulated over many years, now amounted to $1,604,000 with principal and interest. He proposed that one-half of this sum be remitted to the people and that the worthy poor be not required to pay at all. Needless to say, this magnanimous move on the part of President Taylor was accepted by the Saints and caused general rejoicing.

1880

"If you find people owing you who are distressed," he
continued, "if you will go to work and try to relieve them
as much as you can, under the circumstances, God will relieve you when you get into difficulties."

In a circular issued at the close of conference President
Taylor continued his dissertation on debt. "The rich have
a fitting opportunity to remember the Lord's poor. If you
are holding their notes and they are unable to pay, forgive
the interest and the principle or as much thereof as you
might desire them to forgive were their and your circumstances reversed, thus doing unto others as you would that
others should do unto you, for upon this hang the law and
the Prophets. If you have mortgages upon the homes of your
brethren and sisters who are poor, worthy and honest, and
who desire to pay you but cannot, free them in whole or in
part. Extend to them a Jubilee, if you can consistently."

This was an example of practical Christianity worthy
of any church or institution.

At the concluding session of the great conference,
President Taylor bore a powerful testimony of the divinity
of the work in which he was engaged.

"I testify as my brethren have done that this is the
work of God that has been revealed by the Almighty, and
I know it. God will sustain Israel; no power can injure us
if we do what is right. This Kingdom will roll on, the purposes of God will progress, Zion will arise and shine and the
glory of God will rest upon her. We will continue to grow
and increase, until the kingdoms of this world shall become
the Kingdoms of our God and His Christ, and He will reign
forever and forever."

After the death of President Young, the Quorum of the
Twelve, as a body, presided over the affairs of the Church
until the October conference, 1880, when the First Presidency was reorganized. John Taylor was named as President, with George Q. Cannon and Joseph F. Smith as his
counselors. On this important occasion President Taylor desired that the quorums of the priesthood should separately

have the privilege of sustaining the new First Presidency. The impressive scene is well described by B. H. Roberts as follows:

"The Apostles occupied the stand as set apart for their use in the great Tabernacle, the second one in the tier of three. The space south of the stand was occupied by the Patriarchs, Presidents of Stakes and their counselors, and the High Councils of the various stakes. North of the stand, the bishops and their counselors were seated, with Presiding Bishop Hunter and his counselors in front. The High Priests occupied the north center of the body of the great hall, with their presidents in front. The Seventies were seated in the south half of the body of the hall, with the first seven Presidents in front. The space immediately back of the High Priests was reserved for the Elders, while the north side of the house, under the gallery, was set apart for the Quorums of the Lesser Priesthood, the Priests, Teachers, and Deacons. The gallery, capable of seating three thousand people, was reserved for the use of the members of the Church.

"Apostle Orson Pratt, with white hair and full white beard, presented the several motions to be acted upon. The manner of voting was for the proposition to be presented to each quorum severally, except in the case of the Priests, Teachers and Deacons, who voted all together as the Lesser Priesthood. The members of each quorum rose to their feet as the question was presented and raised the right hand in token of assent, or if any were opposed to the proposition, they could make it manifest in the same way, after the affirmative vote had been taken.

"The order in which the quorums voted was as follows:

"First, the Twelve Apostles;

"Second, the Patriarchs, Presidents of Stakes, their counselors and the High Councils;

"Third, the High Priests;

"Fourth, the Seventies;

"Fifth, the Elders;

"Sixth, the Bishops and their counselors;

"Seventh, the Lesser Priesthood.

"After this the President of the quorums voted on the question and it was then put to the entire assembly which arose en masse and voted in the same manner. It was a remarkable scene. There was not a dissenting vote in the vast assembly; and there were probably thirteen thousand people crowded into the great Tabernacle. Perfect unanimity prevailed, and as the several quorums registered their votes, and the entire assembly arose with uplifted hands, sanctioning what they had done, the scene was indescribably grand and impressive, carrying with it a power and influence that can only come from a righteous people."

John Taylor and his counselors were thus sustained, in these solemn and impressive ceremonies, as the First Presidency of the Church. President Taylor at the time was seventy-two years of age, but he was still strong and active and able to carry on with his arduous duties. In 1881 he made two extended trips, visiting the northern and southern settlements. He spoke at many meetings, encouraged the people, and "preached righteousness as essential to the favor of God, and with the favor of God he assured the Saints they need not fear what man or nations could do."

In the fall of 1881 the agitation of the country against the practice of polygamy in Utah and surrounding states became intense. For months the ministers of various religions had been active in urging Congress to pass stringent laws prohibiting this practice. At a conference of Methodist ministers held in Ogden at this time the following resolution was adopted: "Mormonism holds the balance of power in Idaho and Arizona and menaces New Mexico, Colorado, Wyoming and Montana. We believe polygamy is a foul system of licentiousness, practiced in the name of religion, hence hideous and revolting. It should not be reasoned with, but ought to be stamped out." Similar meetings were held in various parts of the nation, and the agitation finally resulted in the passage of the Edmunds Bill in Congress and

Edmunds Bill

its approval by the President of the United States on March
22, 1882. This bill provided fines and imprisonment for
those who practiced polygamy. It also vacated the registration and election offices in Utah and placed the registration
of voters and the management of elections under the federal
returning board, known as the Utah Commission. At the
April conference in 1882, President Taylor took occasion to
make some remarks regarding the Edmunds law.

1882

"We do not wish to place ourselves in a state of antag-
onism, nor act defiantly towards this government," he said;
"we will fulfill the letter, so far as practicable, of that
unjust, inhuman, oppressive and unconstitutional law, so far
as we can without violating principle. . . .

"We shall abide all constitutional law, as we always
have done, but while we are God-fearing and law-abiding,
and respect all honorable men and officers, we are no
craven serfs, and have not learned to lick the feet of oppressors, nor to bow in base submission to unreasonable
clamor. We will contend inch by inch, legally and consti-
tutionally, for our rights as American citizens. . . . We need
have no fears, no trembling in our knees about these at-
tempts to deprive us of our God-given and constitutional
liberties. God will take care of His people if we will only
do right."

It will thus be seen that President Taylor had a firm
and unalterable belief that God was at the helm and that
the Latter-day Saints would be led aright.

In 1883 and in succeeding years to 1890, there were
many prosecutions against the Latter-day Saints under the
Edmunds law. In January, 1885, President Taylor felt that
it was wise for him and a number of his brethren of the
Twelve to leave Utah for a season, until the storm had spent
its fury. These brethren went by train to Denver and Al-
buquerque and thence to the settlements of the Saints in
Arizona. From Arizona he went to California. He returned
on January 27 to Salt Lake City, where he learned that his
arrest had been determined upon by the non-Mormon offi-

1885

cers. On Sunday, February 1, 1885, he addressed the Saints in the Tabernacle and delivered a vigorous sermon, setting forth the wrongs inflicted upon the people. He concluded his sermon, which was his last in public before the Saints, with this significant remark: "I will tell you what you will see by and by. You will see trouble, trouble, trouble enough in these United States. And as I have said before, I say today, I tell you in the name of God, woe to them that fight against Zion, for God will fight against them."

Thereafter President Taylor went into retirement and was not found by the non-Mormon officers who sought his arrest. He continued to direct the policies of the Church and from time to time issued epistles addressed to the Saints. In a letter to his family, which had gathered in Salt Lake City to celebrate his seventy-eighth birthday on November 1, 1886, he did not complain of his exile.

"The protecting care of the Lord over me and my brethren has been very manifest since my absence from home, for which I feel to bless and praise His holy name. I always am very desirous to acknowledge His hand in all things, and I am very anxious that you should do the same. For to the Lord we are indebted for every blessing we enjoy, pertaining to this life, and the life which is to come."

The above was President Taylor's last birthday message to his family. In the summer of 1887 his health began to fail. He passed away peacefully at the home of Thomas F. Rouche in Kaysville, Utah, on the 25th of July. At his bedside were his counselors, George Q. Cannon and Joseph F. Smith, together with members of his immediate family.

VII

The day following his demise his counselors issued a splendid statement in the *Deseret News*, regarding President Taylor's life and labors. It is reproduced here in full:

"Once more the Latter-day Saints are called upon to mourn the death of their leader—the man who has held the keys of the Kingdom of God upon earth. President John Taylor departed this life at five minutes to eight o'clock on the evening of Monday, July 25th, 1887, aged 78 years, 8 months and 25 days.

"In communicating this sad intelligence to the Church, over which he has so worthily presided for nearly ten years past, we are filled with emotion too deep for utterance. A faithful, devoted and fearless servant of God, the Church in his death has lost its most conspicuous and experienced leader. Steadfast to and immovable in the truth, few men have ever lived who have manifested such integrity and such unflinching moral and physical courage as our beloved President who has just gone from us. He never knew the feeling of fear connected with the work of God. But in the face of angry mobs, and at other times when in imminent danger of personal violence from those who threatened his life, and upon occasions when the people were menaced with public peril, he never blanched—his knees never trembled, his hand never shook. Every Latter-day Saint always knew beforehand, on occasions when firmness and courage were needed, where President John Taylor would be found and what his tone would be. He met every issue squarely, boldly and in a way to call forth the admiration of all who saw and heard him. Undaunted courage, unyielding firmness were among his most prominent characteristics, giving him distinction among men who were distinguished for the same qualities. With these were combined an intense love of freedom and hatred of oppression. He was a man whom all could trust, and throughout his life he enjoyed, to an extent surpassed by none, the implicit confidence of the Prophets Joseph, Hyrum and Brigham and all the leading men and members of the Church. The title of 'Champion of Liberty,' which he received at Nauvoo, was always felt to be most appropriate for him to bear. But it was not only in the possession of these qualities that President Taylor was great. His judgment was remarkably sound and clear, and through life he has been noted for the wisdom of his counsels and teachings. His great experience made his suggestions exceedingly valuable; for there has scarcely been a public movement of any kind commenced, carried on, or completed, since he joined the Church, in which he has not taken part.

"But it is not necessary that we should, even if time permitted, rehearse the events of his long and busy life. To do so would only be to give the greater part of his history of the Church; for with it his biography is inseparably interwoven.

"The last time President Taylor appeared in public was on Sunday, February 1st, 1885. On that occasion he delivered a lengthy discourse in the Tabernacle, in Salt Lake City. Rumor had been floating around for some time that his arrest was contemplated. In fact, while returning from a trip to the settlements in Arizona, he was advised in California that he was in great danger, and it was suggested that perhaps it would be better for him not to return to Salt Lake City. He listened to these cautions but still resolved to take the risk, and came back and fearlessly went about his business for some time. But on the evening of Saturday, February 1st, he concluded to withdraw himself from the public performance of his numerous and important duties. In taking this step he did so more to preserve peace and to remove all possible cause of excitement, than from any desire of personal safety. He perceived that there was a determination on the part of men holding official position here to raise an issue, and, if possible, involve the Latter-day Saints in serious trouble. He had not broken any law. He knew he was innocent and that if he were arrested and could have a fair trial, nothing could be brought against him. He had taken every precaution that a man could take under his circumstances to make himself invulnerable to attack. He was determined that, so far as he was concerned, he would furnish no pretext for trouble, but would do everything in his power to prevent the people over whom he presided from being involved in difficulty.

"From that date upwards of two years and a half ago when he left his home in Salt Lake City he had not the opportunity of crossing its threshold again. To home and its joys, its delightful associations and its happy reunions he has been a stranger. He has lived as an exile—a wanderer in the land, to the development and good government of which he has contributed so much! While living in this condition, one of his wives was stricken with disease, and though his heart was torn with anguish at the thought of her condition, and with anxiety to see her and minister to her in her deep distress, her residence was closely watched by spies, and when she was in a dying condition, was even searched with hope of entrapping him. Thus she was deprived of the privilege of looking upon his beloved face, and he had not even the sad consolation of witnessing or taking any part in her funeral ceremonies.

"During the two years and a half that President Taylor has been living in this condition, he has been cut off from all the society and loving ministrations of his family. But though this was so hard to bear at his time of life, he never murmured. He was always full of courage and hope, cheering everyone with whom he was brought in contact, and lifting his companions by his noble example out of despondency and discouragement. With the same courage with which he stood by the Prophet of God and with a walking cane parried the guns of the mob when they vomited their sheets of flame and messengers of death in Carthage Jail, he confronted the difficulties and the trials which he had to meet when compelled to leave his home and the society of those whom he loved. His demeanor throughout this long ordeal has been most admirable. Everyone who has seen him has been impressed by his equanimity and stately bearing. Always distinguished for his courtesy and dignity of character, at no period of his life did he ever exhibit those traits to greater advantage than during his exile. He has never condescended even to speak evil of those who so cruelly persecuted him.

"By the miraculous power of God, President John Taylor escaped the death which the assassins of Carthage Jail assigned for him. His blood was then mingled with the blood of the martyred Prophet and Patriarch. He has stood since then as a living martyr for the truth. But today he occupies the place of a double martyr. President John Taylor has been killed by the cruelty of officials who have, in this Territory, misrepresented the Government of the United States. There is no room to doubt that if he had been permitted to enjoy the comforts of home, the ministrations of his family, the exercise to which he was deprived, he might have lived for many years yet. His blood stains the clothes of the men, who with insensate hate have offered rewards for his arrest and have hounded him to the grave. History will yet call their deeds by their right names; but One greater than the combined voices of all historians will yet pronounce their dreadful sentence.

"It is now some time since President Taylor was attacked by disease. It came upon him by degrees, manifesting itself in the beginning by a swelling of the limbs for the want of proper exercise. He fought disease with his characteristic pluck and determination. He would not yield. He would neither allow himself nor anyone else to think that his sickness was serious. He would not permit his family to know his real condition, as he did not wish them to have any anxiety on his account, and it was almost against his express wishes they were told how sick he was. When messages were sent by him to them, they were always of a reassuring character. Up to the last day or two he was able to sit in his chair, and until quite recently he was able to assist himself in getting in and out of bed. The strength he has exhibited and his tenacity of life have been very wonderful; for though so strong, he had partaken of scarcely any nourishment for the past six weeks. So peacefully did he pass away, and so like a babe falling asleep that a brief period elapsed before those who stood around his bed were sure that his spirit had taken its flight.

"As the sad intelligence which we now communicate
still spreads through these valleys and mountains, sorrow
will fill the hearts of all at hearing of the last days of their
beloved and venerable President. We know how deep has
been the sympathy that has filled the hearts of the Saints
and of his being compelled to live as an exile from his
family and the people. The expressions of esteem and love
which have come to him from all parts of the land have
deeply touched him and caused him great pleasure in
thinking how much he was beloved and how much his
welfare was desired by all the Saints throughout the earth.

"His constant desire was to do everything in his power to relieve the Latter-day Saints from the oppressions
under which they suffer. Every pulsation of his heart beat
with love of Zion and a desire for her redemption. We desired, and the desire was general, we believe, throughout
the Church—that he might live to emerge from his exile
and be once more a free man among the people whom he
loved. But this has been denied us. He has gone to mingle
with the holy and the pure, and to quote his own eloquent
words, written concerning his dear friend, Joseph the Seer:

'Beyond the reach of mobs and strife,
He rests unharmed in endless life;
His home's in the sky, he dwells with the Gods,
Far from the furious rage of mobs.'

"And though we have lost his presence here, his influence will still be felt. Such men may pass from this life
to another, but the love which beats in their hearts for
righteousness and for truth cannot die. They go to an enlarged sphere of usefulness. Their influence is extended and
more widely felt, and Zion will feel the benefit of his labors,
as it has the labors of others who have gone before him.
The work of God will roll forth. One after another of the
mighty men—the men who have spent their lives in the
cause of God—may pass away, but this will not affect the
purposes of our Great Creator concerning His latter-day
work. He will raise up others, and the work will go on

increasing in power, in influence, and in all true greatness, until it will accomplish all that God has predicted concerning it.

"We feel to say to the Latter-day Saints: Be comforted! The same God who took care of the work when Joseph was martyred, who has watched over and guarded and upheld it through the long years that have since elapsed, and who has guided its destinies since the departure of Brigham, still watches over it and makes it the object of His care. John has gone; but God lives. He has founded Zion. He has given His people a testimony of this. Cherish it in your heart of hearts, and live so each day that when the end of your mortal lives shall come, you may be counted worthy to go where Joseph, Brigham, and John have gone, and mingle with that glorious throng whose robes have been washed white in the blood of the Lamb."

VIII

The funeral of President Taylor was held in the great Tabernacle at Salt Lake City at 12 noon on Friday, July 29. The building was filled to capacity with those who mourned the passing of their leader. The speakers were Lorenzo Snow, Franklin D. Richards, Heber J. Grant, A. O. Smoot, Lorenzo D. Young, Joseph B. Noble, and Angus M. Cannon. All paid glowing tributes to the faith and devotion, the courage and ability of President Taylor. At the conclusion of the services the body was laid to rest in the Salt Lake City Cemetery. At the graveside Richard Ballantyne offered the dedicatory prayer.

WILFORD WOODRUFF

WILFORD WOODRUFF

(1807-1898)

"**W**ILFORD the Faithful." That was the title given to Wilford Woodruff in the early days of the Church, and it was a title justly earned. Never was there a more devoted and faithful Latter-day Saint. "His integrity and unbounded devotion to the worship and purposes of his God," writes Matthias F. Cowley, author of the *Life of Wilford Woodruff*, "are not surpassed by any prophet of either ancient or modern times." Here truly was a good and great man who, in his youth, was permitted to ally himself with those who were engaged in the sublime task of building on earth the kingdom of God; and, unlike many of his associates whose days were "cut short in righteousness," Wilford Woodruff was granted ninety-one years of life and labor, and was at last permitted to preside over the organization that he had struggled so long and so diligently to establish and maintain.

Wilford Woodruff, like his distinguished predecessors Joseph Smith and Brigham Young, came from the sturdy pioneers of New England. His ancestors, originally from England, had been for several generations farmers and millers, in and about the neighborhood of Farmington, Connecticut. They were a hardy, long-lived people. "My great-grandfather, Josiah Woodruff," related Wilford, "lived nearly one hundred years. He possessed an iron constitution and performed a great deal of manual work up to the

time of his death." Of his grandfather Wilford remarked
that "he likewise possessed a strong constitution and it was
said of him that for several years he performed more labor
than any man in Hartford County."

Wilford's father, Aphek Woodruff, was born at Farmington in 1778. He continued the reputation of his family,
being known as a man of strong constitution. "At eighteen
years of age he began work in a flour mill and sawmill and
continued at his occupation there for about fifty years.
Most of that time he labored eighteen hours a day." So
wrote his distinguished son.

From the above it is easy to understand why Wilford
Woodruff was such a determined, hardy, and healthy man,
and why his life was continued for ninety-one years. There
is no doubt that here is a clear case of inherited physical
and mental qualities. Wilford was greatly indebted to his
sturdy ancestors.

The date of Wilford Woodruff's birth is given as March
1, 1807, at Farmington. He was the third son of Aphek
and Beulah Woodruff. When he was only fifteen months
old his good mother was stricken with "spotted fever" and
died within a few days. Shortly thereafter the father was
married again, to Azulah Hart. This stepmother was to have
the privilege of rearing Wilford, although she may have
thought at times that it was not exactly a privilege, as he
was an extremely active child and must have caused her
considerable concern. He himself relates the following
interesting and rather amazing account of "accidents" that
befell him in his childhood and youth. Let mothers who
have mischievous children console themselves in the thought
that all the following described ills befell one who became
the greatest missionary and fourth President of The Church
of Jesus Christ of Latter-day Saints, who lived until he
reached his ninety-second year.

"When three years of age, I fell into a caldron of
scalding water and although instantly rescued, I was so
badly burned that it was nine months before I was thought

to be out of the danger of fatal consequences. My fifth and sixth years were interwoven with many accidents. On a certain day, in company with my elder brothers, I entered the barn, and chose the top of a haymow for a place of diversion. We had not been there long before I fell from the great beam upon my face on the bare floor. I was severely hurt, but recovered in a short time, and was again at play.

"One Saturday evening, with my brothers, Azmon and Thompson, while playing in the chamber of my father's house, contrary to his instructions, I made a misstep and fell to the bottom of the stairs, breaking one of my arms in the fall. So much for disobedience. I suffered intensely, but soon recovered, feeling that whatever I suffered in the future, it would not be for disobedience to parents. The Lord has commanded children to obey their parents; and Paul says, 'This is the first commandment with promise.'

"It was only a short time after this that I narrowly escaped with my life. My father owned a number of horned cattle, among which was a surly bull. One evening I was feeding pumpkins to the cattle, and the bull, leaving his own, took the pumpkin I had given to a cow which I called mine. I was incensed at the selfishness of this male beast, and promptly picked up the pumpkin he had left, to give it to the cow. No sooner had I got it in my arms than the bull came plunging toward me with great fury. I ran down the hill with all my might, the bull at my heels. My father, seeing the danger I was in, called to me to throw down the pumpkin, but (forgetting to be obedient) I held on, and as the bull was approaching me with the fierceness of a tiger, I made a misstep and fell flat upon the ground. The pumpkin rolled out of my arms, the bull leaped over me, ran his horns into the pumpkin and tore it to pieces. Undoubtedly he would have done the same thing to me if I had not fallen to the ground. This escape, like all others, I attribute to the mercy and goodness of God.

"During the same year, while visiting at my Uncle Eldad Woodruff's, I fell from a porch across some timber, and broke my other arm.

"Not many months passed before I was called to endure a still greater misfortune. My father owned a sawmill in addition to his flour mill, and one morning, in company with several other boys, I went into the sawmill and got upon the headlock of the carriage to ride, not anticipating any danger; but before I was aware of it my leg was caught between the headlock and the fender post and broken in two. I was taken to the house, and lay nine hours before my bones were replaced. That time was spent in severe pain; but being young, my bones soon knitted together, and in a few weeks I was upon my feet as usual, attending to the sports of youth. During this confinement my brother Thompson was my companion. He was suffering from typhus fever.

"Shortly after this, upon a dark night, I was kicked in the abdomen by an ox; but being too close to the animal to receive the full force of the blow, I was more frightened than hurt.

"It was not long before I made my first effort at loading hay. I was very young, but thought I had loaded it all right. When on the way to the barn, the wheel of the wagon struck a rock, and off went the hay. I fell to the ground with the load on top of me; this was soon removed, and aside from a little smothering I was unhurt.

"When eight years of age, I accompanied my father, with several others, in a one-horse wagon, about three miles from home, to attend to some work. On the way the horse became frightened, ran down a hill, and turned over the wagon, with us in it. We were in danger, but were again saved by the hand of Providence. None of us were injured.

"One day I climbed an elm tree to procure some bark; while about fifteen feet from the ground, the limb upon which I stood, being dry, broke, and I fell to the ground upon my back. The accident apparently knocked the breath out of my body. A cousin ran to the house and told my parents that I was dead, but before my friends reached me I revived, rose to my feet, and met them on the way.

"When twelve years old I was nearly drowned in Farmington River. I sank in thirty feet of water, and was miraculously saved by a young man named Bacon. The restoration to life caused me great suffering.

"At thirteen years of age, while passing through Farmington meadows, in the depths of winter, in a blinding snowstorm, I became so chilled and overcome with cold that I could not travel. I crawled into the hollow of a large apple tree. A man in the distance saw me, and, realizing the danger I was in, hastened to where I was. Before he arrived at the spot I had fallen asleep, and was almost unconscious. He had much difficulty in arousing me to a sense of my critical condition, and promptly had me conveyed to my father's house, where, through a kind Providence, my life was again preserved.

"At fourteen years of age I split my left instep open with an ax which went almost through my foot. I suffered intensely from this injury, and my foot was nine months in getting well.

"When fifteen years old I was bitten in the hand by a mad dog in the last stages of hydrophobia. However, he did not draw blood, and through the mercy and power of God I was again preserved from an awful death.

"At the age of seventeen I met with an accident which caused me much suffering, and came nearly ending my life. I was riding a very ill-tempered horse, which, while going down a very steep, rocky hill, suddenly leaped from the road and amid the thickest of the rocks. At the same time, he commenced kicking, and was about to land me over his head among the rocks, but I lodged on the top of his head, and grabbed each of his ears with my hands, expecting every moment to be dashed to pieces against the rocks. While in this position, sitting astride the horse's neck, with neither bridle nor other means of guiding him except his ears, he plunged down the hill among the rocks with great fury, until he struck a rock nearly breast high, which threw him to the earth. I went over his head, landing squarely upon my feet almost one rod in front of the horse. Alighting upon my feet was probably the means of saving my life; for if I had struck the ground upon any other part of my body, it would probably have killed me instantly. As it was, one of my legs was broken in two places, and both my ankles put out of place in a shocking manner. The horse almost rolled over me in his struggle to get up. My uncle saw me, and came to my assistance. I was carried to his house in an armchair. I lay from 2 o'clock in the afternoon until 10 o'clock at night without medical aid and in great pain, when my father arrived with Dr. Swift, of Farmington. The doctor set my bones, boxed up my limbs, and that night conveyed me eight miles in his carriage to my father's house. I had good attention, and although my sufferings were great, in eight weeks I was out upon my crutches, and was soon restored to a sound condition."

Wilford continued his labors on the farm and in the mill, assisting his father in every way possible. There is some mention of his having attended school during his early years, but we do not know to what extent he continued his education. We do know, however, that he learned to read and write well and that his favorite book was the Bible.

In April, 1827, shortly after Wilford reached his twentieth birthday, he left his father's home and went to East Avon, Connecticut, where he took charge of his Aunt Helen Wheeler's flour mill, "on shares." Here he remained for three years. He then took charge of a mill at Collinsville, but he had been there only a short time when he was persuaded by his brother Azmon to go to western New York and join him in the purchase of a farm. The two brothers located at Richland, Oswego County, and made purchase of 140 acres, "with a good dwelling house," for $1,800. Of this amount they were able to pay $800 down.

II

It was at Richland that two humble elders of The Church of Jesus Christ of Latter-day Saints, Zera Pulsipher and Elijah Cheney, came to Wilford's door on December 29, 1833. These elders left word that they would speak in the Richland schoolhouse the same night. Both Wilford and his brother Azmon attended this meeting; they listened to the sermons of the elders, and they believed. Wilford records the event as follows:

"Elder Pulsipher opened with prayer. He knelt down and asked the Lord in the name of Jesus Christ for what he wanted. His manner of prayer and the influence which went with it impressed me greatly. The spirit of the Lord rested upon me and bore witness that he was a servant of God. After singing, he preached to the people for an hour and a half. The Spirit of God rested mightily upon him and he bore a strong testimony of the divine authenticity of the Book of Mormon and of the mission of the Prophet Joseph Smith. I believed all that he said. The spirit bore witness of its truth. Elder Cheney then arose and added his testimony to the truth of the words of Elder Pulsipher.

"Liberty was then given by the elders to any one in the congregation to arise and speak for or against what they had heard as they might choose. Almost instantly I found myself upon my feet. The Spirit of the Lord urged me to bear testimony to the truth of the message delivered by these elders. I exhorted my neighbors and friends not to oppose these men; for they were the true servants of God. They had preached to us that night the pure Gospel of Jesus Christ. When I sat down, my brother, Azmon, arose and bore a similar testimony. He was followed by several others."

The result of this meeting was that two days later, on a cold day, in water "mixed with ice and snow," Wilford and his brother were baptized by Elder Pulsipher.

Others of the neighborhood came into the Church later. On January 25, 1834, a branch of the Church was organized at Richland, and Wilford Woodruff was ordained to the office of teacher. The real work of his life was now before him.

Early in April Wilford took his horses and wagon; and accompanied by two brethren from the Richland branch, he set out for Kirtland, Ohio, to visit the Prophet Joseph Smith. It took them two weeks to make the journey. Wilford gives us an account of this visit in his journal.

"Here for the first time in my life I met and had an interview with our beloved Prophet Joseph Smith, the man whom God has chosen to bring forth His revelations in these last days. My first introduction was not of a kind to satisfy the preconceived notions of the sectarian mind as to what a prophet ought to be, and how he should appear. It might have shocked the faith of some men. I found him and his brother Hyrum out shooting at a mark with a brace of pistols. When they stopped shooting, I was introduced to Brother Joseph, and he shook hands with me most heartily. He invited me to make his habitation my home while I tarried in Kirtland. This invitation I most eagerly accepted, and was greatly edified and blest during my stay with him. He asked me to help him tan a wolfskin which he said he wished to use upon the seat of his wagon on the way to Missouri. I pulled off my coat, stretched the skin across the back of a chair, and soon had it tanned—although I had to smile at my first experience with the Prophet."

The reason that the Prophet Joseph and his brother Hyrum were practicing shooting "with a brace of pistols" was no doubt due to the fact that they were about to undertake a journey to Missouri to assist the Saints who had been expelled from Jackson County in recovering their farms and homes. A brace of pistols was about the only argument that the Missouri mob would understand.

During the course of his visit to Kirtland, Wilford was invited by the Prophet to become a member of Zion's

Camp, as the expedition to Missouri was now called. Wilford agreed, and on the first of May joined the camp at New Portage, Ohio. After a long march of one thousand miles, the brethren, 205 in number, arrived in Clay County, Missouri, on the 24th of June. In July the camp was disbanded, finding that the Saints were so scattered that it would be impossible to restore them to their lands and that the attempt would mean open warfare with the Missourians. The Prophet advised all the young men of the camp without families to remain in Missouri, and Wilford Woodruff was obedient to this advice. He settled in Clay County near the home of Lyman Wight. In December he dedicated his property and himself to the upbuilding of the kingdom of God: "Be it known that I, Wilford Woodruff, do freely covenant myself, unto the Lord, for the purpose of assisting in the building up of His Kingdom and His Zion upon the earth, that I may keep His law. I lay all before the Bishop of His Church, that I may be lawful heir to the Celestial Kingdom of God."

In November 1834 Wilford received a call from Bishop Partridge to undertake a mission for the Church to the southern states. His particular assignment was to the states of Arkansas and Tennessee. Several other elders accompanied him. "We put some Books of Mormon and some clothing into our valises," he related, "and started on foot." This mission proved to be most trying and difficult. The settlements were few and widely separated. It was while on this mission that Wilford made the longest, hardest day's journey of his life "on foot." He and his companion walked sixty miles "between sunrise and ten o'clock at night, without a morsel of food to eat." After wading through swamps, sleeping out nights in rainstorms, being followed by packs of wolves, and other incredible hardships, in his efforts to preach the gospel, Wilford sums up his labors in Arkansas and Tennessee during the year 1835 as follows:

"I had traveled 3,248 miles, held 170 meetings, baptized 43 persons, assisted Elder Parrish to baptize 20 more, confirmed 35, organized 3 branches, ordained 2 teachers and 1 deacon, procured 30 subscribers for the *Messenger and Advocate*, 173 signers to the petition to the Governor of Missouri for redress of wrongs done the Saints in Jackson County, had 3 mobs rise against me—but was not harmed—wrote 18 letters, received 10 and, finally, closed the labors for the year 1835 by eating 'johnny cake,' butter and honey at Brother A. O. Smoot's."

Wilford had certainly proved his worth as a missionary. Humbly, quietly, consistently he had gone about his duties, but with a determination and persistence that in a few years brought him into prominence as one of the great missionaries of the Church.

Wilford continued his work in Tennessee and Kentucky until September, 1836. At that time he was released, and with Elder A. O. Smoot he made his way to Kirtland, Ohio, the headquarters of the Church.

Wilford was pleased to again mingle at Kirtland with his friends and brethren whom he had not seen for nearly two years. Especially did he enjoy the society of the Prophet. "There is not so great a man as Joseph standing in this generation," he wrote. "The Gentiles look upon him, and he is like a bed of gold, concealed from human view. They know not his principles, his wisdom, his virtue, his calling. His mind, like Enoch's, expands as eternity, and God alone can comprehend his soul." How fortunate for Wilford Woodruff that he was able to associate with and appreciate the Prophet of God.

On April 13, 1837, Wilford was married to Phoebe Carter at Kirtland. At this time he was one month past his thirtieth birthday. His wife was eight days his junior. This marriage was preeminently successful and Wilford had indeed found his true companion.

Although happily married, Wilford felt the necessity of continuing his missionary work. "One month and one day after this important event," he wrote, "I left my wife with Sister Hale, with whom she expected to stay for a season.

I left Kirtland in good spirits, with Elder Jonathan Hale."
This mission took Wilford as far east and north as the Fox
Islands, off the coast of Maine. Here he and Elder Hale
labored with great diligence for three months, establishing
branches of the Church on both the North and South Fox
Islands. In October, Elder Hale departed for his home in
Kirtland. Elder Woodruff sent for his wife, and upon her
arrival, he continued his efforts on the islands until May,
1838, when he visited his old home at Farmington, Connecticut. Here he had the extreme pleasure of baptizing his
father, his stepmother, and his sister. "It was truly a day of
joy to my soul," he relates.

III

On August 9, 1838, "while holding meeting with the
Saints at North Vinal Haven, Fox Islands," Elder Woodruff
received a letter from Thomas B. Marsh, president of the
Quorum of Twelve Apostles, informing him that "the
Prophet Joseph Smith had received a revelation from the
Lord, naming persons who had been chosen to fill the places
of those of the Twelve who had fallen." Wilford Woodruff
was among those named. "Know then, Brother Woodruff,
by this," continued President Marsh, "that you are appointed to fill the place of one of the Twelve Apostles, and that
it is agreeable to the word of the Lord, given very lately,
that you should come speedily to Far West, and, on the
26th of April next, take your leave of the Saints here and
depart for other climes across the mighty deep."
Elder Woodruff at once began preparations to carry
out the instructions of his presiding brethren. However,
as a number of his converts were desirous of accompanying
him to Missouri, the start from Scarboro, Maine, was de-
layed until October 9, which was extremely late in the
season to begin the long, wearisome journey overland to
Missouri by wagon. But no obstacle could deter Brother

Woodruff when he felt that he was carrying out the will of the Lord. The little company departed "in ten new wagons," and after much illness among its members and great difficulty in traveling through rain, mud, and snow, "for two months and sixteen days," Wilford and a part of his caravan arrived at the village of Rochester, Illinois, only to learn that all of the Latter-day Saints who had lived in Missouri were at that time being driven from that state by bloodthirsty armed mobs. Wilford therefore concluded that it was best for himself and his family to remain in Rochester during the winter. "In the spring," he relates, "I took my family and removed to Quincy, Illinois, where I could mingle with my brethren; and I knelt to praise God for His protecting care over me and my family in all our afflictions."

Although the Saints had now been driven out of Missouri, it was necessary, in order to fulfill the revelation of July 8, 1838, that the brethren of the Twelve should return to Far West and from there take leave of the Saints "on the 26th of April next, on the building spot of my house, saith the Lord." The Twelve, trusting in the Lord's protecting care, decided to carry out the command of the revelation. "I took into my wagon," related Elder Woodruff, "Brigham Young and Orson Pratt; Father Cutler took into his wagon John Taylor and George A. Smith. On the way we met John E. Page who was going with his family to Quincy, Illinois. His wagon had turned over, and when we met him he was trying to gather up with his hands a barrel of soft soap. We helped him with his wagon. He then drove into the valley below, left his wagon, and accompanied us on our way. On the night of the 25th of April we arrived at Far West. On the morning of the 26th of April, 1839, notwithstanding the threats of our enemies that the revelation which was to be fulfilled this day should not be fulfilled. . . . We moved on to the Temple lot and fulfilled the revelation and commandment given to us." It was at this same meeting that Wilford was ordained to the apostleship under the hands of President Brigham Young and his fellow apostles.

While the above incident was taking place, the Prophet Joseph, his brother Hyrum, and others escaped from the Missouri officers who had held them in prison for almost six months. They were in Quincy to greet the brethren of the Twelve on their return.

The problem now before the leaders of the Church was to find a new place of gathering for the Saints. A few weeks after his escape from Missouri the Prophet Joseph purchased a tract of land forty miles north of Quincy at a place called Commerce. Here he located and in a few days Wilford Woodruff, with his family in his wagon, followed him. Not finding a suitable place for settlement at Commerce, Wilford crossed the river to Iowa and "moved into a room in the old Military barracks." Here he remained until the time came for him to depart for his mission to England.

I regret that I cannot record more information than a brief paragraph regarding the missionary work Elder Woodruff accomplished in England during the years of 1840 and 1841. But in the annals of our Church history no other missionary ever met with equal success. He left Nauvoo in August, 1839, sick and penniless, and somehow worked his way across the country to New York City. Here the Saints assisted him with $15 to pay his passage in a sailing vessel to Liverpool, where he arrived on January 11, 1840. In March he began his missionary labors in the Herefordshire district, and continued there for three months. On leaving for the Manchester district in June, he recorded the following: "I never before left a field of labor with as much satisfaction with the results of my work; I felt to render unto God the gratitude of my heart for giving me so many souls as seals to my ministry; and I note the remarkable fact that I had been led by the spirit, only a little more than three months before, through a densely populated country for eighty miles, and chose no part of it for my field of labor until I was led by the Lord to the house of John Benbow, at Frome's Hill, where I preached for the first time on the 5th of March, 1840; now, on the 22nd of June, I was going to the Manchester Conference, to represent this fruitful field of my labors with 33 organized churches numbering 541 members, 300 of whom received the ordinance of baptism under my hands." Similar results, though not quite as fruitful, accompanied Elder Woodruff's missionary efforts wherever he went, and hundreds of faithful people were brought into the Church during the short period of his labors in England.

In April, 1841, the brethren of the Twelve left England on their return journey. Arriving in New York City the latter part of May, Wilford left his brethren and went to Scarboro, Maine, where his wife awaited him at the home of her parents. With her he paid a visit to his father at Farmington, Connecticut. It was not until October that he arrived in Nauvoo. "When I left Nauvoo two years before," he wrote, "there were not more than a dozen houses in the place, but on my return to the city, there were several hundred."

Once again with the Saints at the gathering place, Elder Woodruff was unusually active. He was made a member of the Nauvoo city council; he was called to assist in locating emigrants; he worked on the construction of the Nauvoo Temple; he assisted Elder John Taylor in the publication of the *Times and Seasons*, and he labored at the task of building a comfortable dwelling for himself. With the energy he put forth he was successful in every enterprise.

Wilford remained in Nauvoo and the surrounding settlements from October, 1841, to July, 1843, when he was requested by the Prophet to undertake a mission to the East, "for the purpose of holding conferences and gathering funds for the completion of the Temple." This mission took him to St. Louis, Cincinnati, Pittsburgh, Philadelphia, New York City, Boston, and Portland, Maine. The return journey was begun in October, and Nauvoo was reached on November 4.

Elder Woodruff remained in Nauvoo during the winter of 1843-44, and he enjoyed the society of the Prophet and his brethren of the Twelve. Continually active in his Church duties, his diligence and labor enabled him to surround himself with some of the comforts of life. But not long was he to remain at home. In April, 1844, the Prophet requested all of the members of the Twelve, except John Taylor and Willard Richards, to undertake another important mission to the East. His parting with the Prophet on this occasion is described in Wilford's journal as follows: "Joseph stood in the entry of his door when I took his hand to bid him farewell; Brother J. M. Grant was with me. As he took me by the hand he said, 'Brother Woodruff, you are about to start upon your mission.' I answered, 'Yes.' He looked me steadily in the eye for a time without speaking a word; he looked as though he would penetrate my very soul, and at the same time seemed unspeakably sorrowful, as if weighed down by a foreboding of something dreadful. He finally spoke in a mournful voice, 'God bless you, Brother Woodruff; go in peace.' I turned and left him with a sorrowful heart, partaking of the same spirit which rested upon him. This was the last time I ever saw his face or heard his voice —in the flesh."

Wilford's mission to the East during the summer of 1844 was interrupted by the news of the death of the Prophet, which he received at Portland, Maine, on July 9. He at once left for Boston, where he met President Brigham Young. He recorded in his journal under date of July 17: "Elder Brigham Young arrived and we called upon Sister Vose. Brother Young took the bed and I the arm chair, and then we veiled our faces and gave vent to our grief. Until now I had not shed a tear since the death of the Prophet. My soul had been nerved up like steel. After giving vent to our grief in tears we felt more composed."

The brethren of the Twelve gathered at Boston, and by train, boat, and stage they traveled to Nauvoo, arriving

the evening of August 8. "When we landed in the city,"
wrote Wilford, "a deep gloom seemed to rest over Nauvoo,
such as we had never before experienced."

IV

Under the leadership of President Brigham Young and
the Twelve, the confusion that Sidney Rigdon and others at-
tempted to cause in the Church after the death of the
Prophet was soon allayed and order was restored. At a
council meeting of the Twelve held on August 12, Wilford
Woodruff was chosen to preside over the European Mission.
Arrangements were made for his wife to accompany him.
Wilford's letter of appointment follows:

"Nauvoo, August 22, 1844.
"To all Elders and Saints in Great Britain, Greetings:
"We send our beloved Brother Wilford Woodruff to
England to take charge of all business transactions pertaining to The Church of Jesus Christ of Latter-day Saints,
both spiritual and temporal. We wish you to give diligent
heed to his counsel in all things, and as we have not the
opportunity of informing you of what has transpired this
season by letter, our beloved Brother will make known unto
you all things. We wish the brethren to be faithful and
diligent in keeping all the commandments of God, and in
hearkening to the counsels of those who are sent to counsel them. Let no man or set of men think they have power
or authority or the keys of the Kingdom above Apostle
Wilford Woodruff whom we send unto you to instruct you
in the things pertaining to life and salvation. Though our
Prophet be slain for the word of God and the testimony
of Jesus, yet the keys of the Kingdom remain in the Church
and the heavens are not closed, neither is the mouth of
the Almighty sealed up that He cannot speak. The God of
Israel will communicate to His disciples all things necessary for the building up of His Kingdom on the earth until

Israel is gathered, yea even all the blood of Abraham scattered over all the earth, Zion established, Jerusalem rebuilt, and the whole earth be filled with the glory and knowledge of God. We wish all the Saints in England to continue their gathering as usual to the land of America; and they may have the privilege of appointing a committee to visit the land of America to prepare a location for a settlement of the brethren from Europe according to their desire under the direction and counsel of Elder Wilford Woodruff; and further we would say unto the Saints in all the world that may be visited by Elder Wilford Woodruff that inasmuch as they will render him any assistance in his mission they will be doing the will of God and shall not lose their reward; and we desire that all Saints may use their efforts to sustain him in this important mission which he is called to fulfill by their faith, prayers, and brotherly love according to the grace of God; for he is qualified to teach in all things pertaining to the Church and Kingdom of God established in these last days. Therefore, dear brethren, we would say unto you in conclusion: be humble and faithful and hearken diligently unto the counsel of this our beloved brother in the Lord, Elder Wilford Woodruff, and the blessings of the Lord will attend you, in the name of Jesus Christ. Amen.

> BRIGHAM YOUNG,
> President of the Twelve.
> WILLARD RICHARDS,
> Clerk."

Elder Woodruff and his wife, with their two small children, departed from Nauvoo on August 28. After visiting their parents in Connecticut and Maine, they journeyed to New York City, where they went on board a "packet ship" on December 8. After a rough voyage of twenty-seven days, they landed in Liverpool.

This second mission to England was somewhat different than the first had been. Instead of doing individual missionary labor, at which he was preeminently successful, he found himself under the necessity of directing the efforts of others. This was no small task, as the membership of the Saints in the British Mission alone was eleven thousand, with fifteen hundred men holding the priesthood. But Wilford Woodruff was equal to his duties and proved to be an able executive. Every part of the work was built up and advanced during his administration. His release came from President Young in December, 1845, and with it the information that it was the intention of the Saints to remove from Nauvoo early in 1846 and seek out a favorable location, "somewhere west of the Rocky Mountains," where they could worship their God unmolested by mobs. Wilford completed the affairs of the mission as quickly as he could and departed from England on January 23, 1846. After visiting relatives in New England, he reached Nauvoo on April 23. President Young and most of the leaders of the Church had already departed for the West.

While Wilford remained in Nauvoo he held several meetings in the temple with those of the Saints who had been unable to leave. Finally, on May 26, he was ready to take his departure from his comfortable home, his farm, and his possessions, and begin his long journey into the wilderness. "I left the city of the Saints, feeling that I was most likely taking a final farewell of Nauvoo for this life," he related. "I looked back upon the Temple and city as they receded from view and asked the Lord to remember the sacrifices of His Saints."

The season of the year was wet and the journey across Iowa was difficult. There were no roads to follow—only trails in the soft mud made by those who had gone ahead. At one place in the journey, Wilford wrote, "I stopped my carriage on the top of a hill in the midst of a rolling prairie, where I had an extended view of all about me. I beheld the Saints coming in all directions from hills and dales, groves and prairies, with their wagons, flocks and herds, by the thousands. It looked like the movement of a nation."

Council Bluffs, the temporary halting place of the Saints, was finally reached on July 7. Here the brethren *1846* remained in camp about one month while the Mormon Battalion was organized and sent on its journey. Early in August it was decided that as many of the Saints as could possibly do so should cross the river and settle on the Indian lands where a winter settlement was to be formed, named Winter Quarters. This plan was carried out, and Wilford crossed the river and began to build a house to shelter his family An event occurred here which he relates as follows: "On the 15th day of October, 1846, while with the Camp of Israel building up Winter Quarters, on the west side of the Missouri River (then Indian country), I passed through one of the most painful and serious misfortunes of my life. I took my ax and went two and a half miles upon the bluff to cut some shingle timber to cover my cabin. I was accompanied by two men. While felling the third tree, I stepped back of it some eight feet, where I thought I was entirely out of danger. There was, however, a crook in the tree, which, when the tree fell, struck a knoll and caused the tree to bound endwise back of the stump. As it bounded backwards, the butt end of the tree hit me in the breast, and knocked me back and above the ground several feet, against a standing oak. The falling tree followed me in its bounds and severely crushed me against the standing tree. I fell to the ground, alighting upon my feet. My left thigh and hip were badly bruised, also my left arm; my breastbone and three ribs on my left side were broken. I was bruised about my lungs, vitals and left side in a serious manner. After the accident I sat upon a log while Mr. John Garrison went a quarter of a mile and got my horse. Notwithstanding I was so badly hurt, I had to mount my horse and ride two and a half miles over an exceedingly rough road. On account of severe pain I had to dismount twice on my way home. My breast and vitals were so badly injured that at each step of the horse pain went through me like an arrow. I continued on horseback until I arrived at Turkey Creek, on the north side of Winter Quarters. I was then exhausted, and was taken off the horse and carried in a chair to my wagon. I was met in the street by President Brigham Young, Heber C. Kimball, Willard Richards, and others, who assisted in carrying me to the wagon. Before placing me upon my bed they laid hands upon me, and in the name of the Lord rebuked the pain and distress, and said that I should live, and not die. I was then laid upon my bed in the wagon, as my cabin was not yet done. As the Apostles prophesied upon my head, so it came to pass; I did not die. I employed no physician, but was administered to by the elders of Israel, and nursed by my wife. I lay upon my bed, unable to move until my breastbone began to knit together on the ninth day. In about twenty days I began to walk, and in thirty days from the time I was hurt, I returned to my laborious employment."

It was a lonely winter that the Saints spent at Winter Quarters in 1846 and 1847. The cold was intense, and many of the inhabitants were still in their wagons, having been unable to build homes. The hardships caused much suffering and there were several hundred deaths, but the Saints were united and did all they could to assist each other. With the coming of warmer weather in February and March, President Young began preparations to lead a group of men into the western country to search out a permanent location for the Saints. This group, consisting of 143 men, three women, and two children, was ready early in April, and Wilford Woodruff was among the number.

Much has been written and said about the pioneer journey across the plains, and I shall not go into details here. It is perhaps sufficient to say that on July 24, 1847, President Young, riding in Wilford Woodruff's carriage, first viewed Salt Lake Valley and declared, "This is the right place." The brethren had been on the way three months and seventeen days. Of his entrance into the valley Wilford Woodruff recorded the following in his journal:

"We gazed with wonder and admiration upon the vast fertile valley spread out before us for about twenty-five miles in length and sixteen miles in width, clothed with a heavy garment of vegetation, and in the midst of which glistened the waters of the Great Salt Lake, with mountains all around towering to the skies, and streams, rivulets and creeks of pure water running through the beautiful valley.

"After a hard journey from Winter Quarters of more than one thousand miles, through flats of the Platte River and plateaus of the Black Hills and Rocky Mountains and over the burning sands and eternal sage regions, willow swails and rocky regions, to gaze upon a valley of such vast extent surrounded with a perfect chain of everlasting mountains covered with eternal snow, with their innumerable peaks like pyramids towering towards heaven, presented at one view to us the grandest scenery and prospect that we could have obtained on earth. Thoughts of pleasant meditation ran in rapid succession through our minds at the anticipation that not many years hence the House of God would be established in the mountains and exalted above the hills, while the valleys would be converted into orchards, vineyards, fields, etc., planted with cities, and the standard of Zion be unfurled, unto which the nations would gather."

During the short time that Elder Woodruff remained in the valley he and others explored the country as far west as Tooele Valley and as far south as Utah Lake. He also went to the canyons and hauled out logs with which to construct a home. There was no such thing as idleness in this man's life; wherever he went he pursued some useful labor with diligence. Work was the keystone of his successful career.

Elder Woodruff remained in Salt Lake Valley one month and two days and then, with a number of his brethren, began the weary return trip of one thousand miles to Winter Quarters. After an arduous journey the brethren arrived on the banks of the Missouri and were again united with their families on October 31.

V

The year 1848 witnessed a general exodus of the Saints westward from the Missouri River. Wilford Woodruff expected to make the journey with them, but before leaving President Young requested him to undertake a mission to the eastern states and visit the congregations of Latter-day Saints. Ever willing to do his duty as requested by those who presided over him, Wilford left Winter Quarters on June 21. His mission took him to Nauvoo, Chicago, Detroit, and Boston, where he arrived on August 12. During the fall and winter he visited the the branches of the Church in New England. The entire year of 1849 was spent in missionary labor in Canada and the eastern states. Early in 1850 he received word from the First Presidency to return home, and on the 9th of April took his departure from New York City with 209 members. After a long, wearisome journey, Elder Woodruff and his company arrived in Salt Lake City on October 14.

Salt Lake Valley in 1849 presented a different appearance than it did when Elder Woodruff first viewed it in July, 1847. There were now more than 5,000 inhabitants in the city and valley, and many improvements had taken place. Elder Woodruff completed his own home near the temple block and made his family as comfortable as possible. During the seventeen years that he had been a member of the Church he had lived an almost nomadic life, being driven from place to place. But henceforth, Salt Lake Valley was to be his permanent place of residence, although he still was to journey far and wide, in behalf of the Church, until the end of his long life.

In Salt Lake Valley Wilford resumed his customary activities as a member of the Twelve. Weekly meetings of this quorum were held and the affairs of the Church were discussed. In addition to this work he became a member of the territorial legislature. Early in 1851 he joined an expedition that was organized to visit the struggling settlements of the Saints in the southern part of the territory. Returning during the latter part of May, he worked with diligence on his own little farm south of the city. He received no salary from the Church and was under the necessity of supporting himself and family with the labor of his hands.

During the year 1852 Wilford was engaged in the work of building a meeting place for the Saints on the temple block; this structure became known as the Old Tabernacle. He also accompanied the First Presidency on a tour of the southern settlements.

As the new year of 1853 opened, Wilford recorded in his journal: "A new year in a new era! How time flies, and how wonderful, how magnificent are the events which are borne upon its wings! It is the opening of a dispensation that includes all the other dispensations since the world began. The events of the one thousand years past pale into insignificance compared with the work of the present time."

The first day of the year Wilford attended a party at the new Social Hall. On the 14th of February he was present when ground was broken for the Salt Lake Temple. During the fall of the year Wilford, together with Ezra T. Benson, led a colony of Saints to Tooele Valley.

In the summer of 1854, Elder Woodruff accompanied a number of the Twelve on a tour of the southern settlements. When he returned he harvested the crop of his farm which he reports as 369 bushels of wheat, 400 bushels of potatoes, and 200 bushels of corn. In 1855 he called a group of interested people together at the Social Hall and organized a horticultural society, which was to promote the growing of fruit in the Territory. Constantly he labored at every task which would promote the welfare of the Saints in the valleys.

On March 1, 1857, Wilford Woodruff celebrated his fiftieth birthday. On this day he could look back over a well-spent life, filled with truly great accomplishments. On July 24 he was in attendance at a pioneer celebration at Silver Lake, Big Cottonwood Canyon, when word was brought that an army was on its way to Utah, with a new governor to replace Brigham Young. From this time on until June of the following year, Elder Woodruff was extremely busy, attending council meetings with his brethren and making preparations for the Saints to defend themselves against the army. He was indeed pleased when he learned that the army had decided to make camp for the winter at Fort Bridger. In the spring of 1858 Wilford joined the Saints in the move south. He and his family were in Provo when word came that General Johnston had marched his soldiers through Salt Lake Valley and made camp at Cedar Fort. Wilford now returned to Salt Lake City and resumed his customary activities. In the fall he was made president of the Deseret Agricultural and Manufacturing Society.

On March 1, 1860, Elder Woodruff recorded the following in his journal: "I am fifty-three years old today. I feel sensitive when I look upon these years and see how truly short life is—like a weaver's shuttle, it soon passes. Man should strive diligently to make his life useful. He should speak the truth, live honestly, practice virtue and set an example in all things worthy of imitation."

On March 4, 1861, he makes note of the inauguration of President Abraham Lincoln: "President Lincoln's enemies declared that he would never sleep in the White House. . . . Many of the people of the Nation have persecuted the Saints of God, and they now have trouble of their own. The rulers in the nation and states did nothing for us."

In May, 1861, Elder Woodruff undertook a journey to the southern settlements with President Brigham Young and a number of the leading brethren. While he was away from the city his aged father, Aphek Woodruff, passed away. He had been baptized by his son in 1839.

In his *Life of Wilford Woodruff*, Matthias F. Cowley
makes a few comments regarding the activities of Brother
Woodruff during the year 1862.

"It is wonderful how Wilford Woodruff busied himself in a multitude of occupations. His journal furnishes
evidence of a remarkably busy life. One moment he was
recording stirring events in the history of the world; then
he is writing Church History; the next moment tells something of a correspondence received from those who desire
information concerning the Latter-day Saints. The next page
contains an account of his orchard and the work of plant-
ing more fruit trees; later he is found in the irrigation fur-
rows; then he is addressing missionaries upon their duties
and responsibilities; on the same page he opens a prophetic
inspiration of his soul and tells of things to come. In all
he sees the glory and goodness of God. He listens to the
words of the Prophet and makes careful record of them.
Then he discourses upon the principles of a free government and the rights of a people under a constitution."

On January 1, 1864, Elder Woodruff recorded in his
journal, "I have lived to see fifty-six new years, and I have
kept a daily journal of my life for the last thirty-five years.
In some measure it has also been the life of others."

During the years 1865 and 1866 Elder Woodruff continued his usual activities in the valleys. In 1867 he attended the sessions of the general conference held in the new
Tabernacle. "This conference was one of unusual interest to
the Saints. Between eight and ten thousand people met to
honor the occasion. The organ was not quite completed. It
was designed to have two thousand pipes, but then had
only seven hundred and fifty."

In 1868 Elder Woodruff moved to Provo, in response
to a call from President Young. Here he continued to take
an active part in all the affairs of the city and Church.

He seemed to be interested in every phase of human
activity. "We find him," writes Elder Cowley, "grubbing
willows, breaking land, digging ditches, constructing roads,

barns, and homes. He was indeed a model of industry. All honorable work was God's work, whether he dug a ditch, preached a sermon or wrote a history."

At the October conference held at Salt Lake City in 1868, Elder Woodruff recorded, "This is the first time in thirty-two years that all of the Quroum of the Twelve have been together. The last time before this was at the home of Elder Heber C. Kimball in Kirtland." This meeting referred to was held in the year 1836. It does speak for the diligence of this Quorum that some of its members had been away from headquarters engaged in missionary work during all that time.

On July 24, 1869, after a Pioneer Day celebration at Salt Lake City, Elder Woodruff recorded the following in his journal: "Twenty-two years ago today I drove the team which brought President Brigham Young from Emigration Canyon to this city. He lay upon a bed sick, in my carriage. As soon as his eyes rested upon the beautiful, yet desert scene of the valley before us, he said: 'This is the place; for the Lord has shown it to me in a vision.' We now number more than a hundred thousand souls. See what God hath wrought."

On January 10, 1870, Elder Woodruff was present when the Utah Central Railway was completed from Ogden to Salt Lake City. He writes, "This is a great day in Utah. Some twelve or fifteen thousand people of the city and surrounding country, men, women and children, assembled around the railroad depot to celebrate the completion of the Utah Central Railway, and to see the last rail laid and the last spike driven by President Young." The days of the long journey across the plains by ox team, on horseback, or on foot, were over forever.

In 1871 Elder Woodruff, now sixty-four years of age, purchased a ranch at Randolph in Rich County, where he established a home. He subsequently spent several summers there, enjoying himself in harvesting hay and in getting wood from the canyons. Nothing pleased him more than to do a good day's work with his hands.

The years of 1872 to 1875 were spent by Elder Woodruff in his usual activities, visiting the wards and stakes, looking after his farms and ranches, and meeting with brethren in council at home. On September 1, 1875, he recorded the death of his dear friend and associate, George A. Smith. "Time and death are thinning the ranks of the First Presidency, the Twelve Apostles and the first Elders of the Church. No man has ever lived in this Church who has left a cleaner and brighter record for both time and eternity than the Apostle George A. Smith."

The same year, in October, he wrote of the visit of the president of the United States, U. S. Grant, to Ogden and Salt Lake City. It was the first time he had ever seen a president of this country. He had the opportunity of being a member of the party that welcomed the distinguished visitor to the territory.

In the fall of 1876 Elder Woodruff accompanied President Young and party to Saint George. It was the intention of the brethren to remain throughout the winter and attend the dedicatory ceremonies of the St. George Temple, which was nearing completion. On January 1, 1877, the lower portion of the building, including the font, was dedicated by Elder Woodruff. "We are this day blessed with the privilege which very few since the days of Adam have enjoyed," he said. "We assemble in a Temple built by the commandment of the Lord for the salvation of the human family. We have met to dedicate certain portions of this building." Following a few remarks, Elder Woodruff offered a lengthy prayer in which he beautifully expressed the gratitude of the Saints for the privilege of building and working in this temple.

On March 1, 1877, while still at St. George, Elder Woodruff celebrated his seventieth birthday.

Early in April the general conference of the Church convened at St. George, and Elder Woodruff was called to

1877

preside over the St. George Temple. He was engaged in this activity when he learned of the death of President Brigham Young, which occurred on the 29th day of August, 1877.

After the death of President Young, Elder Woodruff again made his residence in Salt Lake City, where he participated in the council meetings of the Twelve. The First Presidency was not reorganized for several years. It was at this time that the federal officials made a determined effort to end the practice of polygamy, and it was necessary for Elder Woodruff to go into exile. He recorded in his journal: "This is the first time in my life I have had to flee from my enemies for the gospel's sake, or for any other cause." During 1879 he spent some months in visiting the Saints in Southern Utah and Arizona. He also called upon the Indian tribes and labored among them as a missionary. He slept out-of-doors, worked in the fields, chopped wood, dressed buckskin, or did whatever was required to aid and assist the people. On April 2, 1880, he was back in Salt Lake City and attended the annual conference of the Church. At the October conference the same year, John Taylor was named as President of the Church and Wilford Woodruff as president of the Quorum of Twelve.

Oct 1880

As president of the Quorum of Twelve it was now Elder Woodruff's duties to direct the activities of his brethren. In this capacity he no doubt should have remained in Salt Lake City, but on account of the Edmunds law passed by Congress in 1882, which again attacked the practice of polygamy and provided severe penalties for those who would not abandon the doctrine, President Woodruff was again forced to leave his home. He visited the stakes and settlements of the Saints in Southern Utah, Eastern Utah, Nevada, and Arizona. Many of the leading brethren of the Church were apprehended and forced to serve terms in the penitentiary, but Elder Woodruff was fortunate in evading arrest. He went about his duties quietly and was ministered to and protected by the Saints.

VI

On July 26, 1887, Elder Woodruff was at Fayette, Sanpete County, when he learned of the death of President John Taylor at Kaysville, Utah. In his journal he wrote at this time: "President Taylor's death places the chief responsibility and care of the Church of Latter-day Saints upon my shoulders, in connection with the Twelve, which now become the Presiding authority of the Church. This places me in a very peculiar situation. It is a position I have never looked for, but in the Providence of God this new responsibility is thrown upon me. I pray God my Heavenly Father to give me grace equal to my day. It is a high responsibility for any man and it is a position which requires great wisdom. I never expected to outlive President Taylor, but God has ordained otherwise. . . . I can only say, marvelous are Thy ways, O Lord Almighty, for Thou hast truly chosen weak instruments to perform in Thy hand Thy work on earth. May Thy servant Wilford be prepared for whatever is required at his hands by the God of Heaven. I ask this blessing of my Heavenly Father, in the name of Jesus Christ, the Son of the living God, even so, Amen."

And so this faithful and diligent missionary, who sought only to go his way and do the will of God humbly and sincerely, stood at last, after a long and useful life, at the head of a great religious people. He had been tried and tested and weighed in the balance, and he had not been found wanting.

Arriving in Salt Lake City, President Woodruff was unable to attend the funeral of President John Taylor or to appear at any public meetings, as he was still subject to arrest in the anti-polygamy crusade. However, he kept closely in touch with his brethren of the Twelve and performed his duties as best he could, under difficult and trying circumstances.

Apr 1889

At the April conference in 1889 Wilford Woodruff was sustained as President of the Church, with George Q. Cannon and Joseph F. Smith as his counselors. On the day this action was taken, President Woodruff recorded the following in his journal: "This 7th day of April, 1889, is one of the most important days in my life, for I was made President of the Church of Jesus Christ of Latter-day Saints, by the unanimous vote of ten thousand of them. The vote was taken by quorums and then by the entire congregation, as in the case of President John Taylor. This is the highest office ever conferred upon any man in the flesh. It came to me in the eighty-third year of my life. I pray God to protect me and give me power to magnify my calling to the end of my days. The Lord has watched over me until the present time."

During the years 1889 and 1890 there was no relaxation on the part of the federal government to suppress polygamy. The persecution that the Saints had suffered for this principle had been very severe. In the fall of 1890, President Woodruff came to the conclusion that the time had come for him to advise the Saints "to refrain from contracting any marriage forbidden by the law of the land." On September 25, he recorded in his journal:

"I have arrived at a point in the history of my life, as the President of the Church of Jesus Christ of Latter-day Saints, when I am under the necessity of acting for the temporal salvation of the Church. The United States government has taken a stand and passed laws to destroy the Latter-day Saints on the subject of polygamy or patriarchal marriage, and after praying to the Lord and feeling inspired, I have issued the following proclamation which is sustained by my counselors and the Twelve Apostles." Hereafter follows the official declaration, known as "The Manifesto," in which the Saints were advised to "refrain from contracting any marriage forbidden by the law of the land."

The issuance of the Manifesto was probably the most important act in the long career of President Woodruff. It brought relief from persecution and left the Saints free to go forward with the great work of preaching the gospel and establishing the kingdom.

In a sermon delivered at Logan, on November 1, 1891, President Woodruff further clarified his position in regard to this important issue.

"The Lord showed me by vision and revelation exactly what would take place if we did not stop this practice. . . . I know there are a good many men, and probably some leading men in this Church, who have been tried and felt as though President Woodruff had lost the Spirit of God and was about to apostatize. Now I want you to understand that he has not lost the spirit nor is he about to apostatize. The Lord is with him, and with this people. He has told me exactly what to do, and what the result would be if we did not do it. . . . I want to say this; I should have let all the Temples go out of our hands, I should have gone to prison myself, and let every other man go there, had not the God of Heaven commanded me to do what I did do; and when the hour came that I was commanded to do that, it was all clear to me."

Another important accomplishment during the administration of President Woodruff was the dedication of the Salt Lake Temple on April 6, 1893. As previously recorded here, the work on the construction of this building had been begun by President Brigham Young in 1853, forty years previously. It had been a heavy task for the Saints to construct this great temple by the donation of labor, material, and money; but at last they had been successful, and the beautiful and imposing structure, a monument to their faith and fidelity, was completed. The aged President offered the dedicatory prayer. On that day he wrote in his journal: "I attended the dedication of the temple. The spirit and power of God rested upon us. The spirit of prophecy and revelation was upon us and the hearts of the people were melted and many things were unfolded to our understanding."

Among the remarks made by President Woodruff at the dedication of the temple were the following: "That from this time on the power of the adversary would be broken; that the enemy would have less power over the Saints and meet with greater failures in oppressing them; that a renewed interest in the gospel message would be awakened throughout the world."

In the fall of 1893 President Woodruff, although now in his eighty-sixth year, took an extended trip to the East with a group of his brethren. Denver, Kansas City, Independence, and Chicago were visited. At Independence he recorded the following: "I went through Jackson County with Harry Brown in 1834 on a mission to the Southern states. At that time we traveled secretly lest our lives should be taken by the mobocrats; now in 1893 the mayor of Independence and hosts of others bid us welcome to the city. How great the contrast, and we ascribe the honor and praise to God our Heavenly Father."

In 1896 statehood was granted to Utah by the United States government. "I feel thankful to God," wrote President Woodruff, "that I have lived to see Utah admitted into the family of states. It is an event that we have looked forward to for a generation."

One of the most important events of President Woodruff's long life was the celebration of his ninetieth birthday on March 1, 1897. On that occasion thousands of Latter-day Saints gathered in the Salt Lake Tabernacle to do him honor. Appropriate remarks were made by his counselors and others of the General Authorities. A silver mounted cane was presented to him by temple workers. The vast congregation sang "We Thank Thee, O God, for a Prophet." On returning to his home President Woodruff recorded his impressions of the day in his journal. "The scene completely overpowered me. The events of my childhood and early manhood came to my mind. I remembered vividly how I prayed to the Lord that I might live to see a Prophet or an Apostle who would teach me the gospel of Christ.

Here I stood in the great Tabernacle filled with ten thousand children, with Prophets, Apostles and Saints. My head
was a fountain of tears. Still I addressed the mighty congregation."

During the week beginning July 20, 1897, there was
a great celebration in Salt Lake City, commemorating the
fiftieth anniversary of the arrival of the pioneers in Salt
Lake Valley. President Woodruff took a prominent part in
this celebration. At the mammoth parade on July 24 he
rode in the first carriage.

In the latter part of 1897 and the early months of 1898
President Woodruff began to fail noticeably in health. Yet
he was able to attend the conferences of the Church in the
Tabernacle and to make a few remarks as occasion required.
In August, 1898, he went with a group of friends to San
Francisco, in order to enjoy a change of climate. It was
while there, at the home of Colonel Isaac Trumbo, that
he passed away on the morning of September 2. George
Q. Cannon, who was with him at the time, recorded the
event:

"I arose about 6 o'clock. The nurse told me he had
been sleeping in the same position all the time. I took
hold of his wrist, felt his pulse, and I could feel that it
was very faint. While I stood there it grew fainter and
fainter until it faded entirely. His head, his hands, and
his feet were warm and his appearance was that of a person
sleeping sweetly and quietly. There was not a quiver of a
muscle nor a movement of his limbs or face; thus he passed
away."

The body of the deceased leader was conveyed to
Utah in a special car attached to a Southern Pacific train.
Church officials, together with members of the President's
family, met the train at Ogden on September 4 and ac-
companied the remains of the President to his home in Salt
Lake City.

The funeral was held in the Tabernacle on Thursday,
September 8, at 10 A.M. Before that hour the great build-

ing was filled to capacity, with Saints and friends who had come to do honor to one who was universally respected and loved. The counselors to the President, George Q. Cannon and Joseph F. Smith, together with others of the leading brethren, paid elegant tributes to the deceased. And when the sun departed over the western hills that autumn evening, the body of Wilford Woodruff, one of the great leaders of Israel, rested peacefully in the soil of the valley that he had first viewed, over fifty-one years previously, with the original group of Mormon pioneers.

VII

A brief synopsis of George Q. Cannon's sermon at the funeral of President Woodruff follows:

"In the passing of President Woodruff, a man has gone from our midst whose character was probably as angelical as that of any person who has ever lived upon the earth. We shall ever miss him. His family will ever miss him, as to them he was the all in all, an honored and respected husband and father.

"In the death of such men it is a consolation to know that they have left behind them the keys of the Priesthood which they held, thus permitting the rolling on of the work of God. President Woodruff was an unassuming man, very unaffected and childlike in his demands. He did no man an injury, nor was he too proud, even in his Apostolic calling, to toil as other men toiled. His traits and characteristics were enobling, and so energetic was he, that nothing was too burdensome for him even in his advanced years. He was of a sweet diposition and possessed a character so lovely as to draw unto him friends in every walk of life. He was straightforward in all his dealings with his fellowmen and never shirked an obligation. He was free, sociable and amiable in every respect. No jealousy lurked in his bosom. He looked upon all mankind as his equals and was one who cherished the most profound respect for all with whom he associated. He was gentle as a woman and his purity was like unto that of the angels themselves. In spite of his high and holy calling, he displayed no dignity; and was unpretentious, unassuming and his character and life were as transparent as glass. He hid nothing from his brethren, but was candid, outspoken and free to all.

"In his office one morning he remarked, 'I am growing old,' the statement being occasioned through the greater ability of a strong wiry grandson in hoeing potatoes. So industrious was President Woodruff, that he felt he was growing old because those stronger and younger could outdo him in cultivating the garden. For years he lived on his 20-acre farm and took pleasure in beautifying his surroundings and wresting from the earth the elements to sustain life.

"In the ministry President Woodruff has accomplished a great deal. He has traveled thousands of miles, preached the Gospel to thousands of people, and succeeded in bringing a great many into the Church. He left behind him a monument for good that time cannot efface or obliterate.

"President Woodruff was a man of God. He has finished the fight and has been called hence to mingle with his brethren and receive his well-earned reward. He was a heavenly being. It was heaven to be in his company, and his departure from this sphere of action, robs the community of a great and good man, and one who fully merited all the blessings promised to those who remain true and steadfast to the end."

LORENZO SNOW

LORENZO SNOW

(1814-1901)

O N September 13, 1898, eleven days after the death of President Wilford Woodruff, the Quorum of Twelve Apostles met in Salt Lake City and sustained Lorenzo Snow as the President of The Church of Jesus Christ of Latter-day Saints. President Snow chose as his counselors George Q. Cannon and Joseph F. Smith, the same men who had served with the two previous presidents. Three weeks later, at the semiannual general conference in October, President Snow was unanimously sustained in his high position by the great assembly of Latter-day Saints present on that occasion.

When this great honor and responsibility came to President Snow, he had arrived at an age when most men have long since retired from the active affairs of life. On the previous April 3 he had passed his eighty-fourth birthday, but he was still mentally and spiritually alert and able to carry on with his arduous duties.

It will be interesting here to follow the path that Lorenzo Snow pursued during his long and active life that led finally to his exalted position.

Lorenzo was the fifth child and first son of Oliver and Rosetta Snow, pioneers of Ohio, who had left the New England states in the early part of the nineteenth century and sought a new home in the West. We are informed that when they first settled in the township where the village

of Mantua was formed, only eleven families had preceded
them. It was here at Mantua, Ohio, that Lorenzo Snow was
born on April 3, 1814.

Of the youth of the boy we know but little, except that
he was a faithful and dutiful child. His sister, Eliza R.
Snow, informs us of a few of his early traits and advantages:

"Although a farmer by occupation, my father was
much abroad on public business, and Lorenzo, being the eldest of three brothers, was left in charge, and early in life
became accustomed to responsibilities, which he discharged
with scrupulous punctuality and that inflexibility of purpose
which insures success; and from early childhood exhibited
the energy and decision of character which have marked his
progress in subsequent life. An unseen hand evidently was
guiding him, for in his boyhood he was energetically, yet
unconsciously, preparing for the position in life he was
destined to occupy. Ever a student, at home as well as
in school, (most of his schooling after his twelfth year was
during the winter terms) his book was his constant companion, and when sought by his associates, 'hid up with his
book' became proverbial. With the exception of one term in
a High School in Ravenna, Ohio, also a special term of
tuition under a Hebrew professor, he completed his scho-
lastic training in Oberlin College, which at that time was
exclusively a Presbyterian institution."

It was while on his way to Oberlin College that Lorenzo fell in company with a traveler named David W. Patten,
a missionary of The Church of Jesus Christ of Latter-day
Saints and one of the original Quorum of Twelve Apostles.
The conversation naturally turned to religion, and the impression that Elder Patten made on Lorenzo's mind at that
time was not to be erased in later years.

Meantime, Eliza, Lorenzo's older sister, had joined the
Church and moved to Kirtland. She wrote to her brother
inviting him to visit her and attend a Hebrew school that
was being opened in Kirtland for members of the Church.
Lorenzo accepted the invitation and in a short time he had

formed an intimate acquaintance with the Prophet Joseph Smith and other leaders of the Church. It was not long until he became a believer in the newly revealed gospel. His own words beautifully describe his conversion:

"I was baptized by Elder John Boynton, then one of the Twelve Apostles, June, 1836, at Kirtland, Ohio. Previous to accepting the ordinance of baptism, in my investigations of the principles taught by the Latter-day Saints, which I proved by comparison to be the same as those mentioned in the New Testament taught by Christ and His Apostles, I was thoroughly convinced that obedience to those principles would impart miraculous powers, manifestations and revelations. With sanguine expectation of this result, I received baptism and the ordinance of laying on of hands by one who professed to have divine authority; and having thus yielded obedience to these ordinances, I was in constant expectation of the fulfillment of the promise of the reception of the Holy Ghost. The manifestation did not immediately follow my baptism as I had expected, but although the time was deferred, when I did receive it, its realization was more perfect, tangible and miraculous than even my strongest hopes had led me to anticipate.

"Some two or three weeks after I was baptized, one day while engaged in my studies, I began to reflect upon the fact that I had not obtained a knowledge of the truth of the work—that I had not realized the fulfillment of that promise, 'he that doeth my will shall know of the doctrine,' and I began to feel very uneasy. I laid aside my books, left the house, and wandered around through the fields under the oppressive influence of a gloomy, disconsolate spirit, while an indescribable cloud of darkness seemed to envelop me. I had been accustomed, at the close of day, to retire for secret prayer, to a grove a short distance from my lodgings, but at this time I felt no inclination to do so. The spirit of prayer had departed and the heavens seemed like brass over my head. At length, realizing that the usual time had come for secret prayer,

I concluded I would not forgo my evening service, and, as a matter of formality, knelt as I was in the habit of doing, and in my accustomed, retired place, but not feeling as I was wont to feel.

"I had no sooner opened my lips in an effort to pray, than I heard a sound, just above my head, like the rustling of silken robes, and immediately the spirit of God descended upon me, completely enveloping my whole person, filling me from the crown of my head to the soles of my feet, and O the joy and happiness I felt! No language can describe the almost instantaneous transition from a dense cloud of mental and spiritual darkness into a refulgence of light and knowledge, that God lives, that Jesus Christ is the Son of God, and of the restoration of the Holy Priesthood, and the fullness of the Gospel. It was a complete baptism—a tangible immersion in the heavenly principle or element, the Holy Ghost; and even more real and physical in its effects upon every party of my system than the immersion by water; dispelling forever, so long as reason and memory last, all possibility of doubt or fear in relation to the fact handed down to us historically that the 'babe of Bethlehem' is truly the Son of God; also the fact that He is now being revealed to the children of men, and communicating knowledge, the same as in the apostolic times. I was perfectly satisfied, as well I might be, for my expectations were more than realized; I think I may safely say, in an infinite degree.

"I cannot tell how long I remained in the full flow of the blissful enjoyment and divine enlightenment, but it was several minutes before the celestial element which filled and surrounded me began gradually to withdraw. On arising from my kneeling posture, with my heart swelling with gratitude to God, beyond the power of expression, I felt—I knew that he had conferred on me what only an omnipotent being can confer—that which is of greater value than all the wealth and honors worlds can bestow. That night as I retired to rest, the same wonderful manifestations were repeated, and continued to be for several suc-

cessive nights. The sweet remembrance of those glorious
experiences, from that time to the present, brings them fresh
before me, imparting an inspiring influence which pervades
my whole being, and I trust will to the close of my earthly
existence."

This baptism by the Spirit constituted a complete conversion to Lorenzo Snow. Thereafter he spent over sixty
active years in the service of the Church.

While still at Kirtland, in the spring of 1837, Lorenzo
was called to undertake a short mission to Ohio. He traveled "without purse or scrip," which was a new and rather
difficult experience for him, as he had always had sufficient
means to pay his own way. But he went forward humbly
and accomplished his tasks.

Returning to Kirtland and finding much disaffection
among the Saints, Lorenzo, with his family, including his
father and mother, brothers and sisters, decided to migrate
to Missouri and join the members of the Church who had
settled there. This was a long and tedious journey of one
thousand miles and occupied the greater part of the summer of 1838. Arriving at Far West, Lorenzo was very ill
with a fever and remained in that condition for several
weeks. He was nursed back to health and life by his faithful sister Eliza.

As soon as he regained his health, in the late fall of
1838, Lorenzo undertook his second mission, this time to
southern Illinois and Kentucky. The first part of the journey
was made by floating down the Missouri River on a raft,
which was a dangerous and hazardous undertaking. Afterwards Lorenzo and his companion walked from town to
town through the snow and cold, but everywhere he labored unceasingly to proclaim the gospel message.

In February, 1839, Elder Snow decided to leave Kentucky and pay a visit to his old home in Ohio. The following from his journal well describes his difficulties at the
time: "On the last of February, 1839, I left the State of
Kentucky with one dollar and twenty-five cents in my

pocket, to visit my former home in Ohio, and to settle up
some unfinished business, having received by letter from
my sister Eliza, the news of the expulsion of our people
from Missouri. The distance of the journey before me was
about five hundred miles, and in the worst season of the
year for traveling, and at a time when very little interest
was felt by the people for Gospel truths, and few opportunities afforded for public preaching. The trip was a tedious
one—on foot and in the midst of snow and rainstorms—
sometimes, hard, frozen ground—sometimes mud and water
soaking through my boots until my socks were wringing wet
at night, and of course, hard and stiff in the morning, when
I was fortunate enough to get them dry. It was a hard pull,
but I accomplished the feat, and worn out by fatigue and
exposure, I arrived among my friends in Ohio. The first
place I reached was Brother Smith's, where one year before I had performed missionary labors, preached and baptized, and at his house made my home. Fatigue and its
consequences had so changed my appearance that at first
Brother Smith and family did not recognize me. As soon
as recognized, and my condition known, every attention
was extended that kindness could suggest, and everything
done for my comfort that warm hearts and willing hands
could bestow. Then came a reaction of the overstraining
of my physical powers, and with a burning fever, I was
confined to my bed, and for days remained in a prostrate
condition, when, through the kind ministrations of my friends
and the blessings of God in the manifestations of His power,
I soon recovered and resumed my missionary labors."

Elder Snow continued his missionary work in Ohio
until the fall of 1839, when he engaged as a schoolteacher
at Shalersville, during the winter of 1839 and 1840. Meantime the Saints had been driven out of Missouri, and with
them the family of Elder Snow. They had now located
at Nauvoo, Illinois, and in May, 1840, Elder Snow set out
to join them. After an absence of eighteen months, he was
happy to again meet with his parents and brothers and
sisters.

Shortly after his arrival in Nauvoo, and while visiting at the home of Elder H. G. Sherwood, Lorenzo relates that the conversation turned to religious matters. "Elder Sherwood was endeavoring to explain the parable of the Savior when speaking of the husbandman who hired servants and sent them forth at different hours of the day to labor in his vineyard." While Lorenzo listened closely to the explanation, "the Spirit of the Lord rested mightily upon me—the eyes of my understanding were opened, and I saw as clear as the sun at noon-day, with wonder and astonishment, the pathway of God and man. I formed the following couplet which expresses the revelation as it was shown to me:

"'As man now is, God once was,
As God now is, man may become.'"

II

In the spring of 1840, Elder Snow received a call from the presidency of the Church to undertake a mission to England. He readily responded to this call and left home the latter part of May. He then proceeded by stage, boat, and on foot to New York City. He describes his voyage across the ocean as follows: "I took steerage passage on board a sailing vessel, having supplied myself with blanket, buffalo robe, and a supply of provisions. I had heard tell of deck passage, but when I experienced deck passage, with its peculiar make-up, on this voyage, I could truly say, with the Queen of Sheba, 'the half has not been told,' and I felt assured that the other half never could be told. And, after all, the almost unbearable discomfort I experienced on the voyage was not attributable particularly to deck passage, but to the unpleasant peculiarities of the situation. I was surrounded with a huddled crowd of rough, uncouth people, very filthy in their appearance and habits. We had a long passage of about six weeks, in which we encountered

storms and tempests and suffered much for want of fresh
water and also a sufficient supply of food."

Arriving in England, Elder Snow was happy to meet
with Brigham Young, Heber C. Kimball, Parley P. Pratt,
and other leading brethren. Nine of the Quorum of Twelve
Apostles were laboring in the British Isles at the time. After a short visit in Manchester and Birmingham, Elder Snow
was appointed to preside over the members of the Church
in London.

I can give only a brief account here of Elder Snow's
splendid missionary labors in the British Mission. But his
experiences were interesting and varied, and he led many
earnest seekers for truth into the waters of baptism. Six
months after his arrival in London he was able to report:
"When I took charge of this conference we numbered less
than one hundred members; since then we have increased
to two hundred and twenty." One year later he was able
to report to the president of the European Mission, Parley
P. Pratt, that the membership of the London Conference
had increased to four hundred. This increase was no doubt
due in part to the splendid leadership and faithful labors
of Elder Lorenzo Snow.

Having been released from his mission, Elder Snow
departed from Europe in January, 1843. The long voyage
homeward took him to New Orleans and thence up the
Mississippi by river steamer to Nauvoo, where he arrived on
April 12. Among those who greeted him at the wharf were
the Prophet Joseph Smith and Elder Snow's sister, Eliza
R. Snow.

The summer of 1843 was spent in visiting relatives
and friends in Illinois and Ohio. In the fall he secured a
position as a schoolteacher at Lima, Illinois, a settlement
thirty miles from Nauvoo. He was engaged in this work
when he received a call from the presidency of the Church
to undertake a mission to Ohio, in the spring of 1844. His
work was to distribute among the people the Prophet's
"Views of the Powers and Policy of the Government of

the United States," and to preach the gospel wherever opportunity afforded. He was in the city of Cincinnati, engaged in this labor, when he learned of the death of the
Prophet at Carthage, Illinois, on the 27th of June. He at
once secured a horse and buggy and returned to Nauvoo.

During the year 1845, Lorenzo was engaged in work
on the Nauvoo Temple and in preparing for the great
move westward. About the middle of February, 1846, with
what wagons and livestock he was able to secure, he
crossed the Mississippi River and joined the Saints in their
journey across Iowa to Council Bluffs. Before reaching
the Bluffs a settlement was formed at a place called Mt.
Pisgah, and a few of the Saints who were unable to continue the journey were instructed to remain there during
the winter. Elder Snow was called to preside over this
settlement. In the spring of 1848 he resumed his journey
across the plains, and after many trying and difficult experiences he arrived in Salt Lake Valley.

III

On February 12, 1849, at Salt Lake City, Lorenzo
was asked to attend a meeting of the Quorum of Twelve
Apostles, and greatly to his surprise he was informed that
he had been selected to become a member of that body.
He was also informed that this appointment had come to
him as a result of his faithfulness and devotion, and that
he would now be called upon to assume greater responsibilities in the Church. He had not long to wait for this
promise to be fulfilled. At the October conference, in 1849,
Elder Snow was selected to carry the gospel message to
the nation of Italy. This call came as a great surprise to
him, and it was difficult for him to leave, as he had a large
family to care for and to provide with the necessities of
life. But he was not a man to shirk his duty when his
church required his services. With less than two weeks prep-

aration, he joined a number of his brethren in the weary trip across the plains eastward, in a very inclement season of the year. Following are a few paragraphs from his journey regarding his adventures at this time:

"Some persons feared that our horses were too enfeebled to bear us over the mighty plains; but when the snows began to fall, winds swept our pathway, and enabled us to pass without difficulty, while on our right and left the country was deeply covered for hundreds of miles.

"One day as we were taking our noontide meal, and our horses were quietly grazing on the prairie, a startling call resounded through our little camp, 'To arms, to arms, the Indians are upon us.' All eyes were turned in the direction, and we beheld a spectacle, grand, imposing and frightful. Two hundred warriors, upon their furious steeds, painted, armed and clothed with all the horrors of war, rushed towards us like a mighty torrent. In a moment we placed ourselves in an attitude of defense. But could we expect, with thirty men, to withstand this powerful host? Onward rushed the savage band with accelerated speed as a huge rock, loosened from the mountain's brow, dashes impetuously downward, sweeping and overturning and burying in its course.

"We saw it was their intention to crush us beneath the feet of the foaming chargers. They approached within a few paces, and in another moment we should be overwhelmed, when lo, an alarm like an electric shock struck through their ranks and stayed their career, as an avalanche, sweeping down the mountain side, stops in the midst of its course by a hand unseen. The Lord had said, 'Touch not mine anointed, and do my prophets no harm.' "

Oh, is not faith in a living God a beautiful thing? It is the highest attainment of the mind of man. But the brethren were to witness still other miraculous events.

"When we arrived on the banks of the great Missouri, her waters immediately congealed for the first time during the season, thus forming a bridge over which we passed to the other side; this was no sooner accomplished than the torrent ran as before."

The missionaries visited for a few days with the Saints who still resided at Kanesville; they then pursued their way eastward. Elder Snow was particularly interested in the appearance of Mt. Pisgah, Garden Grove, and Nauvoo. In the latter city he noted that "the moss was growing upon the buildings, which were fast crumbling down; the windows were broken in; the doors were shaking to and fro by the wind, as they played upon their rusty creaking hinges. The lovely Temple of our God—once the admiration and astonishment of the world and the hope of the Saints, was burned, and its blackened walls were falling upon each other."

From Nauvoo, Elder Snow continued his journey by boat to St. Louis, and thence eastward to New York City. On the 25th of March he sailed for England on the ship Shannon, and on the 19th of April, six months after he had left his home in Salt Lake City, arrived in Liverpool.

Elder Snow remained in England until the 15th of June. During his visit there he made a tour of the larger cities, where there were thriving branches of the Church, and was financially assisted by the members who were interested in his mission to Italy. "Presidents, officers and members," he relates, "received me with kindness and contributed liberally towards my mission, and while I have not had the opportunity of visiting Cambria's hills, the Welsh brethren have sent donations with all the nobility of soul which gives unsolicited."

Thus Elder Snow was enabled to continue his journey. He arrived in Italy sometime during July and located in the city of Genoa. The manners, customs and habits of the Italian people were all strange to him, and he was unacquainted with the language. The religion of the country was almost completely Catholic, and economic conditions were languishing. For a time Elder Snow was unable to find a single opening where the light of the gospel could penetrate. In a letter written at this time he records his reflections as follows: "I am alone and a stranger in this great city . . . eight thousand miles from my beloved family, surrounded by a people with whose manners and peculiarities I am unacquainted. I have come to enlighten their minds and instruct them in the principles of righteousness; but I see no possible means of accomplishing this object. All is darkness in the prospect." In the same letter Elder Snow records a beautiful prayer in behalf of the Italian people and for his own success in proselyting among them: "I ask God my Heavenly Father to look upon this people in mercy. Oh Lord, let them become the objects of Thy compassion, that they may not all perish. Forgive their sins, and let me be known among them, that they may know Thee, and know that Thou hast sent me to establish Thy Kingdom. They do wickedly all the day long and are guilty of many abominations. They have turned their backs upon Thee, though they kneel before the image of Thy Son, and decorate Temples to Thy worship. The priests, the rulers and the people have all gone astray, and have forgotten Thee, the Lord their God. But wilt thou not have mercy upon them? Thou knowest that I bade a heart-trying farewell to the loved and tried partners of my bosom, to obey Thy call; and hast Thou not some chosen ones among this people to whom I have been sent? Lead me unto such, and Thy name shall have the glory, through Jesus, Thy Son."

I do not have space in this short sketch to go into detail regarding this Italian mission, but it is interesting to note that Elder Snow did find a place in Italy where "some chosen ones among this people" accepted the gospel. In the province of Piedmont there was a large Protestant population, and to that place Elder Snow appointed two companions who had joined him, Elders Stenhouse and Toronto, to labor. In a letter to President Brigham Young, Elder Snow gives a beautiful description of the country. "Piedmont is situated at the foot of the Alps, the highest

mountains in Europe. The scenes of this land embrace all
the varieties of a region where the heavens and the earth
seem to meet. The clouds often enwrap these mighty emi-
nences, and hide their frowning grandeur from our view.
At other times they are covered with snow, while at their
feet the vine and fig tree are ripening their fruit." In this
delightful region, Elder Snow and companions, on the
18th of September, 1850, "ascended a very high mountain,
a little distance from La Tour, and having taken our position
on a bold projecting rock, we sang praises to the God of
heaven and offered up a prayer." The elders then proceeded
amongst themselves to organize the Church in Italy. From
this day the work went forward. Converts were made in
La Tour, Turin, and French Switzerland, and the work thus
begun has continued to the present time. Elders were also
dispatched by Elder Snow to the island of Malta and to
Bombay and Calcutta in India, where some converts were
made and small branches of the Church established.

IV

In March, 1852, Elder Snow bade farewell to the Saints
and friends of the Italian Mission and began his return
journey homeward. His route was by way of Gibraltar,
Portsmouth, London, Liverpool, and New York City. From
the latter place he made his way to Kanesville, Iowa, and
thence across the plains to Salt Lake Valley, where he arrived on July 30.

During Elder Snow's absence his family had lived in
very uncomfortable circumstances. "My house," he writes,
"built of logs, with roof made of willows and earth, and
floors of primitive style, just before starting on my mission,
had already become quite uncomfortable and could not be
sufficiently improved to meet the requirements of ordinary
convenience." His first efforts therefore were to build a
home, and without any visible means at hand, he began the

work. "Through the blessings of God upon my efforts—
with great economy and perseverance—I succeeded far
beyond my most sanguine expectations. I erected a large,
two story, adobe house, with nine rooms—finished off several of them and moved into it with all my family, feeling
truly thankful to the giver of all good for the blessings of
a comfortable and respectable habitation."

The first winter after Lorenzo Snow's arrival at home
he occupied the time in teaching school, in serving as a
member of the territorial legislature, and in preaching to
the Saints in the various wards and settlements. At the
April conference in 1853, he found another call awaiting
him. President Young announced to the Saints that Lorenzo
Snow had been selected to lead fifty families into Box Elder
County and strengthen the settlements there. Always obedient to call, Lorenzo arrived at the small settlement on Box
Elder creek in May, 1855. His own account of the same
follows: "When I arrived in Box Elder County, I found the
location where Brigham City now flourishes in a very un-
prosperous condition. Whether its change from a primitive
state should be called improvement, i. e., whether it was
better or worse for what had been done on the premise,
would puzzle an antiquarian. Even the log meeting house,
with its ground floor and earth roof, was more extensively
patronized as a receptacle for bed bugs than for the assemblage of Saints.

"At first, in locating there, I only took a portion of my
family, as a small and incommodious adobe hut was the
only tenement attainable. During the summer and fall, I
succeeded in erecting a house, one story and a half in
height, thirty feet by forty. It being impossible to obtain
shingles, I covered the building with slabs, and for two
winters, the rattling of those slabs, put in motion by the
canyon breezes, supplied us with music, in the absence of
organs and pianos."

Under these conditions Lorenzo Snow took up his
residence in Box Elder County, where he was to succeed
and prosper and make his home for nearly forty years.

Always mindful of the cultural activities of the community where he resided, it is interesting to note that, under the pioneering conditions that prevailed in the Box Elder settlement at the time Elder Snow took up his residence there, he arranged the large room of his new house so that it would serve as a place in which "plays" or "theatricals" could be held. Lorenzo's sister, Eliza R. Snow, tells us the story. "He then organized a dramatic company; and during the long winter evenings, his amateur performers drew crowded audiences of invited guests. Here the old and the young, the gray-headed and the little prattlers, met and mingled—the people were drawn together and a union of feeling was awakened. The effect was very satisfactory, not only in producing pleasurable recreation at the time, but was one of the aids in arousing the partially dormant energies of the people."

Lorenzo continued his work as a community builder at Brigham City until 1864, when he was again called on a short foreign mission—this time to the Hawaiian Islands. Certain problems had arisen among the Saints on the islands that were of sufficient importance to President Brigham Young that he decided to send two of the apostles there to settle the difficulties. Ezra T. Benson and Lorenzo Snow were selected for this task. They were accompanied by Elders Joseph F. Smith, Alma Smith, and W. W. Cluff. These brethren "took stage at Salt Lake City, about the 1st of March, 1864, for San Francisco, California." There they went on board a steamer, and arrived in Honolulu harbor on March 27. As their destination was the island of Maui, they continued on by boat to the little harbor of Lahaina. Here an accident occurred that almost took the life of Lorenzo Snow. The small boat in which the brethren were being conveyed from the ship to the land was capsized by an immense wave, and all the occupants were thrown into the water. In a few moments all were accounted for except Elder Snow. A frantic search was made for him, and in fifteen or twenty minutes he was brought to the surface by a native and quickly taken to the shore by his missionary companions. Elder Cluff relates that "as soon as we got him into our boat, we told the boatman to pull for the shore with all possible speed. His body was stiff and apparently lifeless. Brother A. L. Smith and I were sitting side by side. We laid Brother Snow across our laps, and on the way to shore we quietly administered to him and asked the Lord to spare his life that he might return to his family and home. On reaching the shore we carried him a little way to some large empty barrels that were lying on the sandy beach. We laid him face downwards on one of them and rolled him back and forth until we succeeded in getting the water he had swallowed out of him. . . . Finally we were impressed to place our mouth over his and make an effort to inflate his lungs. . . . After a little, we received very faint indications of returning life. These grew more and more distinct until consciousness was fully restored."

After this miraculous experience Elder Snow quickly regained his strength and performed his mission. About the middle of April, Elders Benson and Snow sailed from Honolulu harbor on their return journey. One month later they joined their friends and relatives in Utah.

V

It was shortly after he returned home, in 1864, that Lorenzo began to develop the splendid cooperative enterprises that for a period of years thrived and prospered under his management and attracted the attention of the entire Church to the community of Brigham City. For years President Brigham Young had been preaching home industry to the Saints, but because of the great distance between Utah and the manufacturing centers of the East, it had been difficult and in most cases impossible to obtain equipment and machinery. However, Lorenzo Snow now proposed to make a beginning. Three substantial members of the Church joined him in raising $3,000, and with this amount to purchase goods, the Brigham City Mercantile and Manufacturing Association was organized. What followed is related by Elder Snow. "We commenced by organizing a mercantile department. The dividends were paid in store goods, amounting, usually to about twenty-five percent per annum. As this enterprise prospered, we continued to receive capital stock, also adding new names to the list of stockholders, until we had a surplus of capital, or means, and succeeded in uniting the interests of the people and securing their patronage. We resolved then to commence home industries and receive our dividends, if any, in the articles produced."

This plan proved to be feasible, and in a short time, according to Elder Snow, he and his brethren who were stockholders in the store began the erection of a "tannery building, two stories, 45 x 80, with modern improvements and conveniences, at a cost of $10,000. Most of the materials, mason and carpenter work were furnished as capital stock by such persons as were able and desired an interest in our institution. The larger portion of this work was done in the winter season, when no other employment could be had, one-fourth being paid in merchandise to such as needed. . . . This tannery has been operated during the past nine years [wrote Elder Snow in 1876] with success and reasonable profits, producing an excellent quality of leather, valued from $8,000 to $10,000 annually."

When the tannery was in successful operation, it called for further industries: "We connected with this branch of industry a boot and shoe shop; also a saddle and harness shop, drawing our dividends in the articles manufactured in those departments."

But the cooperative work did not end here. "Our next enterprise was the establishing of a woolen factory, following the same course as in putting up the tannery. This also added to our capital, increasing the number of our stockholders without interrupting any man's business. The profits of the mercantile department, with some additional capital, purchased the machinery. During the past seven years this factory has done a satisfactory business, and we have not been necessitated to close for lack of wool, winter or summer, and have manufactured about $40,000 worth of goods annually."

One industry continued to add to another. "With the view of probable difficulty in obtaining wool, we next started a sheep herd, commencing with fifteen hundred head, supplied by various individuals who could spare them as capital stock. They now number five thousand, and prove a great help to our factory in times like these, when money is scarce and cash demanded for wool."

It seems that one could go on indefinitely listing President Snow's accomplishments. "Our next business was the establishment of a dairy, and, having selected a suitable ranch, we commenced with sixty cows, erected some temporary buildings, making a small investment in vats, hoops, presses, etc., all of which have been gradually improved, till, perhaps now it is the finest, best and most commodious of any dairy in this Territory. The past two years we have had five hundred milk cows producing each season in the neighborhood of $8,000 in butter, cheese and milk.

"Next, we started a horn stock herd, numbering at present 1,000, which supplies, in connection with the sheep herd, a meat market owned by our association.

"We have a horticultural and agricultural department, the latter divided into several branches, each provided with an experienced overseer.

"Also we have a hat factory, in which are produced all our fur and wool hats. We make our tin ware—have pottery, broom, brush and molasses factories, a shingle mill and two sawmills, operated by water power; and also blacksmith, furniture and tailor departments, and one for putting up and repairing wagons and carriages.

"We have a large, two-story adobe building, occupied by machinery for wood-turning, planing and working mouldings, operated by water power.

"We have established a cotton farm of one hundred and twenty-five acres in the southern part of the Territory for the purpose of supplying warps to our woolen factory, where we maintain a colony of about twenty young men.

"We have a department for manufacturing straw hats, in which we employ from fifteen to twenty girls. Last year we employed twenty-five girls in our dairy, and have them in constant employ in our millinery and tailoring departments, also in making artificial flowers, as hat and shoe binders, as weavers in our woolen mills and clerks in our mercantile department.

"Many of our young men and boys are now learning trades, their parents being highly pleased that they are being furnished employment at home, rather than going abroad, subject to contracting bad habits and morals.

"We have erected a very elegant building, two stories, 32 x 63 feet; the upper part devoted to a seminary, and the lower occupied as a dancing hall. I have considered it of the highest importance to the interest of our community, to provide for and encourage suitable diversions and amusements."

One could go on indefinitely, enumerating the great accomplishments of President Lorenzo Snow in Brigham City, which occupied his time and attention for a period of more than twenty years. But he demonstrated beyond any doubt that the Latter-day Saints are capable of originating and developing cooperative enterprises, if left to pursue their tasks and follow the principles of their holy religion. And yet, it seems that there must always be a capable leader. The businesses founded by President Snow did not long survive his active management, but soon drifted into the hands of private owners. Some prospered for a time and some were abandoned.

In the midst of his prosperity, in 1872 and 1873, Lorenzo Snow and his gifted sister, Eliza R. Snow, joined a party of Church officials in making a trip to Europe and the Holy Land. We are fortunate in having a full account of this trip from the pen of President Snow, who wrote frequent letters to the *Deseret News* while on his journey.

At the head of the "Palestine Tourists," as the group was familiarly known, was George A. Smith, first counselor to President Brigham Young. In making his appointment, President Young had written to George A. Smith as follows: "As you are about to start on an extensive tour through Europe and Asia Minor, where you will doubtless be brought in contact with men of position and influence in society, we desire that you observe closely what openings now exist, or where they may be effected, for the introduction of the Gospel into the various countries you shall visit. When you get to the land of Palestine, we wish you to dedicate and consecrate that land, that it may be blessed with fruitfulness, preparatory to the return of the Jews, in fulfillment of prophecy and the accomplishment of the purposes of our Heavenly Father.

"We pray that you may be preserved to travel in peace and safety; that you may be abundantly blessed with words of wisdom and free utterance in all your conversations pertaining to the holy gospel, dispelling prejudice, and sowing seeds of righteousness among the people."

It was with this spirit that the "Palestine Tourists" embarked on their long journey, which was to consume more than eight months' time. To Lorenzo Snow, it must have been interesting to compare the comfortable train on which he rode to Omaha, Nebraska, with the slow-moving ox teams with which he had previously made several laborious journeys. In his voyage across the ocean, on a splendid steamer, he must have thought of his first trip to England, when he was quartered in the hold of a sailing vessel. The countries visited on the way to Palestine were England, Holland, Belgium, France, Italy, and Egypt. From Egypt, the tourists went in a ship to Jaffa, and from there had the first sight of the Holy Land. A few days later, on Sunday, March 2, 1873, the dedication of the land took place. "President Smith made arrangements with our dragonman," writes Eliza R. Snow, "and had a tent, table, seats and carpet taken up on the Mount of Olives, to which all the brethren of the company, and myself, repaired on horseback. After dismounting on the summit, and committing our animals to the care of servants, we visited the Church of Ascension, a small cathedral, said to stand on the spot from which Jesus ascended. By this time the tent was prepared, which we entered, and after an opening prayer by Brother Carrington, we united in service in the order of the Holy Priesthood, President Smith leading, in humble, fervent supplication, dedicating the land of Palestine for the gathering of the Jews and the rebuilding of Jerusalem, and returning heartfelt thanks and gratitude to God for the fulness of the Gospel and the blessings bestowed on the Latter-day Saints. Other brethren led in turn and we had a very interesting session; to me it seemed the crowning point of the whole tour, realizing as I did that we were worshiping on the summit of the sacred Mount, once the frequent resort of the Prince of Life."

Leaving Palestine late in March, the tourists began their return journey, which took them through the countries of Greece, Turkey, Austria, Germany, and England. From the latter place they sailed in June for the United States. Eliza R. Snow continues the account of the trip from their arrival in New York City: "When we left New York, my brother and I proceeded directly to the place, in the state of Ohio, where he was born, and where we both were brought up—the place of our childhood and youth—also neighboring towns and counties. I had been absent thirty-seven years, my brother returned once within that time. Very many of our relatives and friends have gone the way of all the earth since we left, and everything we remembered has yielded to the strokes of the battle axe of changeful time. Those of our relatives and acquaintances who remain received us with affectionate cordiality; indeed it was one continued ovation from first to last, through the counties of Portage, Geauga, Cuyahoga and Loraine, where we went; even children born since we left that country came distances to see us and converse with us.

"Having been so long abroad we felt anxious to return home; at the same time, being desirous of seeing as many of our friends and relatives as possible, we visited night and day, going from place to place in rapid succession.

"We succeeded in gathering many genealogies, both of the dead and the living; and we think, in many instances, have renewed friendships, revived and created associations that will extend into eternity. We feel that God is with us, and humbly trust that his blessings will attend our efforts."

The last part of the journey was made by train. President Snow arrived in Brigham City on July 8, 1873, and was greeted by members of his family and by many friends. He at once resumed his activities in his business afairs and Church duties.

On April 3, 1884, President Snow reached his seventieth birthday. A few weeks later at a family gathering at Brigham City, he expressed his gratitude for his many blessings: "My heart is filled to overflowing with warmest feelings of gratitude to my Heavenly Father for these marvelous blessings. . . . When I look upon this extensive family—intelligent and gifted sons and daughters—half a score or more of the former having been called, sent forth and performed many years of arduous missionary labor among far-off nations, and upon distant islands; and also behold many of my daughters honored wives and mothers in Israel, surrounded by healthy and happy children, and feel that all this is through the mercy and kindness of God, and the work of the great Jehovah—what shall I say? Language is powerless to express the deep feelings of my heart for this holy and sacred opportunity on this the celebration of my seventieth birthday; of standing here and beholding this glorious and heavenly inspiring spectacle."

President Snow did not contemplate holding another

family reunion, as he was now advanced in years. He continued: "This is the last family reunion we have reason to expect this side of the spirit world. May the God of our fathers help us to keep His laws, live honorable lives, preserve inviolate our virtue and integrity, listen to the whisperings of the Holy Spirit, and seek diligently to purify ourselves, that not a single member of this family be lost by deviating from the straight and narrow path, but may we all prove ourselves worthy to come forth in the morning of the first resurrection, crowned with glory, perpetuating in immortality the family union, and continue down through the endless ages of eternity."

The beautiful spirit of President Lorenzo Snow can be felt and appreciated in his address to his family.

From the time when the first anti-polygamy law was passed by Congress in 1862, until the death of President Brigham Young in 1877, there was constant agitation throughout the United States, and also among non-Mormons in Utah, to enforce the law and convince the leaders of the Church that they should abandon the doctrine. It was believed that with the passing of Brigham Young there would be a change in sentiment among the members of the Church toward the practice of plural marriage; but President John Taylor took a firm stand in the matter and gave no evidence that a change would be made. As a result, the agitation was renewed, and in 1882, the Edmunds law was passed by Congress, which provided severe penalties for those who were convicted of plural marriage, or what was termed "unlawful cohabitation."

On the morning of November 20, 1885, the home of President Lorenzo Snow at Brigham City was surrounded by seven United States deputy marshals, and he was arrested on the charge of "unlawful cohabitation." "There were three regular trials, the first one commencing December 30th, 1885, and the last one ending January 5th, 1886, conviction being the result in each case. He was sentenced by Judge O. W. Powers, January 16th, 1886, the judgment being the full penalty of the law—imprisonment for six months and a fine of $300 and cost—under each conviction. Under this segregation process inaugurated by the Utah courts, President Snow served eleven months, without a murmur or complaint." However, an appeal was taken to the Supreme Court of the United States, and this court reversed the judgment of the lower court and stated that "there was but one entire offense for the continuous time; that the trial court had no jurisdiction to inflict a punishment in respect of more than one of the convictions." President Snow was at once released from the Utah penitentiary, and there was general rejoicing among his family and friends.

VII

At the April conference of the Church in 1889, Lorenzo Snow was sustained as the president of the Quorum of Twelve Apostles. In this position he was active, and with his brethren visited many of the wards and stakes of the Church.

As his years advanced, further honors were given to President Snow. With the completion of the great Salt Lake Temple and its dedication in 1893, he was designated by the First Presidency to preside over the ordinance work in this magnificent structure, which the Saints had toiled and labored to build over a period of more than forty years. One who knew him at this time paid him this tribute: "No more fitting appointment could possibly have been made. He has ever been interested in temple work. He is spiritually minded to a very high degree, and with his heavenly countenance and sweet, gentle dignity, no one living is better, if so well qualified to stand as the watchman at the door which opens between the living and the dead."

On September 2, 1898, President Wilford Woodruff died in San Francisco, California. Before his death President

Woodruff had declared "that it is not the will of the Lord in the future that there should be a lengthy period elapse between the death of the president and the re-organization of the First Presidency." Acting on this advice, the brethren of the Twelve met in Salt Lake City on September 13 and sustained Lorenzo Snow as the President of The Church of Jesus Christ of Latter-day Saints. President Snow at the time was five months past his eighty-fourth birthday, but as stated in the beginning of this chapter, he was still mentally and spiritually alert and physically able to carry on with his arduous duties. He expressed his humility to his brethren when he stated: "I do not want this administration to be known as Lorenzo Snow's administration, but as God's, in and through Lorenzo Snow." President Snow chose as his counselors George Q. Cannon and Joseph F. Smith, the same men who had served with the two previous presidents.

On the afternoon of Sunday, October 9, at the closing session of the semiannual general conference, President Snow and counselors were sustained by the priesthood of the Church, voting in quorums, and then by the vast assembly without a dissenting vote. Following this mighty approval, President Snow addressed a few appropriate remarks to the congregation: "Brethren and Sisters, this much I say, and I say it in the name of the Lord: I will endeavor to be devoted to your interests and the interests of the Kingdom of God. I will serve you to the best of my knowledge and understanding, in reference to that which will promote your interests in connection with the interests of the Almighty. I will do this, the Lord being my helper.

"It is an easy thing for us to rise here and raise our right hands in token of our approval of what is presented before us. I can do that without any trouble, and so can you. But there is something involved in this rising here and raising our right hands in approval of the propositions presented; there is a meaning to it; something that ought to be well considered, and that is, acting in the future in

accordance with this manifestation of our approval. . . .
In this solemn assembly, let us decree in our hearts, let
us inwardly testify to the Lord, that we will be a better
people, a more united people, at our next conference, than
we are today."

The first task that President Snow set for himself as
his administration began was to bring about an improvement
in the finances of the Church. Under the provisions of the
Edmunds-Tucker act, passed by Congress in 1887, the
Church had been disincorporated, its property confiscated
and placed in the hands of an unfriendly receiver. A rental
was charged before the Church was permitted to occupy
its own property, such as the tithing office, the historian's
office, or even the temple block. President Snow therefore
found the finances in a very chaotic condition. To meet
this emergency he proposed to the brethren that bonds
should be issued to meet the pressing obligations of the
Church. "On Thursday, December 1st, 1898," relates Joseph
Fielding Smith, "the first Presidency and the Apostles met
in council and President Snow reviewed the financial condition of the Church and said he deplored it, but it seemed
necessary that the Church issue bonds in the sum of
$500,000. The matter was put to a vote and unanimously
agreed to by the brethren. Later it was determined that
the bond issue should be double that amount, and two
series were issued, A and B, each for $500,000, the first
series to be redeemed December 31st, 1903, and the second
to be redeemed December 31st, 1906."

In May, 1899, President Snow began the work which
was perhaps the most noteworthy of his entire administration—that of encouraging the Saints to pay a full tithing.
At a special conference held at St. George, Utah, May 17,
he made known his important message to the people. His
son, LeRoi C. Snow, who was present on that occasion,
well describes the event: "I was sitting at a table on the
stand, reporting the proceedings, when all at once Father
paused in his discourse. . . . When he commenced to

speak again his voice strengthened and the inspiration of
God seemed to come over him. His eyes seemed to brighten
and his countenance to shine. He was filled with unusual
power. Then he revealed to the Latter-day Saints the vision
that was before him. . . . He told them that he could see,
as he had never realized before, how the law of tithing
had been neglected by the people, also that the Saints
themselves were heavily in debt, as well as the Church, and
now through strict obedience to this law—the paying of
a full, honest tithing—not only would the Church be re-
lieved of its great indebtedness, but through the blessings
of the Lord this would also be the means of freeing the
Latter-day Saints from their individual obligations, and
they would become a prosperous people." Directly on
tithing, President Snow said, "The word of the Lord is:
The time has now come for every Latter-day Saint, who
calculates to be prepared for the future and to hold his
feet upon a proper foundation, to do the will of the Lord
and to pay his tithing in full. That is the word of the Lord
to you, and it will be the word of the Lord to every settlement throughout the land of Zion. . . ."

"When the returning party reached Nephi, where we
were to take the train for home, President Snow called the
members all together in a meeting which will never be
forgotten by those who were present. He commissioned
every one present to be his special witness to the fact
that the Lord had given this revelation to him. He put
all the party under covenant and promise not only to obey
the law of tithing themselves but also that each would bear
witness to this special manifestation and would spread the
tithing message at every opportunity."

Returning to Salt Lake City, President Snow called
an assembly of all the principal officers of the priesthood
of the Church. This assembly, held July 2, 1899, "was in
session from 10 o'clock in the morning, until after 7 o'clock
in the evening," relates LeRoi C. Snow. "Such a gathering
of priesthood had never before been held in the Church.

All twenty-six of the general authorities of the Church were
there. All the forty stakes of Zion and four hundred seventy-
eight wards were represented. The spirit of the meeting was
that of testimony and the promotion of faith, not one of
temporal and business affairs. The renewed tithing revelation was the theme of all the eighteen addresses. Humble,
honest obedience to the tithing law became rather a spiritual gift and privilege than a material duty. The solemnity
of the occasion was impressed upon the assemblage when
President Snow led in the sacred Hosannah shout and pronounced glorious blessings and promises upon the people."
Such was the great work of this man, who was now in his
eighty-sixth year.

At the October conference, held in Salt Lake City in
1899, President Snow expressed his gratitude for the blessings of the Lord that were being poured out upon the
people. "I want to say to everyone that it is our privilege
to be blessed to such an extent that we will feel perfectly
repaid for all the inconveniences that may have resulted
to us in coming to this gathering. As Latter-day Saints,
the Lord has placed us in relation with himself, and, in
order to carry out the condition that we are in, we need
His blessings above any other class of people.

"Our prospects are sufficiently grand and glorious to
cause us to put forth every exertion that we possibly can,
in order to secure the blessings that are before us. Nothing
should deter us from the exercise of every power that God
has bestowed upon us, to make our salvation and exaltation sure. All men and women who are worthy to be
called Latter-day Saints should live hour by hour in such a
way that if they should be called suddenly from this life
into the next, they would be prepared. It is our privilege
to so live to that extent that we shall feel satisfied that
all will be well, if we should be called away at any hour—
If there should be any Latter-day Saints within the sound
of my voice that have not reached this assurance in regard
to their future, they should not rest satisfied until they have

secured it, so that they may know that everything is right with them."

On January 1, 1900, a new year dawned favorably for The Church of Jesus Christ of Latter-day Saints. Progress was being made along all lines, and the aged and honored man at the head of the Church was hopeful that progress would continue. Addressing a body of priesthood on January 11 in Salt Lake City, he said that "although we as a people had met with all kinds of troubles, had suffered from heart burnings, and had been called upon to make all sorts of sacrifices, yet we had never lost hope of arriving in due time at a state of perfect union." Speaking of the apostles, he was pleased to say that more could be said of them in this respect today than at any other time since the days of the Prophet Joseph.

"Notwithstanding the weaknesses which the servants of the Lord and His people manifested in various ways, He had sustained His servants, and given them grace sufficient to meet and overcome every trial and trouble. This being the case, he [the speaker], for one, could look into the future with great assurance. He did not feel to worry one particle as to the present or the future. Everything considered, who, he asked, had such great reasons for thanksgiving and rejoicing as we had."

On April 3, 1900, President Snow celebrated his eighty-sixth birthday. A pleasing party was given for him on the afternoon of that day in the temple annex, which was attended by the General Authorities, their wives, the temple workers, and a group of friends. There were speeches, songs, recitations, and instrumental music. The President thanked the gathering and stated that he had greatly enjoyed the occasion.

Three days later, on the opening day of the general conference, President Snow delivered a lengthy and inspiring sermon. "Seventy years ago," he said, "this Church was organized with six members. We commenced, so to speak, as an infant. We had our prejudices to combat. Our

ignorance troubled us in regard to what the Lord intended
to do and what he wanted us to do. Through the blessings
of the Lord, however, we managed to move along in our
stage of infancy, receiving support from the Lord as he saw
proper to give it. We advanced into boyhood, and still
we undoubtedly made some mistakes, which did not
generally arise from a design to make them but from lack
of experience. We understand very well, when we reflect
back upon our own lives, that we did many foolish things
when we were boys, because of our lack of experience and
because we had not learned fully to obey the instructions
of our fathers and mothers. . . . Many of us afterwards
learned it, but too late perhaps to correct ourselves. Yet
as we advanced, the experience of the past materially assisted us to avoid such mistakes as we had made in our
boyhood.

"It has been so with the Church. Our errors have
generally arisen from a lack of comprehending what the
Lord required us to do. But now, we are pretty well along
to manhood; we are seventy years of age, and one would
imagine that after one had lived through his infancy,
through his boyhood, and on until he had arrived at the
age of seventy years, he would be able through his long
experience, to do a great many things that seemed impossible and in fact were impossible in his boyhood state.
When we examine ourselves, however, we discover that we
are still not doing exactly what we ought to do, notwithstanding all our experiences. We discern that there are
things which we fail to do that the Lord expects us to
perform, some of which he required us to do in our boyhood. But we feel thankful and grateful that we are enabled
now, through our past experience to accomplish many
things that we could not do in former times, and that we
are able to escape individual sins that have brought trouble
upon us in times past. While we congratulate ourselves in
this direction, we certainly ought to feel that we have not
yet arrived at perfection. There are many things for us
to do yet. . . .

"Now, Latter-day Saints, how is it with us? We have received the Gospel. We have received the Kingdom of God, established on earth. We have had trouble; we have been persecuted. We were driven from Ohio. We were driven from Nauvoo; and once we were driven for a time from this beautiful city. Many have lost thousands of dollars; lost their homes and all they had, and some of the brethren have seen their wives and children lay down their lives because of the hardships they had to experience during these changes, these persecutions, these revolutions and these drivings. The people have looked with astonishment at the willingness of the Latter-day Saints to suffer these things. Why do we do this? Why do we adhere to these principles that have caused us at times so much grief and sacrifice? What is it that enables us to endure these persecutions and still rejoice? It is because we have had revelations from the Almighty; because He has spoken to us in our souls and has given to us the Holy Ghost, which is a principle of revelation wherever it exists and is promised to every man, as in the days of the former Apostles, who will believe, repent of his sins and be immersed in water for the remission of them by those who have the authority from the Lord to administer this ordinance.

"This Church will stand, because it is upon a firm basis. It is not from man; it is not from the study of the New Testament or the Old Testament; it is not the result of the learning that we received in colleges or seminaries, but it has come directly from the Lord. The Lord has shown it to us by the revealing principle of the Holy Spirit of light and every man can receive this same spirit."

Such was the manner in which this great man, Lorenzo Snow, addressed the Latter-day Saints, in the eighty-seventh year of his life.

The summer of 1900 was spent by President Snow in Salt Lake City, with the exception of short trips to Brigham City and Logan. Almost every day he was in his office, where he consulted with his brethren and took care of important correspondence. A subject continually in his mind was the financial condition of the Church and the necessity of the Saints' paying a full tithing in order to relieve the Church of its obligations. But the spiritual truths of the gospel were not neglected; they were constantly before him. At the opening session of the conference in October, 1900, he said, in addressing the Saints:

"The religion that we have received, the principles of exaltation and glory that you and I have received, bring upon us persecution, or else they are not those principles which we thought they were. They bring upon us trouble upon the right hand and upon the left, but we should seek to be calm and cool, as Job learned to be calm and cool under circumstances of the most unhappy character. We should learn to do this and there are things that are provided for us by which we can learn this. Think now of how much worse you and I might be, and then think of what superior blessings we actually possess. We know that in the future after we have passed through this life, we will then have our wives and our children with us. We will have our bodies glorified, made free from every sickness and distress, and rendered most beautiful. There is nothing more beautiful to look upon than a resurrected man or woman. There is nothing grander that I can imagine that a man can possess than a resurrected body. There is no Latter-day Saint within the sound of my voice but that certainly has this prospect of coming forth in the morning of the first resurrection and being glorified, exalted in the presence of God, having the privilege of talking with our Father as we talk with our earthly father.

"What a glorious thing! You will know no prison walls, your friends turning away from you, your being dispossessed of your property, being driven from your home, being cast into prison, being defamed. These things do not hurt you one particle. They do not destroy your prospects, which are still glorious before you. And then we should understand that the Lord has provided, when the days of trouble come

upon the nations, a place for you and me, and we will be
preserved as Noah was preserved, not in an ark, but we
will be preserved by going into these principles of union
by which we can accomplish the work of the Lord and
surround ourselves with those things that will preserve us
from the difficulties that are now coming upon the world,
the judgments of the Lord. We can see, as we read the
newspapers, that they are coming upon the nations of the
ungodly; and they would have been upon us if we had
stayed among the nations, if the Lord had not inclined our
ears and brought salvation to us, we would have been as
they are."

On January 1, 1901, President Snow issued an extremely interesting document, which was published in the *Deseret
News* of that day, entitled, "Greeting to the World." It
expresses his great faith and wisdom to such an extent that
I desire to reproduce it here in full.

"A new century dawns upon the world today. The
hundred years just completed were the most momentous in
the history of man upon this planet. It would be impossible
to make even a brief summary of the notable events, the
marvelous developments, the grand achievements and the
beneficial inventions and discoveries, which mark the progress of the ten decades now left behind in the ceaseless
march of humanity. The very mention of the nineteenth
century suggests advancement, improvement, liberty and
light. Happy are we to have lived amidst its wonders and
shared in the riches of its treasures of intelligence.

"The lessons of the past century should have prepared
us for the duties and glories of the opening era. It ought
to be the age of peace, of greater progress, of the universal adoption of the golden rule. Barbarism of the past should
be buried. War with its horrors should be but a memory.
The aim of nations should be fraternity and mutual greatness. The welfare of humanity should be studied instead
of the enrichment of a race or the extension of an empire.
Awake, ye monarchs of the earth and rulers among nations,

and gaze upon the scene on which the early rays of the rising Millennial day gild the morn of the twentieth century! The power is in your hands to pave the way for the coming of the King of kings, whose dominion will be over all the earth. Disband your armies; turn your weapons of strife into implements of industry; take the yoke from the necks of the people; arbitrate your disputes; meet in royal congress and plan for union instead of conquest, for the banishment of poverty, for the uplifting of the masses, and for the health, wealth, enlightenment and happiness of all tribes and peoples and nations. Then shall the twentieth century be to you the glory of your lives and the lustre of your crowns, and posterity shall sing your praises, while the Eternal One shall place you on high among the mighty.

"Ye toiling millions, who in the sweat of your faces earn your daily bread, look up and greet the power from above which shall lift you from bondage! The day of your redemption draweth nigh. Cease to waste your wages in that which helps to keep you in want. Regard not wealth as your enemy and your employers as your oppressors. Seek for the union of capital and labor. Be provident when in prosperity. Do not become a prey to designing men who seek to stir up strife for their own selfish ends. Strive for your rights by lawful means, and desist from violence and destruction. Anarchism and lawlessness are your deadly foes. Dissipation and vice are chains that bind you to slavery. Freedom is coming for you, its light approaches as the century dawns.

"Men and women of wealth, use your riches to give employment to the laborer! Take the idle from the crowded centers of population and place them on the untilled areas that await the hand of industry. Unlock your vaults, unloose your purses and embark in enterprises that will give work to the unemployed, and relieve the wretchedness that leads to the vice and crime which curse your great cities, and that poison the moral atmosphere around you. Make others happy, and you will be happy yourselves.

"As a servant of God I bear witness to the revelation
of His will in the nineteenth century. It came by His own
voice from the heavens, by the personal manifestation of
His Son, and by the ministration of holy angels. He commands all people everywhere to repent, to turn from their
evil ways and unrighteous desires, to be baptized for the
remission of their sins, that they may receive the Holy
Ghost and come into communion with Him. He has commenced the work of redemption spoken of by all the holy
prophets, sages and seers of all the ages and all the races
of mankind. He will assuredly accomplish His work, and the
twentieth century will mark its advancement toward the
great consummation. Every unfoldment of the nineteenth
century in science, in art, in mechanism, in music, in literature, in poetic fancy, in philosophical thought, was prompted by His Spirit, which before long will be poured out
upon all flesh that will receive it. He is the Father of us
all, and He desires to save and exalt us all.

"In the eighty-seventh year of my age on earth, I feel
full of earnest desire for the benefit of humanity. I wish
all a Happy New Year. I hope and look for grand events to
occur in the twentieth century. At its auspicious dawn I
lift my hands and invoke the blessing of heaven upon the
inhabitants of the earth. May the sunshine from above smile
upon you. May the treasures of the ground and the fruits
of the soil be brought forth freely for your good. May the
light of truth chase darkness from your souls. May righteousness increase and iniquity diminish as the years of the century roll on. May justice triumph and corruption be stamped
out. And may virtue, chastity and honor prevail, until evil
shall be overcome and the earth shall be cleansed from
wickedness. Let these sentiments, as the voice of the 'Mormons' in the mountains of Utah, go forth to the whole
world, and let all people know that our wish and our mission are for the blessing and salvation of the entire human
race. May the twentieth century prove the happiest, as
it will be the grandest, of all the ages of time, and may

God be glorified in the victory that is coming over sin, sorrow, misery and death. Peace be unto you all!"

On Wednesday, April 3, 1901, at the Beehive House on East South Temple Street in Salt Lake City, President Snow celebrated his eighty-seventh birthday. An account of festivities of the day, taken from the *Deseret News*, is reproduced here in part.

"The Bee Hive House was very artistically decorated with flowers and potted plants; and on the south mantle in the northeast parlor stood a most gorgeous bouquet of American Beauty roses, the gift of two little girls, and therein is a touching story. Early this morning, before President Snow was up, there came a knock at the door and when it was opened there stood two little tots almost hidden behind a bouquet. They said it was for President Snow, and with radiant faces they were conducted into the house and up to the aged man's bedroom door. They then sang two or three sweet little pieces, and went away as happy as the birds of spring. President Snow was deeply touched by the serenade of these little children, and he says he will cherish it not only as one of the dearest incidents of the memorable day, but of all his life time."

In the afternoon, in the temple annex, a splendid birthday program was rendered by members of the President's family and a few of the General Authorities of the Church.

During the summer of 1901 President Snow continued actively with his duties and was daily at his office on East South Temple Street. Here he met with his brethren to discuss the problems of the Church; frequently visitors would call to make the acquaintance of the venerable President; long hours were spent in taking care of voluminous correspondence. Occasionally he went to one of the outlying wards or stakes to address a conference, and he was always able to thrill the Saints with his fervent testimony.

On the opening day of the semiannual general conference, on October 4, 1901, President Joseph F. Smith took charge and announced that President Snow was suffering from a cold, and thought it not wisdom to venture out. It was not, however, a matter to give alarm to the Saints, as the illness of the President was not severe. He attended no meetings of the conference except on the last day, Sunday afternoon, October 6, when he delivered a *1901* splendid spiritual sermon. His concluding words were:

"There is another subject that I wish to speak of. I am getting along in years now, being nearly 88 years old. I have had only one counselor since President [George Q.] Cannon died. I have chosen another Counselor [Rudger Clawson]. I have sought the guidance of the Lord in the matter, and the Lord has directed the choice. I have chosen a strong, energetic man, and I think he will be a great help to myself and President Smith; I hope therefore you will sustain him. God bless you all."

VII

These were the last words ever spoken in public by this great man and leader. Four days later his noble spirit left his body and departed from this world. The *Deseret News* gives the following brief account of his demise under date of Thursday, October 10:

"The public will be greatly shocked to learn that President Lorenzo Snow, fifth President of the Church of Jesus Christ of Latter-day Saints, passed away at his home in the Bee Hive House at 3:35 o'clock this afternoon. The immediate cause of his demise was hypostatic congestion, superinduced by aggravated bronchitis. The announcement of his death will come like a thunderbolt from the unclouded skies to tens of thousands of people who were entirely unaware of his sickness. His family and friends, however, have known for some time of his serious condition, but not until yesterday was his illness viewed with alarm.

"Several weeks ago President Snow contracted a cold which annoyed him considerably, and which was accompanied by a constant hacking cough. Gradually it grew worse, and about ten days ago became more troublesome than ever. During Conference he was confined to his home and office most of the time, and attended the meeting in the Tabernacle on Sunday afternoon with the greatest difficulty. On Tuesday he attended to business as usual, but yesterday morning stomach complications arose and he was unable to retain the slightest morsel of food. Last evening Doctors Richards and Wilcox were summoned, and announced his condition as being very grave. At 1 o'clock Dr. Richards was again called and returned at 6:30 and 11, since which time the doctors have been constantly at his bedside. At 4 this morning, and again at 9:30, the President experienced severe sinking spells, and has only been conscious and coherent at intervals during the day."

Three days later there follows an account of the funeral:

"Prior to the funeral services, which were held in the Tabernacle commencing at 10:30 a.m., the body lay in state at the family residence, thousands taking a last look at their departed leader, and shedding a silent tear as they glanced at the lifeless form of one whom they had learned to dearly love. The large Tabernacle had been beautifully decorated for the obsequies, and the catafalque, upon which rested the handsome casket containing the mortal remains of Israel's respected son, was a literal bed of roses and sweet smelling flowers, so numerous and beautiful were the floral offerings that had been sent in by admiring friends. One of these bore the words in purple letters, 'As God Is Man May Be,' and illustrated in telling manner a sentiment that for years had been uppermost in President Snow's thoughts and actions. The Tabernacle was filled to overflowing, and the services were in keeping with the strict solemnity of the occasion."

Among those who spoke at the funeral was Brigham

Young, Jr. He paid President Snow this splendid tribute:

"I have looked upon President Lorenzo Snow as a second father. I have loved him as a father, and I mourn his departure; but I feel thankful that he was surrounded with every comfort, that peace prevailed in his home and with the people, and that he passed to his rest in the midst of his loving family and friends. About two hours before his death I laid my hand upon his brow and said, 'President Snow, do you recognize me?' He looked at me with his sweet smile and eyes full of intelligence, and said, 'I rather think I do.' He was intelligent nearly to the last, and he knew that his time had come, for he spoke of it. If the prayers and faith of the people could have saved him, President Snow would be alive today; but God has willed it otherwise, and we are deprived of a man who has been one of the most valiant of those who were raised up by the Almighty to assist in laying the foundations of the great cause which He instituted for the salvation of His sons and daughters.

"I have known President Snow since before the death of the Prophet Joseph Smith. I knew him well before the Prophet was martyred, and I knew he was a friend of the Prophet, a friend of the leaders of the Church, and a friend of God. Though but a boy, I recognized in this man a power that was born of the Holy Spirit. I have known his works since 1843, and no man that has lived among us has been more thorough, more diligent, wiser in all positions where he has been placed, and shown more integrity to the work, than the late President Lorenzo Snow. I loved that man, as I loved his predecessors; and the grand work that he has accomplished in the last three years will live in the history of the Church, showing forth the greatness and the executive and financial ability of the man. He will stand among the foremost of those who have inaugurated this great and glorious work of the latter days. Thank God that I was acquainted with him! Though I mourn the loss of his society, I know that he has gone to a reward that is great and glorious; for him there is a crown laid up that shall never fade. I know his family will miss him, and his brethren will miss him; but Lorenzo Snow has done a magnificent work, and his example is worthy of emulation."

The body of President Snow was laid to rest in the Brigham City cemetery on Sunday afternoon, October 13, 1901.

JOSEPH F. SMITH

JOSEPH F. SMITH

(1838-1913)

I N THE first number of the *Millennial Star,* published at
Manchester, England, in May, 1840, there is an interesting yet pathetic letter from Mary Fielding Smith, wife of
Patriarch Hyrum Smith, to her brother Joseph Fielding, who
was laboring as a missionary in England. In this letter
Mary Smith writes some of the details of the mob persecutions that she and many of the Saints had endured in Missouri. I shall take the opportunity of reproducing a few
paragraphs from this letter. It is dated "Commerce, Illinois, North America, June, 1839."

"My very dear brother,—As the elders are expecting
shortly to take their leave of us again to preach the Gospel
in my native land, I feel as though I would not let the opportunity of writing you pass by unimproved. I believe it
will give you pleasure to hear from us by our own hand,
notwithstanding you will see the brethren face to face, and
have an opportunity of hearing all particulars respecting
us and our families, from their mouths.

"As it respects myself, it is now so long since I wrote
to you, and so many important things have transpired, and
so great have been my afflictions, etc., that I know not
where to begin; but I can say, hitherto has the Lord preserved me, and I am still living to praise him, as I do this
day. I have, to be sure, been called to drink deep of the
bitter cup; but you know, my beloved brother, this makes
the sweet the sweeter. . . .

"You have, I suppose, heard of the imprisonment of my dear husband, with his brother Joseph, Elder Rigdon and others, who were kept from us nearly six months; and I suppose no one felt the painful effects of their confinement more than myself.

"I was left in a way that called for the exercise of all the courage and grace I possessed. My husband was taken from me by an armed force, at a time when I needed, in a particular manner, the kindest care and attention of such a friend; instead of which, the care of a large family was suddenly and unexpectedly left upon myself, and, in a few days after, *my dear little Joseph F. was added to the number.* Shortly after his birth I took a severe cold, which brought on chills and fever; this, together with the anxiety of mind I had to endure, threatened to bring me to the gates of death. I was at least four months unable to take any care of myself or child; but the Lord was merciful in so ordering things that my dear sister could be with me all the time. Her child was five months old when mine was born; so she had strength given her to nurse them both, so as to have them do well and grow fast.

"You will have heard of our being driven, as a people, from the state, and from our homes, but you will hear all particulars from the elders, so as to render it not necessary for me to write them; this happened during my sickness, and I had to be removed more than two hundred miles, chiefly on my bed. I suffered much on my journey; but in three or four weeks after we got to Illinois, I began to mend, and my health is now as good as it ever was. It is now a little more than a month since the Lord, in his marvelous power, returned my dear husband, with the rest of the brethren, to their families in tolerable health. We are now living in Commerce, on the bank of the Mississippi river. The situation is very pleasant; you would be much pleased to see it. How long we may be permitted to enjoy it I know not; but the Lord knows what is best for us. I feel but little concerned about where I am, if I can but

keep my mind staid upon God; for you know, in this, there
is perfect peace."

Under these circumstances then, amidst the most distressing, dangerous, and pathetic conditions, Joseph F.
Smith was born into the world.

I find on looking into the history that it was on Tuesday, October 30, 1838, that a mob-militia, numbering about
two thousand, appeared before Far West. The following
day they made demands upon the Saints, the first of which
was that the Mormon leaders be given up "to be tried
and punished." It was upon this demand and in order to
avoid open hostilities that the Prophet Joseph Smith, Sidney
Rigdon, Parley P. Pratt, and others surrendered to the mob
leaders. On Thursday, November 1, the history states,
"Hyrum Smith and Amasa Lyman were brought into camp."
That night a court martial was held, and General Doniphan
was ordered by Samuel Lucas, the commanding general,
"to take Joseph Smith and the other prisoners into the
public square of Far West and shoot them at 9 o'clock tomorrow morning." May it be said to the everlasting honor
of General Doniphan that he refused to carry out this mali-
cious order. After some debate among the officers, the prisoners were taken to Independence for trial, but in a few
days they were ordered to Richmond, Ray County, where
they arrived on November 9. Here they were imprisoned
in a vacant house. "When they were confined, General
Clark sent Colonel Price with two chains and padlocks,
and had the prisoners fastened together. The windows were
then nailed down; the prisoners were searched, and the only
weapons they had, their pocket knives, were taken away."

Four days later, on Tuesday, November 13, while Hyrum
Smith languished in chains in "a vacant house" at Richmond, his wife Mary was taken in travail at Far West,
and "dear little Joseph F. was added to the number."
The sorrows, the trials, the difficulties of these parents
were manifold; and yet, here was a child who was to be
their great reward. We shall see as we go along how nobly

he added to the illustrious name of his parents, and how, in time, with great ability and honor, he lived to preside over The Church of Jesus Christ of Latter-day Saints, for which they both gave their lives.

Hyrum Smith was first married to a young woman named Jerusha Barden, in Palmyra, New York, in 1826. Six children had been born to these parents when Jerusha, a faithful and good woman, died at Kirtland, Ohio, October 13, 1837. A little more than two months later, on December 24, Hyrum was married to Mary Fielding, an English girl, who had lately come to Kirtland from Toronto, Canada. Mary was cultured, refined, educated, a splendid companion for Hyrum, and fully able and qualified to take care of his motherless children. Shortly after the marriage, Hyrum moved with his family to Missouri, where persecution, as related in the previous pages, took place.

There are some interesting incidents regarding the early childhood of Joseph F. Smith. He himself relates this one, which occurred shortly after his birth:

"After my father's imprisonment by the mob, my mother was taken ill and continued so for several months. In January, 1839, she was taken in a wagon, on her sickbed, to see her husband, who was confined by the mob, a prisoner in Liberty Jail, for no other reason than that he was a Latter-day Saint, and while in this condition of health, and her husband in jail, a company of men led by a Methodist preacher named Bogart, entered her house, searched it, broke open a trunk and carried away papers and valuables belonging to my father. I, being an infant, and lying on the bed, another bed being on the floor, was entirely overlooked by the family (my mother being very sick, the care of me devolved upon my Aunt Mercy and others of the family, during the fright and excitement). So when the mob entered the room where I was, the bed on the floor was thrown on the other, completely smothering me up, and here I was permitted to remain until after the excitement subsided. When thought of, and discovered, my existence was supposed to have come to an end; but subsequent events have proved their suppositions were wrong, however well-founded."

Somehow, during February or March of 1839, Mary Smith, still confined to her bed, was carried out of Missouri in a sleigh or wagon and taken to Quincy, Illinois, where some of the Saints had made temporary headquarters. Here she and her child remained until joined by their husband and father, Hyrum Smith, on April 22, after his escape from the Missouri officers. In a few weeks Hyrum removed his family to Commerce, later named Nauvoo, and here they remained until the great migration westward.

Of Joseph F. Smith's childhood years, which were spent in Nauvoo, I have some knowledge, as I was fortunate in being a member of his party when he visited that abandoned city in 1906. His memory was vivid regarding many interesting events. He pointed out to us the place in the road where he had stood as he watched his father and "Uncle Joseph" ride away to Carthage on that fateful day in June, 1844. "This is the exact spot," he said, "where I stood when the brethren came riding up on their way to Carthage. Without getting off his horse father leaned over in his saddle and picked me up off the ground. He kissed me good-bye and put me down again and I saw him ride away." The child never saw his father again, except in death. "I remember the night of the murder," he continued, "when one of the brethren came from Carthage and knocked on our window after dark and called to my mother, 'Sister Smith, your husband has been killed.'" He remembered his mother's scream on hearing this dreadful news, and her moans and cries throughout the night.

When we went to the old home of the Prophet Joseph Smith, the President said, as we stood in the kitchen, "In this room the bodies of the martyrs lay in their coffins, after they had been brought from Carthage and dressed for burial. I remember my mother lifting me up to look upon the faces of my father and the Prophet, for the last time."

Outside, as we stood on the bank of the Mississippi River, President Smith pointed out to us where he had stood as he had watched the Saints leave Nauvoo in the early months of 1846. "Many of them crossed on the ice," he said, "the river being completely frozen over at times during that winter."

President Smith was only a child when the tragic events here related took place, but they were firm and clear in his mind nearly sixty years later when we visited Nauvoo with him.

Mary Smith remained in Nauvoo until the summer of 1846, when, by her resourcefulness and ability, she had acquired a sufficient number of teams and wagons to follow the Saints to Winter Quarters. There, on the banks of the Missouri, she established herself until she was sufficiently equipped to take up the long journey to the valleys of the mountains.

Joseph F. Smith has left us an account of some of his boyhood experiences while in or near Winter Quarters. The following is well worth reproducing, as it gives us an intimate picture of an incident in the life of the growing boy in which the influence of his loved mother is shown in shaping his own character.

"In the fall of 1847 my mother and her brother, Joseph Fielding, made a trip down the Missouri river to St. Joseph, Mo., about fifty miles, for the purpose of obtaining provisions and clothing for the family for the coming winter, and for the journey across the plains the following spring. They took two wagons with two yokes of oxen on each. I was almost nine years of age at the time, and accompanied my mother and uncle on this journey as a teamster. The weather was unpropitious, the roads were bad, and it rained a great deal during the journey, so that the trip was a very hard, trying and unpleasant one. At St. Joseph we purchased our groceries and drygoods, and at Savannah we laid in our store of flour, meal, corn, bacon and other pro-

visions. Returning to Winter Quarters, we camped one
evening in an open prairie on the Missouri river bottoms,
by the side of a small spring creek, which emptied into
the river about three-quarters of a mile from us. We were
in plain sight of the river, and could see over every foot
of the little open prairie where we were camped. . . . On
the other side of the creek were some men with a herd of
beef cattle which they were driving to Savannah and St.
Joseph for market.

"We usually unyoked our oxen and turned them loose
to feed during our encampments at night, but this time,
on account of the proximity of this herd of cattle, fearing
that they might get mixed up and driven off with them, we
turned our oxen out to feed in their yokes. Next morning
when we came to look for them, to our great disappoint-
ment our best yoke of oxen was not to be found. Uncle
Fielding and I spent all the morning, well nigh until noon,
hunting for them, but without avail. The grass was tall
and in the morning was wet with heavy dew. Tramping
through the grass and through the woods and over the
bluffs, we were soaked to the skin, fatigued, disheartened
and almost exhausted. In this pitiable plight I was the first
to return to our wagons, and as I approached I saw my
mother kneeling down in prayer. I halted for a moment and
then drew gently near enough to hear her pleading with the
Lord not to suffer us to be left in this helpless condition,
but to lead us to recover our lost team, that we might continue our travels in safety. When she arose from her knees
I was standing near by. The first expression I caught upon
her precious face was a lovely smile, which, discouraged
as I was, gave me renewed hope and assurance that I had
not felt before. A few moments later Uncle Fielding came
to the camp, wet with the dews, faint, fatigued, and thoroughly disheartened. His first words were: 'Well, Mary,
the cattle are gone.' Mother replied in a voice which fairly
rang with cheerfulness, 'Never mind, your breakfast has
been waiting for hours, and now, while you and Joseph

are eating, I will just take a walk out and see if I can find the cattle.' My uncle held up his hands in blank astonishment, and if the Missouri river had suddenly turned to run up stream, neither of us could have been much more surprised. 'Why Mary,' he exclaimed, 'what do you mean? We have been all over this country, all through the timber and through the herd of cattle and our oxen are gone— they are not to be found. I believe they have been driven off, and it is useless for you to do such a thing as to attempt to hunt for them.' 'Never mind me,' said mother, 'get your breakfast and I will see,' and she started toward the river, following down, proceeded out of speaking distance. The man in charge of the herd of beef cattle rode up from the opposite side of the creek and called out: 'Madam, I saw your oxen over yonder in that direction this morning about daybreak,' pointing in the opposite direction from that in which mother was going. We heard plainly what he said, but mother went right on, paid no attention to his remark and did not even turn her head to look at him. A moment later the man rode off rapidly toward his herd, which had been gathered in the opening near the edge of the woods, and they were soon under full drive for the road leading toward Savannah, and soon disappeared from view.

"My mother continued straight down the little stream of water, until she stood almost on the bank of the river, and then she beckoned to us. (I was watching her every moment and was determined that she should not get out of my sight.) Instantly we rose from the mess-chest, on which our breakfast had been spread, and started toward her, and, like John who outran the other disciple to the sepulchre, I outran my uncle and came first to the spot where my mother stood. There I saw our oxen fastened to a clump of willows growing in the bottom of a deep gulch which had been washed out of the sandy banks of the river by the little spring creek, perfectly concealed from view. We were not long in releasing them from bondage and getting back to our camp, where the other cattle had been fastened to the wagon wheels all the morning, and we were soon on our way homeward bound, rejoicing. This circumstance was one of the first practical and positive demonstrations of the efficacy of prayer I had ever witnessed. It made an indelible impression upon my mind and has been a source of comfort, assurance and guidance to me throughout my life."

In the spring of 1848 most of the Saints at Winter Quarters made preparations to begin the long journey across the plains to the new gathering place in the valleys of the mountains. Widow Smith was among the number, and although she had done all she could to procure proper equipment, with her limited resources, when the time came to undertake the arduous journey she found herself poorly prepared. She had managed to get together seven old wagons, on which were loaded her household goods and supplies, together with those of her sister, Mrs. Thompson, and others who made up her party, but all of them combined did not possess a sufficient number of cattle to pull the wagons. However, by fastening two wagons together and yoking up the cows and calves and what oxen they had, and undaunted and full of faith, they began the journey. Brave little Joseph F. was there too, nine years of age his last birthday; doing the work of a little man now, driving his four oxen, hitched to one or two wagons; anxious and willing always to help in every way he could.

The experiences of the journey across the plains were never forgotten by Joseph F. Smith. The captain of the company was most unkind to his mother throughout the entire journey. "One cause of his spite at my mother," President Smith relates, "was because she would not allow me to stand guard at nights and perform all the duties of a man. But I did faithfully perform many duties that should have been reserved for one of more mature years. I yoked, unyoked, and drove my teams, and took my turn as day guard with the men."

At one place on the journey "as the company was moving slowly through the hot sand and dust, in the neighborhood of the Sweetwater, the sun pouring down with excessive heat, towards noon one of Widow Smith's best oxen laid down in the yoke, rolled over on its side and stiffened out its legs spasmodically, evidently in the throes of death. The unanimous opinion was that he was poisoned. All the hindmost teams of course stopped, the people coming forward to know what was the matter. In a short time the Captain, who was in advance of the company, perceiving that something was wrong, came to the spot. Probably no one supposed for a moment that the ox would recover, and the Captain's first words on seeing him were: 'He is dead; there is no use working with him; we'll have to fix up some way to take the widow along; I told her she would be a burden upon the company.'

"Meantime Widow Smith had been searching for a bottle of consecrated oil in one of the wagons, and now came forward with it, and asked her brother Joseph Fielding, and others of the brethren, to administer to the ox, thinking that the Lord would raise him up. They did so, pouring a portion of the oil on the top of his head, between and back of the horns, and all laid hands on him, and one prayed, administering the ordinance as they would have done to a human being that was sick. In a moment he gathered up his legs, and at the first word arose to his feet, and traveled right off as well as ever."

It was no doubt the faith and determination of Widow Smith, and the blessings of God, that brought her and her party safely through to Salt Lake Valley, where they arrived on September 23, 1848. The immediate duty now before her was to find some means of subsistence and some way to support her family. She located on Mill Creek, south of Salt Lake City, and in the course of two years built a comfortable home and obtained some valuable farming property. But not long was Widow Smith to survive the rigors and trials of pioneer life. She became ill in the summer of 1852, and on the 21st of September quietly breathed her last, surrounded by her family and friends.

II

Joseph F. Smith was now an orphan boy, a few months before his fourteenth birthday. With the world before him, what would he do and what path would he take? His mother had been his all to him, and from her he had learned valuable lessons; he would remember what she had taught him; he would not disappoint her. He would strive to become one of the strong men of the Church and carry on the good name of both his mother and father.

But the boy had some tendencies to overcome. He was quick with his temper and not afraid to let his fists fly, if sufficiently provoked. He once related to my father, Charles W. Nibley, an incident that occurred shortly after his mother's death, in which he had a clash with his school-teacher. "My little sister Martha," he said, "was called up to be punished. I saw the schoolteacher bring out the leather strap, and he told the child to hold out her hand. I just spoke up loudly and said, 'Don't whip her with that!' and at that he came at me and was going to whip me; but instead of whipping me, I licked him, good and plenty." As nearly as I can find, this episode ended Joseph F. Smith's formal school education.

What to do now? Perhaps "uncle" George A. Smith, one of the twelve apostles, who had formed a strong attachment for the boy, took the matter of his future in hand. At any rate, during the April conference of 1854, four months after his fifteenth birthday, his name was read out as a missionary, called to preach the gospel to the natives of the Hawaiian Islands.

It was exceptional that one so young should have been trusted to undertake this important calling, yet his experiences had been such that for some time he had been doing the work of a man. He was tall and strongly built, unafraid and able to take care of himself in any situation. He had developed in advance of his years. He had a complete and whole-hearted faith in the religion of his parents. The authorities of the Church were well assured that here was a boy who could be depended upon to do his duty.

And so, when the group of missionaries, under the presidency of Parley P. Pratt, left Salt Lake City for the Pacific coast on May 27, 1854, taking the southern route to San Bernardino and traveling with ox teams and wagons, Joseph F. Smith was among the number. The record tells us that he was the youngest of the group.

For the sake of brevity I shall have to omit the details of his journey to the islands; how on reaching San Bernardino he was forced to work in the mountains "making shingles for a man named Morse" in order to obtain ship money to continue his journey to San Francisco; how at San Francisco, again without means, the boy went into nearby harvest fields and worked "to obtain means for clothing" and to purchase passage to the islands. Finally all was in readiness, and on September 8, 1854, nine missionaries went on board the ship Vaquero in San Francisco harbor, bound for the Hawaiian Islands.

The elders tried to obtain steerage accommodation (the cheapest that could be had) but none being obtainable on this boat, "special quarters had to be provided for them with the crew." After a stormy voyage of nineteen days, the Vaquero sailed into Honolulu harbor on September 27. The brethren had been four months to the day on their journey from Salt Lake City. As the missionaries approached the harbor, many of the natives came out to meet the vessel, some of them in their canoes and some swimming. Joseph F. listened to their conversation, as they called to each other and to those on the ship, and wondered how in the world it would ever be possible to understand the native tongue.

In a few days Joseph F. was appointed to labor on the island of Maui, and from there, on October 20, he wrote a lengthy letter to his father's cousin, George A. Smith, in Salt Lake City. I should like to quote all of this splendid letter but cannot do so on account of limited space, but I shall quote two or three paragraphs to show the strength of character, the power of faith and belief, that this young man had developed—and he was not yet sixteen years of age.

"I feel thankful to you for your counsel," he writes, "for I know it is good, and I know that the work in which I am engaged is the work of the living and true God, and I am ready to bear my testimony of the same, at any time or at any place or in whatsoever circumstances I may be placed; and hope and pray that I ever may prove faithful in serving the Lord, my God.

"I am happy to say that I am ready to go through thick and thin for the cause in which I am engaged, and truly hope and pray that I may prove faithful to the end. These are my feelings; and I feel like blessing the valleys of the mountains, and almost all they contain, all the day long. . . .

"Give my love to all the folks; to George and his sister; and remember me to cousin Elias and his folks, and also to cousin Jane and the boys; and tell them that I desire an interest in their prayers, that I may hold out faithful, and bear off my calling with honor to myself and the Cause in which I am engaged. I had rather die on this mission than to disgrace myself or my calling. These are the sentiments of my heart. My prayer is that we may hold out faithful to the end, and eventually be crowned in the Kingdom of God, with those that have gone before us."

A boy who could write a letter like that had good promise in him. He did prove true, and he was successful on this mission—as he proved true and was successful throughout his life. He remained on the Hawaiian Islands a little more than three years and established a reputation as a diligent and faithful missionary, which brought honor and satisfaction to him.

The journey homeward was similar to the outward trip; to San Francisco by boat, then down the California coast to San Bernardino, then across the desert to Salt Lake City. He arrived at his home safe and well on February 24, 1858. He was now three months past his nineteenth birthday.

1858

III

On his arrival Joseph F. found that the leaders of the Church and the Saints generally were greatly concerned regarding the approach of Johnston's army, which for the time being had been stopped at Fort Bridger. "The day following my arrival home," he relates, "I reported myself to President Young and immediately enlisted in the legion to defend ourselves against the encroachments of a hostile and menacing army. From that time until the proclamation of peace and a free and full pardon by President Buchanan came, I was constantly in my saddle, prospecting and exploring the country between Great Salt Lake City and Fort Bridger, under the command of Colonel Thomas Callister and others. I was on picket guard with a party of men under Orrin P. Rockwell, when Commissioners Powell and McCollough met us near the Weber river with the President's proclamation. Subsequently I was on detail in the deserted city of Great Salt Lake, until after the army passed through the city, and thence to Camp Floyd. After this assisted my relatives to return to their homes, from which they had fled, going to the south some time previous."

On April 5, 1859, Joseph F. was married to Levira A. Smith, of Salt Lake City. His thought now was to establish a home and to accumulate sufficient means to take care of himself and family. But again the Church requested his services. At the annual conference in April, 1860, his name was among those read out to the congregation who were requested to do missionary labor. This time his call was to England. Following the April conference he reported himself ready for duty, and shortly thereafter began the weary journey eastward across the plains, "driving a four-mule team," in order to obtain transportation and board. In two and a half months he reached New York City, and on the 14th of July sailed for Liverpool on the steamship *Edinburgh*. After an uneventful voyage he arrived in England.

The principal part of Joseph F.'s time in England was spent in the Sheffield Conference, where he was called to preside. It was on this mission, no doubt, that he developed the beautiful gift of speaking that was his in a supreme degree. Of all men that I have ever heard speak, I think that he was the most eloquent and impressive. His voice was pleasant and appealing; he could speak with the utmost kindness and tenderness; but when aroused or angered, his rebuke to the sinner was terrible. Of all preachers of the gospel, I always think of Joseph F. Smith as the greatest I ever heard.

One incident that occurred while Joseph F. was on this English mission may be of interest to the reader. On a certain Sunday at Sheffield, one of the members of the branch, Brother William Fowler, who was employed as a polisher and grinder in a cutlery works, brought in a song he had composed and requested that the choir learn to sing it. The first line of this song was, "We Thank Thee, O God, for a Prophet." This beautiful song is now one of the best known and most frequently heard of any of the hymns sung by the Latter-day Saints.

Shortly after Joseph F. arrived in England, Elder George Q. Cannon was sent by President Brigham Young to preside over the European Mission. This gave the two men an opportunity to frequently associate together, and a close friendship was formed between them. Later in life they were to serve jointly as the counselors to three Presidents of the Church.

Before returning home, Joseph F. was granted the

opportunity of visiting several of the countries of Europe. He made a tour of the branches of the Church in Denmark in company with President George Q. Cannon, and later was able to visit Paris and other cities in France. Thus was his education broadened by the advantages given to him by his Church. He had crossed two oceans and proclaimed the gospel in many lands before he reached his twenty-third birthday.

Having been released from his second mission, Joseph F. set sail from Liverpool on June 24, 1863, and arrived home in September, after completing his third journey across the plains.

Once more in Salt Lake City with his loved ones and friends, Joseph F.'s thought again was, "now the time has come when I may settle down for a season and take care of my own." But once again President Brigham Young reached out for the young man with the request that he do further service for the Church. It appears that an elder by the name of Gibson had been causing considerable trouble among the Saints in Hawaii, and President Young thought it necessary to send two of the Twelve, Ezra T. Benson and Lorenzo Snow, to straighten out the difficulties. As these brethren were unable to speak the language, Joseph F. Smith and two other elders who had labored on the islands were requested to accompany them. On March 1, 1864, they left Salt Lake City, and Joseph F. now embarked on his third mission, before his twenty-sixth birthday. Truly the Lord was preparing him for the great responsibility that was one day to be his in presiding over the Church. This second mission to the islands was carried out faithfully, and in December, 1864, Joseph F. returned to Salt Lake City, having performed the tasks that were assigned him.

For a time after his return he found employment in the Church Historian's office, and was an assistant to George A. Smith. On July 1, 1866, while still working in this capacity, he was asked to attend a meeting of several of the apostles and President Young in "the upper room of the

Historian's Office." At the conclusion of the meeting,
"President Young turned to his brethren and said, 'Hold
on, shall I do as I feel led? I always feel well to do as the
Spirit constrains me. It is in my mind to ordain Brother
Joseph F. Smith to the apostleship, and to be one of my
counselors." The brethren present approved of President
Young's desired action, and accordingly Joseph F. Smith
was ordained to this high and holy calling by the President.
As there was no vacancy in the quorum at the time, the
matter was not made public until April 8, 1867, when his
name was presented to the conference and he was sustained
as a member of the Quorum of Twelve Apostles, succeeding Amasa M. Lyman. The widow's son, the herd boy of
the plains, the youthful missionary, had now through his
faith and faithfulness, his ability and devotion, been recognized and had taken his place in the leading quorum of
the Church, next to the First Presidency. From this time
on he became one of the strong men of the Church, one
who helped to guide its destiny during the troublesome
years ahead.

IV

It was in this same year, 1867, that my father, Charles
W. Nibley, first became acquainted with Joseph F. Smith.
He relates the event as follows:

"The first time I ever remember having seen Joseph
F. Smith was in the little village of Wellsville, in the year
1867. He was twenty-eight years of age, and had recently
been chosen one of the Twelve Apostles. President Brigham
Young and company were making a tour of the northern
settlements, and the new Apostle, Joseph F. Smith, was
among the number. I heard him preach in the old meetinghouse at Wellsville, and I remarked at the time what a
fine specimen of young manhood he was—strong, powerful,
with a beautiful voice, so full of sympathy and affection,

so appealing in its tone, that he impressed me, although I was a youth of but eighteen. He was a handsome man."

From the time of his return from his second mission to the islands in 1864, until February, 1874, a period of ten years, Joseph F. Smith was allowed to remain at home, except for his visits to the various stakes. During these years, besides providing a living for himself and looking after his church duties, he served as a member of the Territorial House of Representatives.

At the October conference in 1873, Joseph F. Smith was called by the First Presidency of the Church to preside over the European Mission. He immediately began preparations to accept this important position, and on February 28, 1874, he departed for England, where he arrived on the 21st of March. He was now embarking upon his fourth mission.

During the years of 1874 and 1875, President Smith visited the branches of the Church in England and Scotland. He also made a tour of France, Switzerland, Germany, and the Scandinavian countries. In the fall of 1875 he was released to return home following the death of George A. Smith, counselor to President Brigham Young.

During the year 1876, President Smith was called to preside over the settlements in Davis county. In April, 1877, he attended the dedication of the St. George Temple and the annual conference of the Church, which were held at the same time. On the second day of the conference, April 7, he was again called by President Young to take charge of the European Mission. President Young informed him that this would be "a long mission," but Providence ruled otherwise. On August 29, 1877, President Brigham Young died, and the Council of Twelve Apostles sent word for President Smith to return home "as soon as possible."

After his arrival in Salt Lake City, President Smith was daily in consultation with his brethren. The Twelve as a quorum was now the governing body of the Church, with John Taylor as its president.

In the fall of 1878, Joseph F. Smith and Orson Pratt were sent on a mission to the eastern states "to gather up records and data relative to the early history of the Church." These brethren arrived at Independence, Missouri, on September 6, and the same day visited the temple lot. The same evening they went on to Richmond, and the following day called on David Whitmer, the last surviving witness of the Book of Mormon. President Smith has left us an excellent account of this visit, which is too lengthy to be reproduced here, but I shall take the opportunity to quote one paragraph. When asked by Orson Pratt, "Do you remember what time you saw the plates?" David Whitmer replied: "It was in June, 1829, the very last part of the month, and the eight witnesses, I think, the next day. Joseph showed them (the eight witnesses) the plates himself. We not only saw the plates of the Book of Mormon, but the brass plates. . . . The fact is, it was just as though Joseph, Oliver and I were sitting right here on a log, when we were overshadowed by a light. It was not like the light of the sun, nor like that of a fire, but more glorious and beautiful. It extended away around us, I cannot tell how far, but in the midst of this light, immediately before us, about as far off as he sits, (pointing to John C. Whitmer who was sitting 2 or 3 feet from him) there appeared, as it were, a table, with many records on it, besides the plates of the Book of Mormon; also the sword of Laban, the Directors, (i. e. the ball which Lehi had) and the Interpreters. I saw them just as plain as I see this bed (striking his hand upon the bed beside him) and I heard the voice of the Lord as distinctly as I ever heard anything in my life declaring that they (the plates) were translated by the gift and power of God."

It is fortunate that this interview, one of the last that David Whitmer gave, was preserved by Joseph F. Smith.

While on this journey to the East, the brethren visited the Hill Cumorah, the Kirtland Temple, Far West, and other places of interest. They returned to Salt Lake City on September 28.

For more than three years after the death of President
Brigham Young, the Church was governed and regulated
by the Quorum of Twelve Apostles acting as a body. On
Sunday, October 10, 1880, it was announced to the Saints
that the First Presidency had been reorganized with John
Taylor as President of the Church and George Q. Cannon
and Joseph F. Smith as counselors. This was indeed a high
honor to these three brethren. It is worthy of note that
both George Q. Cannon and Joseph F. Smith had been
bereft of their parents in their childhood years. They had
made their way upwards, alone; yet not alone, for they
had been humble and dependent upon Him who does not
desert his faithful children.

With the advent of President Taylor's administration,
the government began a bitter and relentless campaign
against the practice of polygamy. The Edmunds law, passed
by Congress in 1882, was extremely drastic; self-government
was forbidden the people of Utah, and the Latter-day
Saints who practiced plural marriage were denied the right
to vote. As President Joseph F. Smith had been obedient
to this principle, and as he was one of the high officials
of the Church, he was immediately sought by the federal
officials. In October, 1884, word came to him that two
deputies had been assigned to subpoena him to appear before the grand jury. It was therefore necessary for him to
go into seclusion and for the following seven years he was
sought by the federal officers—but not found. During the
fall of 1884 and the winter of 1884-85 he spent considerable
time in visiting the settlements of the Saints in Southern
Utah, Colorado, Arizona, New Mexico, and California. In
January, 1885, with his wife Julina and small daughter,
he departed for the Hawaiian Islands, where he supervised
the work of the mission until July, 1887, when he was requested to return home because of the severe illness of
President John Taylor. He arrived at Kaysville, Utah, on
July 18 and was permitted to be with President Taylor
for several days before his death, which occurred on July 25.

The Council of Twelve Apostles again took charge of the Church, with President Wilford Woodruff at its head. It was not until April 5, 1889, that the First Presidency was again reorganized. At this time President Woodruff chose George Q. Cannon and Joseph F. Smith as his counselors. President Smith was still forced to remain in seclusion, although the Church abandoned the teaching and practice of polygamy, as set forth in the Manifesto issued by President Woodruff in October, 1890. However, it was not until September, 1891, that Joseph F. Smith was granted amnesty by the president of the United States and obtained his full freedom. On Sunday, September 17, he addressed the Saints in the Salt Lake Tabernacle for the first time in seven years. "This is a memorable day to me," he said, "and no words at my command can express my gratitude to God."

The principal event of the succeeding years of President Woodruff's administration was the dedication of the Salt Lake Temple on April 6, 1893. The Saints had been forty years in building this beautiful and imposing structure. Joseph F. Smith, as a boy, had witnessed the laying of the cornerstones, and now he was present and a member of the First Presidency when the building was completed.

On September 2, 1898, President Wilford Woodruff died at San Francisco, where he had gone to try to recover his health. Again the First Presidency of the Church was dissolved and the responsibility of governing the members was upon the Quorum of Twelve Apostles, with Lorenzo Snow at its head. At a meeting of the Twelve on September 13, Lorenzo Snow was sustained as President of the Church, and he chose as his counselors the same men who had served with two previous Presidents, George Q. Cannon and Joseph F. Smith. President Snow was eighty-four years of age when he became President of the Church. He lived only three years to exercise the duties of this important office. At his death on October 10, 1901, Joseph F. Smith became the President. This important action was

taken at a meeting of the twelve apostles, held on October
17.

V

63 yrs old
1901

At the time he was sustained as President of the
Church, Joseph F. Smith was within one month of his
sixty-third birthday. He was strong and vigorous in health;
sound in mind and body; a man qualified by training and
experience for his high position. He was the first President
of the Church to be born of Latter-day Saint parents;
from them he had learned the teachings of the gospel;
from them he had inherited a strong natural desire to be of
service in the work of God and to maintain the good name
with which they had blessed him.

The years of Joseph F. Smith's administration as President of the Church were years of prosperity and advancement. As early as 1906 the Church was cleared entirely
of debt, and due to his good management and the management of his successors, it has been kept clear of financial
obligations since that time. How often, during the administration of President Smith, did the Saints hear his ringing
advice: "Get out of debt; keep out of debt; never mortgage
your homes nor your farms." All his life he personally
practiced the principle of "pay as you go."

Many splendid buildings were constructed during the
administration of President Smith. Among them are the
Bishop's Building, the Hotel Utah, the L.D.S. Church Office
Building, the L.D.S. Hospital, the Alberta Temple, and the
Hawaii Temple. No President since Brigham Young had
conducted a more enterprising building program.

President Smith had a vital interest in the old historic
landmarks of the Church. While he was President he authorized the purchase of the Prophet Joseph Smith's birthplace at Sharon, Vermont, the Carthage jail, and the Joseph Smith farm at Palmyra. Purchases were also made

of portions of the original temple lot at Independence, Missouri.

One of the historic occasions of President Smith's administration was the erection and dedication of the Joseph Smith Monument at Sharon, Vermont, which occurred on December 23, 1905, the one hundreth anniversary of the Prophet's birth. President Smith, his counselor, Anthon H. Lund, and a number of the General Authorities and friends journeyed to Vermont to attend this celebration. The dedicatory services took place at 11 o'clock on that historic day, President Smith offering the prayer. As it reveals the deep feelings of his heart, I should like to reproduce a few paragraphs from this prayer: "Our Father who art in heaven! Hallowed be thy most holy name. We, thy servants and handmaidens, representing The Church of Jesus Christ of Latter-day Saints, have gathered here to dedicate this monument to the memory of thy servant, Joseph Smith, the great Prophet and Seer of the nineteenth century, who was born into the world near this spot, on the 23rd day of December, 1805—one hundred years ago. It was from him that we received the everlasting gospel, revealed to him by the Eternal Father, through Jesus Christ, the Son.

"With hearts full of gratitude to thee for the light of thy gospel, the authority of the Holy Priesthood, and the ordinances of salvation for the living and for the dead, revealed through thy servant Joseph Smith; in loving remembrance of him, and grateful for the privilege of being present on this occasion, we dedicate to thee the ground on which stands this monument, that it may be sacred and most holy. We dedicate the foundation, typical of the foundation thou hast laid, of apostles and prophets, with Jesus Christ, thy Son, as the chief cornerstone. We dedicate the the base as typifying the rock of revelation on which thy church is built. We dedicate the die, with its inscriptions, as appropriate to the whole design. We dedicate the capstone as a sign of the glorious crown that thy servant Joseph has secured unto himself through his integrity to thy cause, and that of similar reward which shall grace the head of each of his faithful followers. We dedicate the spire as a token of the inspired man of God whom thou didst make indeed a polished shaft in thine hand, reflecting the light of heaven, even thy glorious light, unto the children of men. We dedicate the whole monument as signifying the finished work of human redemption. . . ."

At the conclusion of the dedicatory services, President Smith and party assembled in the cottage that had been built around the hearth of the old Smith home. Here, Anthon H. Lund presented President Smith with a watch chain and locket, "in behalf of the Utah party." President Smith replied in part as follows: "I hardly know whether I can trust myself to say anything. It would not be true for anyone in my position to say less than that I esteem above all the riches or any honor that the world can bestow, the love and confidence of my associates—to know that I have a little merit, to be worthy, at least in a small degree, of possessing the confidence and love of good men and women. Of course my heart has been full the whole day. Yesterday while visiting the birthplace of my father and some of his brothers and sisters, and contemplating this rugged country, filled with hills and ravines, the thought that here in this land was where my kindred had birth, that we are perhaps traversing the same roads and the same ravines, and possibly partaking of the products of the same orchard from which our ancestors two or three generations ago partook, and then the thought of dedicating this monument—(here the President broke down, his voice choked with emotion, and his eyes filled with tears, but, making an effort to control himself he continued)—My heart is like that of a child. It is easily touched, especially with love. I can much easier weep for joy than for sorrow. I suppose perhaps it is due to some extent to the fact that all my early remembrances were painful and sorrowful. The persecutions of the Prophet and the people in Missouri and in Illinois, the final martyrdom of the Prophet and my father, the expulsion of the Saints from Nauvoo, the driving out of the widows and orphans from their homes, the journey across the plains, the hardships we endured in the settling of the valley of the Great Salt Lake and trying to make a home there, my experiences on the plains, in standing guard, herding cattle and going to the canyons; and then starting out at the age of fifteen on a mission to the Sandwich Islands, so far away, alone apparently, without father or mother, without kindred or friends, scarcely— all this had a tendency in my youth to depress my spirit. But I have had strength by the grace of God to keep myself from deadly sins. And now, when I experience the expressions of confidence and love of my brethren and sisters, it goes directly to my heart. . . ."

In 1906, President Joseph F. Smith and a party of friends, which included my honored father, Charles W. Nibley, made an extended trip to Europe and visited the congregations of the Latter-day Saints in Germany, Holland, Belgium, Switzerland, France, and the British Isles. On their return journey they stopped at Nauvoo, Carthage, and Far West—historic places in early Church history. It was President Smith's first visit to Carthage jail, the scene of the death of his father. By choice, he had always remained away from this building. I was with him on this occasion and heard him remark to my father, "Charley, I despise this place. It harrows up my feelings to come here."

Four times during President Smith's administration he made trips to the Hawaiian Islands. During the visit there in 1915 he dedicated at Laie the site for a temple. Elder Reed Smoot, who was with him, remarked of this occasion, "I have heard President Smith pray hundreds of times. He has thrilled my soul many times with his wonderful spirit of prayer and his supplications to our Heavenly Father. But never in all my life did I hear such a prayer. The very ground seemed to be sacred, and he seemed as if he were talking face to face with the Father. I cannot and never will forget it if I live a thousand years." From the time of his first mission to the Hawaiian Islands as a boy, President Smith had manifested great love for that country and its people.

During his administration, President Smith made many trips to the outlying wards and stakes. He found complete happiness in his association with the Latter-day Saints; in visiting with them and in teaching them the principles of the gospel. "As a preacher of righteousness," said Charles W. Nibley, "who could compare with him? He was the greatest that I ever heard—strong, powerful, clear, appealing. It was marvelous how the words of living light and fire flowed from him. He was a born preacher, and yet, he did not set himself up to be such. He never thought highly of his own good qualities. Rather, he was simple, plain and unaffected to the last degree; and yet, there was a dignity with it all which enabled anyone and everyone to say: 'Here is a man among men.' "

President Smith's favorite themes in speaking were, first, the divine mission of Jesus Christ, and second, the divine mission of the Prophet Joseph Smith.

"I know that my Redeemer lives," he said on one occasion. "We have all the evidence of this great and glorious truth that the world has, that is, all the so-called Christian world possess; and, in addition to all they have, we have the testimony of the inhabitants of this western continent, to whom the Savior appeared and delivered his gospel, the same as he delivered it to the Jews. In addition to all this new testimony, and the testimony of the Holy Scriptures from the Jews, we have the testimony of the modern Prophet, Joseph Smith, who saw the Father and the Son, and who has borne record of them to the world, whose testimony was sealed with his blood and is in force upon the world today. We have the testimony of others, who witnessed the presence of God in the Kirtland Temple, when he appeared to them there, and the testimony of Joseph and of Sidney Rigdon, who declare that they were

the last witnesses of Jesus Christ. Therefore I say again,
I know that my Redeemer lives; for in the mouths of these
witnesses, this truth has been established in my mind. Besides these testimonies, I have the witness of the Spirit of
God in my own heart, which exceeds all other evidences,
for it bears record to me, to my very soul, of the existence
of my Redeemer, Jesus Christ."

On another occasion President Smith said of the
Prophet Joseph Smith:

"I was acquainted with the Prophet Joseph in my
youth. I was familiar in his home, with his boys and with
his family. I have sat on his knee. I have heard him preach.
I distinctly remember being present in the council with
my father and the Prophet Joseph Smith and others. From
my childhood to youth I believed him to be a prophet of
God. From my youth until the present I have not only
believed that he was a prophet, for I have known that he
was. In other words my knowledge has superseded my belief. I remember seeing him dressed in military uniform
at the head of the Nauvoo Legion. I saw him when he
crossed the river, returning from his intended western trip
into the Rocky Mountains to go to his martyrdom, and I
saw his lifeless body, together with that of my father, after
they were murdered in Carthage jail; and still have the
most palpable remembrance of the gloom and sorrow of
those dreadful days. I believe in the divine mission of the
prophets of the nineteenth century with all my heart, and
in the authenticity of the Book of Mormon, and the inspiration of the book of Doctrine and Covenants, and hope to
be faithful to God and man, and not false to myself, to
the end of my days."

Joseph F. Smith was granted this wish. He was true
to the end of his days.

President Smith's last public trip to visit the Saints
was made in the fall of 1917, when he, with a number of
the Council of Twelve and other leading brethren, journeyed
to Southern Utah by automobile and held meetings in the

various settlements. He counseled the Saints to pay their tithes and offerings; to keep the word of wisdom; to be faithful to every convenant and obligation, and to keep out of debt.

At the general conference in 1917, he remarked of his health: "I begin to feel that I am getting to be an old man, or rather a young man in an old body. I think I am just about as young as I ever was in my life in spirit. I have the truth today more than I ever did before in the world. I believe in it more firmly now than I ever did before, because I see it more clearly. I understand it better from day to day by the promptings and inspiration of the spirit of the Lord that is vouchsafed to me; but my body gets tired, and I want to tell you, sometimes my poor old heart grieves considerably."

In January, 1918, President Smith suffered a severe blow in the death of his eldest son, Hyrum M. This young man, had he lived two months longer, would have reached his forty-sixth birthday. For some years he had been a member of the Quorum of Twelve Apostles. Capable and able and showing splendid qualities of leadership, it was the hope of his friends that he would live long to carry on the great work of his distinguished father—but it was not to be so. The loss of this son preyed heavily upon the President and weakened his declining health. However, he continued on and worked at his tasks. He was present at all the sessions of the general conferences in April and in October, 1918. In his opening address at the latter he expressed the feelings of his heart:

"For more than seventy years I have been a worker in this Cause, with you and your progenitors, who broke the way into these valleys of the mountains; and my heart is just as firmly set with you today as it ever has been. Although weakened in body, my mind is clear with reference to my duty, and with reference to the duties and responsibilities that rest upon the Latter-day Saints; and I am ever anxious for the progress of the work of the Lord, for the prosperity of the people of The Church of Jesus Christ of Latter-day Saints throughout the world. I am as anxious as I ever have been, and as earnest in my desires that Zion shall prosper, and that the Lord shall favor his people and magnify them in his sight, and in the knowledge and understanding of the intelligent people of all the world."

On the 10th of November, 1918, the anniversary of the day on which he was sustained as President of the Church, seventeen years previously, and three days before his eightieth birthday, he addressed the members of his family who had met to do him honor.

"I cannot help reflecting a little on the fact that over sixty years ago I had to start out in the world, without father or mother—but one brother lived and he was not like me; we were very different from each other—and four sisters. My brother has passed and three of my sisters have also passed away, there being one left. Without anything to start with in the world, except the example of my mother, I struggled along with hard knocks in early life . . . and I have had to watch my step, my 'P's' and 'Q's' so to say, for fear I would do something that would diminish my standing and involve my honor and my word. If there is anything on earth I have tried to do as much as anything else, it is to keep my word, my promises, my integrity to do what it was my duty to do."

It was one week after this family meeting, on Sunday, November 17, that President Smith suffered an attack of pleurisy. The following day he was stricken with pneumonia, and on Tuesday morning, November 19, 1918, he quietly breathed his last. The Church of Jesus Christ of Latter-day Saints had lost one of its greatest leaders.

On account of the great influenza epidemic that was raging in the country at the time of President Smith's death, no public funeral was held. At the graveside services in the Salt Lake City cemetery on November 22, President Heber J. Grant was the principal speaker. Charles W. Penrose offered the dedicatory prayer and benediction.

VI

A brief synopsis of the remarks of President Heber J. Grant at the graveside follows:

"I endorse with all my heart every word that has been uttered here by the lifelong friend of President Joseph F. Smith, Bishop Charles W. Nibley. There is no place in the world where men become so attached to each other as they do in the missionary field, where they are laboring without money and without price to carry the gospel of life and salvation to those who know not the truth; and it was during their labors as missionaries in the European Mission that a friendship was formed between President Smith and Bishop Nibley that has been as lasting and as strong, I believe, as the friendship between any two men in all the Church. [At this point President Grant read two appropriate poems—the first entitled "Beloved By All," by Eliza R. Snow; the second, "A Real Man," by Edgar A. Guest. President Grant then continued.]

"I became intimately associated with President Smith before I reached my majority, and for thirty-six years I have been with him, first when he was a counselor, and later when he was President of the Church. During all these years I have never known of anything in his life, in either word or act, that was not worthy of a real man. I could say in all sincerity, 'He was the kind of man I'd like to be.' Standing here by his grave, I desire more than language can tell, the power and the ability to be as kind, as considerate, as forgiving, as brave and noble, and true, and to walk in every deed in his footsteps. I could ask nothing more.

"May God bless and comfort the hearts of his sorrowing family. May they follow his example, and if they will do this, they will meet him and dwell with him eternally. For no man that ever lived had a more powerful testimony of the living God and of our Redeemer than Joseph F. Smith. From my earliest childhood days he has thrilled my

very being with the testimony that he has borne to all
those with whom he has come in contact, bearing witness
that he knew that God lives and that Jesus is the Christ,
the Son of the living God, the Redeemer of the world. The
very spirit of inspiration that was with this man found lodg-
ment in my heart and in the hearts of many others. I loved
Joseph F. Smith as I never loved any other man that I
have ever known. May God bless his memory. May he
comfort the family and help them and every one of us to
be true to his noble example of integrity, of devotion, of
courage, and of love of God and of his fellows; and, particularly, may we all be as kind, as considerate of those
that God has given us as he has been toward his family,
is my prayer, and I ask it in the name of Jesus. Amen."

VII

    A few months after President Smith's death, my father,
Charles W. Nibley, in an article published in the *Improvement Era*, paid him the following tribute:
    "In the Spring of 1877, I was called to accompany
President Smith on a mission to Europe. I was called by
him to labor in the business affairs of the Liverpool office,
and from that time until the day of his death, I think I
have enjoyed his personal confidence more than any man
living. When I look back on it all now, I can see what
a treasure, a blessing, a favor from the Almighty it has
been to me.
    "During the last eleven years, especially, I have trav-
eled with him almost constantly whenever he has gone from
home. I have been with him on three different trips to
Europe, including the first missionary trip above mentioned,
and on four trips to the Sandwich Islands. Everywhere,
and on all occasions, I have found him the same great,
brave, true-hearted, noble and magnificent leader, so simple
and unaffected, so entirely democratic and unassuming.

"One touching little incident I recall which occurred on our first trip to the Sandwich Islands. As we landed at the wharf in Honolulu, the native Saints were out in great numbers with their wreaths of *leis*, beautiful flowers of every variety and hue. We were loaded with them, he, of course, more than anyone else. The noted Hawaiian band was there playing welcome, as it often does to incoming steamship companies. But on this occasion the band had been instructed by the mayor to go up to the 'Mormon' meetinghouse and there play selections during the festivities which the natives had arranged for. It was a beautiful sight to see the deep-seated love, and even tearful affection that these people had for him. In the midst of it all I noticed a poor old blind woman, tottering under the weight of about ninety years, being led in. She had a few choice bananas in her hand. It was her all—her offering. She was calling Iosepa, Iosepa. Instantly when he saw her he ran to her and clasped her in his arms, hugged her, and kissed her over and over again, patting her on her head, saying, 'Mama, mama, my dear mama.'

"And with tears streaming down his cheeks he turned to me and said, 'Charlie, she nursed me when I was a boy, sick and without anyone to care for me. She took me in and was a mother to me.'

"Oh, it was touching—it was pathetic. It was beautiful to see the great, noble soul in loving tender remembrance of kindness extended to him, more than fifty years before; and the poor old soul who had brought her love offering—a few bananas—it was all she had—to put into the hand of her loved Iosepa.

"On these ocean trips there was much spare time, and we often whiled away an hour or two playing checkers. He could play a good game of checkers, much better than I. In fact, he could beat me four times out of five, but once in a while, when I played more cautiously, and no doubt when he was more careless, I could beat him. If he was beating me right along and I made an awkward move,

and could see instantly that I had moved the wrong checker, he would allow me to draw it back if I noticed it immediately; but on the other hand, if I had beaten him
for a game or two and should put my finger on a checker
to draw it back, even though it were on the instant, he
would call out with force enough, and in that positive way
of his, 'No you don't, you leave it right there.' It is in these
little incidents that we show the human side of our natures.

"He was always careful with his expenditures, too. He
abhorred debt, and no man have I ever known who was so
prompt to pay an obligation to the last penny. He could
not rest until the Church was out of debt, and though hundreds of schemes, and many of them extra good schemes,
too, were presented to him, which no doubt would have
meant an increase of wealth for the Church, yet he re-
solutely set his face against debt, and would not, under
any conditions or circumstances, involve the Church in
that way. Neither would he himself become involved in
debt in his own individual affairs, but persistently stuck
to the old motto, 'Pay as you go.'

"Many of the older people now alive can recall that
forty years ago, or even less, he was considered a radical,
and many a one of that time shook his head and said,
'What will become of things if that fiery radical ever becomes president of the Church?' But from the time he was
made president of the Church, and even before that time,
he became one of the most tolerant of men; tolerant of
others' opinions, and while he would denounce sin with
such righteous wrath as you would seldom see in any man,
yet for the poor sinner he had compassion and pity, and
even forgiveness, if sincere repentance were shown. None
more ready than he to forgive and forget.

"He loved a good story and a good joke. There was a
good laugh in him always. He had no patience with vile
stories, but there was a fine vein of humor in him, and he
could relate incidents of his early life and entertain the
crowd about him as few men ever could.

"He was the most methodical in all his work of all persons I ever knew. Every letter that he received had to be endorsed by him with the date and any other information, and all carefully filed away. He could not stand for disorder. Everything in connection with his work was orderly. He could pack his suitcase or trunk and line out and smooth out every piece of clothing in it so that it would hold more and be better packed than if anybody else had done it. His clothes, too, were always clean.

"He was a most strenuous worker, and never considered saving himself at all. You could go up to his office in the Beehive almost any night when he was well, and find him writing letters or attending to some other work. Perhaps some dear old soul had written him a personal letter, and he would work into the night answering it with his own hand. Indeed, he overworked himself, and, no doubt, injured his strong constitution.

"He was careless about eating—careless as to what he ate and when he ate. His living was exceedingly simple and plain. He rarely got to bed before midnight, and the consequence was he did not get sufficient sleep and rest.

"He was very fond of music and loved to sing the songs of Zion.

"His love for children was unbounded. During the trip we took last year down through the southern settlements to St. George and return, when the troops of little children were paraded before him, it was beautiful to see how he adored these little ones. It was my duty to try to get the company started, to make time to the next settlement where the crowds would be waiting for us, but it was a difficult task to pull him away from the little children. He wanted to shake hands with and talk to every one of them.

"Once in a little while someone would come up to him and say, 'President Smith, I believe I am a kinsman of yours.' I knew then that we were good for another ten minutes delay, for that great heart of his, that went out

to every kinsman as well as to the little children, could
not be torn away quickly from anyone claiming kinship
with him.

"I have visited at his home when one of his little children was down sick. I have seen him come home from his
work at night tired, as he naturally would be, and yet he
would walk the floor for hours with that little one in his
arms, petting it and loving it, encouraging it in every way
with such tenderness and such a soul of pity and love as
not one mother in a thousand would show.

"While he was a hard-headed, successful business man,
yet very few in this dispensation have been more gifted
with spiritual insight than he. As we were returning from
an eastern trip, some years ago, on the train, just east of
Green River, I saw him go out to the end of the car, on
the platform, and immediately return and hesitate a moment, and then sit down in the seat just ahead of me. He
had just taken his seat when something went wrong with
the train. A broken rail had been the means of ditching
the engine and had thrown most of the cars off the track.
In the sleeper we were shaken up pretty badly, but our
car remained on the track.

"The President immediately said to me that he had
gone on the platform, when he heard a voice saying, 'Go
in and sit down.'

"He came in, and I noticed him stand a moment, and
he seemed to hesitate, but he sat down.

"He said further that as he came in and stood in the
aisle he thought, 'Oh, pshaw, perhaps it is only my imag-
ination'; when he heard the voice again, 'Sit down,' and
he immediately took his seat, and the result was as I have
stated.

"He, no doubt, would have been seriously injured
had he remained on the platform of that car, as the cars
were all jammed up together pretty badly. He said, 'I
have heard that voice a good many times in my life, and
I have always profited by obeying it.'

"On another occasion, at a function which was held in the palatial home of Mr. and Mrs. A. W. McCune, he made an extended talk to the gathering. He then said that when a certain brother who had been called to a responsible position in the Church was chosen for that position, he himself had never heard the spiritual voice more plainly and more clearly telling him what to do, than in this naming of the individual who was to be called for that certain office.

"He lived in close communion with the Spirit of the Lord, and his life was so exemplary and chaste that the Lord could easily manifest Himself to His servant. Truly he could say, 'Speak, Lord, for thy servant heareth.' Not every servant can hear when He speaks. But the heart of President Smith was attuned to the Celestial melodies—he could hear, and did hear.

"What shall I say of the grand and glorious work that he has done in rearing the large and splendid family that he leaves behind? What a noble work for any man! Indeed, no man without great nobility of soul could have accomplished it. Is not this bringing up a good family, and a large family of good citizens, good men and women, good for the Church, for the State, and for the Nation—is not this, I say, about the most God-like piece of work that man can do in this world? The thinking mind, which goes into this question deeply enough, will see that here is the work, not only of a man, of a great man, but of a God in embryo. The whole Church can take pride in the vindication of the great principle which he has so successfully wrought out. No ordinary man could accomplish that. Happy the wife who can call him husband. Happy and blessed indeed the children who call him father. Never was a man more chaste and virtuous to the fibre of his being than he. Against all forms or thoughts of licentiousness, he was set, and as immovable as a mountain. 'Blessed are the pure in heart'; and he was of the purest—he shall see God.

"It is written that a truly great man is known by the number of beings he loves and blesses, and by the number of beings who love and bless him. Judged by that standard alone, where is his equal to be found in all this world!

"I can say of Joseph F. Smith as Carlyle said of Luther, that he was truly a great man, 'Great in intellect, in courage, in affection, and integrity. Great, not as a hewn obelisk, but as an Alpine mountain.' No heart ever beat truer to every principle of manhood and righteousness and justice and mercy than his; that great heart, encased in his magnificent frame, made him the biggest, the bravest, the tenderest, the purest and best of all men who walked the earth in his time.

"His life was gentle, and the elements
So mix'd in him, that Nature might stand up
And say to all the world, 'This was a man!' "

HEBER J. GRANT

HEBER J. GRANT

(1856-1945)

A MONG the followers of Brigham Young in the trek westward in 1847 was a young man, Jedediah M. Grant, thirty-one years of age, tall, straight, wiry; a man filled with burning zeal for the religion he had espoused. Day after day this ardent adherent of The Church of of Jesus Christ of Latter-day Saints pursued his weary journey toward the new gathering place in Salt Lake Valley. Fearful tragedies befell him on the way. First, his little daughter Margaret died and was buried in a shallow grave. Then his wife, Caroline, unable to withstand the hardships of the journey, sickened and died. Jedediah was unwilling to leave her to the desolation of the prairies and to the ravages of wild beasts. He constructed a rude coffin, which he strapped to his wagon, and brought her body through to Salt Lake City for safe burial. But with all his trials and tribulations, his zeal for his religion did not diminish. It rather increased with the years, and he became one of Brigham Young's most valiant assistants.

On January 19, 1851, Jedediah M. Grant was elected to be the first mayor of Salt Lake City, and on April 7, 1854, he was chosen by President Brigham Young to the office of second counselor in the First Presidency of the Church. The following year Jedediah married Rachel Ridgeway Ivins, a beautiful and accomplished woman. To them a son was born on November 22, 1856, whom they named Heber Jeddy.

I once questioned President Heber J. Grant regarding his zealous and accomplished father. He replied, "I never knew my father. He died nine days after I was born!" He further related to me that his father, on getting up in the winter nights to wait on his wife and infant son, had taken a severe chill, which had soon turned to pneumonia. On December 1, 1856, Jedediah died—a few months past his fortieth birthday. From that time on the widow and her son made their way alone.

Heber J. Grant lived the life of a normal child in Salt Lake City. He himself recounts the following event, which occurred in his childhood and which gives us a picture of two of the Presidents of the Church—the great pioneer President, Brigham Young, and the boy "hanging on" his sleigh.

"When I was about six years old," relates President Grant, "in the winter of 1862, the sleighing was very good and as I had no opportunity of cutter-riding in those days, none of our family possessing a sleigh or team, boy-like, I used quite frequently to run into the street, and 'hang on behind' some of the outfits which passed our home, and after riding a block or two would jump off and run back.

"On one of these occasions I got on the sleigh belonging to President Brigham Young, and as all who were acquainted with him know, he was very fond of a fine team, and was given to driving quite rapidly. I therefore found myself skimming along with such speed that I dared not jump off, and after riding some time I became cold. President Young, happening to notice me hanging on his sleigh, immediately called out—'Brother Isaac, stop!' He then had his driver, Isaac Wilson, get out and pick me up and tuck me snugly under the robes on the front seat. President Young waited some time before saying anything to me, but finally he asked, 'Are you warm?' and when I answered 'Yes,' he inquired my name and where I lived. He then talked to me in the most kindly manner, told me how much he had loved my father and what a good man he was, and expressed the hope that I would be as good as my father. Our conversation ended in his inviting me to come up to his office some day and have a chat with him. This I very soon afterwards did, and from the day of this childhood acquaintance with President Young, I ever found, in calling at his office or home, a most hearty welcome, and I learned not only to respect and venerate him, but to love him with an affection akin to that which I imagine I would have felt for my own father, had I been permitted to know and return a father's love."

The widow of Jedediah M. Grant supported herself by sewing and taking boarders, when Heber was a boy, and only by the sheerest economy was she able to make ends meet. There was a close companionship between the mother and her little son, and she was to be the dominant influence in shaping his career. "So near to the Lord would she get in her prayers," relates her son, "that they were a wonderful source of inspiration to me from childhood to manhood!" She had faith in her little boy and she taught him that he would not only succeed in the business world, but that he would also become a leader in his Church. She would take care of him now, and later on he would be able to provide for her. Such was the stimulating influence that came to the boy, Heber Jeddy Grant, from his noble mother.

As the years advanced, the boy, in himself, felt this inherent desire to win in the battle of life, in every way. He had a natural desire to excel, to get ahead. He relates his baseball experience:

"Being an only child, my mother reared me very carefully; indeed, I grew more or less on the principle of a hot-house plant, the growth of which is 'long and lanky,' but not substantial. I learned to sweep, and to wash and wipe dishes, but did little stone throwing, and little indulging in those sports which are interesting and attractive to boys, and which develop their physical frames; therefore, when I joined a baseball club, the boys of my own age, and a little older, played in the first nine; those younger than myself played in the second, and those still younger in the third and I played with them. One of the reasons for this was that I could not throw the ball from one base to the other; another reason was that I lacked physical strength to run or bat well. When I picked up a ball, the boys would generally shout, 'Throw it here, sissy!' So much fun was engendered on my account by my youthful companions that I solemnly vowed that I would play baseball in the nine that would win the championship of the Territory of Utah.

"My mother was keeping boarders at the time for a living, and I shined their boots until I saved a dollar, which I invested in a baseball. I spent hours and hours throwing the ball at a neighbor's barn, (Edwin D. Woolley's) which caused him to refer to me as the laziest boy in the Thirteenth Ward. Often my arm would ache so that I could scarcely go to sleep at night. But I kept on practicing, and eventually played in the nine that won the championship of the Territory. Having thus made good my promise to myself, I retired from the baseball arena."

Other examples could be given of the ability of this youth to get where he wanted to go. He had an ardent desire to witness the performances or shows in the Salt Lake Theatre but no money with which to buy tickets. Years later, when he became the president of the Salt Lake Theatre, he described, in a humorous mood, his successful efforts to be admitted to the "upper circle."

" 'The tall boy,' the carrier of water to the upper circle, for the privilege of getting in, was your humble servant, and when the thirsty crowd in the third circle emptied the five-gallon coal oil can used as a water bucket, and I had to walk across the road to the nearest well, beyond the Social Hall, to refill it, I often wished that the 'gods of the galleries' had filled up on water before they reached the theatre. Years later, when I was the president of the Salt Lake Theatre Company, and sat in my box and gazed up to the third gallery, I frequently thought of the 'tall boy' who carried water to that section, and my mind went back to the time when he, too, appeared on the stage of the Salt Lake Theatre, as one of the pickaninnies in 'Uncle Tom's Cabin.' "

"I have found nothing in the battle of life," wrote President Heber J. Grant, years ago, in an early number of the *Improvement Era*, "that has been of more value to me, than to perform the duty of today, to the best of my ability; and I know that where young men do this, they will be better prepared for the labors of tomorrow." To illustrate this point, he then recounted one of his early experiences in entering business in Salt Lake City.

"When a youth, attending school, a man was pointed out to me who kept books in Wells, Fargo and Co.'s Bank, in Salt Lake City, and it was said that he received a salary of one hundred and fifty dollars a month. Well do I remember figuring that he was earning six dollars a day, Sundays omitted, which seemed to me an enormous amount. Although I had not yet read the inspiring words of Lord Bulwer Lytton, yet I dreamed of being a bookkeeper, and of working for Wells, Fargo & Co., and immediately joined the bookkeeping class in the Deseret University, in the hope some day of earning what I thought at that time to be an immense salary.

"I quote with pleasure from Lord Bulwer Lytton: 'What man wants is not talent, it is purpose; not power to achieve, but the will to labor.'

"The result was that some years later, I secured a position as bookkeeper and policy clerk in an insurance office. Although at fifteen, I wrote a very nice hand, and it was all that was needed to satisfactorily fill the position which I then held, yet I was not fully satisfied but continued to dream and 'scribble,' when not otherwise occupied. I worked in the front part of A. W. White & Co.'s bank, and when not busy, volunteered to assist with the bank work, and to do anything and everything I could to

employ my time, never thinking whether I was to be paid
for it or not, but having only a desire to work and learn.
Mr. Morf, the bookkeeper in the bank, wrote well, and
took pains to assist me in my efforts to become proficient
as a penman. I learned to write so well that I often earned
more before and after office hours by writing cards, invi-
tations, etc., and making maps, than the amount of my
regular salary. Some years later, a diploma at the Territorial
Fair was awarded me for the finest penmanship in Utah.
When I engaged in business for myself, there was a vacancy
at the university in the position of teacher of penmanship
and bookkeeping, and to make good the promise to myself,
made when a youth of twelve or thirteen, that I would
some day teach these branches, I applied for the situation.
My application was accepted, and my obligation to myself
was thus discharged.

"'Never Despair' has been one of the guiding stars
of my life.

"At nineteen, I was keeping books and acting as policy
clerk for Mr. Henry Wadsworth, the agent of Wells, Fargo
& Co. My time was not fully employed. I was not working
for the company but for the agent personally. I did the
same as I had done in Mr. White's bank—volunteered to
file a lot of bank letters, etc., and to keep a set of books
of the Sandy Smelting Co., which Mr. Wadsworth was
doing personally.

"My action so pleased Mr. Wadsworth that he employed me to do the collecting for Wells, Fargo & Co.,
and paid me twenty dollars a month for this work in addition to my regular compensation of seventy-five dollars
from the insurance business. Thus I was in the employ of
Wells, Fargo & Co., and one of my day dreams had become a reality.

"When New Year's eve arrived, I was at the office
quite late writing calling cards. Mr. Wadsworth came in
and pleasantly remarked that business was good; that it
never rains but it pours, or something to this effect. He

referred to my having kept the books of the Sandy Smelting Co. without compensation, and said a number of com-
plimentary things which made me very happy. He then
handed me a check for one hundred dollars which doubly
compensated me for all my extra labor. The satisfaction
enjoyed by me in feeling that I had won the good will and
confidence of my employer was worth more to me than
twice one hundred dollars."

Before Heber J. Grant was twenty years of age, he
purchased from Mr. Wadsworth, who had been promoted
to the management of the Wells-Fargo Bank at San Francisco, the "good will" of the latter's insurance agency for
$500. In order to raise this amount of money, he placed
a mortgage on his mother's home. It is needless to say,
however, that this obligation was soon repaid.

The enterprise that young Heber J. Grant manifested
in his business affairs attracted the attention of President
Brigham Young. At twenty years of age he was offered
and accepted the position of assistant cashier of Zion's
Savings Bank and Trust Co., which a few years previously
had been established by President Young. Heber had to
furnish a bond in order to qualify for his new position,
and in this connection he tells an interesting story:

"I had to give a bond of $25,000, vouching for my
honesty. I walked up to the office of President Brigham
Young, and just as he opened the door with his cape on
his arm I said: 'President Young, as you know, the other
day I was elected assistant cashier of Zion's Savings Bank
and Trust Co., and they require a bond of $25,000, guaran-
teeing my honesty. I thought it would be a very appropriate
thing for the President of the bank to sign my bond, and
I have come for your signature.' He smiled and said, 'Heber, I don't see how in the world I can get out of signing
your bond. I said so many good things about you at the
director's meeting that if I now refuse to sign your bond
they will accuse me of not telling the truth!' He remarked
that it would be a real pleasure for him to sign it!"

On November 1, 1877, three weeks before his twenty-first birthday, in the newly completed temple at St. George, Utah, Heber J. Grant was married to Lucy Stringham. Lucy has been described to us as "a woman of sweet disposition, excellent character, and one who exercised considerable judgment in business affairs, which contributed in no small manner to her husband's early financial success."

II

The Church now began to recognize the enterprise and ability of Jedediah M. Grant's son and his devotion to the religion of his father and mother. In the fall of 1880, a short time before his twenty-fourth birthday, he was informed by President John Taylor that he had been selected to preside over the Tooele Stake, with headquarters at Tooele. This appointment came as a great surprise to Heber J. Grant, but he did not murmur about accepting it, although he knew that it would now be more difficult for him to make a living and carry on his various business enterprises in Salt Lake City. From the Church he received no material compensation. He had to pay his way to and from Tooele, and besides earn enough to maintain his business and support his family.

President Grant has left us some interesting information regarding his Tooele experiences. I glean the following from one of his sermons:

"As a boy, without experience, never having spoken in public in my life, for any length of time, never ten minutes at once, I was called to preside over a stake of Zion. I remember preaching and telling everything I could think of, and some of it over twice, and ran out of ideas in seven minutes and a half by the watch. Among other things, I told the people that I knew nothing of the duties that devolved upon me, but with the help of the Lord I would do the best I could, and that with his help I had no fear at all but what I could get along. I remember a good brother telling me that I had made a very serious mistake, that I had destroyed my influence by telling the Saints I did not know anything.

"'Well,' I said, 'they may discover that I have a little sense, later on, and that will agreeably surprise them.'

"The next Sunday I did not do any better. I ran out of ideas in six or seven minutes. The next Sunday I did the same. The following Sunday I took a couple of very excellent preachers with me and went away down to the south end of Tooele county, the farthest settlement, to the little town of Vernon, sometimes called String Town, because it covered a long string of ranches. There was a little log meeting house, and, as I was walking to meeting with the late high councilor in the Ensign Stake of Zion, John C. Sharp, who was then the bishop of Vernon, I looked around and said: 'Why, Bishop, there is nobody going to meeting.'

" 'Oh,' he said, 'I think there will be somebody there.' We were walking up a little hill from his home. The meetinghouse was not in sight. When we reached the top of the hill, I saw a number of wagons around the meetinghouse, but I did not see a soul going to meeting. 'Well,' I said, 'there are some wagons there, but I don't see anybody going to meeting.' He said: 'I guess there will be somebody in the meetinghouse.' We walked into the meetinghouse two minutes to 2 o'clock, and the house was full, every seat occupied, and we were the last people to come in. At 2 o'clock, promptly, we began the meeting; Brother Sharp told me he had tried to educate the people to be seated before 2 o'clock; and, apparently, he had succeeded. I got up to make my little speech of five, six or seven minutes, and I talked for forty-five minutes, with as much freedom and as much of the Spirit of the Lord as I have ever enjoyed in preaching the Gospel, during the forty years that have passed since then. I could not restrain the tears of gratitude which I shed that night, as I knelt down

and thanked God for the rich outpouring of his Holy
Spirit, for the testimony that had come into my heart and
soul, confirming the knowledge that I had of the gospel,
giving me increased power, because of the knowledge that
I had that God, by his Holy Spirit, had inspired me to proclaim this gospel.

"I received another lesson the next Sunday for which
I have been just as grateful, although not as happy over
it. I went to Grantsville, the largest ward in the Tooele
Stake of Zion, and I approached the Lord with much the
same attitude as Oliver Cowdery when he told the Lord, 'I
want to translate,' and the Lord told him he could translate.
But, failing, he was later told, he did not study it out, and
he did not pray about it, and he did not do his share. I
told the Lord I would like to talk again to the Saints in
Grantsville; I got up and talked for five minutes, and I
perspired as freely, I believe, as if I had been dipped in a
creek, and I ran out of ideas completely. I made as complete a 'fizzle,' so to speak, of my talk, as a mortal could
make. I did not shed any tears of gratitude, but I walked
several miles away from that meetinghouse, out into the
fields, among the hay and straw stacks, and when I got
far enough away, so that I was sure nobody saw me, I
knelt down behind one of those stacks and I shed tears
of humiliation. I asked God to forgive me for not remem-
bering that men could not preach the gospel of the Lord
Jesus Christ with power, with force, and with inspiration
only as they are blessed with power which comes from
God; and I told him there, as a boy, that if he would forgive me for my egotism, if he would forgive me for imagin-
ing that without his Spirit any man can proclaim the
truth and find willing hearts to receive it, to the day of
my death I would endeavor to remember from whence the
inspiration comes, when we are proclaiming the gospel of
the Lord Jesus Christ, the plan of life and salvation again
revealed to earth. I am grateful to say that during the
forty years that have passed since then, I have never been

humiliated as I was humiliated that day; and why? Because
I have never, thank the Lord, stood upon my feet with an
idea that a man could touch the hearts of his hearers, be
they Latter-day Saints or sinners, except that man shall
possess the Spirit of the living God, and thus be capable
of bearing witness that this is the truth that you and I are
engaged in."

III

After having labored faithfully in the work of presiding
over the Tooele Stake from October, 1880, until October,
1882, Heber J. Grant was called by revelation, through
President John Taylor, to the high position of an apostle.
This call came to him about one month before his twenty-
sixth birthday. It was a responsible position for such a
young man. Yet, when one looks into his early history, there
is ample evidence that the fact had long been known that
he would one day receive his high calling. From a sermon
delivered by President Grant in 1919, I find the following:
"When I was a little child in a Relief Society meeting
held in the home of the late William C. Staines, corner
South Temple and Fifth East Streets, my mother was there,
'Aunt Em' Wells was there, Eliza R. Snow, Zina D. Young,
and many others. After the meeting was over Sister Eliza
R. Snow, by the gift of tongues, gave a blessing to each
and every one of those good sisters, and Sister Zina D.
Young gave the interpretation. After blessing those sisters,
she turned to the boy playing on the floor, and pronounced
a blessing upon my head by the gift of tongues, and Zina D.
Young gave the interpretation. I, of course, did not understand a word, and all I got of the interpretation, as a child,
was that some day I should be a big man. I thought it
meant that I would grow tall. My mother made a record of
that blessing. What was it? It was a prophecy, by the gift
of tongues, that her boy should live to be an apostle of

the Lord Jesus Christ; and ofttimes she told me that if I would behave myself, that honor would come to me. I always laughed at her and said: 'Every mother believes that her son will become president of the United States, or hold some great office. You ought to get that out of your head, Mother.' I did not believe her until that honor came to me."

Even though it had been made known to his mother and himself, through the gift of tongues to Eliza R. Snow, that he would one day "be an apostle of the Lord Jesus Christ," and even though he had been designated for that high calling by President John Taylor, through special revelation, yet Heber J. Grant was extremely doubtful of his qualifications and of his ability to carry on in this important position. Another remarkable experience, which he related in later years, forever removed the doubt from his mind as to the reasons why he was chosen.

The following is from one of his sermons after he became President of the Church:

"From October, 1882, when I was called to be one of the Council of the Twelve, until the following February, I had but little joy and happiness in my labors. There was a spirit following me that told me that I lacked the experience, that I lacked the inspiration, that I lacked the testimony to be worthy of the position of an apostle of the Lord Jesus Christ. My dear mother had inspired me with such a love of the gospel and with such a reverence and admiration for the men who stood at the head of this Church, that when I was called to be one of them I was overpowered; I felt my unworthiness and the adversary taking advantage of that feeling in my heart, day and night, the spirit pursued me, suggesting that I resign, and when I testified of the divinity of the work we are engaged in, the words would come back, 'You haven't seen the Savior; you have no right to bear such testimony,' and I was very unhappy.

"But in February, 1883, while riding along on the

Navajo Indian Reservation, with Elder Brigham Young, Jr., and fifteen or twenty other brethren, including the late president, Lot Smith, of one of the Arizona stakes, on our way to visit the Navajos and Moquis—going through a part of the Navajo Reservation to get to the Moqui Reservation —as we were traveling to the southeast, suddenly the road turned and veered almost to the northeast, but there was a path, a trail, leading on in the direction in which we had been traveling. There were perhaps eight or ten of us on horseback and the rest in wagons. Brother Smith and I were at the rear of our company. When we came to the trail I said, 'Wait a minute, Lot; where does this trail lead to?'

"He said, 'Oh, it leads back into the road three or four miles over here, but we have to make a detour of eight or nine miles to avoid a large gully that no wagons can cross.'

"I asked, 'Can a horseman get over that gully?'

"He answered, 'Yes.'

"I said, 'Any danger from Indians, by being out there alone?'

"He answered, 'No.'

"I said, 'I want to be alone, so you go on with the company and I will meet you over there where the trail and road join.'

"One reason that I asked if there was any danger was because a few days before our company had visited the spot where George A. Smith, Jr., had been killed by the Navajo Indians, and I had that event in my mind at the time I was speaking. I had perhaps gone one mile when in the kind providences of the Lord it was manifested to me perfectly, so far as my intelligence is concerned—I did not see heaven, I did not see a council held there, but like Lehi of old, I seemed to see, and my very being was so saturated with the information that I received, as I stopped my animal and sat there and communed with heaven, that I am as absolutely convinced of the information that came to me upon that occasion as though the voice of God had spoken the words to me.

"It was manifested to me there and then, as I sat there and wept for joy, that it was not because of any particular intelligence that I possessed, that it was not because of any knowledge that I possessed more than a testimony of the gospel, that it was not because of my wisdom, that I had been called to be one of the apostles of the Lord Jesus Christ in this last dispensation, but it was because the Prophet of God, the man who was the chosen instrument in the hands of the living God of establishing again upon the earth the plan of life and salvation, Joseph Smith, desired that I be called, and that my father, Jedediah M. Grant, who gave his life for the gospel, while one of the presidency of the Church, a counselor to President Brigham Young, and who had been dead for nearly twenty-six years, desired that his son should be a member of the Council of the Twelve. It was manifested to me that the Prophet and my father were able to bestow upon me the apostleship because of their faithfulness, inasmuch as I had lived a clean life, that now it remained for me to make a success or a failure of that calling. I can bear witness to you here today that I do not believe that any man on earth from that day, February, 1883, until now, has had sweeter joy, more perfect and exquisite happiness than I have had in lifting up my voice and testifying of the Gospel at home and abroad in every land and in every clime where it has fallen to my lot to go."

The years from 1882, when he was called to the apostleship, to 1901, when he departed for Japan to open a mission for the Church, were spent by Heber J. Grant in visiting the wards and stakes, in attending the councils of the apostles, and in looking after his extensive business enterprises. The following quotation from one of his sermons presents a clear picture of his business ability during those early years:

"In 1890-91, earnest efforts were being made to estab-

lish the beet sugar industry in our territory. Because of *1890-91*
the financial panic of 1891, many who had subscribed for
stock were unable to pay their subscriptions, and I was
sent east to secure the funds needed to establish the industry. Having failed in New York and Hartford to obtain
all of the money required, I was subsequently sent to San
Francisco where one hundred thousand dollars was secured
from Mr. Henry Wadsworth, cashier of Wells, Fargo & Co.'s
bank in that city. I am confident that my having been
faithful when a boy in his employ, at the time he was agent
of Wells, Fargo & Co., in Salt Lake City, had some influence in causing him to loan to my associates such a
large sum, at a time when there was a great demand for
money."

During the year 1893 a severe business depression took *1893*
place throughout the United States. Values of real estate
and all commodities declined; people drew their money
out of banks and hundreds of these institutions were forced
to close their doors; factories were shut down and men
were thrown out of employment. A chaotic condition prevailed in the business world.

Among the thousands who suffered on account of this
depression was Heber J. Grant. At the October conference
in 1893 he described the state of affairs—and his own
financial condition—to the Saints.

"The Latter-day Saints have been through hard times,
and there are a great many of us who are pulling long
faces and thinking we are in a terrible fix, when we are
in no fix at all. This whole financial panic is a great hoax
from first to last, in one sense of the word. The people all
over the country got scared. At what? At nothing. In the
face of good crops of cotton, corn and wheat, and general
prosperity in the whole country, we have had something
over 570 banks fail; and I venture the assertion that out of
that number there were only a very few that failed
because they were in a bad financial condition. Why did
they fail? Simply because the people got scared, drew their

money out of the banks, and in many cases hid it. In nine
cases out of ten there was no earthly reason for taking
their money out of the banks. It is estimated that of the
trade that is transacted ninety-five percent of it is done
on credit, and that there is only five percent of actual
money that changes hands in transacting the business of
a country. We have had such a scare that the ninety-five
percent has been contracted about twenty percent; in
other words, about four times as much contraction as there
was money in existence to do the business with. The result
is that everybody has become frightened of everybody else,
and as I say, 570 banks have failed, and, almost without
exception, they were absolutely sound and solvent.

"I want to confess to you that I and many others have
done wrong. Why? Because we have been so very anxious
to make a dollar that we have run in debt, and now we
cannot promptly pay our honest debts. I cannot, for the
reason that $10,000 collateral securities which are good,
would not raise $1,000. For the first time in my life I
have had people come to me and ask me to pay money that
I owed them, and I have had to ask for an extension of
time. If the Lord will only forgive me this once I will
never be caught again. I have been a borrower of money
since I was eighteen; but if I can only get paid off what
I owe now, I shall be content, I believe, with the blessings
of the Lord, whatever they may be, be it much or little.

"I went out here on the street with $30,000 worth of
securities and tried to borrow $10,000, and I would have
paid twenty percent interest if I could have got it; but
I could not get anything. So far as our property is concerned it is of no actual value to us, only as we are ready
and willing to use it for the advancement of God's kingdom. It is our duty to provide for our families; but it is
not our duty to live in extravagance. It is not our duty to
labor to gain wealth for the adornment of our persons.
Of course I like to see people have good things, and I
hope to live to see the day when the Latter-day Saints will

be wealthy. But I want to say to you that unless we become more humble, more godlike, more faithful in keeping the commandments of God, I do not expect we shall become wealthy. Whenever we learn to be willing to use the means that God gives us for the onward advancement of his kingdom, Latter-day Saints will not have any particular financial trouble; the Lord will bless them with an abundance. What we need to do is to seek for the light and inspiration of his Spirit to guide us at all times, and he will give all other things to us that are necessary."

At the October conference in 1894, Elder Grant preached a vigorous sermon on the subject of home industry and the necessity of keeping money at home. As to the value of the latter advice, he illustrated his point by relating the following story:

"I remember hearing Brother George L. Farrell in the Assembly Hall six months ago make a statement with reference to homemade goods, and I have quoted it at every conference I have been at since, and I expect to go on quoting it. He stated that he bought some homemade shoes, and he met at the depot the man he owed for making these shoes. He went up to him and gave him the $5. This man turned around, saw another person that he owed, and handed him the $5. He saw another and gave it to him; and he saw another and gave it to him; and the fourth man walked up to Brother Farrell and said, 'Brother Farrell, I owe you $6; here is $5 of it, I will give you the other dollar the next time we meet.' The $5 cancelled, in about the same length of time it takes to tell it, $25 of debts. And debt is bondage; therefore, it lifted $25 of bondage from the shoulders of these people."

The doctrine of personal salvation was always a favorite topic with Heber J. Grant. He was a strong believer in the doctrine that the Lord helps those who help themselves. At the October conference in 1895 he brought forth this subject in a forcible manner:

"If you want to know how to be saved, I can tell you;

How to be Saved?

it is by keeping the commandments of God. No power on earth, no power beneath the earth, will ever prevent you or me or any Latter-day Saint from being saved, except ourselves. We are the architects of our own lives, not only of the lives here, but the lives to come in the eternity. We ourselves are able to perform every duty and obligation that God has required of men. No commandment was ever given to us but that God has given us the power to keep that commandment. If we fail, we, and we alone, are responsible for the failure, because God endows his servants, from the President of the Church down to the humblest member, with all the ability, all the knowledge, all the power that is necessary, faithfully, diligently, and properly to discharge every duty and every obligation that rests upon them, and we, and we alone, will have to answer if we fail in this regard."

During 1897 Elder Grant suffered a severe illness and was forced to undergo an operation for appendicitis. For some months he was unable to leave his home and go about his regular duties. On March 12, 1898, he spoke for the first time in nearly one year in the Tabernacle at Salt Lake City, and described his illness and recovery as follows:

"It is a source of great pleasure to me to once more stand before the Latter-day Saints in this Tabernacle. As most of the Latter-day Saints assembled are aware, it has been nearly a year since I have occupied this position, during which time I have undergone a very serious surgical operation, which, according to the medical journals, should have ended my life. It is recorded that it is impossible for a man to recover who is in the condition that I was found to be in at the time of the operation. But I am grateful to be here; and I feel to thank my Heavenly Father, and the brethren of the priesthood who administered to me and blessed me during the ordeal and promised me that I should recover. Since that time I have also been very sick with pneumonia. Some years ago I tried to insure my life, but the companies refused. Their physicians told me that if

I ever took pneumonia I would die. But I am still here, notwithstanding the report of the physicians of the life insurance companies. It is a source of pleasure to me to again mingle my voice with the Latter-day Saints, and to bear testimony to the knowledge that I possess of the divinity of the work in which we are engaged."

Always pursuing the path of achievement and experiencing supreme satisfaction in overcoming any difficulty that lay in his path, Elder Grant undertook in those years the task of learning to sing. His own delightful account of this achievement is taken from an article he published in the *Improvement Era* in 1900. I shall reproduce it here in part:

"Believing there are quite a number who have never sung, who perhaps would be benefited by reading an account of my efforts, and who might be encouraged thereby in learning to sing, I have decided to give my experience to the readers of the *Era*.

"My mother tried to teach me when a small child to sing, but failed because of my inability to carry a tune. Upon joining a singing class taught by Professor Charles J. Thomas, he tried and tried in vain to teach me when ten years of age to run the scale or carry a simple tune, and finally gave up in despair. He said that I could never, in this world, learn to sing. Perhaps he thought I might learn the divine art in another world. Ever since this attempt, I have frequently tried to sing when riding alone many miles from anyone who might hear me, but on such occasions could never succeed in carrying the tune of one of our familiar hymns for a single verse, and quite frequently not for a single line.

"Nearly ten months ago, while listening to Brother Horace S. Ensign sing, I remarked that I would gladly give two or three months of my spare time if by so doing it would result in my being able to sing one or two hymns. He answered that any person could learn to sing who had a reasonably good voice, and who possessed perseverance, and was willing to do plenty of practicing. My response was that I had an abundance of voice, and considerable perseverance. He was in my employ at the time, and I jokingly remarked that while he had not been hired as a music teacher, however, right now I would take my first music lesson of two hours upon the hymn, 'O My Father.' Much to my surprise, at the end of four or five days, I was able to sing this hymn with Brother Ensign without any mistakes. At the end of two weeks, I could sing it alone, with the exception of being a little flat on some of the high notes. My ear, not being cultivated musically, did not detect this, and the only way I knew of it was by having Brother Ensign and other friends tell me of the error.

"One of the leading Church officials, upon hearing me sing, when I first started to practice, remarked that my singing reminded him very much of the late Apostle Orson Pratt's poetry. He said Brother Pratt wrote only one piece of poetry, and this looked like it had been sawed out of boards, and sawed off straight.

"At the end of two or three months, I was able to sing not only, 'O My Father,' but 'God Moves in a Mysterious Way,' 'Come Come, Ye Saints,' and two or three other hymns. Shortly after this, while taking a trip south, I sang one or more hymns in each of the Arizona stakes, and in Juarez, Mexico. Upon my return to Salt Lake City, I attempted to sing 'O My Father,' in the big Tabernacle, hoping to give an object lesson to young people, and to encourage them to learn to sing. I made a failure, getting off the key in nearly every verse, and instead of my effort encouraging the young people, I fear that it tended to discourage them.

"When first starting to practice, if some person would join in and sing bass, tenor or alto, I could not carry the tune. Neither could I sing if anyone accompanied me on the piano or organ, as the variety of sounds confused me.

"I am pleased to be able to say that I can now sing with piano or organ accompaniment, and can also sing the lead in 'God Moves in a Mysterious Way,' in a duet, a trio or quartet. I have learned quite a number of songs, and have been assured by Brother Ensign, and several others well versed in music, to whom I have sung within the past few weeks, that I succeeded without making a mistake in a single note, which I fear would not be the case, were the attempt to be made in public. However, I intended to continue trying to sing the hymn, 'O My Father,' in the Assembly Hall or big Tabernacle until such time as I can sing it without an error.

"Upon my recent trip to Arizona, I asked Elders Rudger Clawson and J. Golden Kimball if they had any objections to my singing one hundred hymns that day. They took it as a joke, and assured me that they would be delighted. We were on the way from Holbrook to St. Johns, a distance of about sixty miles. After I had sung about forty times, they assured me that if I sang the remaining sixty they would both have nervous prostration. I paid no attention whatever to their appeal, but held them to their bargain and sang the full one hundred. One hundred and fifteen songs in one day and four hundred in four days, is the largest amount of practicing I ever did.

"Today, my musical deafness is disappearing, and by sitting down to a piano and playing the lead notes, I can learn a song in less than one-tenth the time required when I first commenced to practice."

IV

On February 14, 1901, the First Presidency announced that a new mission of the Church would be established in Japan, and the Elder Heber J. Grant had been selected to begin the missionary work in that distant island. Elder Grant readily responded to this call and began to make preparations for his departure.

In this connection he relates an interesting story: "The most marvelous experience in all my life, financially speaking, happened between the time I was called to go to Japan, and the time I departed. As I came from the meeting in the Temple where I had accepted the call, Apostle John W. Taylor caught up with me and said, 'Wait, and let all of the other brethren go out.' Then he continued, 'I know that you have made as great a sacrifice today as Abraham of old made when he was willing to offer up his son Isaac. You are not in a position to accept this call because of the debts you owe. The Lord has accepted your sacrifice, and I prophesy that you will go to Japan a free man financially.' In four months I had paid $4,600 tithing. I had paid all obligations where I had friends who were endorsers, and instead of being in financial distress when I left, I was practically a free man."

Prior to leaving Salt Lake City, he addressed the young people of the Church at the June Conference and gave them some excellent advice:

"In bidding good-bye to the young men and the young ladies forming the Mutual Improvement Associations, I desire to impress upon their minds what was said here today by Brother Roberts, that it is work that will count with you boys and girls; it is keeping the Word of Wisdom; it is paying your tithing; it is avoiding bad company; it is valuing your virtue more than your life; it is listening to the counsels and advice of your fathers and your mothers, and the Priesthood of God, and doing your duty—it is these things that will magnify you before God, and that will bring you back into his presence.

"Young men and young ladies, I leave with you my testimony that God lives, that Jesus is the Christ, that Joseph Smith was and is a prophet of God, and that Lorenzo Snow today is a prophet of God. How do I know it? I know it as well as I know that I stand before you tonight. I know heat, I know cold; I know joy and I know sorrow; and I say to you that in the hour of sorrow, in the hour of affliction, in the hour of death, God has heard and answered my prayers, and I know that he lives. I leave my testimony with you."

At a farewell reception held at the home of President Grant on June 11, President Joseph F. Smith stressed the importance of the mission that Elder Grant was about to undertake and offered his congratulations and good wishes for the success and safe return of the elders. I shall quote President Smith in part as follows:

"To Brother Heber J. Grant I say, we are pleased to think that to you has been entrusted the great labor of opening the door of the gospel of Jesus Christ to one of the foremost nations of the earth today. They are the children of God, and have souls to save; they are bright and ingenious. We expect Brother Grant to do his duty in that calling, and we know he will, and we will sustain him by our faith and prayers. I do not care whether he succeeds in learning the language or not, if he will stay there until the servants of God say, 'Come home,' his name will go down to all time in honor and blessing, and hundreds, yea thousands and perhaps millions, will receive the gospel as a result of his labors in the beginning; so that we congratulate Brother Heber on this mission. It is an important one, and we shall do everything in our power to help him to succeed, and to obtain for him the blessing of God and the preservation of his life. May the Lord bless your house while you are away, and bless your children who remain at home, and your wife who shall remain at home, and sustain and bless her until your return, that she shall stand at the head of her family, and be given power of the Lord to direct and control in wisdom and love."

Shortly after his arrival in Japan, President Grant issued the following comprehensive address to the Japanese people, announcing the purpose of his mission. On account of its historic importance, I desire to present this address here in full:

TO THE JAPANESE PEOPLE

"In company with my associates sent to you from the headquarters of the Church of Jesus Christ of Latter-day Saints, in Salt Lake City, Utah, as an Apostle and minister of the Most High God, I salute you and invite you to consider the important message which we bear. We do not come to you for the purpose of trying to deprive you of any truth in which you believe, or any light that you have been privileged to enjoy. We bring to you greater light, more truth and advanced knowledge, which we offer you freely. We recognize you as the children of our common Father, the Creator of the universe. The spirit of man, the intelligent ego, is the offspring of God; therefore men and women of all races and kindreds and tribes and tongues on the face of the earth are brothers and sisters. It is, then, in the spirit of fraternity that we approach you, desiring your welfare now and hereafter. Our mission is one of duty. We have been commanded of God to proclaim His word and will to the world. It is by His divine authority that we act, and not in our own name or for personal ends. We entreat you to listen to our words.

"There have been in all ages some men inspired by the Almighty for the benefit of their own race and nation. The light they brought may be likened to that of the stars in the firmament. It was adapted to the times and conditions when they appeared. They all looked forward to a period when greater light and higher truth should be manifest. We declare to you that this greater revelation has come, and we have been commissioned from on high to expound it to you. The power and might and progress of the nations that are called Christian, proclaim the fact that there is something in their faith which is grand and potent for good. But the division and contention existing among the various sects into which they are separated, give proof that there is something among them that is wrong, and which tends to strife instead of union; to war instead of peace. The truth is that Jesus of Nazareth introduced to the world the divine religion intended to unite all mankind as one family and redeem the earth from evil. Error has crept in among His professed disciples, and darkness has come over the face of the world, and the pure light of heaven has been obscured.

"The great Eternal God in His infinite mercy, has restored that faith introduced by His Son Jesus Christ, who has reappeared, and once more organized His Church on the earth and conferred authority upon His chosen servants to proclaim the Christian faith in all its early simplicity, attended by the same authority and power. This is preparatory to the consummation of all things, spoken of by the seers and sages and poets and prophets of all the centuries from the beginning of time. The great Eternal God has spoken out of the heavens and opened up communication between Him and His people. He commands His children in every country, of every class and creed and position and color, to turn from their evil ways, repent of their sins and approach to Him in Spirit, also to be baptized by immersion in water by one holding authority from Him for the remission of their sins, with the promise that by the laying on of hands of His deputed messengers, the Holy Ghost shall be bestowed upon all persons who thus obey His word. This will constitute a new birth and open the door of the kingdom of heaven to every obedient soul.

"By His authority we turn the divine key which opens the kingdom of heaven to the inhabitants of Japan. We say to them all, come to the light which has been shed forth from the Sun of Righteousness. We offer you blessings that are beyond price. They are not of man, nor do they come by the power of man, but they are from heaven where the true and living God dwells and rules in majesty and glory. That which your ancestors received which was good and which leads to do good, was but as the glimmering of the twilight. We bring to you the truth in all its effulgence, direct from the great Luminary of the day. Come to the light and the truth, and walk in the one way that leads

to the divine and eternal presence! Then shall your souls
be filled with peace and love and joy, and you shall learn
how to unite with the great and pure of all nations and
tribes, for the establishment of the grand empire of righteousness on earth, and hereafter you shall dwell with the
just, and the redeemed, in the immediate presence of our
Eternal Father, and your glory and dominion shall be
celestial and everlasting.

"Your servant for Christ's sake
"HEBER J. GRANT."

After presiding over the Japanese Mission for eighteen
months, President Grant addressed the following interesting
letter to the Saints of the European Mission, in response to
a request from Joseph J. Cannon, the editor of the *Millennial Star.* As it expresses President Grant's feelings at the
time, I desire to reproduce it in part:

"Tokyo, Japan, January 12th, 1903.
To the Saints in the European Mission:

"A few days ago a letter reached me from Elder Joseph J. Cannon, requesting a 'contribution.' The answer in
my heart was prompt, 'Yes, with much pleasure,' but when
I read on and found that what was desired was a literary
production for the *Star,* I did not experience so much
pleasure as I had anticipated.

"I have done but little writing for publication; a few
articles for the *Era* being my principal effort in that line,
and these were written at the request of Elder Edward H.
Anderson, the associate editor, and with the hope that they
would inspire our young men to contribute to the columns
of that worthy magazine, and to try to inspire them with
a desire never to become discouraged in the battle of life,
but to press on to final victory.

"I greet the good people of the European mission,
and although this letter will cross the Pacific and Atlantic
oceans as well as the continent of America, before arriving
at its destination, yet I feel that the Saints in the mission

are not so very far away, and are near and dear to me. My intimate association with Presidents John Taylor and George Q. Cannon and others from the British Isles, particularly President John R. Winder, who has been almost as a father to me, with President Anthon H. Lund from Scandinavia, and the 'grand old man' Karl G. Maeser from Germany, makes me feel as if I were personally acquainted with many of you in all parts of the European mission.

"We are of one faith and have one common hope in life as well as for the eternities to come. I know that you have the same love for the work of God that I have, and that you are equally willing to make sacrifices for the advancement of our Master's work on the earth, a knowledge of which has come to you through the blessings of the Lord. I feel that we are 'one' agreeable to the teachings of our Lord Jesus Christ. There is nothing more true than that the Spirit makes us one. This truth has come to me very forcibly when I have been traveling among the Indians of Arizona, New Mexico and in the republic of Mexico, and since I came to Japan. My heart has gone out in true affection to the Indians, and to the people of this land, and I have a burning desire that they might come to a knowledge of the gospel of life and salvation.

"While sitting here writing this letter to you and thinking of the six or seven times since becoming an apostle that it has all but been decided by the Presidency for me to go to Liverpool, I am reminded of the fact that we never know what is coming to us. The thought never came to me that I would communicate by letter from Japan with you in place of having the pleasure of a personal acquaintance: neither did I think when my name was first considered for the presidency of the European mission, now nearly twenty years ago, that I would not have been with you long before now. When the Lord shall send me to you I am sure there will be a warm welcome in your hearts for me, and from all that Brothers Rulon S. Wells, Joseph and James McMurrin, John Nicholson, Henry W. Naisbitt, the members of my quorum and others who have presided at Liverpool have told me of the many warm and true hearts from one end to the other of the mission, I anticipate great joy in making your personal acquaintance."

The above letter was almost in the nature of a prophecy, for in a few months President Grant was called to return home and was there informed by President Joseph F. Smith that he had been appointed to preside over the European Mission. I have gleaned the following from one of his later sermons:

"I remember that while I was laboring in Japan, on account of my failure to learn the language, I was not entirely happy in my work there. I remember going out into the woods, kneeling down and praying to God that when my work was finished there I would appreciate it if I were called to the British Isles to succeed Brother Francis M. Lyman. Two or three days after uttering that prayer I received a cable: 'Come home on the first vessel.' When I arrived home President Smith told me that they had decided to send me to Europe to succeed Brother Lyman. He said, 'We realize that the two years or more that you have been in Japan have been anything but satisfactory from the standpoint of the joy that comes into the hearts of the missionaries in bringing souls to a knowledge of the truth, and we want you to have at least a year of real genuine missionary experience.' When I went into his office and bade him good-bye, and said, 'I will see you in a year,' he said, 'We have decided to make it a year and a half.' I said, 'Multiply it by two and say nothing about it, and it will please me,' and that is exactly what he did. I was there a little over three years, and never have I had sweeter joy, more genuine satisfaction in my life than during those three years, when I had no thought except spreading of the Gospel of the Lord Jesus Christ."

President Grant arrived in Salt Lake City, on his return from Japan, in September, 1903. A few weeks later he took his departure for Europe. Shortly after arriving in

England, on November 28, he issued the following address
to the European Saints, which is reproduced here in part:
"To the Saints in the European Mission:

1903

"On assuming the duties of president over this mission
at the beginning of a new year, I send greetings to the Elders and Saints of Europe and adjacent countries where the
gospel is being preached.

"While writing I am reminded of how little one knows
of what a day, month or year will bring. On the 12th of
December, 1902, I was seated in Tokyo, the capital city
of Japan, writing to the saints of this mission, and expressed
surprise to be communicating with them from Japan, but
it was not so much of a surprise for me then as it is to be
seated this day in the Liverpool office doing the same thing.

"While we have but a limited idea of what is to hap-
pen to us in the future of our lives, yet there is one thing
for which I feel truly grateful to our Father in heaven,
and that is the perfect assurance which I have that all will
be well with us in the battle of life, and also in the great
eternity to come, provided we as Saints do our full duty
day by day, and can know at the close of each day's labor
that we have done our best.

"While writing from Japan I stated that I anticipated
great joy in meeting the Saints in the European mission,
whenever in the providences of the Lord I should be sent
here. My reasons for this were my intimate association with
Presidents John Taylor, George Q. Cannon, John R. Winder,
Anthon H. Lund, that great educator Karl G. Maeser, and
other noble and good men and women who were gathered
from this mission by the truths of the gospel; and also the
assurances which I had received from President Joseph F.
Smith and the members of my own Quorum, as well as
others of the brethren, who have presided in this land,
of the warm-hearted, true and faithful Saints still located
in this mission.

"If I am to judge of the future by the brief past, then
my mission is to be a happy and busy one, as I have

thoroughly enjoyed my association with the elders and
Saints whom I have met since my arrival in England."

I do not have space in this limited chapter to describe
the great work performed by President Grant during the
three years that he presided over the European Mission. I
can testify that he was a wonderful and inspiring President,
as I served as one of his missionaries and had the privilege
of a close and pleasant association with him. He was untiring in his efforts to promulgate the principles of the gospel. His affable and pleasant manner won him and the
Church thousands of friends. The missionaries loved and
honored him for his splendid leadership.

At the conclusion of his mission, in December, 1906,
he published in the *Millennial Star* a farewell address to
the missionaries and Saints, which I shall reproduce here
in part:

"To the Elders and Saints of the European Mission:

"On November 28th, three years ago, I landed in
Liverpool and was welcomed by President Francis M. Lyman and associates in the Liverpool office. Today it is
thirty-five months since I assumed the presidency of the
European mission. The time has passed very rapidly. I have
been busy and have thoroughly enjoyed my labors. The
mission was in a splendid condition, and I have endeavored
to maintain the high standard set by my predecessor.

"The principal thing during my mission for which I
feel grateful is the visit of the President of the Church to
the European mission for the first time since it was established. The visit of President Joseph F. Smith and party
caused the Elders and Saints to rejoice, and has been pro-
ductive of great good. I earnestly pray that he will come
again, and that his sojourn will be much longer, so that he
can more fully visit the different parts of the mission.

"Since my arrival nine hundred and sixteen missionaries have registered in Liverpool.

"I have nothing but words of the highest commendation and thanks for my associates in the Liverpool office, and all of the mission and conference presidents who have labored under my jurisdiction. I am very grateful and sincerely thank the Elders for their untiring energy and zeal in spreading the gospel. My labors have been principally confined to the British mission. There has been a great increase in the European mission in the amount of labor being done by the Elders, in distributing tracts and books, visiting strangers' houses and securing gospel conversations. In the British mission, August, September and October show over 1,200,000 tracts distributed, an increase of over 400,000 as compared with the same period of last year. The books distributed amounted to over 43,000, an increase of over 28,000. The strangers' houses visited with first tracts for the quarter were 249,390, an increase of 102,-076. The gospel conversations were 86,496, an increase of 39,806. These increases should be reduced nearly thirty per cent on account of having more Elders now than during the same period last year. The one thing that I regret is that the baptisms have not increased in proportion to the large increase in tracts, books and conversations. . . .

"I, with those of my family with me, will depart for home with feelings of love, good will and blessing in our hearts for all the elders and Saints with whom we have been associated, and with earnest prayers for their continued success and happiness. Our experiences during the past three years will always be pleasant memories through the entire journey of life, and we sincerely pray that the strong friendships formed may endure throughout eternity. I again extend my love and blessings to all the elders and Saints in the European mission. I hope sometime to have the privilege of greeting many of the Saints in the land of Zion, and also of returning to this land and meeting others at some future date.

"Liverpool, December 1st, 1906.
"Heber J. Grant."

SLC
1907

Arriving in Salt Lake City a few weeks after his departure from England in December, 1906, President Grant at once became active in Church and business affairs. At the April conference in 1907, he reported his mission to the Saints. My limited space allows me to quote only a few paragraphs:

"After an absence of three years and a half," he said, "I rejoice to return to my mountain home. I rejoice in the progress of the work of God at home or abroad. I wish to say to fathers and mothers who have sons in the European Mission that they are doing their duty; they are boys to be proud of.

"While in Japan, I prayed to the Lord with all my heart, in the woods of that country, that I might be permitted to succeed Brother Lyman as the President of the European Mission. And why? Because I know from my experience in following him in the Tooele Stake of Zion that he would have all the holes filled up, the bridges made, and the roads in good condition. I knew that I would find the Mission well organized and everything in fine shape, with a good foundation upon which to build. I built upon that foundation, and the young missionaries seconded my efforts there. God blessed us in our Church work in that land during my administration. I feel that there will be still greater increase under the administration of Brother Penrose, because of the foundation laid by Brother Lyman, seconded by my efforts. When people say that the Latter-day Saints do not believe in education and investigation, they simply tell that which is not true. Last year, in the British Isle alone, over four million tracts were distributed by the Elders, and those tracts were principally written by Elder Charles W. Penrose."

V

After spending a little over one year at home and attending conferences in the stakes, President Grant noted improvement in the Church, which he expressed in his sermon at the April conference in 1908:

"There is no questions in my mind that Zion prospers, and that all is well. I believe, as was said here this morning, that The Church of Jesus Christ of Latter-day Saints was never in a better condition than it is today, spiritually, and temporally, and every way. During the last year, I have had the privilege of traveling in many stakes of Zion, and I believe that the presidents of stakes, the high councilors, the bishops of wards, and the teachers are more energetic, more diligent in keeping the commandments of God, and in teaching their people to live the laws of God, than they ever have been before. I believe that the auxiliary organizations of this Church are in a flourishing condition, from the Relief Society down to the Primary Association. I believe that the Latter-day Saints as a people are taking more interest in the gospel of Jesus Christ, and are striving to carry out the commandments of the Lord more perfectly than they have ever done before. I rejoice in this fact; I rejoice that the people love the gospel; that they desire the advancement of the work of God upon the earth, and that they are anxious to so order their lives that the example which they set shall be worthy of the imitation of all men."

For a period of ten years, from the time of President Grant's return from England in 1906 to the death of Francis M. Lyman in 1916, President Grant remained at home and occupied his time in his church duties and extensive business affairs. When President Lyman died, Heber J. Grant succeeded him as president of the Quorum of Twelve Apostles and was set apart in this important calling on November 23, 1916.

At the April conference in 1917, he expressed his gratitude for the opportunities that had been his to serve in the work of God:

"For thirty-four years and a half I have been one of the general authorities. I have been associated with them in all of their councils. I know the hearts of these men. I know their desires. I know their devotion to God and to all that is for the uplift and the betterment of mankind. I can bear witness that I know as I live, that every word spoken here this morning by President Joseph F. Smith, bearing witness of the honor, the virtue, the integrity, and the uprightness of the men who presided over this Church, is true. I rejoice that in all my associations with the general authorities of the Church since I was six years of age I have never heard one word, in public or in private, fall from the lips of these men, but what would be for the benefit, for the uplift, for the improvement morally and intellectually, physically and spiritually of the Latter-day Saints.

"I rejoice that in all my travels, at home or abroad, I have never found anything, in all the world, of the teachings of uninspired men, which has had the slightest attraction for me. I rejoice that the more I come in contact with the world and the peoples of the world, the more I rejoice in the strength and the power of the gospel of Jesus Christ. I rejoice beyond my ability to express it that the Lord has given to the Latter-day Saints, as individuals, a testimony, a knowledge, for themselves of the divinity of this work in which we are engaged, that we as individuals do not have to rely upon the testimony of others. I rejoice that all the manifestations of power together with the gifts and graces of the gospel which were had in the Church when the Savior was upon the earth, or immediately following His crucifixion are enjoyed today to the fullest extent by the faithful, loyal, true and patriotic Latter-day Saints. I rejoice in the fact, and have often spoken of it in the various conferences throughout the Church, that as this gospel has been preached the world over, men and women from every denomination and from every clime have yielded obedience to it. I rejoice that in the preaching of the Gospel, men with all their worldly wisdom have never been able to capture any of the loyal, faithful young men who have gone forth to proclaim it."

VI

On November 19, 1918, Joseph F. Smith, the President of the Church, died at the Bee Hive House in Salt Lake City. The death of this great man dissolved the quorum of the First Presidency. Four days later, on November 23, at a meeting of the Council of Twelve Apostles, Heber J. Grant was chosen for this exalted position by the unanimous approval of his brethren. The day previous to this important event President Grant had passed his sixty-second birthday. For thirty-six years he had served as a member of the Twelve. He had traveled far and wide in the interests of the Church. His diligence and zeal for the upbuilding of the kingdom of God had been unflagging. He had observed the laws and commandments; he had been a faithful and devoted servant; and now he was called upon to bear the burden of leadership. All doubts in his own mind as to the wisdom of his choice were removed by the statement that President Joseph F. Smith made to him a few hours before his death:

"The Lord bless you, my boy, the Lord bless you," said President Smith. "You have a great responsibility. Always remember this is the Lord's work and not man's. The Lord is greater than any man. He knows who he wants to lead his Church, and never makes any mistakes. The Lord bless you."

On account of the influenza epidemic that was prevalent in the country in the early months of 1919, the general conference of the Church, which had always convened in April, was postponed until June. At that time the great body of the priesthood, voting by quorums, sustained President Grant as President of the Church. This action was followed by the entire membership voting their unanimous approval of his selection. President Grant then arose and spoke in part as follows:

"I feel humble, beyond any language with which God has endowed me to express it, in standing before you here this morning, occupying the position in which you have just voted to sustain me. I recall standing before an audience in Tooele, after having been sustained as president of that stake, when I was a young man twenty-three years of age, pledging to that audience the best that was in me. I stand here today in all humility, acknowledging my own weakness, my own lack of wisdom and information, and my lack of the ability to occupy the exalted position in which you have voted to sustain me. But as I said as a boy in Tooele, I say here today: that by and with the help of the Lord, I shall do the best that I can to fulfill every obligation that shall rest upon me as President of The Church of Jesus Christ of Latter-day Saints, to the full extent of my ability.

"I will ask no man to be more liberal with his means, than I am with mine, in proportion to what he possesses, for the advancement of God's kingdom. I will ask no man to observe the Word of Wisdom any more closely than I will observe it. I will ask no man to be more conscientious and prompt in the payment of his tithes and his offerings than I will be. I will ask no man to be more ready and willing to come early and to go late, and to labor with full power of mind and body, than I will labor, always in humility. I hope and pray for the blessings of the Lord, acknowledging freely and frankly, that without the Lord's blessings it will be an impossibility for me to make a success of the high calling whereunto I have been called. But, like Nephi of old, I know the Lord makes no requirements of the children of men, save he will prepare a way for them, whereby they can accomplish the thing which he has required. With this knowledge in my heart, I accept the great responsibility, without fear of the consequences, knowing that God will sustain me as he has sustained all of my predecessors who have occupied this position, provided always that I shall labor in humility and in diligence, ever seeking for the guidance of his Holy Spirit: and this I shall endeavor to do."

VII

From November, 1918, until May 1, 1945, President
Grant presided over all the activities of the Latter-day
Saints throughout the world. Of the Presidents of the
Church, his administration exceeded any other in length of
years except that of President Brigham Young. He therefore
had a splendid opportunity to put his policies into effect
and to exercise his influence for the upbuilding and betterment of the great latter-day work.

Perhaps the most outstanding contribution President
Grant made to the Church during the years of his presidency was his ability to meet and mingle with the prominent and influential people of the nation; to break down opposition; to remove prejudice and to make and win friends
for the Latter-day Saints. He was a great and outstanding
missionary. I recall his remarks at the general conference
in 1921, when he mentioned a speech he had delivered
before the Knife and Fork Club of Kansas City, in December of the previous year:

"I think that we as a people have very great cause
to rejoice in the era of good will and fellowship that is
existing today for us as a people, among those not of our
faith, in comparison with the conditions that existed some
years ago. I do not know of any single thing that has happened in my experience, during the long time that I have
been one of the General Authorities of the Church, that has
impressed me more profoundly with the change of sentiment towards the Latter-day Saints than the reception that
was accorded to me December last when I went to Kansas
City and delivered a speech upon the accomplishments
of 'Mormonism.' When I reflect upon the fact that in the
leading hotel in that wonderful and progressive city . . . I
was permitted to stand up within ten miles of Independence, the place from which the Latter-day Saints were expelled, by an expulsion and exterminating order of the
Governor of the State, Governor Boggs, and to proclaim

the accomplishments of the Latter-day Saints; to relate
the prophecies of Joseph Smith, to give to those men that
were there assembled—over three hundred of the leading influential business men of the city—the testimony of Josiah
Quincy regarding the Prophet Joseph Smith; to repeat to
them the great Pioneer hymn, 'Come, Come, Ye Saints';
to relate the hardships, the drivings, and the persecutions
of the Latter-day Saints and to have that body of representative men receive that address with approval, applaud
it in many places, and many of them come to me after the
meeting and shake hands and congratulate me upon the
address; and to have some of the members of the board
of directors of that great club—the Knife and Fork Club
of Kansas City—(which I have been informed is the second
greatest dinner club in the United States, the Gridiron
of Washington standing first) to have them say that they
hoped for a return date so that they could hear more of
our people; and then stop to reflect upon the fact that
the Prophet and his followers, in the early days, were expelled from Missouri, that many of them were murdered;
that all kinds of crimes were committed upon the people;
that their property was confiscated; that we have never
received anything for our property that belonged to us
in that section, that today some of the valuable country
that we traveled over there is the very property that our
people owned, (for when you follow up many abstracts of
valuable property you will find that the title centers in
the bishop of the 'Mormon' Church, and only because of
lapse of time have people secured a proper title to these
lands, and not because it was ever paid for)—I say to
stop and reflect that the drivings and the persecutions of
the Latter-day Saints, of which no tongue can tell and no
pen can paint the conditions; and then to realize that there
is a feeling in that community now, among the people residing in the very place, so to speak, from which President
Joseph Smith, the Prophet of the living God, and others
were driven out; to be invited to go there and be asked to

talk of the accomplishments of 'Mormonism,' and to have that talk received, with open arms, shows the most wonderful change of sentiment."

The above example is only one of hundreds of instances in which President Grant traveled to various parts of the United States to exercise the prestige of his high office to present the truth to the people and win friends for the Latter-day Saints. The change in sentiment toward the Mormon people was largely brought about through his own untiring individual efforts.

The organizations of the Church were greatly extended during President Grant's administration. In 1918, when he came into office, there were 75 stakes and 843 wards and independent branches. The report made at the conference in April, 1943, showed that there were 143 stakes and 1,242 wards and independent branches.

With the rapid growth of the Church there was no lessening in the spiritual qualifications of its members. President Grant made, in October, 1937, what I consider as the most important pronouncement regarding the qualifications of the officers of the Church that has been made since the days of the Prophet Joseph Smith. He said on that occasion:

"I announced here at the priesthood meeting last night, and I decided to announce it again, that we expect all the general officers of the Church, each and every one of them, from this very day, to be absolute, full tithe-payers, to really and truly observe the Word of Wisdom; and we ask all of the officers of the Church and all members of the general boards, and all stake and ward officers, if they are not living the gospel and honestly and conscientiously paying their tithing, to kindly step aside, unless from this day they live up to these provisions.

"We feel that in all the stakes of Zion, every stake president, every counselor to a stake president, every stake clerk, and every high councilor, standing at the head of the people in the stake—we ask them to kindly step aside

unless they are living up to these laws. They are given
the responsibility of presiding, and every officer who is a
presiding officer should say from today: 'I am going to
serve the Lord, so that my example will be worthy of
imitation.'

"No man can teach the Word of Wisdom by the Spirit
of God who does not live it. No man can proclaim this gospel by the Spirit of the living God unless that man is
living his religion; and with this great undertaking that we
have before us now we must renew our loyalty to God,
and I believe beyond a shadow of doubt that God inspires
and blesses, and multiplies our substance when we are honest with him. We do not want in this day a repetition of
what the scriptures tell us was the condition in years gone
by, wherein the Lord delcares that he had been robbed, because of the failure of the people to live the financial law
that God has revealed.

"Now, I pray from the bottom of my heart that God
will give each and every man and woman who holds an
office in any stake or ward the spirit and the feeling and
the determination from this day, to renew his covenants
with God, to live his religion; and if we are too weak to do
these things, we should step aside and let somebody else
take our place."

Again at the April conference in 1938, President Grant
stressed this important point:

"I want to leave with this vast audience my deep appreciation of all that has been said. I endorse it with all
my heart, and I renew again everything that I said in the
ten or fifteen minutes at the close of our conference six
months ago. I ask every man and woman occupying a place
of responsibility whose duty it is to teach the gospel of
Jesus Christ to live it and to keep the commandments of
God, so that their example will teach it; and if they cannot live it we will go on loving them, we will go on putting our arms around them, we will go on praying for
them that they may become strong enough to live it. But

unless they are able to live it we ask them to please step
aside so that those who are living it can teach it. No man
can teach the gospel of Jesus Christ under the inspiration
of the living God and with power from on high unless he
is living it. He can go on as a member and we will never
put a block in his way, because the gospel is one of love
and of forgiveness, but we want true men and women as
our officers in the priesthood and in the Relief Societies.
And a man has no right to be in a high council who can
not stand up and say that he knows the gospel is true
and that he is living it."

VIII

Even as he approached his eighties, President Grant
was still active; still guiding the affairs of a great people.
He could look back over his long life and feel assured
that he had been successful in every way. If, as has been
said, "a man's wealth consists in the number of things
he loves and blesses, and which love and bless him in return," then, truly, President Grant accumulated a great
treasure. He touched the lives of many thousands, and in
return he received their sincere love and appreciation.

In the Portland, Oregon, chapel in October, 1937, he
bore the following fervent testimony:

"I want to bear my testimony to you and tell you that
every drop of blood in my body, every ounce of wisdom
in my brain, testifies to you, that beyond the shadow of
doubt, I am converted to my religion. We have the gospel!
We have the plan of life and salvation, and I know it. We
have all the gifts, the prophecies, the power of healing, and
everything they had in ancient days. I am a living monument of the healing power of Almighty God. I had been
given up to die. My wife, who is dead, visited my wife who
lives, and told her that my life was not ended, and although
blood-poisoning had set in, I got well, and since then I have
lifted up my voice in Ireland, England, Belgium, Norway

and Sweden, from Portland, Maine, to Portland, Oregon, Hawaii, Japan, from California to Florida, and up both coasts, saying that as sure as I live, I know that God lives, because he has heard and answered my prayers, time and time again. I know that Jesus Christ is the Son of God, the Eternal Father. I know that Joseph Smith is a prophet of God, and may God help us so to live, that others, seeing our good deeds, will investigate the plan of life and salvation, I ask, in the name of Jesus Christ. Amen."

IX

In his last years President Grant almost daily, when the weather permitted, took a long automobile ride in the country or in the near-by picturesque canyons. On these rides he and Mrs. Grant were always accompanied by relatives or friends. He was never satisfied until his automobile was filled and others were permitted to enjoy the sights that brought him such keen delight and satisfaction. Mrs. Nibley and I were often invited to be his guests and enjoy his society on these occasions, during his last years. We shall not soon forget his kindness toward us nor his unvarying interest in our welfare.

As long as his health permitted President Grant spent a few hours each day in his office, in the Church Office Building on South Temple Street. There he met in consultation with his brethren, visited with friends or strangers, dictated letters, or attended to whatever matters came to his attention. Though his bodily health was impaired, due to a partial paralysis he had suffered in 1940, his mind was clear, alert, and active.

Having been advised by his physician to refrain from giving a public address during the general conference in April, 1943, he dictated a lengthy statement that was read to the Saints assembled. My regret is that it cannot be reproduced in full, but I shall quote from it briefly.

1943

"I want to thank the people for their prayers in my behalf," he said. "I have not been well for a period of more than three years, and yet during that time I have never suffered any pain. . . . The Lord has been good to me and has answered the prayers of the people, as well as my own prayers, that while the Lord should leave me here upon the earth, I should be able physically and mentally to go forward in the furtherance of his work."

The great war that was raging throughout the earth was a source of continual anxiety to him. He voiced his sentiments in this regard in another statement that was read to the October conference in 1943.

"I am praying with all my heart and soul for the end of this war, as soon as the Lord shall see fit to have it stop, and am earnestly praying for the influence of the spirit of the Lord to be with all who have loved ones in the war."

One full year passed, President Grant's health was gradually failing, but his desire to serve and continue on with his great tasks did not diminish with the years. His spirit seemed to grow brighter as his length of life advanced. At the October conference in 1944, he voiced his gratitude to his Heavenly Father for the blessings he had received.

"Again I am permitted to be with you in another general conference of the Church and I bear testimony that I know it is by the healing and sustaining power of God that I am here. In another six or seven weeks, the Lord being willing, I shall begin the eighty-ninth year of my life, and shall have completed sixty-two years since I became one of the apostles, and shall have served twenty-six years as President of the Church. In all this, and in much else, the Lord has blessed me richly, and I am grateful that I can say that I am better now than I have been during some of the weeks and months just passed."

During the winter of 1944-45 his hours spent in his office were less frequent. But to those who visited him at his home he was the same kind, considerate, and affectionate friend. He was not able to attend the April conference in 1945, but he dictated a lengthy statement that was read to the assembled multitude. It was one of the most fervent and beautiful expressions that ever came from his mind and heart. In this stirring appeal to the Latter-day Saints, he bore his last and final testimony.

"The most glorious thing that has ever happened in the history of the world, since the Savior himself lived on earth, is that God himself saw fit to visit the earth, with his beloved Only Begotten Son, our Redeemer and Savior, and appear to the boy Joseph Smith. . . .

"The gospel in its purity has been restored to earth."

"I bear witness to you that I do know that God lives; that he hears and answers prayers; that Jesus is the Christ, the Redeemer of the world; that Joseph Smith was and is a prophet of the Living God, and that Brigham Young and those who have succeeded him were likewise. . . .

"I do not have the language at my command to express the gratitude to God for this knowledge that I possess."

X

On Monday evening, May 14, 1945, about an hour before sunset, the press and radio announced to the world that President Heber J. Grant had died at his home in Salt Lake City. Although the news was not unexpected, it came as a shock to his many personal friends and to the members of the Church throughout the world. A great and good man, a wise counselor, an able executive, the seventh President of the Church, a prophet of God, had departed to his heavenly home.

The funeral of President Grant was held in the historic Tabernacle in Salt Lake City, on Friday, May 18, at 12:15 p.m. An hour before the service, the great building was filled to capacity with those who came to pay him

a parting tribute and do him honor. The first speaker was
George Albert Smith, president of the Council of Twelve.

"Assembled on this solemn occasion," he said, "near the
casket containing a dear one, our feelings are naturally sub-
dued, and if this were the last time we were to be with
him, it would to me be a most distressing situation; but
it is not so in this case. This man who has been summoned
home by our Heavenly Father has concluded his mortal
life in honor, but we will be with him again in immortality
if we are worthy. Born eighty-eight years ago, most of his
life has been devoted to faithfully seeking to divide the
truth of our Lord with his fellowmen. For more than forty
years I have been one of his companions, who have upon
their shoulders the responsibility of disseminating the gospel
of Jesus Christ in all parts of the world. . . .

"President Grant's training was that of character. He
lived in a home where there was family and individual
prayer, morning and evening, and where thanks for the
food partaken of was always given. In his home he was
taught to honor father and mother, to honor his Heavenly
Father, and to love his neighbor as himself. I know of
no man who has been more generous in his contribution
of himself and of the means that have come into his hands.
He tried to make his brothers and sisters of all faiths and
creeds happier."

President David O. McKay, the second speaker, spoke
feelingly.

"President Grant's voice is silent; his heartbeats are
stilled, but he still lives, for to such as he is given the divine promise: 'I am the resurrection, and the life: he that
believeth in me, though he were dead, yet shall he live:
and whosoever liveth and believeth in me shall never die.'"

"Persevering in accomplishment, sincere, honest, up-
right in all his dealings, positive in expression, dynamic in
action, uncompromising with evil, sympathetic with the
unfortunate, magnanimous in the highest degree, faithful
in life to every trust, tender and considerate of loved ones,

loyal to friends, to truth, to God—such was our honored
and beloved President—a distinguished leader, a worthy
exemplar to the Church and to mankind the world over."

The concluding remarks were made by President J.
Reuben Clark, Jr.

"I want to endorse every good thing—and all has been
good today that has been said about President Grant—I
endorse every good thing that anybody shall say about him,
for he was a rare spirit who lived righteously and drew
from our Heavenly Father the blessings which come to those
who keep and obey his commandments. . . .

"God bless his memory to all of us; keep it clean
and bright with us. May we, day by day, come to understand and appreciate, that we may be able to follow along
and live as he lived."

After the funeral service the body of President Grant
was conveyed to the city cemetery, where it was laid away
in the family plot. The dedicatory prayer at the graveside
was offered by Antoine R. Ivins.

GEORGE ALBERT SMITH

GEORGE ALBERT SMITH

(1870-1951)

O N Monday, May 21, 1945, one week after the death of President Heber J. Grant, at a meeting of the Quorum of the Twelve Apostles in the Salt Lake Temple, George Albert Smith, the president of the quorum, was sustained and set apart by his brethren as the President of The Church of Jesus Christ of Latter-day Saints. At the time this high honor came to President Smith he was in his seventy-sixth year, having passed his seventy-fifth birthday on the fourth of April, about six weeks previously. Though not in robust health, he was physically and mentally alert and active, and well qualified by birth, training, and long experience to carry on the great responsibility that had been delegated to him.

President Smith was a member of the fourth generation of a family that had distinguished itself for faithful devoted service in the Church from its organization. His great-grandfather, John Smith, an uncle of the Prophet Joseph Smith, was an early convert to the teachings of his brilliant nephew, having been baptized at Potsdam, New York, on January 9, 1832.

Uncle John, as he is familiarly known in Church history, emigrated to Kirtland in 1833, and thence he followed the Saints in all their wanderings—to Missouri, to Illinois, to Winter Quarters, and to the Great Basin. In the fall of 1847 he reached Salt Lake Valley, a few weeks after the original company of pioneers, and was selected by President Brigham Young to preside over the isolated settlement of the Saints until the return of the First Presidency from Winter Quarters, which took place in September, 1848.

On January 1, 1849, John Smith was ordained to the office of Patriarch to the Church, and he died while faithfully fulfilling his duties in that high calling on May 23, 1854. Humble and sincere, faithful and true, loyal to his brethren and to the Church, he left a good name and a posterity that has done him honor.

Uncle John Smith's eldest son, George Albert, or George A., as he was familiarly called, was approaching his thirty-seventh birthday at the time of the death of his worthy father. Already a seasoned veteran in the Church, he had made a distinguished name for himself as a missionary, an apostle, a statesman, a pioneer of the original company to Salt Lake Valley in 1847, and a colonizer of Southern Utah.

George A. was fifteen years of age when he was baptized at Potsdam, New York, in September, 1832. The following year he moved with his parents to Kirtland, Ohio, the headquarters of the Church, and there met his cousin, the Prophet Joseph Smith, for the first time. They became fast friends, and the faith of George A. in the divine mission of the Prophet and his teachings grew with the passing years.

In the spring of 1834, George A., sixteen years old at the time, accompanied a group of his brethren, known as Zion's Camp, on the long and difficult march to Missouri and return, a distance of nearly 2,000 miles. During the summers of 1835, 1836, and 1837 he was absent in the eastern states, serving as a missionary for the Church. In 1838 he moved with his parents to Missouri and there endured the troubles and difficulties to which the Saints were subjected in their expulsion from that state.

On April 26, 1839, George A. Smith was ordained an apostle, two months before his twenty-second birthday, the

youngest man to be selected for that high office in the
history of the Church. In the fall of the same year he departed from Nauvoo, with his brethren of the Twelve, for
a mission to the British Isles. After a remarkably successful
mission, he returned to his home in the summer of 1841.
The principal part of his time during the next few years
was spent in building up the settlement of the Saints in
Nauvoo and vicinity, and in undertaking short missions to
the eastern states. He was in Michigan in June, 1844, when
he received word of the death of the Prophet and the
Patriarch. He hastened to Nauvoo, and thereafter the
Twelve Apostles became the governing body of the Church.
From this time on, all the active years of his life were spent
in promoting the welfare of the organization to which he
had given such wholehearted allegiance.

He took part in the exodus from Nauvoo; he was, as
we stated previously, a member of the original band of
pioneers who made their way to the Salt Lake Valley in
the summer of 1847, to seek out a new home for the Saints.
Returning to Winter Quarters in the fall, he was requested
by President Brigham Young to remain "on the river" and
look after the welfare of the members of the Church who
were making preparations to begin the journey across the
plains. It was not until the fall of 1849 that he was able
to join his parents and the Saints in Utah.

In the winter of 1850-51, George A. led a colony of
emigrants to the southern part of the territory and founded
the settlement of Parowan. In 1852 he was called to preside over the members of the Church in Utah County, and
two years later, at the April conference of the Church, he
was sustained as historian and general recorder. At the
October conference in 1868 he was selected by President
Young to be the first counselor in the First Presidency, in
place of Heber C. Kimball, who died a few months previously. This position he held until his death, which occurred on September 1, 1875, in the fifty-ninth year of his
life. Viewed from any standpoint, George A. Smith was

John Henry

b 1848

one of the great men of the Church during its early history.

The seventh child and third son of George A. Smith was named John Henry. He was born near Kanesville, Pottawattamie County, Iowa, on September 18, 1848. In June of the following year George A. and his wife, Sarah Ann Libby, began the long journey across the plains to Utah, traveling in the wagon drawn by ox teams. In her arms the brave mother carried her infant son. After the usual hardships they reached Salt Lake City on October 27, 1849. Not long, however, was Sarah Ann Libby Smith to enjoy the peaceful surroundings of her new home. On June 12, 1851, she died, a victim of the dread disease of those pioneer days known as consumption. A sister of the departed woman, Hannah Libby, also a wife of George A. Smith, took the infant boy and reared him, giving him all the affection and tender care that would have been bestowed by his own mother.

In July, 1852, when John Henry was four years old, he moved with his foster mother and family to Provo, where his father had been requested by Brigham Young to locate and preside over the settlements of the Saints in Utah County. Here he grew to manhood, and here he brought his young wife, Sarah Farr, to whom he was married on October 20, 1866.

1866

At the general conference of the Church held in May, 1874, John Henry was called to undertake a mission to the British Isles. He departed from his home in June of that year and was successfully engaged in missionary work in England until July 1875, when he was requested to return home on account of the severe illness of his father. Arriving in Salt Lake City on August 15, he was able to spend only fifteen days at the bedside of the man whom he most loved and honored. President George A. Smith departed from this life on September 1, 1875.

1874

John Henry now established his home in Salt Lake City. His activities were so numerous during the years to come that I can find space to mention only a few of them.

In 1876 he was elected to be a member of the city council of Salt Lake City. Four years later, at the October conference in 1880, his name was presented and he was sustained a member of the Quorum of Twelve Apostles, following in the footsteps of his worthy father. Two years later, in October 1882, he was sent by the President of the Church, John Taylor, to preside over the European Mission, with headquarters in Liverpool, England. In the spring of 1885 he returned to Salt Lake City, and thereafter his time was spent in religious, secular, and political activities, all designed to promote the betterment and welfare of mankind. At the April conference in 1910, John Henry Smith was selected by President Joseph F. Smith to be the second counselor in the First Presidency of the Church. He was engaged in the duties of this high office at the time of his death, which occurred after a brief illness on October 13, 1911.

II

President George Albert Smith was the second son of John Henry and Sarah Farr Smith, an elder brother having died as an infant. President Smith was born in Salt Lake City on April 4, 1870. From the beginning good fortune favored the boy; the home life of the parents was regarded by the neighbors and friends as an ideal. Love and affection abounded there; the highest principles of morality and religion were taught and observed. Living close by was President George A. Smith, the grandfather, after whom the child was named. The family was distinguished; the name they bore was among the most honored in the Church. There were no doubt many fond wishes and expectations expressed for this boy, for where much is given, much is expected. He lived to fulfill all these expectations and add honors to accomplishments of his illustrious forebears. Happy are the parents who can call him their son!

On June 6, 1878, a little over two months past his eighth birthday, he was baptized in City Creek, which then ran down the west side of the temple block, by Elder James Moyle. He was confirmed the same day by his father, John Henry Smith.

I had the privilege of questioning President George Albert Smith regarding the early influences of his childhood. It was plain to see that his own father was his ideal. "I have never met a greater man than my father," he said. The fact that he bore his grandfather's name influenced him in shaping his career. "That has meant much to me," he continued. "I have had that sacred name to take care of."

He told me also that once, when he was recovering from a long illness, he dreamed that he saw and spoke to his grandfather. "I thought I was on the shore of a lake," he related, "and I found that I was alone. I saw a trail through the woods and concluded that I would follow it. Soon I saw a man coming toward me. As he neared me I discovered that he was my grandfather. As we met he said, 'I'd like to know what you have done with my name.' 'Grandfather,' I answered, 'I have never done anything with your name that you need be ashamed of.' I then became conscious, and I made up my mind that I would never do anything to harm his good name."

After a few years of preliminary education in the schools of Salt Lake City, the boy was sent, when twelve years of age, to live with relatives in Provo, where he would have an opportunity to attend the Brigham Young Academy. There he came under the influence of that remarkable educator of pioneer days, Karl G. Maeser. One of the memorable precepts taught him by that noted man which President Smith related to me and which he said had influenced his life, is as follows: "Not only will you be held accountable for the things that you do, but you will also be held responsible for the thoughts that you think."

After the departure of his father for England, early

in 1883, where he had been called to preside over the
European Mission, George Albert returned to Salt Lake
City. After spending one year at the University of Utah,
which he entered when he was eighteen, he left school
and began work as a salesman for Zion's Cooperative Mercantile Institution. This employment appears to have been
to his liking and he made a success of it from the beginning. He was energetic, kind, agreeable, pleasant in conversation, and conscientious in his work. Before me as I write
this sketch I have a diary that he kept during one of his
commercial journeys to Southern Utah in the spring and
summer of 1890. At the time he was only a few weeks past
his twentieth birthday. He left Salt Lake City with his companion, James Poulton, traveling with team and wagon,
bound for the southern settlements. It took them seven
hours to reach their first stopping place, American Fork.
But they were happy; James Poulton had his flute and
George Albert had brought his guitar, and together they
played and sang. Orders for goods were taken from the
merchants in the various settlements. They traveled as far
south as St. George and Panguitch and after a successful
journey returned to Salt Lake City on June 30.

It was in the fall of the following year, 1891, when
he was twenty-one years of age, that he undertook his
first missionary work. He received a call from the Presidency of the Church to labor among the young people in
the stakes of Juab, Millard, Beaver, and Parowan in the
interest of the Mutual Improvement Association. He undertook this work willingly. After receiving his endowments
in the Manti Temple, he departed for the southern part
of the state on September 7. He and his companion, William B. Dougall, Jr., held meetings in the various towns,
organized Mutual Improvement associations, and encouraged
the young people to live in accordance with the principles
of their religion. Their mission being successfully completed,
they returned to their homes during the latter part of
November, 1891.

1892

On Wednesday, May 25, 1892, in the temple at Manti, George Albert Smith was married to his childhood sweetheart, Lucy Emily Woodruff. Lucy was the daughter of Wilford Woodruff, Jr., and Emily Jane Smith. She was the granddaughter of two well-known men in Church history, President Wilford Woodruff and Judge Elias Smith. Gentle, refined, sincere, with complete faith in the religion of her parents and grandparents, Lucy was to make an ideal companion for her husband. They enjoyed many happy years together, until death parted them.

1892

One week after his marriage, George Albert departed for his second mission, this time to the southern states. On his arrival in Chattanooga, Tennessee, he was assigned by the mission president, J. Golden Kimball, to the Middle Tennessee Conference, where he labored with diligence until September. At that time he was transferred to the mission office in Chattanooga, to act as secretary of the Southern States Mission. In a few weeks his wife Lucy joined him, and together they labored happily until June, 1894, when they were honorably released to return to their homes.

In reporting his mission in the Salt Lake Tabernacle on Sunday, July 22, 1894, he stated that the Southern States Mission was in a flourishing condition.

"The prejudice that formerly existed against the servants of God sent among them, and toward the Latter-day Saints located here, has almost died out. Our elders are treated well wherever they go. In former times we only had access to the people in the rural districts, but we now have the privilege of visiting those in the cities, and we are received by many of them kindly. . . .

"The speaker rejoiced at being home again and having the privilege of mingling with the Saints here. He enjoyed his labors greatly while on his mission, and uttered words of praise for the people of the South, who, he said, are among the most hospitable to be found anywhere."

III

At home again, George Albert resumed his employ- ment with Zion's Cooperative Mercantile Institution. He was a natural salesman and found no difficulty in making a good living in that occupation. He also took an active part in politics, and during the presidential campaign in the fall of 1896 vigorously supported William McKinley, the Republican candidate for president. McKinley was elected, and when he appointed a receiver of the Land Office for Utah, on January 5, 1898, George Albert Smith received the appointment. This honor came to the young man three months before his twenty-eighth birthday. Four years later the appointment was renewed without solicitation by Pres- ident Theodore Roosevelt.

Meantime, since his return from his mission, George Albert had been active in his Church duties. He was made superintendent of the Seventeenth Ward Sunday School, and in 1902 was selected to head the YMMIA organiza- tions of Salt Lake Stake, which then embraced the whole of Salt Lake Valley.

On Tuesday, October 6, 1903, at the afternoon ses- sion of the semiannual general conference of the Church held in the Salt Lake Tabernacle, the name of George Al- bert Smith was presented, and he was sustained, as a mem- ber of the Quorum of the Twelve. The appointment came as a complete surprise to Elder Smith, although, he stated to this writer, "My patriarchal blessing given under the hands of Zebedee Coltrin when I was twelve years of age indicated that I would some day become an Apostle." On Thursday, October 8, in the Salt Lake Temple, he was ordained and set apart in his new office and calling by President Joseph F. Smith.

His first stake conference in his new capacity as an apostle was that of Utah Stake, held at Provo on Sunday, October 11, 1903, three days after his ordination. From that date he traveled hundreds of thousands of miles in

visiting the stakes of Zion and the far-flung missions of the
Church. He exercised great diligence in his calling and
unweariedly carried on his work as an advocate of the
gospel of Jesus Christ, which was restored to earth by the
Prophet Joseph Smith.

In reading President Smith's diary, during his early
years as an apostle, one finds many interesting items. On
February 22, 1904, he was elected to the office of chaplain
in the local organization of the Sons of the American Revolution. He subsequently took a real interest in the success
of this group and in 1918 became the president of the
Utah society. At the national convention held at Nashville,
Tennessee, on May 23, 1923, he was elected vice-president
general of the national organization. He served in this office
for seven terms.

On April 13, 1904, he was named a member of the
general board of YMMIA and later on presided as general
superintendent for many years.

On July 24, 1904, he notes in his diary that he "rode
in an automobile in the parade for the pioneers." This
appears to have been his first ride in the new horseless
carriage that was making its appearance on the streets of
Salt Lake City about this time. Again on June 21, 1905,
he writes: "Enjoyed a ride in an automobile by the courtesy
of LeRoi C. Snow."

He took an active interest in the sport of fishing whenever the opportunity was afforded. I find this item under
the date of July 19, 1904. "I went fishing with Willard R.
Smith. He caught ten trout; I didn't catch any. I couldn't
see the fish in time." However, he made a better record
the following year. While at Morgan, after a stake conference held during the last week of September, he was invited to go on a fishing trip by Daniel Heiner, president of
the Morgan Stake, to the East Canyon Reservoir. There he
caught a trout weighing $5^5/_8$ pounds. He was so delighted
with this catch that he had the brethren who were with
him sign a certificate to the effect that it was really a fact

and not just another fish story. As this certificate is included in his diary, I shall reproduce it here.

Morgan, Saturday, Sept, 23/05.

This is to certify that today while fishing in the East Canyon reservoir, we saw George Albert Smith catch and land in the boat a trout weighing $5\frac{5}{8}$ pounds, same being weighed at the Drug Store in Morgan.

(Signed) D. Heiner,
W. Rich,
M. Heiner.

He took an active part in politics and during the presidential campaign of 1904 spoke at Republican rallies in Kaysville, Manti, Provo, Heber City, and Charleston.

On May 6, 1905, Elder Smith accompanied a group of Church officials, including his father, John Henry Smith, and C. W. Penrose, Reed Smoot, and others, on a trip in a private car over the newly completed Salt Lake route, from Salt Lake City to Los Angeles. He noted on his arrival that he had an excellent room with bath at one of the best (if not the best) hotels in the city for $1.35 per day. The same room, with meals, was $3.00 per day.

During these years he met and associated with many interesting people. On October 7, 1904, he writes of having been introduced to the vice-president of the United States, Charles W. Fairbanks, who was visiting in Salt Lake City.

On June 27, 1905, he was present in Ogden to celebrate the eighty-fifth birthday of his maternal grandfather, Lorin Farr. This great pioneer had a remarkable history. He became a member of the Church in 1832 when he was twelve years of age. In 1837 he went with his parents to Kirtland and from that time followed the leaders of the Church in their migrations from place to place, and finally to Salt Lake Valley, where he arrived in September 1847. He subsequently moved to Ogden and became the first president of Weber Stake. He was also the first mayor of Ogden and served as such for twenty-three years; he held many other responsible offices during his long life. Lorin Farr died at Ogden on January 12, 1909. George Albert Smith bore a remarkable resemblance to his distinguished grandfather, both in his physical features and in his ability as a leader among the people.

On August 20, 1905, Elder Smith was at Layton, Utah, where he visited with a distant relative, Silas S. Smith, a cousin of the Prophet Joseph Smith and an early pioneer of Utah.

On September 8, 1905, George Albert assisted Reed Smoot and others in entertaining Gifford Pinchot, chief of the Forestry Division of the United States, who was spending a few days in Salt Lake City.

Two days later, September 10, he recorded a most important event in his diary—the birth of his only son, George Albert Smith, Jr.

During the same month he met and took for a ride around the city Joseph Smith, the founder and first president of the Reorganized Church.

During all this time he was in constant attendance at stake conferences in the various parts of the Church and his own quorum meetings at home. His life was a busy one.

In December, 1905, Elder Smith accompanied President Joseph F. Smith and a party of prominent Church officials to Sharon, Vermont, where, on the 23rd of the month, a granite shaft was dedicated in honor of the Prophet Joseph Smith, on the one hundredth anniversary of his birth.

Eighteen months later, in June, 1907, in company with German E. Ellsworth and Ashby Snow, Elder Smith journeyed to Palmyra, New York, where he succeeded in making a purchase for the Church of the farm formerly owned by Joseph Smith, Sr. This beautiful farm, which includes the Sacred Grove, the scene of the Prophet's first vision, and the old Smith home, is now visited annually by thousands of Latter-day Saints.

IV

In the midst of his busy life, when his travels amounted to almost 30,000 miles per year in behalf of his Church, George Albert Smith suffered a severe illness in February, 1909, which completely incapacitated him for a period of more than two years and weakened him for a number of months beyond that time. In his ardor and zeal for the work of the Lord he had gone beyond his strength; he had exhausted his supply of nervous energy, and a long period of rest and recuperation was required to bring him back to normal health.

The summer of 1909 was spent at Ocean Park, California, where the sea breezes and ocean bathing were helpful. The winter of 1909-10 was spent in St. George, in the mild climate of the valley of the Virgin, and the following year he went again to southern California. Gradually his strength returned, but it was several years before he could carry on the strenuous duties attendant to his apostleship.

During the period of his recuperation Elder Smith received a severe shock, and his life was saddened, with the news of the sudden death of his esteemed and worthy father, President John Henry Smith, on October 13, 1911. The *Deseret News* said of him editorially: "It is difficult to reconcile oneself to the thought that President John Henry Smith, the tender husband and father, the wise counselor, the genial friend, the delightful pulpit and platform orator, the strong defender of the truth, the faithful witness and messenger of the Master, has left us. But such is the decree of him whose servant he was."

George Albert noted the physical effect upon his system due to the death of his father. On November 7, 1911, he wrote in his journal: "Since my father's death I have not regained my strength." He was thus forced to spend most of the winter of 1911 in California, seeking rest and recuperation. In May, 1912, he rented a house in Ocean Park for one year and moved his family to that location. In Octo-

ber he returned to Utah and attended the semiannual conference of the Church. He was called to speak and addressed the Saints briefly in the Tabernacle for the first
time in more than three years.

It was in the latter part of 1912 that Elder Smith noted definite improvement in his health. He was able to attend a stake conference held at Mesa, Arizona, in December,
and in April, 1913, he traveled to Salt Lake City and at-

tended all the sessions of the general conference. Shortly
afterward he resumed his work of visiting one of the stakes
each week as the assignments were given to him.

On July 24, 1913, George Albert accompanied President Joseph F. Smith and party on a trip to Cardston,
Canada. There, on Sunday, July 27, the site for a new
temple was dedicated. This temple was subsequently built,
the first to be erected outside the boundaries of the United
States.

Shortly after his return from Canada, Elder Smith departed for the East on an extended journey that consumed
more than a month's time. On his arrival in New York City
he called on his uncle, President Ben E. Rich of the Eastern
States Mission. He found President Rich suffering a very
severe illness, from which he died a few days later, September 13, 1913. Elder Smith set apart Elder Laurence W.
Richards to preside over the mission temporarily until a
new president could be appointed. After disposing of other
business pertaining to the Church, and making visits to
Albany, Rochester, and Washington, D. C., he returned
home in time to attend the semiannual conference in October.

Elder Smith was now enjoying greatly improved health,
as we learn from his journals during this and succeeding
years. In the fall and early winter of 1913 he accompanied
President Joseph F. Smith, Bishop Charles W. Nibley, and
others to Chicago to dedicate a new chapel. From that
city the party returned by way of Arizona and spent several
days visiting the Latter-day Saints in the Arizona stakes.

Almost every Sunday during 1914, Elder Smith attended a stake conference in one of the stakes.

An item of special interest in his journal in May, 1914, informs us that he had purchased a lot in the new subdivision of Yale Park in Salt Lake City. He subsequently purchased a home on the lot adjoining this beautiful property.

In October 1914 he attended sessions of the International Irrigation Congress at Calgary, Canada in company with Richard W. Young of Utah, who was president of the organization. Latter in the year he made a tour of the Southern States Mission.

On April 4, 1915, George Albert celebrated his forty-fifth birthday. During the same week he attended all the sessions of the general conference in the great Tabernacle. He was one of the speakers at the closing meeting.

"My heart has been made glad during this conference," he said, "at the outpouring of the Spirit of the Lord, and I feel that it has been well for us to be together. In the midst of the turmoil that exists in the world today [World War I was raging at the time] I have felt to praise my maker for the peace and quiet that reigns in Israel; for all the blessings that abound in this great land of America; that our lot has been cast under the folds of the stars and stripes and that our Heavenly Father has seen fit to plant the feet of his people in this grand intermountain country."

This was always the gist of President Smith's teaching. Since his boyhood his heart overflowed to God for his many blessings and for the blessings that were poured out upon the Saints.

In July, 1915, Elder Smith left Salt Lake City to visit the Eastern States Mission. This journey occupied six weeks' time and took him to many of the important cities in that part of the country. Toronto was reached on July 7; the following day he was at Rochester; and on the 8 he spent the day at Palmyra, where he met and visited with Mr. Sexton, the owner of the Cumorah farm. On July 10 he returned to Toronto, and the next day he journeyed to Ottawa, where he called twice to see the governor-general of Canada "but he was reported to be occupied with pressing business." He visited the U. S. Consul Foster "and was received kindly." On the 15 Elder Smith was at Halifax, where he had an interview with Lieutenant Governor Mc-Gregor, "a fine old man." On the 17th he reached St. Johns, N. B., where he called on the mayor, James H. Frick. All these calls were made in addition to lengthy meetings that he held with the missionaries and Saints.

On July 20 George Albert journeyed back to the states and called at the village of Whitefield, New Hampshire, the home of his paternal grandmother, Sarah Ann Libby. Here he had the pleasure of meeting her brother, J. A. Libby, eighty-five years old.

Traveling now to Sharon, Vermont, the birthplace of the Prophet Joseph Smith, he had the pleasure of attending three meetings of missionaries and Saints when "one hundred and eleven testified of the mercy of the Lord and their knowledge of the gospel."

In September, 1916, Elder Smith attended the International Irrigation Congress at Sacramento, California, where, he relates, "I was both temporary and permanent chairman. I was elected second vice-president for the next Congress."

The year 1917 opened with the usual activities. There were quarterly conferences to attend in the stakes and missions to visit. On April 4, George Albert observed his forty-seventh birthday, and May 25 he celebrated the twenty-fifth anniversary of his marriage, "to one of the best women in the world." On June 14 he attended the funeral of Samuel H. B. Smith, son of Samuel H. Smith, brother of the Prophet. Each week through the summer there was a stake conference to attend. Of special interest to this writer is a note in Elder Smith's journal under the date of September 19, 1917: "Left for Duchesne Stake with Preston Nibley." I well remember this trip and the trouble we had with punctures and blow-outs, traveling on dirt and graveled roads the entire distance.

In October Elder Smith spent two weeks visiting the Northwestern States Mission. On the 21st of the same month he was in Arizona attending a stake conference. On November 27 he states that he played his first game of golf "in company with President Smith and Bishop Nibley." Such were his varied activities.

On Monday, July 29, 1918, Elder Smith was in attendance and represented the Church with Samuel O. Bennion at the dedication of a monument erected in honor of General Alexander W. Doniphan, at Richmond, Missouri. General Doniphan is gratefully remembered by the Saints for his valiant and courageous action at Far West, Missouri, in 1838, when the life of the Prophet Joseph Smith would have been taken had it not been for Doniphan's prompt intervention.

The year 1918 was the year of the great influenza epidemic that swept through the country, taking thousands of lives. In the interest of the health of the people, all public meetings were discontinued for a number of weeks until conditions improved. George Albert therefore remained at home in the fall and early winter of this year. It was during this time that the venerable President of the Church, Joseph F. Smith, died at Salt Lake City, on November 19, six days past his eightieth birthday. George Albert offered the opening prayer at the funeral service held in the city cemetery on the 21st, and felt keenly the loss of his distinguished relative. "Personally," he wrote, "I feel that I have lost another father. He has always been very kind to me, and I love him and his memory most sincerely."

V

On January 27, 1919, Elder Smith noted in his journal the rather startling information that "President Grant has asked me to prepare to go to England." The presidency of the European Mission at that time, and for many years previously, had been occupied by a member of the Twelve, and it was therefore in order that Elder Smith should in time be called to take his turn. He began immediately to make preparations to respond to the call, but it was May 19 before passports for himself and family were obtained. On June 4, with his wife, Lucy, his daughter Edith, and his son George Albert, Jr., President Smith left Salt Lake City for his new field of labor. The journey to England was without special incident, and the members of the party were welcomed to the mission home at 295 Edge Lane, Liverpool, on June 25.

As England was recovering at the time from devastation caused by the first World War, and as food of all kinds was scarce, it was difficult for the American elders to obtain permission to enter the country. However, President Smith went to work on this problem with a will and determination to succeed. One of his first visits was to London, where he enlisted the help of the United States Ambassador Davis. British government officials referred him to the Minister of Labor, Sir Robert Horn. After repeated calls on this gentleman and others who were interested, he was able to record in his journal on May 31, 1920, "Today I received word that our missionaries would be allowed to come in."

Meantime he had been most active in have various duties as mission president. In September 1919 he visited the Saints in Ireland, and during the following month he held a conference with the members in Glasgow, Scotland. In November he made a tour of France and Switzerland, accompanied by his son, and held many meetings.

In February, 1920, President Smith journeyed again to Scotland, where he delivered a very enlightening address to the Rotary Club of Edinburgh on the history and doctrines of the Latter-day Saints.

On June 20, 1920, President Smith received the disquieting news from Salt Lake City that his mother had been stricken with partial paralysis. On that day he wrote in his journal: "Received word that my mother is partly paralyzed and feel quite disturbed about it. She is seventy years old and one of the best mothers in the world. I do hope the Lord will heal her."

Norway, Sweden, and Germany were visited in the fall of 1920, and a busy winter was experienced thereafter in getting the missionary work reestablished in Great Britain. On February 1, 1921, President Smith received a cablegram from Salt Lake City with the sad news that his mother had died. Shortly thereafter came word from the First Presidency that his successor had been appointed and that he would be allowed to return home. Only one important engagement remained. He had been appointed to represent Zion's Cooperative Mercantile Institution in accompanying a delegation of American dry goods merchants on a tour of the larger cities of England and Scotland. This journey, which occupied a month's time, afforded him an excellent opportunity to make new friends and advocate the doctrines of the Church.

Just prior to his departure from England he published the following farewell message in the *Millennial Star* under the date of June 30, 1921.

"To the Missionaries and Saints of the European Mission:

"After two years of strenuous effort to further the interests of The Church of Jesus Christ of Latter-day Saints, in Great Britain and on the continent, the time has arrived for me to say farewell to you, my beloved co-laborers, brethren and sisters. I have been released by the First Presidency, and Elder Orson F. Whitney has arrived to succeed me as President of the European Mission. All being well I shall depart from Liverpool July 15th, accompanied by my family, to return to our mountain home in Utah. . . .

"It has been my privilege to travel in the British Isles, Norway, Sweden, Denmark, Holland, Belgium, Germany, France and Switzerland, and to visit the conferences of those missions. We were received with the utmost kindness

and were made to rejoice on account of the faith of the
people . . . . American Ambassadors, Ministers and Con-
suls, received us kindly everywhere and extended every
courtesy that could be expected. We have called and met
government officials, members of parliaments, Lord Mayors,
Lord Provosts, mayors of towns and other officers, titled
gentlemen, business men and manufacturers of importance.
With these we have had many pleasant conversations, and
have supplied many pictures and our literature whenever
it has been acceptable. . . .

"We must not forget, Latter-day Saints, that we have
been made partakers of the Gospel of Jesus Christ and the
responsibility is on us to share our blessings with our fellow
creatures. We have been warned and should continue to
warn our neighbors. The Lord has spoken in our day and
organized His Church. He has conferred divine authority
on men and his all-powerful arm is making bare to prepare
the way for his second coming. . . .

"I thank you all for the assistance you have rendered
and the encouragement you have given me while here, and
I beg of you to as loyally sustain our beloved brother, Elder
Orson F. Whitney, during the period of his presidency.

"I leave my testimony with you, that I know God lives,
that Jesus Christ is his son and our Redeemer, whose gospel
has been restored through the Prophet Joseph Smith. His
Church is established on earth for the last time, in preparation for his coming in power and glory, to reign on earth
as Lord of Lords and King of Kings. We are its members
and I pray that we may so order our lives that we shall
receive eternal life in His Celestial Kingdom, among those
whom we have known and loved here on earth.

(Signed) George Albert Smith."

On July 15, 1921, Elder Smith, accompanied by his
wife, his daughters, and his son, sailed from Liverpool on
his return journey. Nineteen days later they arrived at their
home in Salt Lake City, after an absence of twenty-six
months.

VI

George Albert now resumed his duties in the work of the Quorum of the Twelve, with its many committee meetings and conferences. During the balance of the year he attended quarterly conferences in the stakes of Blackfoot, Panguitch, Kanab, Logan, St. Johns, Snowflake, Mesa, St. Joseph, and Juarez. He also had an added responsibility given him on September 21, shortly after his return, when he was selected by the First Presidency to be the general superintendent of the YMMIA of the Church.

The year 1922 opened favorably for Elder Smith. His health was good; he was enjoying his work; he and his family were comfortably situated in their new home, one of the most beautiful locations in Salt Lake City.

On May 8 he began a journey to the East. On arriving in Springfield, Mass., he attended the national convention of the Sons of the American Revolution and was elected vice-president general for the Pacific and Rocky Mountain states. Four days later he was in Washington and went with Senator Reed Smoot to call on President Warren G. Harding. The following day he had a pleasant interview with Chief Justice William Howard Taft.

On his return to Utah, Elder Smith resumed his visits to the stakes and wards. In November he made a second trip to Washington, D. C., in the interest of the Church.

The year 1923 was also a busy one for Elder Smith. He was absent from Salt Lake City during the entire month of January, traveling on the Pacific coast with President-General Adams of the S. A. R. On the 23rd of the month he was present in Los Angeles when the first stake was organized in California with George W. McCune as president. On the following day this writer took him in an auto to San Bernardino, where he boarded a train for Salt Lake City.

The following incident took place a few weeks later, on March 1, and is recorded in Elder Smith's diary. While his car was parked on a downtown street in Salt Lake City, someone stole his auto robe. That night he wrote as follows: "If I thought the man who took it really needed it I would have presented it to him and he would not have been a thief."

Stake conferences were attended regularly during the summer. In addition he made two trips east during the fall and winter, the latter being a visit to the Southern States Mission, which occupied six weeks time and which took him as far as Havana, Cuba.

On January 1, 1924, George Albert wrote in his diary: "My heart is full of gratitude to my Father in heaven for his blessings during the past year and for the promise of 1924." This was indeed an active year for him. Besides attending twenty-five stake conferences, he was present at all sessions of two general conferences of the Church and in addition made two trips to the eastern states. His travels for many years had averaged more than 30,000 miles per year.

On April 4, 1924, Elder Smith noted in his diary that he was "54 years old today." Some weeks later, on June 13, he began a journey to the East to transact business for the Church. In the course of his travels he visited Chicago, Toronto, Montreal, and New York. He returned home on July 4 and two weeks later took an active part in the national S. A. R. convention, which was held in Salt Lake City. Stake conferences were attended during almost every Sunday for the balance of the year.

On February 5, 1925, George Albert began another extensive journey to the East, which consumed more than six weeks time and took him into twenty-one states. During this time he attended thirty-one meetings with members of the Church "and spoke in all but one." In April he made a tour of the Western States Mission in company with President John M. Knight. In May he attended an S. A. R. convention in Swampscott, Mass., where he was elected vice-president general for the fourth time. On his way home he noted in his diary that he had traveled 22,000 miles since January. One more trip was made to the East in October. During the weeks he was at home he was busy attending stake conferences and presiding over the YMMIA organizations of the Church.

As his responsibilities increased he noted that his many activities were again having an adverse effect upon his health. "I am tired out," he wrote in his diary under the date of February 23, 1926. "I have too many irons in the fire." Nevertheless, there seemed to be no way of removing any of the irons and he continued on. He was in attendance at the general conference in April and spoke at the closing session. Following is a paragraph from the sermon: "We are living in a marvelous age, in the Dispensation of the Fulness of Times. All other dispensations that have gone before are culminating in this one. The Lord tells us in the Book of Mormon that at the time of the coming forth of that book, he would commence his work among all the nations, and it is remarkable that since the publication of the Book of Mormon, more important inventions and discoveries have been presented to mankind than in all the ages that have gone before."

Two weeks after the conference Elder Smith left for a trip to the East. At Washington, D. C., he met President Heber J. Grant and the two attended national meetings of the Boy Scouts organization, where they listened to speeches by President Calvin Coolidge and Sir Robert Baden-Powell, the latter being the founder of the Boy Scout movement. It was on this occasion that the first Silver Buffalo ever awarded by the Boy Scouts of America was presented to the distinguished Englishman. At the close of the convention Elder Smith returned to Salt Lake City and spent the summer in attending conferences in the stakes and in his various duties at the Church headquarters.

During the first six months of 1927 the California and Southern States missions were visited. In Washington, D. C., he met Phillip St. George Cook, grandson of the leader of the Mormon Battalion. In Richmond, Virginia, he visited the church where Patrick Henry made his famous speech. In August, after his return home, he made his first airplane ride to Los Angeles—August 3, 1927. He left Salt Lake City in an open plane at 3:45 p.m. and arrived at Las Vegas four hours later, at 7:45 p.m. Here he remained overnight and the following morning flew to Los Angeles, "in two hours time, making six hours in all to cover a distance of 675 miles." Two days later he flew to Salt Lake City on his return journey. When directly over St. George he dropped a note to Brigham Jarvis, which the latter received and acknowledged.

On January 1, 1928, Elder Smith noted in his diary that his health was definitely improving. "I have been blessed with better health than for years," he wrote. During this year he attended many stake conferences, but there is no record of any extensive eastern trips. The following year, however, he was traveling out of the state most of the time. Before the April conference he had visited the California Mission, which at that time included California and Arizona. On May 9 he left for New York City to attend a meeting of the Boy Scouts of America. On the 16th of the month he was at Washington and enjoyed a short visit with President Herbert Hoover. Two days later, at Akron, Ohio, he had lunch with the founder of the Firestone Tire and Rubber Company, Harvey Firestone.

In June Elder Smith toured the Western States Mission, and in November, in company with Elder Charles A. Callis, he made his ninth visit to the Southern States Mission. His travels during this year were again over 30,000 miles.

The year following, 1930, was the centennial year of the founding of the Church, and George Albert Smith was made general chairman of the centennial celebration. This was a heavy responsibility and it took the major part of his time for a number of months, but under his able management the centennial was a great success. Perhaps the chief event was the great pageant attended by approximately 200,000 people, many of whom came from various parts of the United States.

His second activity of importance during the year was the leading of a caravan of automobiles eastward along the famous emigrant road to Independence Rock in Wyoming. The event took place in July and was part of a national celebration sponsored by the Oregon Trail Memorial Association. On his return he assisted in organizing and was made president of the Utah Pioneer Trails and Landmarks Association on September 11, 1930.

During 1931 Elder Smith traveled 35,694 miles in the interest of the Church. During January he visited the Texas Mission; in February he visited the Arizona stakes and also the Mormon colonies of Mexico; during April he traveled to Memphis, Tennessee, to attend a meeting of the National Council of the Boy Scouts of America; in June he drove to Independence Rock, Wyoming, where a large group of Boy Scouts had gathered from all sections of the United States, and his own ward troop was awarded first place for their excellence. During August he traveled by train and boat as far as Sitka, Skagway, and Juneau, Alaska, and in September, on his return, he made an extensive tour of the North Central States Mission. This was one of the most active years of his life, and he was now sixty-one years of age.

On January 6, 1932, George Albert made note in his diary that he had received the award of the Silver Beaver from the regional society of Boy Scouts of America. This award was given on account of his distinguished service to the organization.

In February, Elder Smith made a trip to Springfield, Illinois, where he addressed a group of two hundred delegates of the S. A. R. society on Washington's birthday. He also had the privilege of laying a wreath on Abraham Lincoln's tomb.

During April he toured the Northwestern States Mission, and in May he journeyed to the East to be present at a banquet of the national Scout organization, at which time he was elected to the national executive board, Boy Scouts of America.

George Albert had a unique and rather disastrous experience in August of this year, when he journeyed with members of his family to the Grand Canyon of the Colorado in northern Arizona. On the last day of the month he and his son took a mule-back ride to the river in the bottom of the canyon. They remained overnight and the following morning were informed by telephone that the Grand Canyon lodge had burned. Fortunately Elder Smith and his family were housed in a nearby cabin; however, some of their possessions were burned in the fire. His son's "effects left in the office were destroyed, including journal and other valuable papers. My clothing in the pressing room was completely destroyed. My purse in the safe was burned to a crisp, with railroad passes and about $25 to $35 in bills."

During the balance of 1932 and the early part of 1933 there were the usual stake conferences to attend. There was also a trip to New York City in April to attend a meeting of the Boy Scout council and another to Nauvoo and Independence in July to attend to business for the Church.

On January 1, 1934, Elder Smith wrote in his diary: "I start the New Year with gratitude to the Lord and with hope for a successful future." On April 4, he noted: "I am sixty-four years old today." However, despite his increasing years, he continued on faithfully with his work. At home his time was completely occupied with varied activities; the meetings of the Twelve; his duties as general superintendent of the YMMIA; the B. S. A. and S. A. R. organizations; the Utah Trails Association, and his various business interests.

Shortly after the April conference in 1934 Elder Smith made a tour of the Eastern States Mission. It was during this visit that he met the eminent scientist, Dr. Michael Pupin. This delightful experience, which was made possible by Dr. Harvey Fletcher, a native Utahn, made a deep impression on Elder Smith, and thereafter, in many of his sermons he referred to the inspiring career of this great man. On this same journey, while at Washington, D. C., George Albert enjoyed a pleasant half hour with George H. Dern, Secretary of War and former governor of Utah. At Buffalo he attended the national convention of the Boy Scouts of America.

It was on this occasion that he received the Silver Buffalo, the highest award in Scouting in the United States. The award was made for outstanding and meritorious service to boyhood, and when it was given, the following citation was read:

"George Albert Smith, Business Executive, religious leader, former President of the International Irrigation Congress and International Farm Congress, Federal Receiver of Public Moneys and special Disbursing Agent for the State of Utah. Member of the Quorum of Twelve Apostles of the Church of Jesus Christ of Latter-day Saints and General Superintendent of the Young Men's Mutual Improvement Associations of the Church. Organizer and President of the Utah Pioneer Trails and Land-Marks Association. Member of the National Executive Board of the Boy Scouts of America, Program Divisional Committee, Committee on Relationships and of its Region Twelve Executive Committee, and identified with its local activities since its organization. He has been indefatigable in serving the cause of scouting and to his enthusiasm for its program must be largely traced the fact that Utah stands above all other states in the percentage of boys who are Scouts."

On his return journey to Utah, during the first week of June, he noted in his diary that he had traveled 5,500 miles on this trip and that he had been treated kindly everywhere and was thankful for the opportunity which had been afforded him "to teach the gospel of Jesus Christ." With the exception of another short trip to the East in the fall, the balance of the year was spent in visiting the stakes and attending to his duties at home.

During 1935 Elder Smith continued his travels. There was a trip to Chicago in May to attend the national council of the B. S. A., and a few days later he was present in Louisville, Kentucky, where he took part in an S. A. R. convention. In June he presided over the great MIA conference in Salt Lake City. On July 6 he officiated in the temple in uniting in marriage his son, George Albert, Jr., and Ruth Nowell.

In July he attended a large reception and banquet in New York City in honor of Sir Robert Baden-Powell, who again was on a visit to the United States. During September he spent two weeks visiting the Northern States Mission.

The year 1936 was another busy year. Stake conferences were attended during January. In February he was in New York City on business for the Church. In March he visited in Louisville, Kentucky, and in May he attended the national S. A. R. congress in Portland, Maine. At home, in his capacity as president of the Utah Trails and Landmarks Association, he dedicated monuments at Old Fort Harmony and Parowan, in Southern Utah.

On January 21, 1937, Elder Smith noted in his journal that he had spent part of the day with a committee of the Utah Pioneer Trails Association. The subject discussed was the erection of a suitable monument at the mouth of Emigration Canyon to honor the pioneers. Thus for ten years George Albert Smith labored faithfully and diligently to bring into realization the great masterpiece of art, which was completed and dedicated on July 24, 1947, in commemoration of the one hundredth anniversary of the arrival of President Brigham Young and the original pioneer band. To George Albert Smith, more than any other man, belongs the honor of having conceived of this monumental work and of having labored faithfully and diligently, against manifold obstructions and discouragements, to bring about its realization.

VII

Throughout the years 1936 and 1937 Elder Smith was greatly concerned about the health of his dear and beloved wife, who for some time had been seriously ailing with arthritis. During April, 1937, her life was despaired of and members of her family were summoned to her bedside. However, she rallied from this illness and became somewhat stronger during the summer, so that she could ride out in a car and enjoy the sunshine and the scenery. On May 25 she and her husband observed the forty-fifth anniversary of their marriage. During September and October her health visibly declined. Late in October she suffered a serious relapse, and on Friday, November 5, she passed peacefully away.

The death of his beloved wife was a heavy blow to Elder George Albert Smith. He was not in robust health himself and had difficulty in maintaining his normal strength so that he could carry on with his tasks. The authorities of the Church were mindful of his loss, and realizing that a change of environment might be beneficial, he was offered and accepted an opportunity to visit the missions of the Church in the South Pacific.

Elder Smith departed from Salt Lake City on January 17, 1938, for San Francisco. The following day he boarded the ship *Lurline,* bound for Honolulu. He arrived on the 28th and immediately began his work, holding meetings with the Saints and missionaries. On February 7, Elders Rufus K. Hardy and Matthew Cowley and family arrived in Honolulu and the same evening the group sailed for the South Seas. En route the Fiji Islands were visited; and on February 18 Auckland, New Zealand, was reached, where Elder Cowley left his brethren to remain and preside over the New Zealand Mission. Elders Smith and Hardy proceeded to Australia. Sydney was reached on February 21, and the visitors were met by Dr. Thomas D. Rees, the mission president, and taken to the mission home. After

remaining one day at the mission headquarters the voy-
agers continued on to Melbourne, where they arrived on
the 25th. From Melbourne they journeyed to Tasmania;
thence to Adelaide, and from there to Perth, the western
port of Australia. In all these cities meetings were held
with Saints and missionaries.

After traveling through various parts of Australia where
the Saints were located, which occupied the time of the
visitors during the month of March, the brethren departed
for New Zealand on April 1. They arrived at Auckland on
April 4, Elder Smith's sixty-eighth birthday. Wellington,
Palmerston, and other districts were visited. On April 7, in
company with Elder Alexander Wishart, Elder Smith left
for Tonga, where he and his companion arrived on May
10. At Nukualofa the Queen of Tonga and the Prime Minister were visited and much prejudice that had heretofore
existed was allayed by the missionaries.

On June 8, Elders Smith and Hardy arrived in Apia,
Samoa. Here the brethren continued their missionary work.
The Governor of British Samoa attended and spoke at their
conference meetings. On July 6 they arrived in Honolulu
on their way home; five days later they docked safely at
Wilmington harbor, where Elder Smith was met by members of his family, and on the 14th they reached Salt Lake
City. Elder Smith had been absent from home for six months
and had traveled 27,000 miles.

After his mission to the South Seas Elder Smith resumed his activities at home and abroad for a period of
five years. During this time he enjoyed good health, which
enabled him to attend to his multifarious duties.

On Monday, June 21, 1943, the members of the Church
were notified by the press and radio that President Rudger
Clawson had died at his home in Salt Lake City. His death
left a vacancy in the important position of president of the
Twelve, and Elder George Albert Smith, being the highest
ranking member in point of service in his quorum, was
sustained by his brethren of the First Presidency and the

Twelve to succeed President Clawson. He was set apart
for this position by President Heber J. Grant on July 8,
1943.

Two years later, on May 14, 1945, came the startling
news that President Heber J. Grant, the venerable head of
the Church, had passed away at his home in Salt Lake City.
At the time Elder George Albert Smith was on his way
east, on business for the Church. He received a telegram
at Buffalo, New York, conveying the sad news and immediately began the return journey to Salt Lake City, where
he arrived in time to be present at the funeral on the 18th.
He was one of the speakers on that occasion. Three days
later, on May 21, at a meeting of the Quorum of the
Twelve held in the Salt Lake Temple, Elder Smith was
sustained by his brethren as the President of The Church
of Jesus Christ of Latter-day Saints.

1945

At the semiannual general conference of the Church
held in October, 1945, in the historic Tabernacle at Salt
Lake City, President Smith was sustained by the great body
of the priesthood voting in quorums. The First Presidency,
the Twelve, the patriarchs, the high priests, the seventies,
the elders, and all members of the lesser priesthood voted
in groups. Finally the entire assembly, including the priesthood, arose in a body and gave the First Presidency a
unanimous sustaining vote by upraised hands. There was
not a negative vote cast in the entire procedure.

After the vote had been taken the President arose to
speak to the people.

"I wonder if anyone here feels as weak and as humble
as the man who stands before you," he said. "I have been
coming to this house since my infancy. I have seen all the
Presidents of the Church since that time, sustained by the
congregations here, as their names have been presented
from this stand. I have seen the Church continue to grow
in numbers, and have realized throughout all my years that
the Church of Jesus Christ is what its name implies. We
who are members of this Church are indeed fortunate to

have found the light and to have accepted the truth. . . .

"And so today, my brethren, standing here in humility before you, I would like to express to you my gratitude that you have seen fit to promise that you will help the humble man who has been called to preside over this Church, as he strives to carry on by the inspiration of the Almighty. For this promise I am grateful and I thank you that you have offered to do the same thing with regard to the two men who stand by my side as counselors, loyal and true and devoted Latter-day Saints, who have done everything to make my responsibility easier for me to carry. You voted to sustain the Quorum of the Twelve, the Quorum that I belonged to for so many years, that I felt like a stranger almost, when I walked out of it to occupy the position of President of the Church."

On the second day President Smith gave the Saints some excellent advice.

"I think I would like to repeat something I have told many times as a guide to some of these younger men. It was an expression of advice of my grandfather for whom I was named. He said: 'There is a line of demarcation well-defined between the Lord's territory and the devil's territory. If you will remain on the Lord's side of the line, the adversary cannot come there to tempt you. You are perfectly safe as long as you stay on the Lord's side of the line. But,' he said, 'if you cross onto the devil's side of the line, you are in his territory, and you are in his power, and he will work on you to get you just as far from that line as he possibly can, knowing that he can only succeed in destroying you by keeping you away from the place where there is safety.'

"All safety, all righteousness, all happiness are on the Lord's side of the line. If you are keeping the commandments of God by observing the Sabbath day, you are on the Lord's side of the line. If you attend to your secret prayers and your family prayers, you are on the Lord's side of the line."

VIII

The first trip outside of Salt Lake City made by President Smith after he became President was to Logan, where, on the afternoon of Sunday, June 4, he delivered an address to the graduates of the Logan LDS Institute. Three days later he journeyed to Provo and spoke to the graduates of the Brigham Young University.

As chairman of "This Is the Place" Monument Commission, President Smith presided at ceremonies held on July 24, 1945, when the first ground was broken on the site where the great monument was to be erected. The same afternoon he addressed an immense group of people, thirty thousand or more, who had assembled at Liberty Park to attend exercises in honor of the pioneers. Two months later the General Authorities of the Church, under the leadership of President Smith, gathered at Idaho Falls on September 23, 1945, to dedicate the magnificent new temple that had been erected in that city. The impressive and solemn ceremonies continued for three days.

President Smith, accompanied by a number of the officials of the Church, journeyed to Washington, D.C., early in November, 1945, and there held a conference with President Harry S Truman relative to the shipment of welfare goods to members of the Church residing in Europe.

President Smith observed his seventy-sixth birthday on April 4, 1946. Two days later he presided at the opening session of the annual conference and delivered a stirring address to the Saints assembled. Five weeks after the conference, on May 13, President Smith left Salt Lake City on a journey to Mexico to visit the members of the Church residing in that country. This was a history-making journey. It was the first time that a President of the Church had visited the southern republic. At Mexico City President Smith had an interview with Manuel Arvilla Camacho, president of the southern republic, and presented him with a Book of Mormon.

Upon his return to Salt Lake City, President Smith fulfilled a long-cherished desire when he journeyed eastward with a few friends in July, 1946, to retrace the memorable trek made by the Mormon pioneers westward from Nauvoo to Salt Lake Valley in 1846-47. The writer of this sketch had the honor of accompanying him on this journey. The party returned to Salt Lake City on July 24, in time for President Smith to lay the cornerstone of the great "This Is the Place" Monument at the mouth of Emigration Canyon.

In October, 1946, President Smith presided at the semi-annual conference of the Church and spoke at several of the sessions.

The entire year of 1947 was a busy one for President George Albert Smith. This was the year in which the inhabitants of Utah were to celebrate the one hundredth anniversary of the arrival of the Mormon pioneers.

During the forepart of the year President Smith delivered several addresses in the eastern and western parts of the United States, stressing the pioneer theme. In April he celebrated his seventy-seventh birthday, and during the same week he presided at all sessions of the annual conference.

A notable gathering of the governors of the states and territories was held in Salt Lake City during the week of July 13 to 17, 1947. On the evening of July 15, these distinguished visitors were entertained by President Smith and members of his family on the spacious grounds of the President's home on Yale Avenue.

The great day of the centennial celebration, July 24, finally arrived. By ten o'clock in the morning fully 50,000 people had gathered at the mouth of Emigration Canyon to witness the unveiling of the magnificent pioneer monument. President Smith was in charge of the services. After a short speech of welcome the monument was unveiled and President Smith offered the dedicatory prayer.

During the first week of October President Smith spoke at length at the opening session of the semiannual conference. He stressed the necessity of righteous living and pointed out that peace and happiness could not be obtained in any other way.

President Smith continued his usual strenuous activities during 1948. On January 29 he spoke at a banquet honoring employees of the *Deseret News* for long periods of service. In February he attended the annual Founder's Day exercises at the University of Utah. On March 1 he was the principal speaker at a reunion of the descendants of Wilford Woodruff. On March 8 he addressed a large audience at Brigham Young University during leadership week. On April 4 he observed his seventy-eighth birthday, and on the same day presided at the opening session of the annual conference of the Church.

In June President Smith journeyed to Garland, Utah, to attend and speak at services in honor of the four sons of Mr. and Mrs. Alben Borgstrom, who had lost their lives in World War II.

In September President Harry S Truman and candidate Thomas E. Dewey visited Salt Lake City while making campaign tours throughout the country. President Smith honored both of these men by greeting them at the railroad station and attending their meetings in the Tabernacle.

The birthday of John Henry Smith, father of President George Albert Smith, was celebrated by his descendants on September 18, 1948. One hundred years had passed since the distinguished churchman and pioneer was born near Council Bluffs, Iowa. President Smith spoke on this occasion and related many incidents pertaining to his worthy father.

At the semiannual conference held during the first week of October, 1948, President Smith presided at all sessions. In his opening sermon he expressed his feelings as follows: "It is glorious to live in this age of the world, despite the fears and sorrows that exist . . . the Lord will protect us as long as we follow his word."

President Smith left Salt Lake City on January 15, 1949, on a trip to Los Angeles, where he had business in connection with the building of the Los Angeles Temple. A few days after his arrival he was seized with a sudden illness, which caused him to be confined to a hospital until February 9. He was then taken to the home of David Stoddard at Laguna Beach, where he remained for rest and recuperation until March 31, when he returned to Salt Lake City. This illness weakened President Smith, and he did not again recover his usual strength and vigor.

President Smith's seventy-ninth birthday occurred on April 4, 1949, and he enjoyed himself at a family dinner. The same day he presided and spoke at some length at the opening session of the annual conference. "I wonder if any of you are as happy as I am to be at this conference," he said. "I started praying about two and a half months ago that I might be here, and I am grateful to the Lord that he has heard not only my prayers, but also your prayers, and I take this occasion to thank every one of you for the interest you have had in me and for the kind words that have been written and the prayers that have been offered."

Besides being at his office for a few hours each day, President Smith made three trips outside of Salt Lake City during the summer—one to Jackson, Wyoming, where he took part in the dedication of the Menor Ferry; a short trip to San Francisco; and a longer journey to Kansas City and St. Louis, where he dedicated two chapels.

On January 13, 1950, President Smith left for another extended visit to California. This journey proved beneficial for his health and he did not return to Salt Lake City until the middle of March.

On April 4, he celebrated his eightieth birthday. At a large reception held in the evening at the Hotel Utah he personally greeted several thousand of his friends. Congratulatory letters and telegrams were received from all parts of the country from both members and nonmembers of the Church. President Smith had spent his lifetime in making friends, and their numbers were legion.

A notable journey for President Smith took place in May, 1950, when he traveled eastward to Whitingham, Vermont, and on May 28 dedicated a monument at the birthplace of President Brigham Young. Two days later he took part and gave the dedicatory prayer at ceremonies in Washington, D.C., when a marble statue of the great pioneer was unveiled in the rotunda of the Capitol.

Another event of special interest to President Smith during 1950 was the centennial celebration of the arrival of the first Mormon missionaries on the Hawaiian Islands. This celebration was scheduled to take place during the week of August 9 to 16, and President Smith made the journey in order to take part with the Latter-day Saints residing on the islands. On his return to Salt Lake he paid a glowing tribute to the hospitality of the Hawaiian people.

The semiannual conference of the Church convened earlier than usual in the fall of 1950. The meetings were held on September 29 and 30 and October 1. President Smith attended all the sessions, presided, and spoke at some length at three of the meetings. His sermons were deeply spiritual, and he voiced his love and affection for good people everywhere. "They are all our Father's children," he said, using an expression he had frequently used throughout his life. His concluding words on the last day of the conference were as follows:

"I pray that the power of our Heavenly Father may go with you workers of this Church, you members, wherever you go, that your homes may be the abiding place of the Spirit of our Heavenly Father, that your sons and daughters may grow up in the nurture and admonition of the Lord, that you may love your neighbors—and that means those who are members of the Church and those who are not—that means all who seek to be what the Lord would have them be.

"I pray that each of us may feel day by day the assurance that so many of you have, that God lives, that

Jesus is the Christ, that Joseph Smith was a prophet of the living God. I know that as well as I know that I live, and I bear witness to you in humility, and realizing the seriousness of such a statement if it were not true, I still bear this testimony to you in the name of Jesus Christ, our Lord. Amen."

President Smith made only one more trip outside Salt Lake City during the balance of 1950. He went by train to Denver, Colorado, on October 17 and on the following day spoke to a large congregation and pronounced the dedicatory prayer at the new Denver Stake Tabernacle. On his return he stopped at Provo to dedicate the new science building at Brigham Young University.

At a meeting of the employees of the Church Office Building on December 22, 1950, three days before Christmas, President Smith, despite his weakening health, spoke with vigor and animation for half an hour. He commented on the unsettled conditions in the world:

"There would be no war in Korea and threats of war everywhere else in the world," he said, "if the people accepted and lived the gospel. . . . These wars come solely because the Adversary is able to deceive the bulk of the people. This makes it all the more important that we who have a testimony of the divinity of Jesus should live the gospel and promulgate it."

This was the last occasion that President Smith addressed a public gathering. His health steadily declined during January, 1951, and on February 3 it was announced over the radio and the newspapers that he had been taken to the LDS Hospital for observation and treatment. The following three weeks, under the constant care of doctors and nurses, he seemed to regain some of his strength, but he grew weary and asked to be returned to his hime. This request was granted, and on February 24 he was removed to his comfortable home on Yale Avenue. There, despite the best of care that could be given, his strength continued to fail, and on the evening of Wednesday, April 4, his eighty-first birthday, he passed away peacefully.

IX

The funeral of President Smith was held in the Tabernacle on Saturday, April 7, at 2 p.m. Before that hour the great building was filled to its utmost capacity, and thousands of people were on the grounds outside. Among the speakers were the two counselors of the departed President, J. Reuben Clark, Jr., and David O. McKay.

"Throughout our association together, which has been close and intimate," said President Clark, "and under various and trying circumstances, I have never known him to even indicate that he was impatient, that he had lost his temper, or even that he was under the necessity of controlling it.

"He was universally kind and considerate of both of us who were privileged and honored to work with him. I fully endorse from my own knowledge and observation all of the good that has been said of him here today, and nothing but good has been said or could be said. Evil slunk away from him at all times. It could not abide the presence of his righteous living. I do not know what more I can say in tribute to him than that."

President McKay followed and spoke feelingly to the members of President Smith's family.

"In the highest degree you children and kinsfolk should find peace and consolation from these three contributing factors:

"First, your father, our beloved leader, has lived as nearly as it is humanly possible for a man to live a Christ-like life. He found the answer to the yearning of the human heart for fullness lies in living outside of oneself by love. President George Albert Smith has proved the truth of Christ's paradoxical saying, 'He that will lose his life for my sake shall find it.'

"Secondly—and I speak advisedly here, for I have seen these children, sons and daughters, in action—the tender attention, thoughtful, efficient care rendered by you daughters and by Albert and other members of the family, your having left nothing undone, nothing unapplied which might contribute to your father's restoration or to his comfort, should now, in this hour of bereavement, bring consolation to your aching hearts. And not only in this hour but throughout the coming years.

"And thirdly, as sure, as certain as Christ's spirit visited other spirits in the eternal realm, while his body lay in the borrowed tomb of Joseph of Arimathea, so lives the immortal spirit of your father, our friend, our beloved leader, President George Albert Smith. . . .

"God bless his memory and bring comfort to your souls today and always, you choice children and members of an illustrious family, I pray in the name of Jesus. Amen."

After the funeral, the body of the departed President was taken to the city cemetery and there laid away in the family plot, near his parents, grandparents, and great-grandparents, all of whom had distinguished themselves in the Church.

The dedicatory prayer at the graveside was given by Winslow Farr Smith, brother of the deceased.

DAVID O. McKAY

DAVID O. MCKAY

(1873-1970)

A "solemn assembly," attended by the priesthood and members of The Church of Jesus Christ of Latter-day Saints, was held in the Tabernacle at Salt Lake City on Monday, April 9, 1951, the day after the close of the regular annual conference and two days after the funeral of President George Albert Smith. At this meeting a new First Presidency was sustained, with David O. McKay as President of the Church and Stephen L Richards and J. Reuben Clark, Jr., as counselors. In the voting by quorums, and finally by the entire congregation, these brethren received a unanimous vote of approval.

President McKay at this time was seven months past his seventy-seventh birthday, vigorous, alert, in excellent health, and fully prepared by years of experience and training to carry on the duties of his great office. Let us glance briefly over the life of this man who thus became the ninth President of the Church.

The grandparents of President McKay, William and Ellen Oman McKay, were residents of Thurso, Scotland, in 1850, when they were converted and baptized by Latter-day Saint missionaries who had come from Edinburgh.

In 1852 William McKay was ordained an elder and labored to build up a small branch of the Church at Thurso. On June 30, 1855, he baptized his eleven-year-old son David in the North Sea, and the following day confirmed him a member of the Church. This boy David, who was born at Thurso on May 2, 1844, grew to manhood and became the father of President David O. McKay.

William McKay prepared to emigrate to Utah in 1856 and establish himself at the gathering place of the Saints in the valleys of the mountains. Early in May, with his wife and five children, he journeyed to Liverpool, and from there, on May 4, took passage on the sailing ship *Thornton*, bound for New York City. There were 764 emigrating Saints on board.

The voyage across the Atlantic occupied five weeks' time and was not without its tragedies, as the record states that there were seven deaths among the members of the Church at sea. On June 12 the *Thornton* docked at New York City; two days later the emigrating Saints were on the train, bound for Iowa City, Iowa, then the western terminus of the railroad.

At Iowa City a handcart company was formed for the journey across the plains, under the leadership of Captain James G. Willie. This was the ill-fated expedition in which sixty-six people perished from cold and exposure before they reached Salt Lake Valley.

The McKay family fortunately did not join the Willie handcart company, and thus they escaped the disaster that befell many of those with whom they had crossed the ocean. They remained in Iowa for three years, until they had acquired teams and equipment to make the journey safely and comfortably.

In the summer of 1859 William McKay and family joined the James Brown company, which consisted of 387 persons with 66 wagons and 415 cattle. They left Florence, Nebraska, on June 13 and arrived in Salt Lake Valley on August 29. Almost immediately after their arrival the McKay family moved to Ogden, Utah, where they subsequently made their home.

II

In the fall of 1859 a wagon road was completed through Ogden Canyon, a distance of seven miles, to another beautiful little valley, which the settlers named Ogden Valley. In the summer of 1860 the two sons of William McKay, Isaac and David, undertook the task of looking after a herd of cattle in Ogden Valley. Isaac was twenty-three years of age, and David was sixteen. In 1861 Isaac took up land in what was known as the south field and decided to make his home there. Other settlers moved in rapidly and soon a community was formed, named Huntsville, after Jefferson Hunt, one of the original settlers. David McKay also acquired land and established a home in Ogden Valley. It was here that he brought his sixteen-year-old bride, Jennette Evans, whom he married on April 9, 1867, at Salt Lake City.

The third child and first son of this marriage was David Oman McKay, born at Huntsville September 8, 1873. As there was no doctor nearer than Ogden, the boy was assisted into the world by a local midwife named Mary Heathman Smith. It was fortunate for the boy that he came to the home of such exceptional and worthy parents. Both the father and mother were consistent, faithful Latter-day Saints. In their home the performance of every religious duty was a part of life.

David O. McKay always had a full and complete appreciation of his devoted parents. He once told this writer that his father was the greatest man he had ever known. On various occasions he paid eloquent tributes to his mother; the following is but one instance.

"I cannot think of a womanly virtue that my mother did not possess. . . . To make home the most pleasant place in the world for her husband and her children, was her constant aim, which she achieved naturally and supremely. . . . In tenderness, watchful care, loving patience, loyalty to home and to right, she seemed to me in boyhood, and she seems to me now, after these years, to have been supreme." (*Improvement Era*, May, 1932.)

The mother's devotion to her infant son is also well illustrated in the following story, which President McKay related shortly after he became a member of the First Presidency in 1934.

"Recent events have given me a yearning to meet again my father and mother, just to tell them what their lives, their daily example and willing sacrifice for their children, have meant to me. I want to acknowledge to them my unpayable debt of eternal gratitude. I should like to see the expression on Mother's countenance as she would recall the following incident that occurred when I was a bouncing boisterous baby. As related to me by her brother, my uncle, it is as follows: 'One day, as I watched you toddling around on the floor, I teasingly made a deprecating remark about you. I remember your mother picked you up and said, as she cuddled you to her cheek, "You do not know, he may be an apostle some day." '

"Of course it may have been, and undoubtedly was just an expression of an ardent wish of a fond mother. All mothers hope for great things for their boys; but, oh, in my heart I have wished she might have lived to see her hopes fulfilled." (*Journal History*, Oct. 27, 1934.)

In his boyhood home David O. McKay had perfect training for the work he was to perform later in life. His father was a religious man, a good man in every sense of the word—devoted to his Church, his country and the welfare of his fellowmen. When the first branch of the Church was organized in Huntsville in 1865, David McKay, twenty-one years of age, was chosen as second counselor to Francis A. Hammond, the presiding elder. He was serving in this capacity when his son David O. was born.

In 1881, at the April conference held in Salt Lake City, David McKay was called to go on a mission to the British Isles. He responded readily to this call and departed from Ogden on April 19, leaving his capable wife to manage the farm and look after the little family of five children during his absence.

In the fall of the same year the boy David O. reached his eighth birthday. On that day—September 8, 1881—he was baptized at Huntsville by Peter Geertsen and confirmed a member of the Church by Francis A. Hammond.

The father returned from his mission in April, 1883, and on November 20 of the same year was ordained bishop of Eden Ward by Elder Franklin D. Richards of the Council of the Twelve. Sixteen months later, on March 29, 1885, he was released from his position in Eden and sustained as bishop of Huntsville, to succeed Francis A. Hammond.

III

David O. McKay served in all the offices of the priesthood in the ward of which his father was the bishop. Three months after his twelfth birthday, on December 14, 1885, at a deacon's quorum meeting held in Huntsville, the boy was ordained a deacon by C. F. Schade, counselor in the bishopric. The following year he gave what was perhaps his first public speech. In an old record that has been found of the "Minutes of the Teachers and Deacons Quorums" of the Huntsville Ward, there is this little item under date of November 13, 1886: "David O. McKay bore his testimony and said he felt pleased in coming to meeting."

An event of considerable importance occurred in the McKay family in July, 1887, when John Smith, the Patriarch to the Church, arrived in Ogden Valley to give blessings to the faithful Saints. He stopped at the home of Bishop David McKay, and the bishop requested the Patriarch to give blessings to his children. This was done on Tuesday, July 17, 1887.

The first to receive a blessing was David O., thirteen

years of age. When the Patriarch placed his hands on the boy's head he uttered words of prophecy:

"Brother David Oman McKay, thou art in thy youth and need instruction, therefore I say unto thee, be taught of thy parents the way of life and salvation, that at an early day you may be prepared for a responsible position, *for the eye of the Lord is upon thee.* . . .

"The Lord has a work for thee to do, in which thou shalt see much of the world, assist in gathering scattered Israel and also labor in the ministry. It shall be thy lot to sit in council with thy brethren *and preside among the people* and exhort the Saints to faithfulness." (Italics added.)

All the prophecies uttered that day upon the head of the thirteen-year-old boy were fulfilled. A responsible position came to him early in life; he traveled throughout the world in the interest of the Church; and he presided "among the people."

David O. McKay was ordained a teacher on January 19, 1891, and two years later, on August 4, 1893, a month before his twentieth birthday, he was advanced to the office of priest.

Meantime he had attended school regularly in Huntsville and had completed the grades there; he also attended the Weber Stake Academy in Ogden, and was offered and accepted the principalship of the school in Huntsville. He was now twenty years of age.

After teaching one year David O. decided to continue his education and make teaching his profession. He therefore entered the University of Utah at Salt Lake City, in September, 1894, and registered for a three-year course in the Normal School. He pursued his studies with diligence while at the university and became an outstanding student. At the graduation exercises in June, 1897, David O. McKay was chosen to represent his class and give the "oration." In reporting this speech the *Deseret News* stated "The essence of the oration was that an unsatisfied appetite for knowledge means progress and is the state of a normal mind."

The following day, at the commencement exercises held in the Salt Lake Theatre (June 9, 1897), he received his teacher's certificate from President Joseph Kingsbury, the head of the university.

Being strong and agile, David O. took part in athletics while at school and became a member of the second football team organized at the University of Utah.

Returning to his home in Huntsville, he was no doubt surprised and pleased when, in July, 1897, he received a call from the First Presidency to undertake a mission to Great Britain. He responded readily to this call, having received the full approval of his worthy parents, and was set apart for his mission on August 6 at Salt Lake City. Shortly afterward he left for New York City, where he boarded the steamship *Belgenland.* After a safe and pleasant voyage the *Belgenland* arrived in Liverpool on August 25, and David O. reported to the headquarters of the mission at 42 Islington. He was assigned by the president of the mission, Rulon S. Wells, to labor in the Scottish Conference.

Arriving in his field of labor, he began his work in the Lanark District, thus following in the footsteps of his illustrious father, who had been a missionary in this vicinity fourteen years previously. He then labored in the cities of Glasgow and Stirling until December 4, 1898, when he was selected by the president of the mission to preside over the Scottish Conference. This position also had been previously held by his father.

It was during the time that he was president of the Scottish District that the following incident occurred, as related by President McKay in 1934.

"I was on my first mission, president, at the time, of the Scottish conference, in the year 1899. Presiding over the European Mission were Elders Platte D. Lyman, Henry W. Naisbett and James McMurrin. President McMurrin represented the European Presidency at a conference held in Glasgow, Scotland. Following a series of meetings we held a most remarkable priesthood meeting, one that will never be forgotten by any man that was present.

"I remember, as if it were yesterday, the intensity of the inspiration of that occasion. Everybody felt the rich outpouring of the spirit of the Lord. All present were truly of one heart and one mind. Never before had I experienced such an emotion. It was a manifestation for which, as a doubting youth, I had secretly prayed most earnestly on hillside and meadow. It was an assurance to me that sincere prayer is answered 'sometime, somewhere.'

"During the progress of the meeting, an Elder on his own initiative arose and said, 'Brethren, there are angels in this room.' Strange as it may seem the announcement was not startling, indeed it seemed wholly proper, though it had not occurred to me that there were divine beings present. I only knew that I was overflowing with gratitude for the presence of the Holy Spirit. I was profoundly impressed, however, when President James McMurrin arose and confirmed that statement by pointing to one brother, just in front of me, and saying, 'Yes, brethren, there are angels in this room and one of them is the guardian angel of that young man sitting there' and he designated one who today is a patriarch in the Church.

"Pointing to another Elder, he said, 'and one is the guardian angel of that young man there,' and he singled out one whom I had known from childhood. Tears were rolling down the cheeks of both of these missionaries, not in sorrow or grief, but an expression of the overflowing spirit. Indeed we were all weeping.

"Such was the setting in which James McMurrin gave what has since proved to be a prophecy. I had learned by intimate association with him that James McMurrin was pure gold; his faith in the gospel implicit; that no truer man, no more loyal man ever lived; so when he turned to me and gave me what I thought then was more of a word of caution than a promise, his words made an indelible impression upon me. Paraphrasing the words of the Savior to Peter, he said, 'Let me say unto you, Brother David, Satan hath desired you, that he may sift you as wheat, but God is mindful of you.' Then he added, 'If you will keep the faith you will yet sit in the leading councils of the Church.' At that moment there flashed into my mind temptations that had beset my path, and I realized even better than President McMurrin, or any other man, how truly he had spoken. With the resolve then and there to keep the faith, there was born a desire to be of service to my fellow men, and with it a realization, a glimpse at least, of what I owed to the Elder who first carried the message of the Restored Gospel to my grandfather and grandmother, who had accepted the message years before in the north of Scotland.

"Following that meeting I had an occasion to visit the scenes of my grandparents' childhood, and I more fully and completely comprehended what the Gospel had done for them and their descendants." (*Journal History*, Oct. 27, 1934.)

After having labored faithfully for two years, David O. McKay was released from his mission in August, 1899. He sailed from Glasgow on August 26 for New York City on the steamship *City of Rome*, and early in September he arrived at his home in Huntsville. He had previously been informed that a position was awaiting him as an instructor in the Weber Stake Academy at Ogden; he was now launched in what he expected would be his life's work.

IV

Shortly after making his residence in Ogden, Elder McKay became a member of the Weber Stake Sunday School board. On September 20, 1900, he was appointed to the position of second assistant to Thomas B. Evans in the stake superintendency of Sunday Schools.

In this organization he made a distinct contribution, which was noted by Andrew Jenson as follows:

"In the beginning of his labors in the Stake Superintendency, preparation meetings for teachers were established, individual and cooperative outlines for the lessons were prepared, through which each Sunday School lesson became a unit. Subsequently 'aim,' 'illustration' and 'application' became household terms. So firmly did he believe, and so enthusiastically did he explain this new class work system, that even brethren and sisters who had been teaching in the good old way for many years became converted and were soon among the strongest supporters of the new method." (*Biographical Encyclopedia*, vol. 3, p. 762.)

A most important event in the life of David O. McKay took place at this time; on January 2, 1901, he was married to Emma Rae Riggs, the sweetheart of his university days. The ceremony was performed in the Salt Lake Temple by Elder John Henry Smith.

In April, 1902, Louis F. Moench, the principal of the Weber Stake Academy, resigned his office after serving twelve years. The directors of the institution met on April 17 and offered the position to David O. McKay. A news item of that day states:

"The board of directors have tendered the position as principal of the Academy for the coming year to Professor David O. McKay, who is at the present time one of the instructors of the Institution and is thoroughly competent and acquainted with the school. Professor McKay will accept the position."

The choice was very popular with the citizens of Ogden, as David O. McKay was fast becoming known, through his church and school work, as one of the prominent men of the city.

On January 6, 1905, Elder McKay suffered a severe loss in the sudden and unexpected death of his beloved mother, Jennette Evans McKay, who passed away in her fifty-fifth year as a result of a stroke of apoplexy. There was a strong bond of love between David O. McKay and his mother that did not diminish with the passing of the years. In his sermons throughout his public career in the Church he frequently paid eloquent tributes to his noble mother.

V

At the closing session of the annual general conference of the Church held in the Tabernacle at Salt Lake City on Sunday, April 8, 1906, the name of David O. McKay was presented to fill a vacancy in the Quorum of the Twelve, *1906* and he was unanimously sustained by the vast congregation assembled. The following day, April 9, at a meeting of the First Presidency and the Twelve held in the Salt Lake Temple, Elder McKay was ordained an apostle and set apart as a member of the Quorum of the Twelve by President Joseph F. Smith.

At the time this high honor came to him he was a few months past his thirty-second birthday, still a young man; but his training in his home, under the supervision of his excellent parents, his missionary experiences in Scotland, his work in the local organizations of the Church, and the education he had acquired, fully qualified him for his exalted position.

Shortly after his elevation to the apostleship David O. McKay was made a member of the Deseret Sunday School board, and on October 6, 1906, was sustained as second assistant general superintendent of the Deseret Sunday School Union. The general superintendent at the time was President Joseph F. Smith.

The years 1906 and 1907 were busy years for Elder McKay. During this time he was retained in his position as principal of the Weber Stake Academy, and in addition he devoted many days in visiting the various stakes of the Church and attending conferences, in his labors as an apostle and assistant general superintendent of the Sunday School Union. The work became too heavy, and in June, 1908, he resigned his position as head of the Academy. He was retained as president of Weber Stake Academy board.

At the annual general conference of the Church held in April, 1909, President Joseph F. Smith made the important announcement that George Reynolds, first assistant superintendent of the Deseret Sunday School Union, would be released on account of ill health and that Elder David O. McKay would be advanced to first assistant; also that Stephen L Richards would be named as second assistant.

In the May issue of the *Juvenile Instructor*, in 1909, that publication said editorially:

"Apostle David O. McKay is well known to the Church at large. His phenomenally successful labors in the superintendency of the Weber Stake Sunday School Union were watched with interest, before he became one of the Lord's special witnesses. His great influence for better Sunday Schools since he became Second Assistant General Superintendent of the Deseret Sunday School Union Board, has been felt not only on that board, but also throughout the Stakes of Zion."

It was during this same year, 1909, that Elder McKay had an unusual and thrilling experience while attending conference meetings in Southern Utah. Together with his small son, David Lawrence, he and three or four brethren were making the journey from Tropic to Kanab, during the first week of September. I shall let President McKay relate the story:

"All day we plodded along up Red Canyon, now going through deep washes, now wading the river or driving over sagebrush, always in mud or water. It was five o'clock in the afternoon when we arrived at Tropic, and our faithful teams were tired. Here we learned that the wash between Tropic and Cannonville was impassable, so we had to take a round-about road; in doing so we met with a series of mishaps, and thereby hangs a tale.

"First, in pulling out of a deep wash, a singletree hook broke, and we were nearly precipitated over an embarkment. This tied with wire, we started again, only to encounter mud which clogged our wheels until the horses could not pull us. To add to the difficulty, a singletree broke, also another hook. By this time the storm had doubled in fury and seemed to be holding a jubilee over our predicament. About all we were conscious of was lightning, thunder, rain and mud.

"When the main road was finally reached it was a question whether we could get to the crossing of the main channel before the floods filled it. We urged our worn-out horses to a last effort and made the first crossing all right, also the second, though the current there was swift. Only one more and we should be safe. But the floods beat us. Between the two main crossings we found a mad torrent, ten feet deep, sweeping down the hillside and rushing along a channel across our road at a terrific rate.

"By this time our retreat was cut off; so just at dark, within two miles of our destination, we were compelled to sit in our buggies all night, in the midst of the noise of the worst flood southern Utah has seen for many, many years.

"In the middle of the night the rain ceased, and at daylight we were guided through the subsiding torrent by two men on horseback." (*Journal History*, Sept. 16, 1909.)

Such were the experiences that came to David O. McKay as he traveled through the stakes in the horse and buggy days.

For a period of seven years Elder McKay continued his strenuous labors in looking after the Sunday Schools of the Church and visiting the various stakes and missions. Then, in March, 1916, he met with a painful accident that temporarily disabled him from his work. It appears from the newspaper account that the road through Ogden Canyon had been damaged by the high waters of the river and that the county officials had attempted to block travel to Ogden Valley by stretching a rope across the highway. Due to fog in the canyon Elder McKay, who was driving his car, did not see this rope, which struck him in the face and severely lacerated his mouth and cheek. His brother, Thomas E., who was with him and uninjured, drove him to the hospital, where he remained several days under a doctor's care until he was able to go to his home.

On November 10, 1917, David O. McKay suffered

1917

another severe shock in the death of his beloved father, Patriarch David McKay. David O. had unbounded love and admiration for his father, and through a long life of service to the people the whole community mourned his loss. The *Improvement Era* said of him at his death:

"He was a leader in the community, a man beloved by all with whom he came in contact; a man continually rendering service to his fellows; kind, lovable, affectionate, full of directing counsel, helpful to the poor and unfortunate, doing good in every walk of life."

Following the death of President Joseph F. Smith, which occurred on November 19, 1918, the Deseret Sunday School Union Board was reorganized, with David O. McKay as superintendent and Stephen L Richards and George D. Pyper as assistants. Elder McKay was set apart for this important position on November 27, 1918, at a meeting of the General Authorities of the Church held in the Salt Lake Temple.

Further honors came to him the following year. On May 9, 1919, Elder McKay was appointed by the First Presidency to be the commissioner of education for the Church, with Stephen L Richards and Richard R. Lyman as his assistants.

1919

VI

Having been appointed by the First Presidency to make a worldwide tour of the missions of the Church, David O. McKay departed from his home in Ogden on December 4, 1920. His traveling companion on this journey was Hugh J. Cannon, former president of the Swiss-German Mission and at the time of his departure president of Liberty Stake.

1920

The two brethren went first by train to Vancouver, British Columbia, and from there they sailed on December 7 for Yokohama, Japan. From Yokohama they traveled again by boat to Shanghai, China, and thence by rail to Peking. In the ancient city of Peking, on Sunday, January

9, 1921, Elder McKay dedicated the land of China for the preaching of the gospel. Here are his own words describing the event:

"At noon, on Sunday, January 9, Brother Cannon and I had a short service in a grove of Cypress trees, almost in the heart of the historic old city of Peking, and I dedicated and set apart the Chinese Realm for the preaching of the gospel of Jesus Christ, as revealed to the Prophet Joseph Smith.

"This official act unlocked the door for the entrance of the authorized servants of the Lord, into this land, at such time in the future as the Presiding Authorities feel impressed to call them. It was a most solemn and memorable occasion, one never to be forgotten by the two humble missionaries participating therein." (*Journal History*, Jan. 9, 1921.)

Leaving China a few days after the dedication of that land, the brethren again visited Japan, then continued their voyage on to Honolulu, where they arrived on February 2, 1921. They remained on the Hawaiian Islands nineteen days, visiting and holding meetings with Saints and missionaries. On their departure they described their visit as having been "very enjoyable."

Elders McKay and Cannon were now under the necessity of sailing to the mainland in order to board a ship for the South Sea Islands. They arrived at San Francisco on March 1, "in the midst of a heavy fog." Here a pleasant surprise awaited them. I shall let Elder Cannon tell the story:

"Our plan had been to sail for Tahiti March 3rd. Accommodations on the 'S. S. Tahiti' had been secured. However, to our delight we found that President Grant and Ivins had come to San Francisco to meet us and had brought with them Sisters McKay and Cannon. And right here it may not be out of place to mention that busy men, men who are burdened with vast responsibilities, who will take two women, each with a baby six months of age, on such a trip, are surely thinking more of the happiness of others than of their own personal comfort.

"While we were endeavoring to meet some difficulties in connection with our transportation, word came of the death of President Anthon H. Lund, and it was decided that we should return home and wait the sailing of the next boat." (*Journal History*, Mar. 28, 1921.)

Boarding a Southern Pacific train at San Francisco on Friday, March 4, 1921, the missionaries and their wives arrived at Ogden the following day. Here Elder and Sister McKay left the train and went to their home. The brethren now remained in Utah until Friday, March 25, during which time they attended the funeral of President Anthon H. Lund, visited with Church officials and members of their families, and made preparations for their extensive journey. Returning by train, they arrived in San Francisco on Saturday, March 26, and three days later boarded the steamship *Marama* bound for the Tahitian Islands.

While en route on this voyage, Hugh J. Cannon wrote a letter to the *Deseret News*, under date of April 7, in which he described a few of the events of the trip. He paid this witty compliment to his distinguished companion.

"Brother McKay has rounded into perfect form as a sailor. Since leaving San Francisco he had not been seasick for a moment; but there have been times when, after looking at the pictures of his wife and kiddies, he has seemed to be see-sick."

On April 12, the *Marama* docked at Papeete, Tahiti. Here the missionaries sent a telegram to the First Presidency in Salt Lake City announcing that they were well and enjoying the voyage.

As their first appointment was Wellington, New Zealand, near which place the annual "Hui Tau" or mission conference was to be held, the missionaries remained on the boat until Wellington was reached on April 21. Here they were welcomed by the mission president George S. Taylor and a group of missionaries. "This was a glorious day for the Saints of New Zealand," wrote President Taylor, "being the first time for an apostle of the Savior to set foot on their soil."

The "Hui Tau" was greatly enjoyed by Elder McKay, and he wrote an account of the event that was subsequently published in the *Improvement Era* of July, 1921. The concluding paragraph of this article is as follows: "Success and long life to the 'Hui Tau.' May each succeeding one be more successful than the last. May its influence extend until it becomes a power, not only to cement the love and increase the faith of Church members, as it does even now, but also to break down the barriers erected by the ignorant and vicious, to impede the progress of the Church of Christ."

After visiting nine days with the Saints and missionaries in New Zealand, Elders McKay and Cannon left Auckland on the steamship *Tofua*, on April 30, 1921, to tour the Tongan and Samoan islands, where there were also many members of the Church. Arriving at Nukualofa in the Tongan group, they were prevented from landing since the ship in which they were traveling had docked in the Samoan islands where there was an epidemic of measles. However, the president of the mission, Mark Coombs, came aboard and accompanied them to Apia, Samoa, where they arrived on May 10.

The visit of Elder McKay in the Samoan islands was a triumph from beginning to end. "It seemed that all Apia was at the pier," wrote Hugh J. Cannon (*Journal History*, July 4, 1921). "For the first time in history an apostle was to visit Samoa. . . . During our stay of four weeks, respect and esteem for the Church official were everywhere apparent, and even veneration was manifested in many unexpected quarters."

As the missionaries took leave of the Saints at Sauniatu, Samoa, Elder McKay called the people around him and offered a prayer for their welfare and for the prosperity of the work of the Lord in the islands. After his departure the natives erected a monument on the spot in commemoration of his visit.

Leaving Samoa on June 10, 1921, Elders McKay and Cannon proceeded southward toward New Zealand. At Nukualofa, in the Tongan group, Elder McKay left the vessel to make a tour of the Tongan Mission, while Elder Cannon continued on to New Zealand. It was not until July 18 that Elder McKay reached Auckland and joined his companion.

The two Church officials now continued their tour of the New Zealand Mission. On July 21 they arrived in Kaikohe and held meetings. Returning to Auckland on Sunday, July 24, they held a large public meeting in the town hall. Many prominent people of the city were in attendance and heard Elder McKay deliver a masterful sermon describing the Mormon Church and its teachings. From Auckland the brethren traveled to Porirua, Palmerston, and Hastings. Returning to Auckland, they sailed on the afternoon of Tuesday, August 2, 1921, for Sydney, Australia.

The visit to Australia, on account of the distances between the cities, was very strenuous. However, in the course of a month, the branches of the Church in Sydney, Melbourne, Hobart, Adelaide, and Brisbane were visited and meetings were held with the Saints and missionaries. On September 4 the tour was completed and Elders McKay and Cannon boarded the steamship *Marcella* bound for Java and the Malayan Peninsula. Of their stay in Java Elder Cannon wrote: "There being no mission of our Church here, our stay in Java was limited to the time the *Marcella* was loading and unloading in Sourabaya and Batavia."

Leaving Java, the missionaries passed on to Singapore, where they arrived on September 28. After remaining in this interesting city two days, they boarded the ship *Bharata* and continued their journey toward Burma and India. In turn the boat stopped at Rangoon, Calcutta, Delhi, and Bombay. Leaving India on the ship *Egypt*, they sailed toward the Suez Canal, through which they passed during the last week of October, 1921. After visiting in Cairo and vicinity a few days, they traveled by train to Jerusalem, where they arrived on November 2. Journeying northward in search of President J. Wilford Booth, president of the Palestine-Armenian Mission, they accidently or rather providentially met him in the railroad station at Haifa. A brief tour of the mission was now made, after which Elders McKay and Cannon returned by train to Port Said.

Taking a boat at Port Said, the elders sailed to Naples, Italy. From Naples they went by train to Rome, and thence to Lausanne, Switzerland, where Elder McKay was overjoyed to meet his eldest son, David Lawrence, who was laboring in that city as a missionary. Here a meeting was held, and also at Basel, the headquarters of the mission. Continuing their journey, the visitors made brief stops at Frankfurt and also at Cologne in Germany. They then traveled on to Liege, Paris, London, and Liverpool, holding meetings with Saints and missionaries.

While at London Elder McKay decided to make a brief trip to Glasgow, Scotland, where he had labored as a humble missionary twenty-two years previously.

"Arriving in the city he visited some of the old Saints of the branch, who were overjoyed on seeing him. Many of the older members he used to know have long since passed to the great beyond. A pathetic scene was witnessed when he called on Sister Noble, his old 'Scotch mother' and landlady. Through her tears she said that she hardly knew her boy. . . . Elder McKay visited the old Conference House at 53 Holmhead street, and although under new tenancy, his request to enter was granted. 'What a flood of memories came to me,' he later remarked, 'as I stood in the same old rooms and viewed the familiar sights of twenty-two years ago; the breakfast room where I used to eat Scotch porridge, the office and the bedroom where I used to sleep in a hole in the wall.'" (*Millennial Star*, vol. 83, p. 826.)

On Saturday, December 10, 1921, at Liverpool, Elders McKay and Cannon boarded the ship *Cedric*, bound for New York City. Arriving in New York, they traveled by train to Utah. On the afternoon of December 24, the day before Christmas, David O. McKay stepped off the train at Ogden into the arms of his waiting family. To a reporter he said, "After traveling 62,500 miles through the world, the dearest spot to me is home."

VII

Once again at the headquarters of the Church after his long absence, Elder McKay resumed his labors as general superintendent of the Deseret Sunday School Union board and his activities in visiting the stakes.

At the April conference in 1922, President Heber J. Grant expressed his gratitude that Elder McKay had returned safely from his long journey.

"I rejoice in the fact that Brother McKay is with us today. Brother McKay has circled the globe since he was last at our conference. He has visited our missions in nearly every part of the world, and has returned, as every missionary has returned who goes out to proclaim this gospel, and comes in contact with the people of the world and with all the varieties of faiths in the world, with increased light, knowledge and testimony regarding the divinity of the work in which we are engaged." (*Conference Report*, April, 1922.)

In his own lengthy report to the conference, Elder McKay related many faith-promoting incidents that he and his companion, Elder Cannon, had experienced while on their missionary journey.

"I should like this afternoon," he said, "to choose some part of that wonderful trip and take you over it, but throughout this conference I have been prompted to try and give the message that seemed to be the most precious to me of all our experiences, namely, the manifestations of the nearness of the Lord and of his guiding hand."

An unexpected honor came to Elder McKay on June 2, 1922, when, at the annual commencement exercises at Brigham Young University in Provo, the degree of Master of Arts was conferred upon him. On that day the *Deseret News* said editorially:

"The degree of Master of Arts, which was conferred on David O. McKay, is fitting recognition of his loving, intelligent and enthusiastic service to his fellow men. Reared on a farm in one of the best of Utah's rural communities, Elder McKay has always understood the vital connection between the soil and sound national morality; trained in the University, he has sensed the vast possibilities of intellectual conquest for the good of man; disciplined in the class room as a teacher, and in the school as an administrator, he has learned to know 'the tender grace' of the human heart; tempered for many years in the unselfish special service of the Master, he has become a mighty and merciful saver of humanity. David O. McKay has stirred thousands into better lives and firmer characters—and is not that the greatest of human achievements?"

VIII

After having remained at home a little more than eight months, following his return from his trip around the world, Elder McKay was appointed by the First Presidency, on September 14, 1922, to succeed Orson F. Whitney as president of the European Mission. This appointment came as a surprise to Elder McKay, but he readily accepted it and began at once to make preparations to depart for his field of labor. One week after he was called, the papers announced that he would sail from Montreal, Canada, on October 27, but this date was subsequently changed to November 17. On that day he and his wife and five children boarded the steamship *Montcalm*, bound for Liverpool.

The retiring mission president was not in Liverpool to greet the new president when he arrived on November 25. On account of ill health, Elder Whitney had already departed for his home in Salt Lake City.

President McKay was enthusiastically greeted by the Saints in Great Britain, many of whom knew him, as this was his third visit to the British Isles in the capacity of a missionary.

It will be impossible in this limited sketch to give a detailed account of the activities of President McKay during the two years that he presided over the European Mission. His labors were strenuous and his travel was almost constant. At the time of his arrival, in November, 1922, the British conferences were in progress, and he attended them until he had completed the tour that had been planned by President Whitney.

In January, 1923, President McKay crossed the English Channel to Holland and held a four-day conference with missionaries and Saints at Rotterdam. During the following month he made a tour of the German Mission and held well-attended meetings in Koenigsberg, Berlin, Dresden, and Basel. In May he attended a conference of the Irish District, at Dublin. Perhaps the most joyful to President McKay of all the conferences held this year was one at Glasgow, Scotland, on May 7. This was the city in which he had labored twenty-five years previously, on his first mission.

"The congregation listened with rapt attention while President McKay brought back memories of his labors in Scotland twenty-five years ago," wrote the elder who reported the meeting to the *Millennial Star*, "mentioning the names of many of the Saints with whom he was well-acquainted and the experiences and good times they had had together."

On July 11, 1923, President McKay was surprised to learn that two of his fellow apostles, Reed Smoot and John A. Widtsoe, had arrived in England. President McKay met them in London, where conference meetings were held for two days with the British missionaries and the London Saints. After these meetings the three apostles departed for Norway, Denmark, and Sweden, where Elder Smoot attended to special business for the government and the three held meetings with the Church members.

Returning from the north, President and Mrs. McKay journeyed to Switzerland in August, and on the 19th and 20th of that month they held meetings with the missionaries and Saints at Lausanne. Sixty-nine missionaries were present on this occasion, and all were inspired by the admonition and instruction given by President McKay.

In September the British conferences began again, and one was held each week until the end of the year.

Early in January, 1924, President and Mrs. McKay journeyed to Marseilles, France, where, on January 8, they boarded the steamship *Lotus* bound for Syria, to visit the Armenian Mission. They arrived at Beirut on January 18 and were met by the mission president, J. Wilford Booth; they then traveled by auto and train to Aleppo, the headquarters of the mission, where they arrived the following day. Meetings were held for three days with the Armenian Saints. It was a time of great rejoicing for those neglected and persecuted people. They expressed their gratitude to God for the privilege of having an apostle in their midst. Both President and Mrs. McKay admonished them "to live the good life and hold firmly to the faith."

On January 24, 1924, the visitors began their journey homeward. Before returning to Liverpool they held meetings with the missionaries and Saints in the Swiss, German, and French missions.

The spring and summer months of 1924 were spent by President McKay in attending various conferences in the British Mission. During July he journeyed to Sweden and held the annual conference of that prosperous mission, which was then under the presidency of Hugo D. E. Peterson. Similar conferences were also held in Norway and Denmark. In August President McKay was back in Liverpool, and the balance of the year was spent principally in Britain, though he traveled to the continent several times to hold important meetings. Then, in October, 1924, word came from the First Presidency of the Church in Salt Lake City that Elder James E. Talmage had been appointed to preside over the European Mission and that upon his arrival in Liverpool, President McKay would be released.

In his farewell message to the European Saints, published in the *Millennial Star* on November 13, 1924, President McKay expressed his affection for his fellow missionaries and the European Saints from whom he was soon to take his departure, in these beautiful words:

"To all our beloved associates at the headquarters of the mission; to the true devoted presidents of the missions; to the willing, capable conference presidents and the five hundred superior men who represent the authority and who perform the service of Christ's Church in these missions; to the brave and fearless Saints who constitute the membership of the branches, we now extend a tender farewell.

"In so doing, may we express the hope and the earnest desire, that as friends and co-workers, we ever remain steadfast to the eternal principles of Truth. Though enemies and a misinformed, credulous public may sneer at us and continue to heap contumely upon us, though difficulties may arise and cause us pain, yet if we will remain true to a firm and unwavering testimony of the divinity of the Restored Gospel, we shall have strength to bear ridicule, power to overcome obstacles and wisdom to manifest restraint under provocation. If we 'let virtue garnish our thoughts unceasingly,' then, as the Lord has promised, our confidence shall wax strong in his presence, the doctrine of the priesthood shall distill upon our souls as the dew from Heaven, and the Holy Ghost shall be our constant companion and guide.

"The strongest testimony is that which is obtained by 'doing the will of the Father,' therefore, may we find joy in performing regularly and faithfully every duty in the Church. Let us pray continually in secret and in our households, pay our tithes and offerings, speak kindly of each other, sustain the Priesthood, be honest in our dealings and kind even with our enemies; let us be strict observers of the Word of Wisdom and keep ourselves pure and unspotted from the sins of immorality. If we will observe these simple duties, no power on earth can deprive us of our membership in the Church of God, or of our fellowship with one another and with Christ our Lord.

"There are in these lands millions of honest men and women waiting to receive the 'glad tidings of great joy'—may we so conduct ourselves that our lives may be an incentive to all to seek the truth and to live righteously.

"The Lord watch between me and thee while we are absent from one another."

On Saturday, December 6, 1924, President and Mrs. McKay, with four children, boarded the steamship *Montcalm* on their return voyage to their native land. Fifteen days later they arrived at their home in Ogden, Utah, after an absence of a little more than two years.

IX

Once again at home, Elder McKay took up his strenuous duties as general superintendent of the Sunday School Union and his labors as a member of the Twelve in visiting the stakes and missions. In April, 1925, at the general conference of the Church, he reported his recent mission to Europe and informed the Saints that "the work of God is growing by leaps and bounds in the European mission." He had rejoiced to find that wherever a group of Latter-day Saints met, "whether in the islands of the sea, in Japan, in Syria, in the Scandinavian countries, in England, Germany, France, Holland—there one finds the spirit of oneness, the spirit of love, the spirit of willing sacrifice for the good of humanity."

In the fall of 1926 Elder McKay made a tour of the Southern States Mission and dedicated a new chapel at Jacksonville, Florida.

In November of the following year he left his home again to visit the Central States Mission, with headquarters at Independence, Missouri. During his tour of the mission he visited branches of the Church in Kansas, Missouri, Oklahoma, Louisiana, Arkansas, and Texas.

Elder McKay was in attendance at the annual conference of the Church held in April, 1930, which celebrated the one hundredth anniversary of the founding of the organization.

In March, 1931, David O. McKay was named by Governor George H. Dern as general chairman of Utah's Conference on Child Health. In May of the same year he was elected president of the Weber College Alumni Association. Two days later, May 30, 1931, he delivered the commencement address to the graduates of that institution.

A tour of the East Central States Mission was made by Elder McKay during November and December, 1932. With mission president Miles L. Jones, he visited the eight districts of the mission and dedicated chapels at Howard, North Carolina, and Durham and Craig in Tennessee. Before returning home he visited his daughter, Mrs. Russell H. Blood, in Philadelphia, and his son, David L. McKay, in Washington, D. C.

During the entire year of 1933 Elder McKay was active in visiting the various stakes of the Church and laboring at his tasks as general superintendent of the Sunday School Union.

X

Elder McKay observed his sixty-first birthday on September 8, 1934. One month later, lacking two days, further honor came to him in the announcement by President

Heber, J. Grant, at the opening session of the semiannual
conference of the Church (October 6, 1934), that he had
chosen David O. McKay to be his second counselor in the
First Presidency. The same day the *Deseret News* said of
him:

"President McKay is one of the most beloved of all
the authorities of the Church. By his long and successful
ministry he has won the complete confidence and hearty
esteem of all among whom he has labored.

"His life has been an unbroken series of outstanding
accomplishments, as a missionary while a young man, as an
educator, as a Sunday School executive, as an Apostle, as
a mission president, and as a special ambassador of the
Church on a world tour, during which time he visited
every mission in the world outside of the United States,
(excepting only South Africa and South America).

"His work in the Council of the Twelve has carried
him into all parts of the Church, into the various stakes
on quarterly conference appointments and Sunday School
and affiliated conventions.

"He has been one of the outstanding leaders of the
youth of the Church, and by his magnetic personality
and marked humility he has directed young men and young
women, as well as those more advanced in age, into paths
of progress in temporal and religious lines.

"He has been exceptional in his teachings of faith in
the Deity and in the principles of the Church. By written
and spoken word he has pointed the way; by a life filled
with honor and distinction he has set the example, and
thousands have happily followed him. His appointment to
the First Presidency comes as a welcome announcement to
the hundreds of thousands in the Church." (*Deseret News*,
Oct. 6, 1934.)

A reorganization of the general superintendency of the
Deseret Sunday School Union took place on October 31,
1934. President David O. McKay was released as general
superintendent—a position he had held since November,

1918—and George D. Pyper was chosen to take his place. A report rendered by the secretary at the time showed that the Sunday School work of the Church had experienced great growth under the leadership of President McKay. From 1918 to the end of 1933 there had been an increase of 572 Sunday Schools and 144,821 enrolled members.

In the *Instructor* for November, 1934, President McKay expressed a few soul-revealing thoughts regarding the approaching Thanksgiving Day.

"As Thanksgiving day, 1934, approaches, I am thankful to know that the members of the Church, and so many people generally, realizing the fact that material possessions alone do not give happiness, are appreciating more than ever before those things which are of most value. I am happy to enjoy with my friends these most worthwhile possessions. To name a few I would say that I am most grateful: For a noble parentage and a worthy name; for an abiding faith in a Supreme Being and in the divinity of the Gospel of Jesus Christ; for ability, though limited, and opportunities so ample, to enjoy the gifts of God as manifest in nature—all the beautiful things of creation are mine merely for the seeing and the seeking; for affectionate family relationships—loved ones and loyal friends— he who has even one friend is rich and I have many who have proved themselves true and loyal. God bless them! For opportunities to render helpful service in the Church of Christ; and above all for the knowledge that a kind and loving Father will give helpful guidance to all who seek him in sincerity:

"For these and many other blessings . . . my heart is full of gratitude." (P. 477.)

In February, 1935, President and Mrs. McKay made a trip to the eastern and southern states. At Washington, D.C., they visited their son and daughter-in-law, Mr. and Mrs. David L. McKay, and saw for the first time their three-month-old granddaughter. On Sunday, February 24, President McKay addressed a capacity audience in the

Washington chapel. The following day, through the courtesy
of Senator Elbert D. Thomas, the couple enjoyed a visit
with Vice-President John Nance Garner and also met several
of the prominent senators.

Leaving Washington, President and Mrs. McKay traveled to Philadelphia, where they visited for several days
with their daughter and son-in-law, Dr. and Mrs. Russell
H. Blood. The journey was then continued to Jacksonville,
Florida, where they met President and Mrs. LeGrand
Richards of the Southern States Mission. From Jacksonville
they traveled westward to New Orleans, where they met
President and Mrs. Charles Rowan and a group of missionaries from the Texas-Louisiana Mission. While there they
were also guests of James H. Moyle, a Utah citizen, who
at the time was serving as U. S. Commissioner of Customs.

President and Mrs. McKay returned to Salt Lake City
on Sunday, May 10, 1935. One month later, on Sunday,
June 10, President McKay delivered the baccalaureate
sermon to 550 graduating students at the University of Utah.
His subject was "The Two Roads of Life," and he pointed
out the necessity of seeking after the finer things of life,
in preference to the sordid, materialistic things. His address
was well received.

During the balance of 1935 President McKay visited
many of the wards and stakes and filled speaking engage-
ments.

The year 1936 was a busy one, as the previous year
had been. On January 15, President and Mrs. McKay departed for Honolulu, where he was scheduled to attend a conference of the Oahu Stake on January 25 and 26. He
remained on the Islands about two weeks, held twenty-five
meetings, and attended several banquets and gatherings.
"Hawaii is a paradise," he said on his return, "and the
Hawaiian people are most hospitable, kind, and generous."

During the latter part of April, 1936, President McKay
and President J. Reuben Clark, Jr., journeyed to Omaha,
Nebraska, where they inspected the old Mormon cemetery,

six miles north of that city, and decided on plans for land-scaping and improving it and installing a suitable monu-ment in honor of the Latter-day Saints who were buried there.

At a sunrise service held at the mouth of Emigration Canyon on July 23 of that year, President McKay delivered an eloquent address on the significance of the settlement of Utah by the Mormon pioneers.

In September he returned to Omaha, Nebraska, and there, with Presidents Grant and Clark, participated in the unveiling and dedication of the beautiful pioneer monu-ment, designed and executed by Avard Fairbanks, at the Old Mormon Cemetery.

During October President McKay made a tour of the Northern States Mission in company with the mission president, Bryant S. Hinckley.

In December he journeyed to San Francisco where, on the 20th of the month, he dedicated the San Francisco Ward chapel.

In 1937, President McKay's labors were, for the most part, confined to the state of Utah. During every day of the week, except Sunday, he spent long hours in his office, attending meetings, keeping appointments, and looking after official correspondence. On Sunday he was in demand in the wards and stakes.

He was at Provo on January 25, where he spoke to a large audience in College Hall on the subject "Eternal Progression." Three weeks later he delivered a notable address to ward and stake workers of the Salt Lake region on "Four Fundamentals of the Church Security Program."

On Sunday, April 4, 1937, at the second session of the general conference, he spoke on "Reverence for the Law." Before a select group of General Authorities and Church workers on July 2, at a meeting in Barrett Hall, President McKay outlined the stand of the Church on "Labor and Labor Unions." His pronouncement on this occasion was to the effect that it is un-American to say to a young man,

"You can't work on this job unless you pay the dues and join our union." "We will make no discrimination against a man who is or is not a member of a union," he continued, "but request that a good day's work be given for compensation received."

On August 20 of that year President McKay attended dedication ceremonies at Brigham City, Utah, when a monument was erected to honor Brigham Young on the spot where the great leader had given his last public address. Two days later he journeyed to Paris, Idaho, and attended the unveiling and dedication ceremonies of a monument erected to honor the memory of Charles C. Rich, pioneer of that city and county.

On September 8, 1937, President McKay observed his sixty-fourth birthday.

Early in 1938, President McKay, together with Mrs. McKay, traveled to Chicago, where he attended a stake conference in that city on February 27.

In April he was appointed by Governor Henry H. Blood to be chairman of the Utah Centennial Exposition Commission. The task of this commission, composed of seventy-five prominent citizens, was to prepare for a great celebration in 1947 in honor of the one hundredth anniversary of the arrival of the Utah pioneers.

President McKay journeyed to Portland, Oregon, in June, 1938, and on the 26th of that month, together with Elder Melvin J. Ballard, organized the Portland Stake, the one hundred twenty-fourth in the Church.

Mrs. Nibley and the writer of this sketch had the privilege of entertaining these brethren in the mission home during their brief stay in Portland and assisting them in effecting the stake organization.

A distinct honor came to President McKay when, on May 3, 1940, he was named by Governor Henry H. Blood as a member of the board of trustees of Utah Agricultural College. Ten days later, on May 13, the board of directors of the Layton Sugar Company elected President McKay to the office of president of that institution.

In October, 1940, he journeyed to Idaho Falls and on the 19th of that month laid the cornerstone of the Idaho Falls Temple and pronounced the dedicatory prayer.

Perhaps the chief event of the year 1941 for President McKay was his visit to Honolulu, in August, and his participation in the dedication ceremonies of the beautiful Oahu Stake Tabernacle. This event took place on Sunday, August 17. It had been twenty years since President McKay had first visited these islands and had developed a real love for the Hawaiian Saints. In his opening remarks he said:

"My soul is deeply stirred this morning, due, I am sure, to a combination of circumstances and experiences. It has been my privilege and duty to attend many dedicatory services, not only in the Church, but in civic and educational circles, and as I have recalled those experiences this morning, I believe that this stands out as the most unique and impressive. It is made so, I believe, largely because of the love the people of the Pacific have for one another and for the Church." (*Deseret News*, Dec. 13, 1941.)

Returning to the mainland, President McKay renewed his activities with diligence. It was during these years that the health of President Heber J. Grant declined measurably, due to his advanced age, and more and more work devolved upon his counselors. However, in addition to his meetings and appointments, President McKay found time to visit many of the wards and stakes. The Saints were always delighted to have him with them.

On September 8, 1943, President McKay celebrated his seventieth birthday. The usual working hours of that day he spent in his office, but in the evening a family dinner was given in his honor at his home. Thirty-six members of his immediate family were present, and the honored guest enjoyed and merited the love and affection that were manifested by those who were nearest and dearest to him.

In addition to President McKay's regular work in 1944, he delivered two notable addresses, one on the subject of motherhood at the 26th Ward in Salt Lake City, and the other, "A Tribute to the Prophet Joseph Smith," before the faculty and students of the LDS Institute at Logan.

XI

The death of Heber J. Grant, the venerable President of The Church of Jesus Christ of Latter-day Saints, on May 14, 1945, dissolved the First Presidency and brought about a reorganization of that quorum. On May 21, 1945, the Council of the Twelve met in Salt Lake City and sustained George Albert Smith as President of the Church. He chose as his counselors J. Reuben Clark, Jr., and David O. McKay, the same brethren who had served with the previous President. President McKay now resumed his place in the First Presidency, with its many activities and great responsibilities.

Early in June President McKay delivered the baccalaureate sermon before the 1945 graduates of the University of Utah. This sermon was a model of clearness and lucidity, and he closed with these eloquent words:

"Even while the glories of youthful prime gladden your hearts and brighten your hopes with anticipated success, there rests unfelt upon your shoulders the weight of a coming responsibility. Yours is the challenge to shape the future. Into your hands and into the hands of a million other youths will be placed the banner of civilization. . . .

"Young men and young women, the future awaits you! It is yours! If you would end war and give peace to the world, you have campaigns to organize and conquests to achieve. These are campaigns planned for the establishment of justice—these are conquests of the soul. Whether it is better to walk along the easy road to selfishness and indulgence, than to strive through self-mastery and service for the realm of spirituality, you must decide." (*Deseret News*, June 8, 1945.)

At the April conference in 1946 President McKay spoke of the great celebration that was planned for 1947,

to honor the Utah pioneers who, one hundred years previously, had made the trek across the plains and entered
Salt Lake Valley.

"No state in the Union can look with greater pride
upon the achievements of its pioneers than the state of
Utah," he said. "It is commendable and highly fitting
therefore that the Governor and State Legislature have set
apart the year 1947 as the centennial year, in which to pay
tribute to these great empire builders. In so doing we confer honor upon ourselves."

As chairman of the Centennial Commission, President
McKay worked untiringly to perfect the arrangements for
the great celebration.

At the general priesthood meeting held on the evening
of April 6, 1946, President McKay gave an enlightening address on the importance and significance of the sacrament.

"No more sacred ordinance is administered in the
Church of Christ than the administration of the sacrament. . . .

"The greatest comfort in life is the assurance of having
close relationship with God. . . '. The sacrament period
should be a factor in awakening the sense of relationship."

On October 18, 1946, the press and radio in Salt Lake
City announced that President David O. McKay had that
day submitted to a surgical operation at the LDS Hospital. His recovery was less rapid than he had anticipated,
due to an embolism that threatened his life, and it was not
until January, 1947, that he was able to resume his duties
in the First Presidency.

Despite his tremendous responsibilities during the centennial year, when he was meeting almost daily with his
various committees, President McKay found time in May
to drive to Klamath Falls, Oregon, and dedicate a beautiful
new chapel that had been erected by the Church in that
thriving community. Mrs. McKay accompanied her husband,
and they kindly invited the writer of this article and Mrs.
Nibley to be their guests on this journey.

The dedicatory services took place on May 24, before an audience of more than one thousand people, which included the city officials of Klamath Falls and many who were not members of the Church. President McKay delivered an excellent sermon, explaining the principles of the gospel, and he also pronounced an inspiring dedicatory prayer.

The month of July, 1947, brought to a culmination the efforts of the Centennial Commission, with the unveiling of the "This Is the Place" Monument at the mouth of Emigration Canyon and the massive parade through the business district of Salt Lake City on the 24th, Pioneer Day. As chairman of the commission, President McKay had directed the planning of these great events.

At the dedication of the Pioneer Monument, President McKay was one of the speakers. He said, in part, "One hundred years ago today the great leader Brigham Young looked over this valley and said, 'This is the right place. Drive on.' What did he have in his mind when he said, 'This is the place'? By reading the reports of his sermons we find that he had in mind first, the prophetic utterance of a man whom he loved, the Prophet Joseph, who said the Saints would go to the west, build cities, and become a mighty people in the midst of the Rocky Mountains.

"Secondly, when that great leader uttered the sentence, 'This is the place,' he had in mind that here they would find a place of refuge and peace.

"Thirdly, he had in mind that from this center there would radiate to all the world a message of truth, in so far as it would be possible for that little band and those who followed them to declare that truth to the world, to establish brotherhood, peace and above all, faith in God our Father.

"Fourthly, he had in mind in this place to establish worship, industry, education and mutual service." (*Deseret News*, Aug. 2, 1947.)

At the semiannual conference, held in October, 1947,

President McKay took occasion to express his gratitude to all who had assisted in the centennial celebration.

"May I take one moment," he stated, as he began his remarks, "in behalf of the Utah Centennial Commission, and so far as I may, the Governor and other state officials, who have sustained the commission, to express to the people of Utah, heartfelt commendation for their cooperation and united effort during the centennial year."

In the same sermon he expressed his love for the noble men with whom he was working in the Church.

"I am happy in my love for my immediate associates, President George Albert Smith and President J. Reuben Clark, Jr., and for these noble men of the Council of the Twelve, the Assistants to the Council of the Twelve, the Council of the Seventy, the Presiding Bishopric, the Patriarch. It is a privilege to work with you and to recognize your unselfish devotion to the Church. Life, though freighted with great responsibilities and a consciousness of my inability, and regrets for failures, is still wholesome and sweet." (*Conference Report*, October, 1947.)

The year 1948 was filled with activity for President David O. McKay. On February 4 he and Sister McKay departed from Salt Lake City for El Paso, Texas, where they arrived on February 7. Here, in company with President and Sister Arwell L. Pierce, they began a tour of the Mexican Mission. They traveled directly to Mexico City and then continued their journey by automobile, visiting various branches and journeying 2,600 miles. At Cuautla President McKay addressed an audience of 900 people and dedicated a new chapel. Upon his return to Salt Lake City early in March he gave a brief report of his trip.

"He explained that the chapel at Cuautla was really an achievement; a credit to Mexico and the Church. He described the apparent harmony existing in the mission. All former misunderstandings are cleared up and the more than 1,200 Mexican members who were reunited with the Church two years ago by President George Albert Smith

are among the stalwart active leaders and members.
. . . President McKay told of the baptism of fifty new
members at the time of the chapel dedication, February
14. . . . 'The mission is in excellent condition,' President
McKay said. "President and Sister Pierce, aided by their
counselors and the missionaries, are doing a splendid work.'"
(*Deseret News*.)

At the general conference of the Church held in April,
President McKay delivered two noteworthy sermons, one
on the struggle of the world to achieve peace and the
second on the obligations and duties of the men who hold
the priesthood.

Ten days after the conference he was a speaker at a
welfare banquet in the Woodruff Stake, and on May 16 he
addressed a youth conference of four stakes in the Logan
area, held in the Logan Tabernacle. On May 23 he was
the principal speaker at a conference of the Mesa Stake
in Arizona.

During the entire summer there were few Sundays
that did not find President McKay filling a speaking engagement in one of the wards or at a stake conference.
All this was in addition to his strenuous work in his office,
where he spent long hours every week day.

In October he again returned to Mesa, Arizona, and
attended a conference of the Spanish-speaking members of
the Mexican and Spanish-American Mission.

During January, 1949, President George Albert Smith,
the loved and honored head of the Church, suffered a
severe illness while on a visit to southern California and
was confined for a short time in a Los Angeles hospital.
President McKay visited his leader there during the latter
part of January and reported that President Smith was recovering satisfactorily. However, this illness, which appeared
at first to be of a temporary nature, weakened the health
of the venerable President.

President McKay was in attendance at all the sessions
of the general conference in April, 1949. Twice he was

called upon to speak and delivered excellent sermons on the progress of the Church and the calling of missionaries. Soon after the close of the conference he returned to southern California and on April 17 attended the meetings of the Long Beach Stake conference, where he spoke and pronounced the dedicatory prayer at the Long Beach Ward chapel, which had recently been completed.

To follow President McKay's activities during 1949 would require more space than has been allotted to me here, and I can mention only a few of his many visits to the wards and stakes. However, here is a partial list of the cities he visited and where he held meetings during the balance of the year: Cedar City, May 15; Lynwood, California, May 27; Ogden, Utah, June 5; Pasadena, California, July 3; Huntsville, Utah, July 9; Vernal, Utah, July 14; Darbey Ward, Teton Stake, July 24; Moose, Wyoming, August 20; Jackson, Wyoming, August 21; Huntsville, Utah, August 28; Lethbridge, Canada, September 3; Raymond, Canada, September 6; Provo, Utah, September 16; Sugar House Ward, September 18; Phoenix, Arizona, October 16; Mesa, Arizona, October 17; Inglewood, California, October 23; Las Vegas, Nevada, November 13; Kaysville, Utah, December 6, and Granger, Utah, December 18. Such were the strenuous activities of President David O. McKay, who, on September 8, 1949, passed his seventy-sixth birthday.

The year 1950—which was to be the last of his years as a counselor in the First Presidency—was no less strenuous than 1949 had been. Both weekdays and Sundays he was using his magnificent ability to forward the cause of Zion and build up the Church and kingdom of God. From his youth on he had been taught to work, and he had worked hard and persistently all his life, believing that work was a privilege as well as a duty.

For exercise throughout the years, he had spent a few brief hours, whenever opportunity afforded, at his father's farm, where he was born and where he had spent his child-

hood in Huntsville, Utah. This farm remained in the possession of the McKay family, and to President McKay it
was a cherished haven where he could ride horses, plow,
plant, reap, and relax from the cares and burdens of his
official duties.

On January 2, 1951, at their home on East South
Temple Street in Salt Lake City, President and Mrs. Mc-
Kay celebrated their golden wedding anniversary. It was a
day of rejoicing for President McKay, who, throughout the
fifty years of his married life, had been truly devoted to
his wife and children. To a friend who congratulated him
on this occasion he wrote:

"Reawakening precious memories, recounting wonderful experiences together, receiving love and devotion of
children and grandchildren, are in themselves sufficient to
have made truly Golden, for my sweetheart and me, the
fiftieth anniversary of our wedding."

Early in the year 1951 the health of President George
Albert Smith began to fail visibly. He spent a few hours
each working day during January at his office, but on
February 3 he was taken to the LDS Hospital for observation and treatment. He remained there about four weeks,
and as his general condition did not improve, he requested
to be taken to his home. His health continued to decline,
and on the evening of April 4, his eighty-first birthday, he
passed away peacefully, surrounded by members of his
family.

XII

The death of President Smith occurred on the eve of
annual general conference of the Church, and it was therefore necessary to rearrange the schedule of the meetings,
as follows: The regular conference sessions were to be held
on Friday, April 6, with meetings at 10 a.m. and 2 p.m.;
the funeral of President Smith was to be held at 2 p.m.

on Saturday in the Tabernacle; the general priesthood meeting was to be held in the evening. On Sunday the regular sessions of the Conference were to continue, and on Monday, April 9, 10 a.m., a solemn assembly was to convene in the Tabernacle, at which time the quorum of the First Presidency was to be reorganized.

All these meetings took place as scheduled, and at the solemn assembly President David O. McKay was unanimously sustained as President of the Church, with Stephen L Richards and J. Reuben Clark, Jr., as his counselors. President McKay then arose and spoke feelingly to the vast congregation in part as follows:

"My beloved fellow workers, brethren and sisters: I wish it were within my power of expression to let you know just what my true feelings are on this momentous occasion. I would wish that you might look into my heart and see there for yourselves just what those feelings are.

"It is just one week ago today that the realization came to me that this responsibility of leadership would probably fall upon my shoulders. I received word that President George Albert Smith had taken a turn for the worse, and that the doctor thought the end was not far off. I hastened to his bedside, and with his weeping daughters, son, and other kinfolk, I entered his sickroom. For the first time he failed to recognize me.

"Then I had to accept the realization that the Lord had chosen not to answer our pleadings as we would have had them answered, and that He was going to take him home to Himself. Thankfully, he rallied again later in the day. Several days preceding that visit, as President Clark and I were considering problems of import pertaining to the Church, he, ever solicitous of the welfare of the Church and of my feelings, would say, 'The responsibility will be yours to make this decision,' but each time I would refuse to face what to him seemed a reality.

"When that reality came, as I tell you, I was deeply moved. And I am today, and pray that I may, even though inadequately, be able to tell you how weighty this responsibility seems.

"The Lord has said that the three presiding high priests chosen by the body, appointed and ordained to this office of presidency, are to be 'upheld by the confidence, faith, and prayer of the Church.' No one can preside over this Church without first being in tune with the head of the Church, our Lord and Savior, Jesus Christ. He is our head. This is his Church. Without his divine guidance and constant inspiration we cannot succeed. With his guidance, with his inspiration, we cannot fail.

"Next to that as a sustaining potent power comes the confidence, faith, prayers, and united support of the Church.

"I pledge to you that I shall do my best so to live as to merit the companionship of the Holy Spirit, and pray here in your presence that my counselors and I may indeed be 'partakers of the divine spirit.'

"Next to that, unitedly we plead with you for a continuation of your love and confidence as you have expressed it today. From you members of the Twelve, we ask for that love and sympathy expressed in our sacred Council. From the Assistants to the Twelve, the Patriarch, the First Council of the Seventy, the Presiding Bishopric, we ask that the spirit of unity expressed so fervently by our Lord and Savior when he was saying good-bye to the Twelve, may be manifested by us all.

"You remember he said, as he left them: 'And now I am no more in the world, but these are in the world, and I come to thee. Holy Father, keep through thine own name those whom thou hast given me, *that they may be one, as we are*. Neither pray I for these alone, but for them also which shall believe on me through their word; that they all may be one; as thou, Father, art in me, and I in thee, that they also may be one in us; that the world may believe that thou hast sent me.'

"Brethren and sisters, brethren of the General Authorities, God keep us as one, overlooking weaknesses we may see, keeping an eye single to the glory of God and the advancement of his work. . . . "

XIII

Three days after he was sustained by the unanimous vote of the members, President McKay was ordained and set apart as President of the Church by his brethren of the Twelve, with President Joseph Fielding Smith officiating. This event took place on April 12, 1951. The following day he left for California where, on Sunday, April 15, he attended the dedicatory services of the combined chapel and stake house at Gridley, California.

Illness confined President McKay to his home during part of the month of May, but in June he again resumed his strenuous activities. During the first two weeks of the month he delivered three notable addresses to the graduates of three great universities—the first at Brigham Young University in Provo, on June 3; the second at the University of Utah, on June 9, and the third at Temple University at Philadelphia, Pennsylvania, on June 14. At each of these universities an honorary doctor's degree was conferred upon him.

In these talks to the graduating groups President McKay stressed the idea that the best we cherish in our present-day civilization can be preserved through education.

During July the President delivered three addresses away from Salt Lake City. The first was at his hometown of Huntsville, Utah, where, on Independence Day, he made an eloquent plea for his hearers to preserve the principles and ideals of the Constitution.

Three days later he journeyed to Castle Dale, Utah, and on July 8 dedicated the Emery Stake Tabernacle. On this occasion he declared that only the observance of the teachings of Christ can bring peace to the world.

President McKay left Salt Lake City by train on July 21 for Hood River, Oregon, where, on the following day, he dedicated a new ward chapel. The same afternoon he went by car to Portland and in the evening spoke to a congregation of more than two thousand people in the Portland Stake Tabernacle.

During the first week of August, President McKay left Salt Lake City by train for Palmyra, New York, to participate in the tenth annual pageant, *America's Witness for Christ*, held at the Hill Cumorah. This great pageant, which he saw for the first time, President McKay designated as "an impressive presentation of the message of the Book of Mormon." He also attended a meeting of the Eastern States missionaries, held in the Sacred Grove, and bore a powerful testimony to those present.

Late in September the President journeyed to Los Angeles, accompanied by a group of his brethren, and there, on September 22, 1951, broke ground for the Los Angeles Temple with these words, "I now declare the first shovel of dirt raised over the site of the Los Angeles Temple, which is to be reared to the glory of God and the salvation of his people." This was indeed an impressive occasion.

Shortly after his return to Salt Lake City President McKay again visited his hometown, Huntsville, where, on September 30 the people gathered to honor him as their most distinguished fellow citizen. The President replied warmly to their greeting, saying, "With all my soul I can say that I love you. I am proud of this valley; I am never happier than when I can come to this valley. It is a glorious place, and added to it are all the memories that I hold dear."

During the first week of October the President presided at all sessions of the semiannual general conference in Salt Lake City. In his opening address he expressed his satisfaction with the manner in which the work of the Lord was prospering. "From all parts of the world where the gospel is preached, reports show substantial advancement in nearly every line of endeavor." In his closing sermon he made a plea for exemplary living.

The day after the close of the conference President McKay went to Provo to attend the inauguration ceremonies of Ernest L. Wilkinson as president of Brigham Young University.

Later the President traveled by train to Washington, D.C., where, on October 22, he attended a conference of a group of prominent men in the nation who had been called together by President Harry S Truman to consider problems confronting the United States.

During November his time was occupied in his office, except for brief trips to outlying wards on Sundays. Early in December he traveled to Randolph, Rich County, where he attended a banquet given for the young people of the stake who were being honored for their unusual activity in the Church. On this occasion President McKay gave them excellent inspirational advice.

The last week of the year the President spent in Salt Lake City. On December 23 he addressed a congregation composed of the combined membership of the 27th and East 27th wards.

XIV

In January, 1952, President McKay traveled by train to Los Angeles to speak to over one thousand young people who had assembled at the South Los Angeles Stake Center to hear their leader on the subject of temple marriage. The meeting was held on January 31, and the young people who were present were uplifted and inspired.

On February 3 the President attended the opening session of the Los Angeles Stake conference; in the afternoon of the same day he met with the leaders of fourteen

stakes and the California Mission and launched a campaign
to raise one million dollars to aid in the construction of the
Los Angeles Temple.

Learning of the death of Elder Joseph F. Merrill of
the Council of the Twelve, President McKay returned to
Salt Lake City by air on February 6 and was the principal
speaker at the funeral of the distinguished apostle, held in
the Tabernacle on the following day.

During a snowstorm of blizzard proportions on the
afternoon of March 2, President McKay attended dedicatory
exercises at the newly completed Primary Children's Hospital, where he spoke and offered the dedicatory prayer.

Three days later, on March 5, he drove to Ogden to
attend exercises at Weber College, when ground was broken
on its new campus for the erection of four buildings.
President McKay's address on this occasion was largely
retrospective, covering his early associations with the school.

On March 7, the President drove to Logan and attended
Founder's Day exercises at Utah State Agricultural College.
Here he delivered a masterful address on education—a
free people's best investment.

President McKay went to Overton, Nevada, on March
15 and before a capacity audience gave an address and
dedicated a new chapel. The following day he continued
his journey to southern California. He returned to Salt Lake
City in time to be present and preside over the annual conference during the first week of April, 1952.

On Sunday following the conference, April 13, President McKay delivered an impressive Easter address over
the National Broadcasting System. On April 30 he left Salt
Lake City by train for Varnell Station, Georgia, to dedicate
a monument that had been placed on the spot where Elder
Joseph Standing had been shot and killed by a mob on July
21, 1879. The dedication was held on May 3, and on the
following day he spoke to a conference of missionaries of
the Southern States Mission at Atlanta.

Returning to Salt Lake City, the President spent a
few days in his office and then on Sunday, May 11, gave a
beautiful Mother's Day talk to a crowded audience in the
East Mill Creek Ward chapel.

There was no slowing down in the President's activities
during 1952. On the 17th and 18th of May he went to
California by auto and dedicated two chapels in the Fresno
Stake, one at the Avenal Branch and the other in the Mer-
ced Ward.

XV

On his return home the President prepared to take
one of the greatest, if not the greatest, tour of his career—
a trip to Europe by air to visit all the European missions.
He was accompanied by Sister McKay and his son and
daughter-in-law, David Lawrence and Mildred McKay.
Boarding a plane at New York City on June 1, 1952, he and
his party crossed the ocean during the night and arrived at
the airport at Glasgow, Scotland, the next day, where
they were met by the president of the British Mission,
Stayner Richards, and Sister Richards. The same evening
they attended services in the Glasgow chapel. Here the
President received a royal welcome.

"You do not know what this reunion means to me,"
he said. "Some of the dearest friends I have, I met here in
the Scottish conference over fifty-four years ago, when I
first came to Glasgow, a young unmarried lad just out of
school. To see you members here tonight fills my heart with
gratitude." (*Church Section*, June 11, 1952.)

Two days later he addressed a large meeting of Saints
and friends in Edinburgh, and on the following day the
party went by air to London, where meetings were held
attended by approximately 1,000 members of the British
Mission.

From London the President and party traveled by air
to Holland, where they landed at the Schipol Airport on

June 11. Here they were met by President and Sister Dono-
van H. Van Dam of the Netherlands Mission. That night
they stopped in a hotel in Scheveningen, and the next day
President and Sister McKay had an audience with Queen
Juliana of Holland. The President presented the Queen with
a copy of the Book of Mormon. The following day a mis-
sionwide conference of the missionaries and Saints of the
Netherlands Mission was held in Rotterdam, and the President was the principal speaker.

From Holland the party flew to Copenhagen, Denmark,
where they were greeted by the mission president, Edward
H. Sorensen, and his wife, together with a large group of
Saints. The next day three large congregations were addressed in the Copenhagen chapel by President McKay.

After remaining four days in Denmark, he and his
party flew to Stockholm, Sweden, where they arrived on
June 19. Here also the President was greeted by the mission president, Clarence F. Johnson, and Sister Johnson,
and by Saints and missionaries and representatives of the
press. Large meetings were held here, and the reception
accorded the Church leader was extremely cordial.

The party continued on to Helsinki, Finland, where
they arrived on June 23. This was the birthday of Sister Mc-
Kay, and a dinner was held in her honor in the mission
home, given by President and Sister Henry A. Matis.
Enthusiastic meetings were also held in this city, attended
by members and friends.

From Finland they flew to Berlin, where they spent
four days, June 25 to June 29. The President spoke to
hundreds of Saints in the meetings held in this city and
also dedicated two chapels—in Charlottenburg and in Dah-
lem. President Arthur Glaus was their host during this visit.

After leaving Berlin, they made a tour through the West
German Mission, with President and Sister Edwin Q. Cannon. Large gatherings greeted them in Hamburg, Frankfurt,
and other places where meetings were held.

Leaving Frankfurt on July 3, they flew to Zurich, Switzerland, where they were greeted by President and Sister Samuel E. Bringhurst. Here the Saints were filled with the same enthusiasm for their President that he had met with elsewhere. At Bern, he looked the situation over for the building of the first temple of the Latter-day Saints in Europe. Property was subsequently purchased for this purpose.

From Switzerland they flew to Paris, where they were met by President and Sister Golden L. Woolf and a group of missionaries and Saints, and where, on July 12, the President said in a meeting, "If the world will accept the message of the restored gospel, we shall have peace more quickly and effectually than in any other way."

On July 16 the President visited Wales, where he sought out the birthplace of his mother. The next day, in London, he and Sister McKay attended a garden party given by Queen Elizabeth at Buckingham Palace.

Meetings were held with the missionaries and Saints again in London, and on July 20 the party flew back to Glasgow, the point of the beginning of the European tour. It was here that President McKay announced that a temple would be built in Switzerland.

On July 21, 1952, the party boarded a plane for New York City, where they arrived the following day. The President was in Europe fifty days, during which time he held forty-five meetings. Four days later (July 26) a large group of friends greeted the McKays at the Salt Lake Depot and welcomed them home.

XVI

The first trip by President McKay after his return from Europe was to Los Angeles, where on August 9 and 10 he consulted with Church leaders regarding the construction of the Los Angeles Temple. Two weeks later he went to Brigham City, Utah, where he dedicated a chapel on August 24. One week later he dedicated an enlarged stake tabernacle at Hyrum, Utah.

President McKay observed his seventy-ninth birthday on September 8, 1952. He spent most of the day in his office, where he received congratulations from many friends. In the evening there was a family party at his home.

At the semiannual conference of the Church held during the first week of October, 1952, President McKay presided at all sessions. In his opening address he gave a lengthy account of his European tour.

Two weeks after the close of the conference he dedicated a new stake and ward chapel at Lake View Ward, Lake View Stake. On November 26 he spoke to the combined Kiwanis and Rotary clubs of Ogden. His subject was "Loyalty to the Government and Constitution."

At the funeral of the distinguished apostle John A. Widtsoe, held in the Tabernacle on December 2, President McKay delivered an eloquent tribute, emphasizing the fact that the deceased had used his talents and ability in forwarding the Church. Five days later he spoke at the Idaho Falls Stake conference. His subject was "Home and Family—Source of Happiness."

Two days before Christmas, on December 23, 1952, he spoke in his own ward, the 27th in Salt Lake City, on the subject "Godliness, as Exemplified by Jesus." Thus closed a very eventful year.

XVII

Shortly after the first of January, 1953, President McKay journeyed to Los Angeles, where, on January 3 and 4, he addressed large meetings in the Wilshire Ward chapel.

On Sunday he dedicated a branch chapel at Laguna Beach. The next day, Monday, January 5, he broke ground for a new mission home to be built near the Los Angeles Temple.

Returning to Salt Lake City, he took the train to Nyssa, Oregon, on January 10 and on the following day dedicated a beautiful chapel of the Ontario Ward and Nyssa Stake at Ontario, Oregon.

Again returning home he remained in Salt Lake City until February 21, when he went by train to Palo Alto, California, where on the 22nd he dedicated a new chapel at San Mateo.

During March the President made only one trip out of the city and that was to North Ogden, where he spoke at the centennial observance of the founding of North Ogden Ward.

As President McKay's strenuous second year as President of the Church closed, his time was occupied in presiding over the 123rd annual conference of the Church.

Shortly after the general conference, in April, 1953, President McKay journeyed to Phoenix, Arizona, where, on April 19, he spoke to a large group of Mormons and non-Mormons in an open air service at Litchfield Park. The meeting was held under the direction of Paul W. Litchfield, chairman of the board of the Goodyear Tire and Rubber Company. Earlier in the day the President had spoken to 3,600 members of the Church in the Phoenix First Ward chapel.

From Phoenix he traveled to Dallas, Texas, and on Sunday, April 26, dedicated a newly completed branch chapel and spoke to a congregation of over 1,200 people.

Returning to Utah, President McKay was invited to attend the commencement exercises of the Branch Agricultural College at Cedar City. There he delivered a thought-provoking address on the subject of "Four Conditions of Success."

During the last week of May, 1953, President McKay

headed a large group of Church officials and their wives on a journey by train to Omaha, Nebraska. There, on the anniversary of President Brigham Young's birth, June 1, he dedicated a large new steel bridge, named "The Mormon Pioneer Bridge," which spans the Missouri River where the Mormons crossed by ferry in pioneer days. The President spoke and reviewed pioneer history to the immense audience assembled.

After the ceremonies at Omaha, President McKay traveled eastward to Washington, D.C., and attended a conference on U.S. foreign policy that had been called by Secretary of State John Foster Dulles. A group of the leading men in the nation had been invited to attend this conference. The President returned to Salt Lake City in time to be present at the annual MIA conference, where he delivered a magnificent address on the subject "The Responsibility and Mission of Youth."

During July, 1953, President McKay was honored with an invitation to address the national council of Boy Scouts of America at a luncheon held at the Statler Hotel in Los Angeles on July 17. In this splendid address he urged his hearers to uphold the ideals of their country. At the close of the meeting he was honored with the award of the Silver Buffalo, the highest award in scouting. A citation accompanying the award read as follows:

"To Dr. David O. McKay, Salt Lake City, Utah: Church official, missionary, executive, educator, President of The Church of Jesus Christ of Latter-day Saints; ninth president in succession since Joseph Smith, the founder and first Prophet of the Church: Holds honorary degrees from several colleges: In his missionary activity he has been world-wide in his travels and service.

"He has filled important public responsibilities, including the chairmanship of the Utah State Centennial Celebration of 1947, commemorating the arrival of the Mormon Pioneers in Salt Lake Valley under the leadership of Brigham Young.

"An ardent supporter of scouting, one of his outstanding decisions as president of the Church was the recommendation that the Cub Scout program be adopted for the younger boys of the Church. He is greatly interested in young people, especially in the organizations of the Sunday School and the Young Men's and Young Women's Mutual Improvement Associations.

"Virile pioneer, colonist, he maintains and promotes the traditions of the western country."

The day following the Scout meeting in Los Angeles, President McKay traveled to Salt Lake City by air to attend the funeral of Elder Albert E. Bowen, a member of the Council of the Twelve. Five days later he was the principal speaker at a celebration in Snowflake, Arizona, which was held in honor of the pioneers of that community.

And now President McKay began another epoch-making journey to Europe by air, to dedicate sites for LDS temples in Switzerland and England. He and his wife and son Llewelyn boarded a plane at New York City on August 2, 1953, and arrived in London next morning. Without taking any rest, they drove the same day to Newchapel, twenty-four miles south of London, and on a thirty-two-acre estate that had been purchased by the Church, President McKay selected the location for the first LDS temple in England.

The following day, August 4, he and his party traveled by air from London to Basel, Switzerland. They remained in Basel overnight and on Wednesday, August 5, journeyed by auto to Bern, where President McKay, in an impressive ceremony, dedicated the temple site.

The party then returned to England on August 7. On Monday the 10th, they proceeded to Newchapel and, after a brief service, during which all present felt the importance of the occasion, President McKay dedicated the site for the first temple to be built in England. In the short space of ten days he had made history that will be remembered for many generations to come.

President McKay and party arrived back in New York City on Saturday, August 15, on their return journey, and four days later stepped off the train in Salt Lake City, where they were greeted by members of their family and many friends.

XVIII

Tuesday, September 8, 1953, was the eightieth birthday of President David O. McKay. From the time of his arrival at his office until evening, the day was filled with many events in which the people had opportunity to show their love for their leader. Telegrams and letters were received from friends and well-wishers in all parts of the world. Many friends called at his office to offer their congratulations. At noon time approximately five hundred business men and civic leaders gathered at the Hotel Utah to do him honor. In the evening President and Sister McKay, with children and granchildren, assembled at the home of Robert R. McKay to celebrate the occasion.

"As I realize the fact that I am eighty years old, I am astonished at the fleetness of time," he said to a reporter. "Now as I look in retrospect, the days of childhood and youth and all its associations—all the cherished memories and aspirations of just a normal farm boy, seem but a decade."

The semiannual conference of the Church convened in October, with President McKay presiding at all sessions. On October 1 he broke ground for the new Relief Society Building on North Main Street, in an imposing ceremony. Speaking to the group assembled, he said, "Today I have nothing but commendation in my heart for the Relief Society of the Church."

At the end of October he made a business trip to the Northwest, to inspect sugar factories at Yakima and Moses Lake, Washington, the properties of the Utah-Idaho Sugar Company, of which he was president.

The principal event in December was the laying of the cornerstone of the Los Angeles Temple, which took place on the 11th. President McKay presided on this occasion and welcomed the hundreds who had assembled. President Stephen L Richards announced that the cornerstone had been laid and then offered the dedicatory prayer. In his prayer he expressed his gratitude for the life of President McKay.

"We thank thee, O Lord, for thy servant, the present president of The Church of Jesus Christ of Latter-day Saints, David O. McKay. We are grateful for the teachings and example of his life. We thank thee for his effective, untiring efforts to promote thy cause throughout the world. We thank thee for his vision and his courage to go ever forward in building and strengthening the Church, at home and abroad."

Two days after the exercises held at the laying of the cornerstone of the Los Angeles Temple, Matthew Cowley, a member of the Council of the Twelve, died in Los Angeles. The funeral of the distinguished Church official was held in the Salt Lake Tabernacle on Wednesday, December 17, 1953, with President McKay as the principal speaker. He praised Elder Cowley as "one of nature's true noblemen."

On Sunday, December 20, President McKay delivered a Christmas message over the Columbia Broadcasting System's "Church of the Air" program.

XIX

On Tuesday, December 29, 1953, President David O. McKay, accompanied by Sister McKay, began a journey of 32,000 miles—a journey that was to take them to the British, South African, and South and Central American missions. This was the longest and most strenuous trip of the President's entire career, and he was now in his eighty-first year.

Leaving Salt Lake City by train, President and Sister McKay traveled to New York City, where, on Saturday, January 2, 1954, they boarded a Pan American Airways Clipper for London, England.

Arriving the following day, they remained in London until January 7, at which time they departed by plane for South Africa, accompanied by A. Hamer Reiser, president of the British Mission. The journey by air was made by way of Lisbon and Dakar, Africa. During this journey Elder Reiser wrote:

"President and Mrs. McKay are the world's most wonderful travelers; always pleasant, relaxed, thoughtful of everyone; everything always in order, forthright and cheerful. They are always conscious of the people back home, who help so much in working out arrangements in advance."

We do not have space to go into all the interesting details of this trip, except to say that the President and party arrived safely at Johannesburg, South Africa, at 7:30 p.m., Saturday, January 9. There they were welcomed by President Leroy H. Duncan and a people who never before had seen a President of their Church.

"These South African Saints," wrote Elder Reiser, "with all the hunger of a devoted people, who never before have seen one of the general authorities of the Church, were beside themselves with joy and did everything to show the fervor of their welcome."

On Sunday, January 10, 1954, the President spoke to 450 members of the Transvaal District, in Duncan Hall. "What wonderful inspiration everyone enjoyed as he poured out wisdom and affection," wrote Elder Reiser.

At Pretoria, near Johannesburg, President McKay had an interview with W. J. Gallman, United States ambassador to the Union of South Africa.

After spending two days in Johannesburg, the President and party flew to Capetown, a distance of nine hundred miles. "The greeting the President received was like the one at Johannesburg, moving and beautiful!"

Three busy days were spent at Capetown and the hearts of the people were warmed by the presence of their President. Then, on January 19, the return journey was begun. The party boarded a plane for Dakar, which was reached after a long journey on the morning of January 21, 1954.

On the evening of the same day they again boarded a plane to cross the Atlantic westward to Brazil. This journey was made in safety, and they arrived at Rio de Janeiro on January 22. There they were met by a group of Brazilian Saints and President Asael Sorenson. The next morning they were greeted by their son Robert McKay, who had flown from Salt Lake City to accompany them on the South American tour and act as interpreter during the South American visit. While in Rio de Janeiro, they paid a visit to James S. Kemper, United States ambassador to Brazil.

Leaving Rio de Janeiro by air, they went to Sao Paulo, the headquarters of the Brazilian Mission. Three meetings were held during the day, and President McKay spoke at each. On the following day a conference of the Brazilian missionaries was held.

On January 26 the journey was continued to Montevideo, Uruguay. Here the party were greeted by President and Sister Lyman S. Shreeve. Meetings were held with the Saints, and President McKay had an interview with U. S. Ambassador McIntosh. He also laid the cornerstone for a new LDS chapel in Montevideo, the second to be erected by the Church in South America.

The visit to Uruguay concluded, on February 1 President McKay and party flew to Buenos Aires, Argentina. Here they were met by the mission president and his wife, Lee and Amy Valentine, and a group of Saints.

In Buenos Aires President McKay had an interesting but strenuous visit. He first spoke to a group of two hundred American business men and their wives. He then had

a personal interview with President Juan D. Peron, after
which he made a call on the U. S. Ambassador, Alfred F.
Nufer. He also attended many church meetings, at times
driving several hundred miles to address groups of Saints.
The largest meeting held was in the Cervantes Theatre, in
Buenos Aires, attended by eight hundred members and investigators.

The President and party departed by plane on February 8 for Santiago, Chile, where they arrived the following
day. At Santiago they found only two members of the
Church. Lima, Peru, was reached the following day. Here
President McKay met with a small number of members who
had organized a Sunday School. He said on this occasion,
"Who knows but that in very fact, this little meeting may
sometime be referred to as the beginning of a mission in
this great state of Peru?"

Again boarding a plane, the party flew to Panama
City, where they met President Gordon Romney of the
Central American Mission. Here a meeting was held with
the few LDS members who reside in the Canal Zone, and
then the journey was continued northward to Guatemala
City. After a short stay the party departed for Los Angeles,
California, where they arrived on February 16. On his arrival President McKay stated to a reporter of the *Deseret
News*, "Our anticipations and desires before leaving have
been more than realized, regarding church conditions and
prospects for future work in South Africa and South and
Central America. There was never a time in the history
of the Church when opportunities for preaching the gospel
in the world were so favorable."

XX

After remaining in Los Angeles one week, resting from
from their long journey, President and Sister McKay returned to Salt Lake City, where they were warmly greeted
by members of their family and friends.

At the ceremony installing Dr. Henry Aldous Dixon as president of Utah State Agricultural College at Logan, held on March 8, 1954, President David O. McKay delivered a magnificent inaugural address on the subject of the American way of life.

Then, on March 18, he began another journey by air to visit a mission of the Church that he had had to bypass during his recent extensive journey—the Mexican Mission. Three days were spent in Mexico City, in which he held meetings with the Saints and missionaries. On his return he stated to the press, "The three-day tour was marked by an overwhelming hospitality. Everywhere we went we not only had our hands shaken but were hugged and embraced. The sincerity and friendliness of the Mexican people thrilled us constantly."

The annual conference of the Church was held during the first week of April, 1954, with President McKay presiding at all sessions. In his opening address he referred to his recent lengthy missionary journey:

"Recent visits to the various missions of the world have impressed me more deeply than ever with the importance and magnitude of the Church, and with its responsibility to make more potent the proclaiming of the gospel of Jesus Christ."

In his closing remarks he expressed a desire that "the spirit of this great conference" should accompany the people "and bring peace to their hearts and harmony in their homes."

His first appointment outside the city after the conference was in Ogden, where, on April 16, he attended the Founder's Day exercises at Weber College. In his talk to the group assembled he said, "We must cherish the ideals and character of the Founding Fathers, as character is higher than intellect."

President McKay, accompanied by Sister McKay, left Salt Lake City by train on April 23 on a trip to the East. On Sunday, April 25, he dedicated a chapel at Madison,

Wisconsin. In New York City Sister McKay, who had been selected as the Utah Mother of the Year, took part in honoring the American Mother of the Year. On the return journey the President dedicated a chapel at Cleveland, Ohio. On May 8, he was again in Salt Lake City, where he delivered a Mother's Day address in Stratford Ward.

The President journeyed to Provo on May 26, where he presided at a ceremony held at Brigham Young University. He dedicated twenty-two buildings erected for student housing and named after prominent individuals in the Church. In his sermon on this occasion he spoke on "True Greatness."

At the MIA June Conference the President delivered a stirring address to the vast assembly on the subject of "Ideals for a Happy Home Life."

"David O. McKay Day" was observed at Ogden, Utah, the former home of President McKay, on July 16, 1954. At noon on that day he was honored at a luncheon held at the Ben Lomond Hotel, at which four hundred prominent men and women of the city were present. In the afternoon he presided at the laying of the cornerstone of the new Ogden Tabernacle. "This day," he said, "has been delightful to experience and will be held sacredly in my memory."

During the first week of August the President traveled to Los Angeles, where on the 8th he spoke to 16,000 people in the Hollywood Bowl, at an MIA conference of the southern California stakes. His subject was "The Abundant Life."

President McKay celebrated his eighty-first birthday on September 8, 1954. On that occasion he said, "The secret of a happy life, and my life has been a happy one, is to learn to love one's work and to give it one's best."

President McKay was in Chicago on September 10, 1954, where he attended the nineteenth annual congress of the United States and Canadian section of the International College of Surgeons, at which his son, Dr. Edward McKay, was a speaker. On this occasion President McKay was given honorary membership in the International College of Surgeons.

On September 17 he was in Provo, where he spoke to the faculty of the Brigham Young University on the subject "Some Fundamental Objectives of the Church University."

During the first week of October he presided at the semiannual conference of the Church. The theme of his opening address was that all members should seek first the kingdom of God.

In his closing remarks he admonished all present to make God the center of their lives.

The President was at Las Vegas, Nevada, on November 14, where he dedicated a chapel of the fifth and sixth wards of Las Vegas Stake. He spoke to the people on the subject "Contentment and Progress."

One week later he addressed a large group in Ogden, when he dedicated a chapel built by the 34th and 37th wards. His subject was "Two Fundamental Purposes of the Church."

At a dinner at the Hotel Utah on November 29, 1954, sponsored by the College of Pharmacy of the University of Utah, international honors were again conferred on President McKay when he received from John Tzounis, Greek Consul at San Francisco, acting for King Paul of Greece, "The Cross of Commander of the Royal Order of Phoenix." This honor was bestowed in part because of the contribution made by the LDS Church to the relief of the Greek people during the great earthquake of 1953.

President McKay was at Brigham Young University on December 14, 1954, to attend the dedication of a building that had been named in his honor. After the dedicatory prayer by Stephen L Richards, President McKay spoke briefly. "This is a soul-stirring hour," he said. "In my educational career, the most significant of my life. I sense a feeling of expanding gratitude and increased responsibility such as I have never before experienced."

XXI

And now President McKay began another of his great journeys to visit the missions of the Church—this time to the South Pacific. Accompanied by Sister McKay and the Church transportation agent, Franklin J. Murdock, who acted as his secretary, he left Salt Lake City on January 2, 1955, by train for San Francisco. There the party boarded an airliner on January 4, bound for Honolulu, which they reached the evening of the same day. From Honolulu the journey was continued by plane until they arrived at Nandi in the Fiji islands. After a day at Nandi the party drove to Suva, where two meetings were held with missionaries and members. Taking a boat at Suva, the party arrived at Nukualofa, Tonga, on January 11. Here they were met by President and Sister D'Monte W. Coombs of the Tongan Mission. A meeting was held here attended by twelve hundred native people. Two days later meetings were held at Vavau. The people everywhere were overjoyed to meet and hear their president. Never before had a president of the Church visited the South Pacific missions.

On January 14, Pago Pago was reached. Here President McKay and his party were greeted by President and Sister Howard B. Stone of the Samoan Mission. Apia was reached on January 15. This was the headquarters of the mission. The shore was lined with enthusiastic members to greet them as they stepped from the boat. The party then motored to the mission home.

On the following day meetings were held with the Saints and missionaries, and the President and party visited Sauniatu, where a beautiful monument had been erected in memory of the apostolic blessing President McKay gave the people on his first visit to the islands in 1921.

Leaving Apia on January 18, they continued their journey to Aitutaki and then to Papeete, Tahiti. Here also meetings were held with missionaries and Saints. On Monday, January 20, 1955, the flight was continued to New

Zealand. At Auckland the President and party were met by President and Sister Sidney J. Ottley of the New Zealand Mission.

The visit to this mission was thoroughly enjoyed by President McKay, and everywhere he went he was loved and venerated by missionaries and Saints. After five days of continuous activity the party continued their journey by air to Sydney, Australia, which they reached on the afternoon of January 31. Here they were met by President and Sister Charles V. Liljenquist of the Australian Mission. Meetings were held in Sydney and then the journey was continued to Brisbane. The President was welcomed there by groups of Saints and missionaries and gave them words of comfort and cheer. Later Adelaide and Melbourne were visited.

On February 8, 1955, the long journey from Australia by air to the United States was begun. Honolulu was reached February 9. After an interesting but strenuous visit with Hawaiian Saints and missionaries, the President and party returned to the mainland on February 14. The same evening they reached Salt Lake City, Utah. The great heartwarming visit of President McKay to the Pacific missions was completed.

XXII

After his return to the mainland the President announced that a temple would be built in New Zealand. This word caused great rejoicing among the members of the Church in the Pacific missions.

The general conference of the Church was held during the first week of April, 1955, in the Salt Lake Tabernacle. In his opening address the President spoke of promoting peace in the world; he also related incidents of his recent journey.

After conference the President journeyed to St. George, where, on April 17, he dedicated the Fifth and Sixth Ward chapel.

On April 24, 1955, President McKay was in Los Angeles, where he spoke to a large group of LDS seminary students on the subject of character development.

On May 9 he was in Washington, D. C., where he was present at a dinner at the White House, as a guest of President Dwight D. Eisenhower.

In June he was the principal speaker at the MIA conference in the Tabernacle in Salt Lake City. His theme was "Our responsibility should enable us to resist wrongdoing."

On June 19 he was at East Ensign Ward in Salt Lake City, where he dedicated a new ward chapel.

During July he filled various appointments in the wards and stakes, and on the 10th of the month delivered a notable Pioneer Day address on the subject of the "Ideals of the Utah Pioneers." On the 31st he dedicated the Park and University wards chapel in Utah Stake.

XXIII

The Salt Lake Tabernacle Choir left Salt Lake City on Wednesday, August 10, 1955, on its history-making trip to Europe. Six days later President McKay, accompanied by Sister McKay, his son Dr. Edward McKay and wife, and his secretary, Miss Clare Middlemiss, departed from Salt Lake City by air for Glasgow, Scotland, where they arrived on August 18. The same day the President and party welcomed the Tabernacle Choir as they disembarked from the *Saxonia* at Greenock; and the next evening they enjoyed the concert by the choir in Kelvin Hall, Glasgow. They also received an official welcome to the city of Glasgow by Lord Provost John Porter.

On the evening of August 20 President McKay and party journeyed to London by air, while the choir continued its tour through the principal cities of Europe. The President was able to attend the concerts in London, Bern, and Zurich.

At Newchapel, twenty-four miles south of London, the President officially broke ground for the British Temple on Saturday, August 27, 1955. The ceremony was witnessed by approximately twenty-five hundred people.

On September 1, the President and party traveled by air to Paris, where, three days later, he held a missionary conference and dedicated a mission home and chapel, the first to be owned by the Church in France. From Paris the party continued their journey by auto to Bern, Switzerland, where they arrived on September 7. The following day, September 8, the President observed his eighty-second birthday. Three days later, on Sunday, September 11, 1955, amidst the most solemn ceremonies, with the great Tabernacle Choir present, President McKay dedicated the temple at Bern, the first temple to be constructed by the Latter-day Saints in Europe. This indeed was a history-making event.

The President remained in Bern from the 11th to the 16th of September and presided at nine dedicatory services, which were attended by thousands of Saints, missionaries, and servicemen from all parts of Europe.

XXIV

After leaving Bern, the President and party returned by air to Salt Lake City, where they arrived on September 22, 1955. The President was delighted with what he had witnessed in Europe. "The temple in Bern," he said, "is one of the best investments the Church has ever made." As for the trip of the Tabernacle Choir: "Every performance has surprised the people and wherever the Choir appeared the press has printed most favorable reviews—all of them merited."

On October 3, he was in his hometown, Huntsville, where he broke ground for a new church edifice.

At the semiannual conference of the Church held in

Salt Lake City during the first week of October, President McKay gave a lengthy review of the trip of the choir and the dedication of the Swiss Temple. He concluded by saying, "My heart rejoices that we have the privilege of working together to establish the kingdom of God on earth."

On Tuesday, October 11, the President was in Provo, where he spoke to the students of Brigham Young University on the subject of "Ideals Contributive to a Happy, Enduring Marriage."

At a luncheon of the Sons of the Utah Pioneers, held in Salt Lake City on October 12, Horace Sorenson, president of the national organization, presented President McKay with an honorary life membership.

He traveled to Mesa, Arizona, during the third week of October and addressed a Lamanite conference held in that city. On his return to Utah he took part in a testimonial to Bishop Thorpe B. Isaacson, held in Ephraim, Utah.

The President attended the dedication of the San Fernando Stake Center at Van Nuys, California, on Sunday, October 30, and delivered a splendid address on the "Key to Happiness, in Home and Society." The following Sunday he dedicated a combined chapel and stake house in Stockton, Calif.

A second honor came from the Greek people when President McKay received, on November 20, a gold medal from the Greek Orthodox Church, in recognition of assistance rendered by the Church to the Greek people following the war and earthquake.

He was at Monument Park Stake on Thanksgiving Day and spoke to a capacity audience at the dedication of the new Third and Fourth Ward chapel. On December 18 he gave an address over the Columbia Broadcasting System "Church of the Air" program. His subject was "The Prophet Joseph Smith—The Source of His Greatness."

On the last Sunday of 1955, he delivered a Christmas message to the members of his own ward—the 27th in Salt Lake City.

XXV

President and Mrs. McKay celebrated the fifty-fifth anniversary of their wedding, on January 2, 1956.

Six days later the President was at Brigham City, Utah, where he dedicated an Indian chapel, built by the Church at the Intermountain Indian School.

During the third week of January he was in Los Angeles, making arrangements for the dedication of the Los Angeles Temple, which was scheduled to take place on Sunday, March 11, 1956. On this trip he conducted Cecil B. De Mille, noted motion picture producer, on a tour through the temple.

At the Fairgrounds Coliseum, on January 25, President David O. McKay was presented with the coveted Silver Beaver award, for his outstanding contributions to Boy Scout work.

Sunday, February 12, was Lincoln's birthday and also an auspicious occasion for the people of Ogden, as on that day President McKay dedicated the beautiful new Ogden Tabernacle. He also delivered a magnificent address on the subject "Jesus Christ—Man's Surest Guide."

During the second week of March, 1956, all roads converged on Los Angeles, as far as the Church in the West was concerned. Thousands traveled to that city by buses, trains, and cars to witness the temple dedication. The General Authorities of the Church, with President McKay at their head, departed from Salt Lake City by train on March 8 and arrived in Los Angeles the following morning. At noon they attended luncheons given in their honor by the Los Angeles Chamber of Commerce and the Los Angeles Rotary Club. The following day the General Authorities and special guests were conducted through the temple by President McKay.

The dedicatory services of the magnificent temple began at 9:30 a.m. on Sunday, March 11, with President

McKay presiding. Two sessions were held each day for four days until, it was estimated, fifty thousand members had participated. This was one of the great events in the history of the Church and marked the beginning of a new era for the Latter-day Saints in southern California.

Returning to Salt Lake City after the temple dedication, President McKay presided at all sessions of the annual general conference held in April. This conference was of special significance to the President, as it marked the completion of fifty years of service as a General Authority of the Church. He had been called to be a member of the Twelve in April, 1906.

At the opening sessions he expressed his gratitude for the condition of the Church. "On behalf of the First Presidency and other General Authorities of the Church, I take great satisfaction," he said, "in reporting that all departments of the Church are progressing very satisfactorily, and expressing gratitude to our Heavenly Father for his divine guidance and inspiration." Then he followed by warning the Saints of the evils in the world that would have to be avoided.

Returning to his hometown and the scene of his birthplace, Huntsville, on May 30, 1956, the President had the pleasure of laying the cornerstone of a new chapel. The old chapel had been erected in 1883, when he was a boy ten years of age.

During the first week of June he attended the annual commencement exercises at Brigham Young University in Provo. He admonished the students to place their trust in Jesus Christ, counseling them to remember the admonition of the apostle Peter when he said, "There is none other name under heaven given among men, whereby we must be saved."

Flying to northern California in June, President McKay dedicated a new and beautiful chapel and stake center at Napa, Santa Rosa Stake. Returning to Salt Lake City, he was a speaker at the MIA June Conference. "I should like to direct my remarks this morning to just one phase of Mutual Improvement work," he said. "I hold in my hand the June Conference program. On the cover is the picture of a bride and bridegroom. Behind them are sketches of happy family life. The caption beneath is, 'Be honest with yourself.' Being true means loyalty. Loyalty means fidelity. Its antonyms are: treason, treachery and perfidy. Young men and young women: You must stand adamant against the false ideologies that would undermine the tried and trusted ideals and truths of the pioneers, who worshipped the God of truth and chose the gospel of Jesus Christ as their philosophy of life."

The President visited Oakley, Idaho, on June 24 and dedicated a chapel there that had been erected by the members of Cassia Stake. On August 4 he was at Paris, Idaho, where he addressed a large group of the family of Charles C. Rich, who were holding a family reunion. On September 8, his eighty-third birthday, he was at his home in Salt Lake City. On that occasion he said, "I appreciate with all my heart the knowledge of Christ's plan for the establishment of peace among mankind. The assurance of the efficiency of that plan brings peace to the soul, beyond the power of expression."

One week after his birthday the President was in Calgary, Canada, where he dedicated a new and beautiful stake center, a $400,000 structure, erected by the members of Calgary Stake. Returning to his home, he journeyed to Cambridge, Massachusetts, the following week, and on September 23 presided at the dedication of a chapel erected by the New England Mission and the Cambridge Branch. During the first week of October he was again in Salt Lake City, where he spoke and offered the prayer at the dedication of the new Relief Society Building on North Main Street.

The first session of the October conference of the Church was held on Friday, October 5. President McKay was the principal speaker.

"The passing of years and the repetition of experience fail to lessen the sense of great responsibility of addressing the congregation in this great Tabernacle, and others listening in over the radio," he said. "I have prayed and now pray for the inspiration of the Lord that I may be able to perform this duty acceptably to him and to you, my brethren and sisters." At this conference the President presided at all sessions and spoke vigorously in giving advice and counsel to those present.

During the last week of November, 1956, President McKay traveled to Jacksonville, Florida, where he dedicated a new and beautiful tabernacle erected by the members of Florida Stake. He afterwards visited the extensive Church ranches in Florida.

His activities for the year 1956 were concluded by a visit to Mesa, Arizona, during the last week of December, where he attended a five stake high priests' annual dinner party, with approximately twenty-five hundred persons in attendance.

XXVI

Despite his advancing years, President McKay continued his strenuous activities during 1957. His first journey out of the city was to Fort Wayne, Indiana, in the Great Lakes Mission, where he dedicated a chapel on January 20, in the presence of more than one thousand members and nonmembers. On February 10 he had returned to Utah and was present and spoke in the remodeled Bountiful Tabernacle.

In April he presided at all sessions of the general conference. "Happy is the man," he said in the closing session, "who has experienced that relationship to his Maker, wherein we are made partakers of the divine nature. That is a reality, and I so testify to you in this sacred hour."

On May 4 in the Pasadena (California) Stake Center, the President spoke to 568 seminary graduates. "I wish the whole world of young people could be within observing distance of this group tonight," he said. "This group of young people have decided that God is God, and that right is right; that wrong brings misery, no matter in what form it comes."

During the second week of June, 1957, the President was again in Los Angeles, where he received resolutions from the city and the state of California, memorializing the activities of the Mormon Battalion in the early history of California.

On September 8, the President's eighty-fourth birthday, he attended a quarterly conference of the Wells Stake in Salt Lake City. Reminding those present that the Church had been established for their benefit, he said, "Live in accordance with the covenants undertaken. Fill a noble mission and God will reward you." Five days later he attended an Aaronic Priesthood banquet in Pioneer Stake.

On account of a prevailing flu epidemic, the semiannual conference of the Church was not held in October, 1957.

In November the President journeyed to Florida and at Miami dedicated a new chapel on November 30. On the last Sunday in the year 1957 he addressed a large group of members in his home ward, the 27th, in Salt Lake City.

XXVII

During the first week of January, 1958, President McKay, with Sister McKay, visited southern California. The President was present at the groundbreaking for a new chapel in Garden Grove. He spoke freely on this occasion. "Any nation that denies God," he said, "that breaks up the home, that robs men of their freedom, will sooner or later fail."

The annual conference of the Church was held as usual in Salt Lake City during the first week of April. At the opening session President McKay expressed his feelings:

"It is over fifty years since I stood here for the first time, as one of the General Authorities of the Church. I remember well then my trembling and humility at facing such an audience, and accepting a position as one of the leaders. The passing of half a century has made it no easier to face this vast audience and to realize the responsibility one holds in discharging such a responsibility. This morning, as then, and during the intervening years, I solicit your sympathy and your prayers."

Five days after the close of the conference, President McKay departed, on April 12, on another of his great world trips—this time to preside at the dedication of the New Zealand Temple. Accompanied by Sister McKay and his acting secretary, Rulon H. Tingey, the party traveled by car to Los Angeles. There they boarded a plane for Hawaii, and on April 14 they arrived at the Honolulu Airport. After remaining overnight in Honolulu, they again boarded a plane and Auckland was reached on April 17. Several hundred members of the New Zealand Mission, with President Ariel S. Ballif at their head, were at the airport to greet the President and his party.

The dedicatory services began at the temple on April 20 and continued until the afternoon of April 23, with two sessions daily. The dedicatory prayer was read at each session by President McKay.

This sacred service was followed by the dedication of the Church College of New Zealand, which took place on April 24. This also was a significant event, which meant much for the Mormon and non-Mormon inhabitants of New Zealand.

President McKay remained in New Zealand until May 1. On the return flight he made brief stops in the Fiji and Hawaiian islands, and arrived in Los Angeles on May 8. On May 10 he was back in Salt Lake City.

A few weeks after his return to his home, President McKay entered the LDS Hospital for the removal of a cataract from his right eye. The operation, though painful,

was successful, and he recovered in a remarkably short
time. In July he began planning for the dedication of the
London Temple, which was nearing completion. This
event he had looked forward to for a long time. Finally
the dates were set, September 7, 8, and 9, with two sessions
daily.

Flying across land and sea, the President left the Salt
Lake City Airport on Tuesday, September 2, 1958. With
him were President and Sister Joseph Fielding Smith and
his acting secretary, A. Hamer Reiser. On account of illness, Sister McKay, who had been his constant companion
on all his trips, was not able to accompany him. Arriving
in the evening at LaGuardia Airport, New York City, the
party spent the night at the Plaza Hotel. The following
afternoon they were driven to Idlewild Airport, where they
boarded a plane for London. After a brief stop in Shannon,
Ireland, the plane came down at 9 a.m., September 4, at
London Airport. There to greet the party were Henry D.
Moyle, Richard L. Evans, and Hugh B. Brown of the
Council of the Twelve; Gordon B. Hinckley, Bishop Thorpe
B. Isaacson, Edward O. Anderson, President and Sister Clif-
ton G. M. Kerr, and others. The President was driven to
the Grosvenor House, where rooms had been reserved for
him and his party.

The dedicatory sessions at the London Temple began
on Sunday, September 7, and continued for three days,
with two sessions daily. At each session the venerable President read the dedicatory prayer and spoke to the people.
Present at all these sessions were the European mission
presidents and their wives and President and Sister ElRay
L. Christiansen of the Salt Lake Temple. The writer of
this volume, with Mrs. Nibley and their daughter, Mrs.
William Murdoch, was also present.

The second day of the temple exercises, September 8,
was the President's eighty-fifth birthday. In the evening
Elders Henry D. Moyle and Leo Ellsworth entertained
for him at the Claridge House. About sixty-five Utah, Ari-

zona, and California people were present at this elaborate
dinner. The President gave a delightful, reminiscent talk,
referring to his past experiences. He regretted that Mrs.
McKay was unable to be with him but was delighted that
his sister, Mrs. Joseph Morrell, and her daughter could be
present.

At the close of the temple dedication the President
made a brief trip to the birthplace of his mother, near
Merthyr Tydfil, Wales.

XXVIII

On his return from England, President McKay arrived
in Salt Lake City by plane on Monday afternoon, September 15. Two days later his family tendered him a belated
birthday party. During his absence Sister McKay had improved in health, which cheered him greatly.

The October conference of the Church in 1958 brought
the usual large number of members to Salt Lake City. At
the opening session, held in the Tabernacle on October 10,
the President welcomed the people.

Three days later, at the closing session, he expressed
his satisfaction with the conference.

"My brethren and sisters, we have come to the closing exercises of a great conference. My soul, with yours,
has been filled with thanksgiving and gratitude to our
Heavenly Father for the outpourings of his Holy Spirit.
We have heard some great messages from the leaders of
the Church, and what I have noticed with satisfaction are
the receptive audiences, showing that the messages were
received graciously, with gratitude."

One week after the close of the conference, the President entered the LDS Hospital as a patient. There he endured the painful but successful operation of having a
cataract removed from his left eye.

Recovering his health sufficiently to take a long jour-

ney, President McKay, with Sister McKay and Elder Marion
G. Romney of the Council of the Twelve, traveled by plane
to Hawaii. There, at Laie, Oahu, on December 17, he
dedicated the newly completed College of Hawaii. This
was an outstanding event in the educational program of
the Church. Among many messages, it brought the following telegram from the president of the United States,
Dwight D. Eisenhower:

"Please give my greetings to all assembled at the dedication of the Church College of Hawaii. This splendid
new campus, built by the faith and work of your Church
members, adds much to the resources of the Hawaiian
community. I am sure that the young people who study
here will be forever inspired by the devoted example of
their many benefactors. Congratulations and best wishes.
(Signed) Dwight D. Eisenhower, President of the United
States of America."

According to a custom that President McKay had followed for a number of years, he spoke to the members of
his own ward, the 27th, on Sunday evening, December
21. The subject of his address was "The Divinity of the
Savior." Approximately one thousand persons were present
at the meeting.

On Christmas Eve, 1958, President and Sister McKay
entertained the members of their family at a Christmas
party at the Hotel Utah.

XXIX

On April 26, 1959, President McKay traveled to Bloom-
field, Michigan, where he dedicated the new Detroit Stake
Center. He told those who attended to fight the "godless
teachings of Communism," and hailed the erection of the
Church building as another bulwark against the teachings
of Communism. He deplored the destructive Communist
forces that had recently established a university of atheism,

which was dedicated to the destruction of belief in God and
its resulting destruction of the human mind.

Three weeks later, on May 17, the President spoke at
a special service commemorating the seventy-fifth anniversary of the dedication of the Logan Temple. On this occasion he stated that "temples of the Church are one of the
greatest means of character building and have a special
place in the Church aside from the ordinances given and
performed within." He elaborated upon this, stating: "Every
temple erected by the Church attracts people who pass,
tells those who read and hear by radio and every other
means of publicity that this is a house of God. It is a temple
to the Most High. Its very existence, its walls, and all pertaining to it declare his reality, his love and his plan of
salvation. We'd like every boy and every girl in the world
and particularly in the Church to recognize this house as
His house. That's what I mean by temples building character."

An event of grave impact occurred on May 19 when
President McKay's lifelong friend, associate, and counselor,
Elder Stephen L. Richards, passed away. Speaking at the
funeral on May 22, the Prophet eulogized his close friend
as "one of the noblest souls that ever mingled among men."
He said, "Goodbye for the present, Stephen L, my beloved
friend and associate. We shall miss you—Oh! how we shall
miss you! but we shall continue to carry on until we meet
again."

At the meeting of the Council of Twelve and First
Presidency on Thursday, June 18, in the Salt Lake Temple,
President J. Reuben Clark, Jr., who had served many years
in the First Presidency, was set apart as first counselor to
President McKay and Elder Henry D. Moyle was set apart
as second counselor.

At the annual MIA June Conference on June 14, President McKay was the keynote speaker: "If you were to ask
me what has contributed most to the happiness of my life
and to the success that I might have obtained, I would

say it was the master control exercised in our home by Sister McKay. Never a condition that could ruffle her character, no tardiness on my part for meals, never a hasty or impetuous answer or accusation, always a feeling of control over children and family and all; no chance for entrance of enmity or fault-finding. Let self-mastery and acceptance of conditions reign and there will always be peace in the home. Self-mastery is always an active virtue."

A few days later, when Sister McKay was approached by reporters on the eve of her birthday, she noted four important conditions or standards that make for marital success. These she listed as "the same religious life, the same social life, about the same education, and the same ideals and desires in life." She explained that President McKay had been called to the apostleship after their first five years of marriage, and that she had been alone much of the time. "But when he was home his advice was so priceless and so helpful with the children that our life has been one round of joy. I have been a very happy wife and mother for fifty-eight years."

In his keynote address given at the opening session of the 129th semiannual conference of the Church, the Prophet cited Communism as the overshadowing problem of our time and stated: "I should say that the most urgent problem of our day is a spiritual problem. . . . Today civilized nations are sitting on a mountain of explosives, accumulated in defiance of Christ's teachings. Let the heat of hatred, suspicion, and greed become a little more intense, and there will be such an international explosion as will greatly retard, if not forcibly drive from the midst of mankind, the hoped-for peace heralded by the heavenly hosts when Christ as a babe was born in Bethlehem."

XXX

In January, 1960, an intensive three-month program designed to reach all the youth of the Church was undertaken *excellent*

1960

in a series of firesides. The purpose of the firesides was to influence the young people "to a renewal of interest in the standards and precepts of the Church." On January 3 nearly 200,000 persons were assembled in 170 gathering places throughout the Church to hear President McKay give the initial message in this series. In an inspiring address he reviewed the ideals of LDS courtship and marriage.

In April, President McKay opened the 130th annual conference of the Church. He observed that "120,000 young people from Asia and Africa each year are indoctrinated with the false ideology of Communism. . . . I thought as I read that how important it is for members of the Church, particularly the leaders who are sent out to these various missions, to exemplify the one source of peace—the Lord and Savior, Jesus Christ. . . . The duty of the Church is to teach and practice the fundamental principles of the good life. Obedience to the gospel of Jesus Christ, no matter what the financial or physical conditions may be, will bring peace in the soul. . . . The purpose of membership in the kingdom of God is for the fostering of spiritual life—I repeat—and the achievement of moral and charitable ends; in other words, for the developing of the religious senti-ment, the true religious spirit."

On May 7 the Prophet paid a surprise visit to Rexburg, Idaho, where he addressed the students of Ricks College in a devotional assembly; and on May 28 he spoke to the stu-dents of Brigham Young University.

On June 5 a capacity audience of twelve hundred heard him stress the need for unity in the Church at the dedication of the Grant Sixth-Seventh Ward chapel in Salt Lake City. A week later he addressed the MIA conference in the Salt Lake Tabernacle.

Ground was broken on July 1 for the new $1.5 million Pioneer Memorial Theatre on the University of Utah cam-pus, at which President McKay expressed his appreciation for the pioneers and paid tribute to the great pioneer heri-tage of his listeners.

In ceremonies that preceded the annual Days of '47 pageant, the Prophet was accorded special tribute as one whose peerless personality reflected his religion, which "made him a composite of all we expect to find in a great man."

Nearing the eighty-seventh anniversary of his birth in September, President McKay considered himself to "be in one of the most wholesome, contributive periods of life. In childhood and throughout the gay and happy years of youth, the seventieth and eightieth birthdays seemed far in the future, and unsteady and feeble many who reached that advanced age. Today, however, I know that what seemed in youth to be a long journey is very short, indeed; and what in anticipation seemed might be a joyless existence is one of the most wholesome, contributive periods of life—full of opportunities for service and resultant satisfaction. Loved ones, loyal friends and precious memories make it so. Faith in a loving Father and confidence in one's friends and associates make life worth living." He further noted: "If one would be happy, one must feel immortality. Every soul is part of divinity—by that I mean this 'aging coat'—this body—is mine; this mind with its power to think and to make decisions is also mine. The spirit and soul never grow old. They are a part of divinity."

He stated that whenever he visited the old homestead in Ogden Valley, he had the same "youthful feelings, the same desires to be active, to mount my favorite horse, Sonny Boy—the same enthusiasm to jump on his back—as when I was young, but the physical body is now too stiff. . . . That which comes from God is always young—it is as eternal as the Author. That, I believe, is literally true. The sky is just as blue, the moon is just as bright as when I was young. Nature is just as full of beauty, if we open our eyes to see it."

On September 25 President McKay dedicated the impressive two million dollar East Bay Interstake Center at Oakland, California. Begun in 1957, the building was dedicated before a capacity crowd of 5,540. The President was accompanied by his son and daughter-in-law, Mr. and Mrs. David Lawrence McKay. The services were conducted by Presidents Stone, Creer, and Ream of the neighboring stakes. A highlight of the proceedings was the address of the Prophet in which he set forth the ideals of Christ as a way to peace in a "world antagonistic to the establishment of peace."

The overwhelming success of the series of youth firesides at the beginning of the year led to a second series of such gatherings, which commenced on October 2. President McKay delivered the first address in the series from the Salt Lake Tabernacle, which was broadcast to 207 other gatherings of youth from coast to coast. He told them, "Your tools are ideas. The thought in your mind at this moment is contributing, however infinitesimally, almost imperceptibly to the shaping of your soul, even to the linaments of your countenance. It is the dominant and recurring ideas that affect us most; but even passing and idle thoughts leave their impression. Trees that can withstand the hurricane sometimes yield to destroying pests that can scarcely be seen except with a microscope. Likewise, the greatest foes of the individuals are not always the glaring evils of humanity, but subtle influences of thought and association in society that are undermining the manhood and womanhood of today."

The first hour of the fireside in each of the 208 assemblies was devoted to a tribute to the first couple of the Church.

On Friday, October 7, President McKay addressed the general conference of the Church. He noted recent threats made by the Premier of Soviet Russia against the United Nations, and added, "Who is this man who presumes to tell the United Nations what to do? He is a man who rejects the divinity of Jesus Christ and denies the existence of God, who is imbued with the false philosophy of Karl Marx, whose aim in life was 'to dethrone God and destroy capitalism.' He is a follower of Lenin, who said, 'I want children to hate their parents who are not Communists.' The followers of these men, to gain their ends, 'resort to all sorts of stratagems, maneuvers, illegal methods, evasions, and subterfuges.' This atheistic attitude, and the advice to hate others, even one's own family, is just the opposite of the spirit of love as manifest and taught by the Savior. In sessions in another part of the United States are men who believe as I have indicated and who are willing to resort to any subterfuge, any scheme, that will further their ends to dethrone God. We appeal to God, who exists and lives, and with whom we are in harmony this morning—we have met in the name of his Beloved Son."

On Thanksgiving Day President McKay dedicated the newly constructed Holladay 11th-14th Ward chapel. He told those present that "faith in God and free agency—the right to worship God according to the dictates of our own conscience—are the blessings for which we should be abundantly grateful this day." He stated that Thanksgiving was essentially a religious festival in the United States, the only country in the world that has set aside a day on which to give thanks to the Lord.

Again on December 18, President McKay spoke to a local congregation. To a gathering of the Saints of the combined 27th and East 27th wards in Salt Lake City he said, "In anticipating this meeting, I have changed my mind two or three times regarding my theme. Conditions in the world are such that I cannot get my thought off the fact that there are two great forces, more potent than ever before, operating in this world, each more determined to achieve success. Each perhaps more active in planning and on one side scheming, than ever before. These two great forces are hate and love. . . ."

During the year 1960 President McKay entertained several prominent visitors, among whom were Eric Johnston, president of the Motion Picture Association of America

and former United States ambassador to the Near East,
Sir Harold Caccia, British ambassador to the United States,
and Masao Yagi, Japan's consul general from San Francisco.

XXXI

After returning from a brief Christmas-New Year's
vacation at Laguna Beach, California, President and Sister
McKay opened the year 1961 by celebrating their sixtieth
wedding anniversary at the home of their son, Dr. Edward
McKay. "We've had sixty happy years," said the President.
"This happiness springs from the fact that we have had
seven choice children, six of whom are now living, all
happily married. We have twenty grandchildren and six
great-grandchildren—treasures of eternity. That is some of
our happiness." He paid tribute to his wife in these words:
"The one thing that has made our home happy is Mama
Ray's self control. She may have thought some things, but
never said them. She is always sweet spoken—a thing to
make a happy life. Her motto seems to be 'never say anything that makes things unpleasant.'"

An important milestone in the progress of the Church
occurred on Sunday, January 15, 1961, when President Mc-
Kay dedicated a newly completed chapel at Palmyra, New
York, the birthplace of Mormonism. More than nine hundred attended the services. The President directed most of
his remarks to the subject of the Prophet Joseph Smith.
"There were those who scorned Joseph Smith and scoffed
at his teachings. Likewise there were those who loved him
and would have died for him. . . . There was something
great about a man who could so impress others that they
were willing to die for him. . . . Just as it was with the
Savior, so it will be with Joseph Smith—he will grow in
greatness and honor as the centuries pass."

An interesting sidelight of this dedication was the arrival, prior to the dedication, of a charred letter marked

"damaged en route" in the office of the Eastern States Mission president, Gerald G. Smith. Although the letter arrived a few days late, it enabled President Smith to make the necessary plans for the dedication, which he otherwise could not have done. The damaged letter bore mute evidence of tragedy. It was one of a few letters salvaged from the wreckage of two transport planes that collided over New York City on Friday, December 16, killing 128 persons and strewing wreckage over a wide area.

On Monday, January 23, President McKay flew to the Bay area of California, where he met the presidencies of nineteen stakes and the Northern California Mission who had assembled at the Hilton Inn, adjacent to the San Francisco Airport, to announce that an imposing temple would soon be built in Oakland, California. The proposed architect's design was presented to those assembled, who pledged to contribute $500,000 toward the cost of the temple. President McKay then attended a press conference and returned to Salt Lake City the same evening.

A momentous event in the history of the British Mission occurred in February, when President McKay dedicated the Hyde Park chapel in London and organized a stake of the Church in London. He left Salt Lake City on February 22 with his wife, family members, and Church officials. On Sunday, February 26, he dedicated the new chapel in the cultural heart of the city before a crowd of more than fourteen hundred members of the Church. In an accompanying address he appealed for world peace through adherence to the fundamental principles of righteousness as found in the true gospel of Jesus Christ.

Upon his arrival in London on Friday, February 24, President McKay held a press conference attended by a large number of representatives of the communications media. Many highly favorable news reports resulted from this conference. On Tuesday, following the dedication, he returned to Scotland, the field of his missionary labors sixty-two years previously. He addressed a meeting of missionaries of the Scottish-Irish Mission and visited places of interest in his old field of labor. On Wednesday he met with missionaries of the British North Mission at Manchester; and he concluded his eventful stay in England with a visit on Thursday to the birthplace of his mother at Merthyr-Tydfil, Wales. Here the Church leader unveiled a plaque at the old home where his mother, Jennette Evelyn Evans, was born in August, 1850.

President McKay conducted the 131st annual conference of the Church on April 6 through 9. In his keynote address he stated: "If the question were asked this morning, 'In what respect during the last year has the Church made the most commendable progress?' I would not answer: 'In financial matters,' although it is a fact that perhaps never before have the financial interests of the Church been more prosperous. I would not say: 'In the increase of the number of new houses of worship,' although members of the Church have put forth more effort and built and paid for more chapels than in any other similar period of the past. . . . I would not answer: 'In the increased membership,' although in the last thirteen months the growth of the Church in numbers in the stakes and in the missions has been most encouraging. . . . I would not answer that the most commendable progress has been in better understanding among the leaders of municipalities, newspaper editors, and well-informed people generally regarding the purposes, organization, and contributions of the Church toward peace and the ultimate destiny of the world. I would answer that the most encouraging progress of the Church during the last year is seen in the increased number of young people participating in Church activity. . . ."

This conference marked the tenth anniversary of President McKay's appointment as ninth Prophet and President of the Church of Jesus Christ in this dispensation.

On Tuesday, May 2, President McKay was in Logan, Utah, where he officiated at the groundbreaking of Church buildings adjacent to the Utah State University campus.

These comprised a stake center and four ward buildings for the Utah State University Stake, an LDS student living center, and a Delta Phi fraternity house. The Prophet took this occasion to review the Church's position regarding the separation of Church and state: "The Church and state must and will remain separate. We declare here . . . that we are not in favor of the bill which is put before Congress that taxes should be taken by churches to foster their own religious instruction. The land which is to be used here is paid for by the Church, and we will do all we can to observe the phrase in the Constitution which declares the Church and state shall remain separate."

The following week, on May 10, President McKay addressed the studentbody at Brigham Young University, following which he unveiled and presented a portrait of Ernest L. Wilkinson in a tribute to the BYU president.

At a gathering of family members and a few specially invited guests at the newly restored home of George C. and Adelaide R. Wood, parents of Wilford C. Wood of Woods Cross, Utah, on May 22, President McKay gave a short message and prayer. A highlight of the evening was a rendition of "Come, Come, Ye Saints" by President McKay on the old organ brought by William Clayton across the plains.

On June 11 the Prophet spoke at the Sunday morning session of the MIA conference. Of the MIA he said, "I wish parents would appreciate the value of the Mutual Improvement Association to the home and to their children in character building. If it did nothing else, it furnishes opportunity for keeping good companions. Parents should know where their children are and what companionship is theirs. Companionship in personality is a great educator. Education is gained not only in school in a formal way, not only in Church in a religious way, but it is acquired daily in our contacts with one another. That is one of the most effective sources of education. . . ."

The First Presidency of the Church was increased to

four members on June 22 when President McKay announced the appointment of Elder Hugh B. Brown of the Council of the Twelve as a counselor in the First Presidency.

Two days later, on June 26, the Prophet presided over the historic gathering in Salt Lake City of the first worldwide meeting of mission presidents in the history of the Church. President McKay announced the theme of the conference, "every member a missionary," and elaborated upon the fundamental objectives of missionary work. This seminar marked the launching of a new uniform method of teaching the gospel in all the missions of the Church and the emphasis on a cooperating program wherein every member is a missionary.

The year 1961 saw the termination of the great service of President McKay's first councilor, President J. Reuben Clark, Jr., who died on October 6 at his home in Salt Lake City. Funeral services for the beloved counselor were held in the Salt Lake Tabernacle on October 10. President McKay conducted the services for the man who had served with him twenty-seven years in the First Presidency. "I feel now," said the Prophet, "that a truly great man [has] gone back to his Creator, and can say truly as Paul said to Timothy: 'I have fought a good fight, I have finished my course, I have kept the faith. Henceforth there is laid up for me a crown of righteousness, which the Lord, the righteous judge, shall give me at that day: and not to me only but unto all them also that love his appearing.'"

The First Presidency was reorganized on Thursday, October 12, when President Henry D. Moyle, formerly the second counselor, was named first counselor and President Hugh B. Brown was named second counselor.

XXXII

At the beginning of the year 1962, while resting at Laguna Beach in southern California, President McKay

1962

traveled to Glendale, California, on January 28 to dedicate the new Glendale Stake Center. In addressing those present he noted that salvation is "a daily occurrence," and then discussed the "animal instincts" and "passions" from which humanity needs to be saved.

The 132nd annual conference of the Church that convened in April was a historical highlight in Church history. Proceedings of the conference were beamed to a potential audience of sixty million people in Europe, South Africa, South America, Central America, and Mexico. Never before had an international audience listened to a session of conference from the Salt Lake Tabernacle. On this occasion the beloved eighty-eight-year-old Prophet spoke on "The Divine Church."

A special Easter message by President McKay was beamed by shortwave radio on April 22 to South America, the Caribbean Islands, and Mexico. His message was centered around the text of Job 19:25: "For I know that my Redeemer liveth, and that he shall stand at the latter day upon the earth."

On May 6 the President dedicated the newly completed Chicago Stake Center and two-ward chapel, which he regarded as "one of the most impressive built by the Church." Nearly three thousand people were in attendance. President McKay spoke on "The Responsibility of Parenthood," and he reviewed ten conditions that contribute to a happy home: "(1) Keeping in mind that you begin to lay the foundation of a happy home in your premarital life; (2) choosing of a mate by judgment and inspiration as well as by emotion; (3) approaching marriage with the lofty view it merits; (4) realizing that the noblest purpose of marriage is procreation; (5) letting the spirit of reverence pervade the home; (6) letting husband or wife never speak in loud tones to each other; (7) learning the value of self-control; (8) fostering home ties by continued companionship; (9) making accessible to children proper literature, music, and appropriate moving pictures; and (10) by example and precept, encouraging participation in Church activity."

A gathering of nearly five thousand Aaronic Priesthood members and their leaders from fourteen stakes held at the public square in Huntsville, Utah, on May 12, heard President McKay relate inspirational experiences of his life and tell of the events leading to the restoration of the Aaronic Priesthood. "Your presence here hallows this ground," he said.

A highlight of the year 1962 was the return of President McKay to Scotland, the land of his ancestors, where he officiated in the creation of the first stake of the Church in that country. He left Salt Lake City on August 23, accompanied by his son and daughter-in-law, Mr. and Mrs. Robert R. McKay. The stake organization occurred on August 28 at a conference gathering of more than twenty-five hundred members and investigators in Glasgow's famed St. Andrews Hall. President McKay spoke at both morning and afternoon sessions of the conference before returning to Salt Lake City on the 29th.

Speaking to the annual Relief Society conference of the Church on October 3 in the Tabernacle, President McKay urged more parental responsibility. "The real tragedy in America is not that we have permitted the Bible to slip out of our public schools, but that we have so openly neglected to teach it in either the home or the Church. Never before was there such need of revitalizing the teaching of faith and repentance on the part of parents."

Business and civic leaders of Utah congregated at the Hotel Utah on December 10 to honor President and Sister McKay at a testimonial dinner, which came at the commencement of the beloved Church leader's ninetieth year. A highlight of the evening was the presentation of an organ to be installed in the newly constructed chapel in Merthyr-Tydfil, Wales, the birthplace of President McKay's mother. A tribute to the President read during the evening stated in part: "Notwithstanding his position of great responsibility

and importance in his church, President McKay always has
kept the common touch. Perfectly at home with the great
and renowned, or with the lowliest, his deep sympathy
for people, and his understanding heart, have opened chan-
nels of communication and influence to inspire and moti-
vate thousands, especially the young people. These attri-
butes have endeared him to everyone with whom he has
come in contact."

XXXIII

A significant event of 1963 was the launching of the
priesthood home teaching program. Addressing the newly
appointed priesthood home teaching committee on May
15, President McKay gave the challenge to "bring about
a rejuvenation throughout the Church of home teaching so
each member will come under the full influence of the
gospel of Jesus Christ."

On May 22 President McKay officiated at special
rites in the Salt Lake Temple at which additions and new
facilities installed during a ten-month renovation period
were dedicated. The meeting was held in the Terrestrial
Room of the temple and attended by special invitation.
In his remarks President McKay related having attended
the Salt Lake Temple dedication in 1893 as a student and
listening to the dedicatory prayer of President Woodruff.
He also discussed the importance and meaning of temple
ordinances.

On June 30 the President dedicated the Federal Heights
chapel in Salt Lake City. He elaborated upon the thought
that "meditation is one of the most secret, most sacred
doors through which we pass into the presence of the
Lord."

At the MIA annual conference held in June, a special
tribute was paid to President McKay by Ellsworth H.
Augustus, president of the Boy Scouts of America, who
stated, "The presentation of a tribute is frequently a per-

functory act, sometimes a mere duty. I can assure you from
the bottom of my heart that this presentation is a great
privilege and pleasure, which I have traveled nearly two
thousand miles to enjoy. And then it reflects my own personal, and the Boy Scouts of America, high regard for The
Church of Jesus Christ of Latter-day Saints, its officers
and members, thousands and tens of thousands of whom
have dedicated their lives in the improvement of youth.
No one has ever done a better job of it."

President McKay left Salt Lake City on August 22 for
Merthyr-Tydfil, where he dedicated a new $340,000 chapel,
not far from the home where his mother was born. The
six-day journey was filled with meetings with missionaries
and mission leaders. The Prophet declared it as one of the
greatest trips he had ever made.

Henry D. Moyle, first counselor in the First Presidency,
passed away on September 18. At the funeral service held
three days later, President McKay eulogized his devoted
counselor in these words: "Among the basic virtues that
stand out in President Moyle's life are: first, his unwavering
faith in the gospel; second, his courageous defense of truth;
third, his cheerfulness, even in the face of frowns or rebuke; fourth, his responsiveness and loyalty to duty; and
fifth, his reverence for God and all things sacred."

The First Presidency was reorganized on Thursday,
October 10, when Hugh B. Brown was set apart as first
counselor and Nathan Eldon Tanner as second counselor,
during the weekly meeting of the First Presidency and
Council of the Twelve.

On November 1 at noon, President McKay officiated
at the dedication of the new Eagle Gate spanning State
Street at the South Temple intersection in Salt Lake City.
In dedicating the new monument, which stands at the one-
time entrance to the farmlands of President Brigham Young,
the President said, ". . . may the Eagle Gate, with its grand
old eagle and the bee hive upon which it stands, continue
to radiate to future generations the virtues of the pioneers

exemplified as follows: loyalty, industry, freedom, faith and worship."

Less than two weeks later, President McKay entered the LDS Hospital in Salt Lake City for a much-needed rest; he was released to his home on November 18.

Ever concerned with the troubles and sorrows of others, the President issued the following statement of deep grief upon learning of the assassination of President John F. Kennedy in November, 1963: "Only a few weeks ago it was our privilege to entertain the president, and now to think that he has gone we are stunned as well as shocked. It is terrible to think that such a tragedy could occur in this age of the world."

XXXIV

Of importance at the commencement of the year 1964 was the visit of the venerable Mormon Church leader with President Lyndon B. Johnson in the White House at Washington, D.C. Making the trip at the invitation of the president, the Prophet left Salt Lake City on January 30 and returned on February 7. A dispatch from Washington reported that "the president of the United States asked for and received a pledge of spiritual help and strength from the President of the Church, at a meeting between the two. . . . It was learned that the spiritual and moral fiber of the nation was discussed and that President Johnson asked for President McKay's prayers in behalf of the nation."

Noteworthy events in the life of President McKay during 1964 included a citation bestowed by the Veterans of Foreign Wars for his loyalty and Americanism; the unveiling of a portrait by the noted portrait artist, Alvin Gittins, at a special unveiling at the Pioneer Memorial Theater; participation in the Days of '47 parade on July 24; and a two-week rest at his home in Huntsville.

On August 2 he made a surprise visit to Oakland, California, where he attended an informal meeting to finalize plans for the Oakland Temple dedication in October. Speaking to those assembled, the President said, "Temple work is as broad as humanity or as life itself. It would be an unjust God who would not save us all, even generations past." He asked the Lord's blessings upon the assembled leaders and commended them for their faithfulness in building the temple. Of the dedication planned for October he said, "When you dedicate, if these legs will do their duty, I will be here with you."

Upon his return to Salt Lake City, President McKay was hospitalized with a heart ailment. Amidst this affliction, the President's keen sense of humor was evident. Dr. Llewelyn R. McKay reported that his father's oft-repeated philosophy was "when you stop you're dead." During one visit to the hospital President McKay told his family, "As soon as this little affair is over and I get home, we'll talk over plans for the next ten years."

Sufficiently recovered from his illness by November 17. President McKay traveled to Oakland, California, to dedicate the new temple there. He was accompanied by his counselors, Presidents Brown and Tanner; Joseph Fielding Smith, president of the Quorum of Twelve; and others of the General Authorities. This was the fifth temple dedicated by the Prophet since he became President of the Church in 1951. More than six thousand people witnessed the proceedings in the temple and the adjacent interstake center. President McKay addressed each of six dedicatory services and gave the dedicatory prayer in four of the meetings.

XXXV

On January 2, 1965, the McKays noted their sixty-fourth wedding anniversary. On this occasion President McKay spoke on the subject of happiness: "If one would be happy one must feel immortality. Every soul is a part of divinity—by that I mean this aging coat—this body—is also mine; this mind with its power to think and to make decisions is also mine. The spirit and soul never grow old. They are a part of divinity. . . . That which comes from God is always young—it is as eternal as the Author. That, I believe, is literally true. The sky is just as blue, the moon is just as bright as when I was young. Nature is just as full of beauty if we open our eyes to see it."

One week after his anniversary President McKay presided at the dedication of the new Deseret Gymnasium in Salt Lake City. Sister McKay was also in attendance. Heeding the advice of his physician, the President did not speak on this occasion.

Upon returning from a two-week rest in southern California in February, President McKay remarked, "I feel great and plan to get right back to work"; however, he was hospitalized again on February 14, with a lung congestion secondary to his heart condition. Two weeks later he had improved enough to return to his Hotel Utah apartment.

The 135th annual conference of the Church convened in April. Many things made it outstanding. Foremost was the presence of the ninety-one-year-old prophet. He spoke a few words of greeting during the sessions and had three important messages read to the congregation. His keynote address contained a fervent appeal for effective safeguards of LDS youth against delinquency. President McKay attended all but two of the seven general sessions. The Sunday morning session began at 8 a.m. to permit the first live nationwide telecast in the history of the Church. This session—televised coast to coast by approximately two hundred television and radio stations—was the most widely disseminated of any conference session in the history of the Church.

In September, on the eve of his ninety-second birthday, President McKay remarked, "I feel fine. I haven't an ache or a pain. I have no drudgery, and every moment of life is a pleasure. Indeed life is glorious."

On Friday, October 1, when the Prophet stood at the pulpit to call the general conference of the Church to order, and when, a few minutes later, he arose to give an inspiring message, it was apparent to the vast congregation that their beloved leader was remarkably renewed in spirit and physical ability. Not since April, 1964, had they heard him speak from the pulpit at conference time. In addition to his opening message, he spoke to seventy thousand holders of the priesthood on Saturday night. He also addressed the closing session of the conference on Sunday, October 3.

In a surprise announcement later in October, President McKay reported the appointment of Joseph Fielding Smith and Thorpe B. Isaacson as additional counselors to serve in the First Presidency. He cited increased work of the First Presidency and the rapid growth of the Church as factors that created the need for additional help.

XXXVI

On February 8, 1966, President McKay addressed Scouts and Scouters of Salt Lake City in a program entitled "Recommittal 1966," in which he outlined the principles of the Scout Oath and Law.

At the general conference of the Church held on April 6, 9, and 10, 1966, which was broadcast to countries in Europe, Asia, Africa, and South America, totaling nearly two-thirds of the earth's population, President McKay once again presided. Speaking a few brief words of greeting in the April 6 opening session, he said, "It is with feelings profoundly appreciated that I appear before you on this occasion. One never appreciates the value of good health until it is lost. I am glad to greet you at this opening session and pray that the Lord's blessings will be with each one who stands in this pulpit and fulfills the assignment made of him." He gave his keynote address on April 9, in which he testified of the reality of the resurrection of Christ.

On April 22 President McKay was in Ogden, where he pulled a switch that signaled the start of construction of the new LDS hospital that would carry his name. He said, "I am very happy and honored that you think highly enough of me to perpetuate my name and memory. . . . I am happy to meet my dear friends on this occasion and I do appreciate your kindnesses. May the Lord bless you and your friendships, for they shine, and for the kindness of perpetuating me and my association with this town and country."

Previous speakers had expressed the wish that President McKay would be with them two years later for the hospital dedication. To this he replied, "I'm not going anywhere. This is the beginning of many happy times ahead of us."

On May 15 the largest convocation of Mormon students ever gathered from the University of Utah assembled at the Salt Lake Tabernacle for a special tribute to their Prophet. Those participating raised their voices in speech and song to President McKay, who was watching the program on closed circuit television in his Hotel Utah apartment. Members of the First Presidency were also present. Highlights of the evening were the presentation of an oil painting of the President and a special message read by his son Robert.

Another "first" occurred in the life of President McKay on June 1 and 2 when he visited historic Church history sites in Missouri at Far West, Independence, Liberty, and Adam-ondi-Ahman. This was the Prophet's first visit to these places. On this visit the purchase of 140 additional acres of land by the Church at Adam-ondi-Ahman was approved.

When the October, 1966, general conference convened, President McKay was on the stand and personally delivered his keynote address. Showing remarkable courage and determination, the ninety-three-year-old Church leader delivered a forty-minute address that set the theme for the conference. He noted the perils facing the world and urged the preaching of the gospel as the only effective solution for them.

On December 24, LDS servicemen in war-torn Asia received a special greeting from President McKay. The message was filmed in Salt Lake City and flown to the area by the Utah Air National Guard on a regularly scheduled flight. The President gave these words of counsel: "You are constantly in our thoughts and prayers. . . . We earnestly hope that regardless of the circumstances in which you find yourselves, you will live as becomes members of The Church of Jesus Christ of Latter-day Saints and as men holding the priesthood of God. In such living you will find the inner 'peace which passeth understanding' in spite of the turmoil of war in which you may find yourselves."

XXXVII

As President and Sister McKay reflected upon sixty-six years of married life during the first week of 1967, they visited the old home at 56 North 2nd West in Salt Lake City where they held their wedding reception on January 2, 1901, following their marriage in the Salt Lake Temple. The old home was the residence of Sister McKay's family at the time young David O. first met her. He was renting a room in the home while attending the University of Utah. After the visit, President McKay was asked if he still loved his sweetheart as much as he did sixty-six years ago. His response was typical of his humor: "No, I love her sixty-six times as much."

At the 137th annual conference of the Church held in April, President McKay attended two sessions on Thursday and Sunday. His three vital messages were read by his son Robert. In his opening message he cited the glaring evils of the day and warned the youth against them. This conference was carried in the Spanish language in a special broadcast to eight cities in Mexico. It was the first such transmission of conference proceedings into Mexico. The Sunday morning session was also carried live to Hawaii for the first time by use of the "Lani Bird" satellite, in orbit 22,000 miles above the Pacific Ocean.

At the priesthood session of conference, Robert McKay was asked to say a few words of his own prior to delivering his father's message to the assembled brethren of the Church. He responded by saying that he and his brothers were often asked how it felt to be the sons of the Prophet of God. "You don't feel it, you live it," he said. He testified further: "My father has my obedience and my sustaining vote. In the home, on the farm, in business, in the Church, I have never been shown one action or one word which would throw any doubt that he should be the Prophet of the Lord."

While visiting his home town at Huntsville on July 12, President McKay was taken ill and was hospitalized. However, he had recovered sufficiently to ride at the head of the Days of '47 parade on the 24th.

Presiding over the general conference in October, President McKay attended the first session but viewed the remainder of the conference from his Hotel Utah apartment. His three messages to the Saints were read by his son Robert. At this conference sixty-nine Regional Representatives to the Twelve were called to assist in meeting the expanding organizational needs of the Church.

Following the conference the Prophet spent nearly a month resting at his summer home in Huntsville.

Among the prominent visitors who paid their respects to the President in 1967 were Edward M. Lindsey, president of the world's 800,000 Lions Club members, Governor George Romney of Michigan, and Tonga's Prince Tu'ipelehake.

XXXVIII

An honor was bestowed upon President McKay in March, 1968, when the Exemplary Manhood Award of the BYU Associated Men Students organization was presented to him in a special devotional assembly at that school. Dr. Edward R. McKay accepted the honor in behalf of his father. The tribute read: "The Associated Men Students of Brigham Young University are proud to present the Exemplary Manhood Award to a man who has given the world a standard of excellence. It is with great honor that this award be presented to David O. McKay, the man who has best exemplified manhood to this generation." In accepting the award, Dr. McKay recalled some of the boyhood experiences of his father, noting, "Father's recipe for success included always careful planning of his day ahead." As a father he always counseled his children to "do the nearest job at hand and do it well. He always told them to do everything with the inspiration and help of the Lord."

Although he was present at two sessions of the April conference, President McKay's messages were read by his son David Lawrence. At this conference Elder Alvin R. Dyer was called to serve as a counselor in the First Presidency.

In September a new one hundred foot flagpole was dedicated on Temple Square. The Prophet's message on this occasion was read by his son Robert: "If we would make the world better, let us foster a keener appreciation of the freedom and liberty guaranteed by the government of the United States, as framed by the founders of this nation. There are some self-proclaimed progressives who cry that such old-time adherence is out-of-date. But there are some fundamental principles of this Republic which, like eternal truths, never get out-of-date; and which are applicable at all times to liberty-loving peoples. Such are the underlying principles of the Constitution, a document framed by patriotic, freedom-loving men, who we declare

were inspired by the Lord. Actuated by these two fundamental and eternal principles—the free agency of the individual, and faith in an over-ruling Providence—those
fifty-six men who signed the Declaration of Independence,
those who drew up the Constitution of the United States
nine years later, gave to the world a concept of government
which, if applied, will strike from the arms of down-trodden
humanity the shackels of tyranny, and give hope, ambition,
and freedom to the teeming millions throughout the world.
. . . I love the Stars and Stripes! I love the people who
make this country great, and I believe in their loyalty. In
its leadership is the greatest responsibility that ever came
to a nation. We pray to God to guide our president and
Congress. I know that they and we do not want war, but
there are things that are worse than death—one is to be
deprived of our liberty!"

When the general conference convened in October,
President McKay presided but was not present at any of
the sessions. His sons Robert and David Lawrence read his
three addresses to the conference. In his opening remarks,
the Prophet said: "I believe that only through a truly educated citizenry can the ideals that inspired the Founding
Fathers of our nation be preserved and perpetuated. . . .
We cannot, must not, be insensible to the evil forces around
us, and especially the Communistic conspiracy, the avowed
object of which is to destroy faith in God, to sow discord
and contention among men with the view of undermining,
weakening, if not entirely destroying, our constitutional
form of government, and to weaken and subvert the ideals
of our younger generation. When acts and schemes are
manifestly contrary to the revealed word of the Lord, I
feel, as do my associates, justified in warning our people
against them. . . ."

In December, President McKay received the Distinguished American Award from the National Football Foundation and Hall of Fame. Believed to be the nation's oldest
former football player, the President received the award in

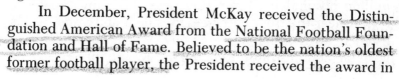

absentia at the eleventh annual awards dinner of the foundation in the Waldorf-Astoria Hotel in New York City on December 3. Accepting the award for him was Frederick S. Schluter of Princeton, New Jersey, a convert to the Church and president of the Delaware Valley chapter of the foundation.

XXXIX

In January 1969 it was reported that President McKay had been numbered among the top five church leaders listed in the public opinion poll released by Dr. George Gallop's Institute of Public Opinion. A total of 1,501 adults in the United States were asked "What man that you have heard or read about, living today in any part of the world, do you admire the most?" In addition to President McKay, others listed were Cardinal Cushing, the Reverend Norman Vincent Peale, the Reverend Paul Roberts, and Bishop Fulton J. Sheen. Men in public life, journalism, entertainment, sports, and medicine were listed along with religious leaders.

The general conference of the Church, which convened on April 4 in Salt Lake City, heard President Mc-Kay's opening message read by his son Robert. President McKay was not present at any of the conference sessions by order of his physician. In his keynote address he elaborated upon this statement: "During the past months I have been most apprehensive of mankind's welfare in a world of tribulation and of false ideals. . . ." His remarks were directed specifically to the subject of the sacredness of the marriage covenant and the evils of divorce.

On July 9 President McKay fulfilled a desire and promise when he attended the opening ceremonies of the $11 million hospital in Ogden that bears his name. Seated in his car near the front entrance, President and Sister McKay listened to the opening ceremony, which concluded with hospital administrator Kenneth E. Knapp presenting the

key to the hospital's front door to President McKay and a
sheaf of red roses to Mrs. McKay. David Lawrence read a
message from his father.

Two weeks later, President McKay rode in the Days
of '47 parade in Salt Lake City.

When he noted his ninety-sixth birthday in September,
physical frailties prevented President McKay from participating in many activities in which he would have normally
taken part. However, he still worked from his Hotel Utah
apartment office and met frequently with his counselors
and others as he directed the affairs of the Church. His
birthday was marked by the groundbreaking for the new
Ogden temple, and two days later for the temple at Provo.

Although unable to be present at the Tabernacle for
any of the sessions of the October general conference,
President McKay challenged priesthood holders of the
Church to "take the responsibility of bringing one member
into the Church each year." In his closing address to the
conference, read by his son Robert, he stated: "Spirituality
is the consciousness of victory over self. It is the realization
of communion with Deity. No higher attainment can be
reached than that. . . ."

XL

President McKay had been failing in health for several
months, no one was quite ready to hear that he had passed
away on Sunday morning, January 18, 1970, in his ninety-
seventh year. At the time of his death he had served as a
General Authority longer than anyone else since the organization of the Church. The previous service record was
held by Charles W. Penrose, who lived to be ninety-three
years, three months, and eight days.

Under the presidency of David O. McKay, the Church
had seen phenomenal growth. Membership during his tenure
as President nearly tripled—from one million to slightly

under three million—and the number of stakes grew from
180 to 500. In directing this growth, President McKay became the most widely traveled President in the Church's
history, traveling about one million miles. Five temples
were completed and ground was broken for three more.
The missions of the Church doubled, and the missionary
force grew from 2,000 to more than 12,000. Of great significance was the organization of the correlation program, designed to increase the effectiveness of the Church teaching
programs and auxiliaries, which was begun during his presidency; added emphasis was also placed upon the importance of the home by the family home evening program,
which came in response to growing world social problems.

Funeral services were held for President McKay in
the Salt Lake Tabernacle on January 22. Presidents Nathan
Eldon Tanner, Hugh B. Brown, Harold B. Lee, and Joseph
Fielding Smith spoke to those assembled. Of President Mc-
Kay, Elder Tanner said, "His life of outstanding service and
leadership has been acknowledged, and great tribute expressed, by newspapers, radio, and television from all over
the continent, and elsewhere in the world, and by telegrams,
letters, and phone calls from admirers far and near.

"As one of the greatest prophets and leaders of this
dispensation, his counsel has been sought and his influence
felt by leaders in all walks of life, including presidents of
the United States. He was loved and respected and revered
by millions of people who now mourn his passing.

"During his whole life he was a true exemplar of the
life of Christ. . . ."

President McKay was buried on a beautiful hillside
in the Salt Lake City cemetery.

A fitting benediction upon the life of President Mc-
Kay is the remark of a prominent businessman who visited
him in 1955: "There is the most God-like man I have ever
met. If you wanted to make man in the image of God,
there is the pattern."

JOSEPH FIELDING SMITH

JOSEPH FIELDING SMITH

(1876-   )

The year 1876 was the centennial year of America's independence. Rutherford B. Hayes was in his first year as president of the United States. In Utah, Brigham Young called men to colonize along the Little Colorado River in Arizona; the first Mormon missionaries were sent into Mexico; Feramorz Little was elected mayor of Salt Lake City; three prison breaks occured at the Utah State prison, in which one guard was fatally wounded; the new ZCMI building on Main Street in Salt Lake City was opened for business; forty tons of powder in a magazine on Arsenal Hill, north of Salt Lake City, exploded, resulting in the deaths of four persons and great destruction of property; President Brigham Young, Daniel H. Wells, and others visited Saint George; much property was destroyed by spring floods; Bishop Lorenzo W. Roundy, a member of a missionary party being led by Daniel H. Wells to Arizona, was drowned by the sinking of the ferry on the Colorado River, and President Wells narrowly escaped death himself; the mail coach was robbed near the Sevier River in Juab County; a band of Navajo Indians arrived in Salt Lake City; John D. Lee was tried and convicted in Beaver County for participation in the Mountain Meadow massacre; and a central committee of the YMMIA was organized.

The year 1876 was also the year that Joseph Fielding Smith, later to become tenth President of the Church, was

1876

born at the family residence at 333 West 2nd North in Salt Lake City. His parents were Julina Lambson Smith and Joseph F. Smith.

Among the ancestors of Joseph Fielding Smith are five who crossed the Atlantic Ocean on the *Mayflower* in 1620. Others of his forebears were active in the Revolutionary War. His grandfather, Hyrum Smith, who was characterized by Joseph the Prophet as one "who possesses the mildness of a lamb, and the integrity of a Job, and the meekness and humility of Christ," was killed with his brother on June 27, 1844, in Carthage jail. His father, Joseph Fielding Smith, born in 1838 during the trials of the Church in Missouri, later became the sixth President of the Church.

Julina Lambson Smith, the mother of Joseph Fielding, was born in Utah in 1849, less than two years after the arrival of the Mormon pioneers. After her marriage to Joseph F. Smith, she became a licensed midwife, which proved to be monetary benefit to a family struggling to get a start in the world. Of note in the account book in which she kept record of her activities as a midwife is the entry on July 19, 1876, the day of Joseph Fielding's birth, that she delivered to herself a son—this, with no medical aid except the assistance of her husband. Joseph was the first son and fourth child of his parents.

Young Joseph spent his early years working on the family farm and assisting his mother in her travels as a midwife. "I remember getting up in the middle of the night, taking the lantern to the dark barn, and hitching up the horse to the buggy. I would then drive my mother to the home of an expectant mother so she could serve as midwife and help with the new baby. I would sit in the buggy and wait. I wondered why babies were so often born in the middle of the night," he recalls.

During Joseph's boyhood years (between eight and fifteen), his father was forced into seclusion in his service to the Church as a General Authority because of government pressure against the Church on the issue of plural marriage. During this time his father fulfilled assignments for the Church in Hawaii and Washington, D.C. However, he was also able to spend time at home with his family. "On such occasions," writes Joseph Fielding, "frequently family meetings were held and he spent his time instructing his children in the principles of the gospel, and they one and all rejoiced in his presence and were grateful for the wonderful words of counsel and instruction which he imparted on these occasions. It can be said in truth that the older children who remember these happy scenes in the midst of anxiety have never forgotten what they were taught, and the impressions have remained with them and will likely do so forever."

Hours such as these with his father prepared young Joseph with the knowledge and understanding that has characterized his public life in the later years. "Among my fondest memories are the hours I spent by his side discussing principles of the gospel and receiving instruction as only he could give it. In this way the foundation for my own knowledge was laid in truth," he has recalled.

Joseph was baptized on the eighth anniversary of his birth, on July 19, 1884, by his father; and he subsequently served in the various offices of the Aaronic Priesthood.

In his youth he was an avid reader, devoting much time to the study of the scriptures. His father on one occasion was able to purchase a copy of the Book of Mormon at a reduced rate because of the faulty numbering sequence of its pages. He gave the book to Joseph, who spent innumerable hours studying its contents. His brothers recall that as a boy he would be missed at a ball game, only to be found in the hay loft reading the scriptures.

He was also fond of sports. He played baseball and developed great skill in handball, which he continued to play for almost a score of years. His sons remember his taking them to the Deseret Gymnasium and "with one hand— either hand, he gave us our choice—behind him he would beat the socks off us playing handball." His love for sports is reflected in the fact that his son Milton played quarterback on the University of Utah football team in 1950.

After completing high school, Joseph attended the Latter-day Saints College for two years. In the years prior to his mission in 1899 he was employed at ZCMI.

His activity in the Church has been diverse. On September 8, 1897, he was ordained an elder. He was active in the YMMIA; he served as Sunday School superintendent and instructor in the 16th and 17th wards; and in 1898-99 he served on the YMMIA board of the Salt Lake Stake.

On May 12, 1899, Joseph was ordained a seventy and set apart to serve a mission in England, where he labored in the Nottingham Conference. He returned home in July 1901 and in May 1903 was called as an aid in the MIA general board. He was instructor of the Seventeenth Ward MIA senior class from 1905 to 1907.

In 1903 he was set apart as a president of the twenty-fourth quorum of seventy and also served as quorum instructor. When the Salt Lake Stake was divided in 1904, he was ordained a high priest and set apart as a high councilor of the stake. On January 6, 1909, he was called as a member of the general board of Religion Classes; and between 1901 and 1910 he labored as a home missionary in the Salt Lake Stake.

President Smith has made a significant contribution to record-keeping in the Church. In 1907 he commenced work with the Genealogical Society; he was appointed a director and librarian in 1908, and served as secretary from 1910-1922. He became vice-president in 1925 and served as president from 1934 to 1963. During his tenure with the society he established the *Utah Genealogical and Historical Magazine*, which he edited in 1910, the beginning year of its publication. He was instrumental in defining the objectives of the Genealogical Society. During the time that he was one of its directors, ward and stake genealogy committees were organized throughout the Church, the Temple Index Bureau was created, and the family group sheets so widely used by genealogists were developed. Under his direction as president, the massive microfilming work of the society was begun.

In addition to the Genealogical Society, Joseph Fielding Smith's name has been synonymous with the Historian's Office for many years. His labor there began on October 1, 1901, and continued until January, 1970. His talent in matters of history is indicated by his diversified responsibilities over the years. In 1902 he traveled on special assignment to Massachusetts to gather genealogical data on the Smith family; he was engaged with Anthon H. Lund, Brigham H. Roberts, and Andrew Jenson in reading the manuscript of Joseph Smith's "History of the Church" in preparation for the publication of that work; he assisted in the compilation of evidence that was used in the Reed Smoot case before the Senate Judiciary Committee in the years 1903-1906; and he personally penned the Historian's Office daily journal during seven years, from 1903 to 1910. In addition, he was engaged in indexing, writing articles for publication, answering correspondence, compiling Church history, proofreading manuscripts, and serving as scribe for the First Presidency.

After being sustained as an assistant church historian on April 8, 1906, Joseph Fielding directed the compilation of the "Journal History of the Church" for the years following 1900. In 1907 he was commissioned by the United States Department of Commerce and Labor to collect statistics of the Church for the religious census being compiled by the government at that time.

When Anthon H. Lund died on March 2, 1921, Joseph Fielding Smith succeeded him as church historian and recorder. During his service as church historian, he directed that valuable historical records of the Church be preserved through an extensive microfilming program; histories of wards and stakes of the Church were standardized; and modern methods of cataloging, filing, and preserving of historical records were inaugurated.

In addition to the administration of the record-keeping departments of the Church, President Smith has also written extensively on church history and doctrine. He has written study courses for priesthood and auxiliary organizations and published numerous books and articles, including a series of "Answers to Gospel Questions" that appeared monthly in the *Improvement Era* between 1953 and 1967. The authorship of twenty-three books is attributed to him. As chairman of the Church reading committee, he read innumerable manuscripts for auxiliaries, priesthood quorums, and many individual authors.

Devoted to education, President Smith has been a member of the BYU board of trustees since 1912 and the Church Board of Education since 1917. In 1951 he was the recipient of an honorary doctor's degree from Brigham Young University.

Another side of his varied service has been twenty-four years in the leadership of the Salt Lake Temple. From 1915 to 1935 he assisted Presidents Anthon H. Lund and George F. Richards as counselor; and between 1945 and 1949 he served as president of the temple.

President Smith's family life has been one of devotion and sacrifice. One year prior to his mission in April, 1898, he was married to Louie E. Shurtliff. On March 30, 1908, his wife died, leaving two small children, five and one half and two years of age. On November 2, 1908, he was married to Ethel Georgina Reynolds, a co-worker in the Historian's Office. To this union were born five sons and four daughters. On August 26, 1937, he once again was deprived of the earthly association of his companion. His marriage to Jessie Ella Evans, who had attained renown as a concert singer, occurred on April 12, 1938.

His family members remember him as a man of love and kindness. His wife Ethel stated: "I have often thought when he is gone people will say, 'He is a very good man, sincere, orthodox, etc.' They will speak of him as the public knows him; but the man they have in mind is very different from the man I know. The man I know is a kind, loving husband and father whose greatest ambition in life is to make his family happy, entirely forgetful of self in his efforts to do this. He is the man who lulls to sleep the fretful child, who tells bedtime stories to the little ones, who is never too tired or too busy to sit up late at night or to get up early in the morning to help the older children solve perplexing school problems. When illness comes the man I know watches tenderly over the afflicted one and waits upon him. It is their father for whom they cry, feeling his presence a panacea for all ills. It is his hands that bind up the wounds, his arms that give courage to the sufferer, his voice that remonstrates with them gently when they err, until it becomes their happiness to do the thing that will make him happy.

"The man I know is most gentle, and if he feels that he has been unjust to anyone the distance is never too far for him to go and, with loving words or kind deeds, erase the hurt. He welcomes gladly the young people to his home and is never happier than when discussing with them topics of the day—sports or whatever interests them most. He enjoys a good story and is quick to see the humor of a situation, to laugh and to be laughed at, always willing to join in any wholesome activity.

"The man I know is unselfish, uncomplaining, considerate, thoughtful, sympathetic, doing everything within his power to make life a supreme joy for his loved ones. That is the man I know."

Jessie Evans Smith spoke of him after twenty-five years of marriage in these words: "He is the kindest man I have ever known. I have never heard him speak an unkind word in our home."

Physical punishment was not his way of disciplining his children. They recall that "he just put both hands on our shoulders, and looking down into our eyes, he would say, 'I wish my kiddies would be good,' and we got the message."

Like his father before him, President Smith is possessed of a keen sense of humor. Speaking of a fine horse that his father bought from George Q. Cannon, President Smith related: "She was so smart she learned how to unlock one kind of corral fastener after another that I contrived, until Father said to me, half humorously, that Juney seemed to be smarter than I was. So Father himself fastened her in with a strap and buckle. As he did so, the mare eyed him coolly; and, as soon as our backs were turned, she set to work with her teeth until she actually undid the buckle and followed us out, somewhat to my delight. I could not refrain from suggesting to Father that I was not the only one whose head compared unfavorably with the mare's."

On another occasion, a listener who heard him speak in a stake conference reported: "As I sat on the front row, almost within arm's reach, he shook his finger again and again at his audience for emphasis, as he preached repentance. It seemed, as I sat directly below the pulpit, that he was pointing directly at me. After the meeting I asked him if I had been his special target for that sermon. As I imitated with my own forefinger his gestures, his face lit up with a friendly smile as he repeated, in fun, his finger-pointing performance. For a long time afterward this finger-pointing became a friendly sign of salutation between us."

The *Deseret News* summarized his personality in these words: "He is fearless and plain-spoken in his preaching, strict and uncompromising in upholding the right, and stern and inflexible in his determined opposition to the forces of evil as they affect the citizenry as well as the members of the Church.

"Yet this guise of stern soldier in the cause of truth presents only half a picture of the man. On the personal side, he is counted by those who know him intimately as a tender and generous friend, in need or otherwise; as a liberal supporter of missionary work; and as a kind-hearted father of eleven children, all of whom are active in the

Church. His personality is courteous and mellow; his advice in trouble constructive, sympathetic, and understanding. Much of the help he has given through such sympathy is scarcely known except to the missionaries he has aided and those who have benefited from his tender-hearted help."

On April 6, 1910, at the age of thirty-three, President Smith was ordained an apostle and set apart as a member of the Quorum of Twelve. He filled the vacancy created by the calling of John Henry Smith to the First Presidency. His travels as a member of the Quorum of Twelve took him into nearly every stake of the Church.

He was visiting missions of the Church in Europe during the summer of 1939, immediately preceding the outbreak of World War II, when he was directed to oversee the evacuation of missionaries from Germany. He and Sister Smith arrived in England in May and subsequently met with missionaries in Britain, Holland, Belgium, France, Switzerland, Sweden, Norway, Denmark, and Germany. While visiting with missionaries in Hanover, Germany, on August 24, they received word from the First Presidency for all missionaries to pack and be ready at a moment's notice to leave the country. On August 25, when notice came for the missionaries to leave, President Smith supervised the work. After successfully completing this assignment, he and Sister Smith returned to Salt Lake City in November, 1939.

During his tour of missions in the Far East in 1955, President Smith divided the Japanese Mission, creating the Northern and Southern Far East missions. He visited LDS servicemen in military installations and dedicated Korea, Okinawa, the Philippine Islands, and Guam for the preaching of the gospel.

Another highlight in his life was the dedication of historical landmarks at Liberty and Kansas City, Missouri, in September, 1963. Speaking at the dedication of the newly constructed bureau of information that shelters the Liberty jail in Clay County, Missouri, President Smith spoke about the suffering of Christ: "It was in that jail, under the hard sufferings that they went through, that the Prophet, in the spirit of humility, knelt before the Lord and prayed and asked the Lord how long this suffering would have to go on, and the Lord answered him. Part of this is written on the walls down there.

"The Lord told the Prophet Joseph Smith that he too had suffered, and nobody ever suffered more than the Son of God. I do not believe that many of the members of the Church fully realize the suffering of the Son of God in the Garden of Gethsemane.

"No man ever suffered, no matter who he was, such torment as Jesus did in the Garden of Gethsemane. He was carrying a load that no one else could carry, in some way that we, I suppose—at least I—cannot fully comprehend. The Savior was carrying my transgressions and yours, and the transgressions of every soul that comes into this Church, and through that suffering, he redeemed us from having to pay the price of our transgressions, if we would believe in him and keep his commandments. He took it upon himself to do that for every soul born into this world, from Adam down to the end of time, who will accept the gospel of Jesus Christ."

After dedicating the bureau of information at Liberty, President Smith performed a similar ceremony in Troost Park in Kansas City, marking the spot where a Mormon chapel stood that served as the first school building in the area now occupied by metropolitan Kansas City. He also visited Far West, Missouri, where his father was born in 1838, at the time Joseph and Hyrum Smith were incarcerated in the Liberty jail.

At the solemn assembly on April 9, 1951, in which David O. McKay was sustained as ninth President of the Church, Joseph Fielding Smith was sustained as president of the Quorum of the Twelve Apostles. He was serving in this capacity on October 29, 1965, when he was selected

to assist President McKay as a counselor in the First *1965*
Presidency.

With the passing of David O. McKay in January, 1970, Joseph Fielding Smith became the tenth President of the Church. On January 23 he was ordained and set apart to this high calling and announced the selection of Harold B. Lee as his first counselor and Nathan Eldon Tanner as second. At the time of his appointment he had served with the Council of Twelve for nearly sixty years, during which time he saw the Church membership increase from 393,437 to nearly three million. The number of stakes grew from 62 to 519, the wards from 694 to nearly 5,000, and missions from 21 to 90.

The first statement of the newly appointed Prophet to the Latter-day Saints was given at a press conference held on January 24: "Every member of this Church is supposed to be acquainted with the fundamental truths of the gospel and be a teacher therein. . . . The scriptures impress upon us the need for faithfulness, integrity, and obedience and the declaration of his truth as we mingle with our fellow-men."

President Smith was sustained by the general conference of the Church in solemn assembly on April 6, 1970. On that occasion he said: "As a Church and as a people, we have been greatly blessed for many years by the inspired leadership, the great spiritual insight, and the firm hand of President David O. McKay. Now that his valiant work here is finished and he has been called home to serve in other ways, the Lord has given the reigns of responsibility and leadership in his earthly kingdom to others of us who remain.

"And since we know the Lord 'giveth no commandments unto the children of men, save he shall prepare a way for them that they may accomplish the thing which he commandeth them,' we are most humbly confident that under his guidance and direction this work will continue to prosper.

"I desire to say that no man of himself can lead this church. It is the Church of the Lord Jesus Christ; he is at the head. The Church bears his name, has his priesthood, administers his gospel, preaches his doctrine, and does his work.

"He chooses men and calls them to be instruments in his hands to accomplish his purposes, and he guides and directs them in their labors. But men are only instruments in the Lord's hands, and the honor and glory for all that his servants accomplish is and should be ascribed unto him forever."

In June President Smith addressed the MIA conference of the Church. He spoke on the role of the auxiliaries, which, he said, were "set up to help members of the Church perfect their lives and do those things which assure them of joy and happiness in this life and eternal life in the life to come.

"The Church auxiliaries are organized to help meet the needs of the people in whatever social conditions may exist. . . . The chief responsibility to do those things which lead to salvation rests with each individual. All of us have been placed on earth to undergo the testing experiences of mortality. We are here to see if we will keep the commandments and overcome the world, and we must do all that we can for ourselves.

"The next responsibility for our salvation rests with our family. Parents are set to be lights and guides to their children and are commanded to bring them up in light and truth, teaching them the gospel and setting proper examples."

He stated that the Church and all its agencies constitute a service organization to help the family and the individual carry out their responsibilities.

"Home teachers, priesthood leaders, and bishops are appointed to lead those with whom they labor to eternal life in our Father's kingdom, and the auxiliary organizations are appointed to assist in this great work of salvation.

"We cannot stress too strongly the great need to utilize all of these programs for the benefit and blessing of all our Father's children."

In September President and Sister Smith were in Hawaii upon invitation of Church College president Owen J. Cook, who had asked the Prophet to speak at the college's fifteenth anniversary commemoration. On this occasion he spoke of the second coming of Christ. "We are living in the last days; these are the days when the signs of the times are being fulfilled. Much that has been promised by the prophets to precede the Second Coming has already taken place. In this present day, confusion, bloodshed, misery, plague, famine, earthquake, and other calamities shall cover the face of the earth. The distress and perplexity, bloodshed and terror, selfish ambition of despotic rulers, such as the world has never before seen, all indicate that the great and dreadful day of the Lord is very near, even at our doors."

President Smith also spoke at the largest conference gathering in the history of the Oahu Stake, admonishing his listeners: "Our real concern in life is one of being humble and faithful and of keeping the commandments so we shall be entitled to the blessings of full salvation in the world to come. Everything we do in the Church centers around the divine law that we are to love and worship God and love and serve our fellow beings."

INDEX